THE
KOVELS'
BOTTLE PRICE LIST

Books by Ralph and Terry Kovel

Dictionary of Marks—Pottery and Porcelain

A Directory of American Silver, Pewter and Silver Plate

American Country Furniture, 1780–1875

The Kovels' Antiques Price List

The Kovels' Bottle Price List

The Kovels' Collector's Guide to American Art Pottery

Kovels' Organizer for Collectors

The Kovels' Price Guide for Collector Plates, Figurines, Paperweights, and Other Limited Editions

The Kovels' Illustrated Price Guide to Royal Doulton

The Kovels' Illustrated Price Guide to Depression Glass and American Dinnerware

Kovels' Know Your Antiques

Kovels' Know Your Collectibles

The Kovels' Book of Antique Labels

THE
KOVELS'
BOTTLE PRICE LIST

SIXTH EDITION

BY RALPH AND TERRY KOVEL

Illustrated

Crown Publishers, Inc. New York

Published by Crown Publishers, Inc.,
One Park Avenue, New York, New York 10016 and simultaneously in Canada
by General Publishing Company Limited
Printed in the United States of America

Library of Congress Catalog Card Number: 75-12542

ISBN: 0-517-54587X

An Important Announcement to Collectors and Dealers

Every second year *The Kovels' Bottle Price List* is completely rewritten. Every entry and every picture is new because of the rapidly changing antiques market. The only way so complete a revision can be accomplished is by using a computer, making it possible to publish the book two months after the last price is received.

Yet many price changes occur between editions of *The Kovels' Bottle Price List.* Important sales produce new record prices. Rarities are discovered. Fakes appear.

The serious collector will want to keep up with developments from month to month rather than from year to year. Therefore, we call your attention to a new service to provide price information: "Kovels on Antiques and Collectibles," a nationally distributed illustrated newsletter, published monthly.

This monthly newsletter reports current prices, collecting trends, landmark auction results for all types of antiques, and tax, estate, security, and other pertinent news for collectors.

Additional information about the newsletter is available from the authors at P.O. Box 22200, Dept. BPL, Beachwood, Ohio 44122.

How to Use This Book

Bottle clubs and bottle shows have set the rules for this edition of *The Kovels' Bottle Price List*. We have taken the terms from those in common usage and tried to organize the thousands of listings in easy-to-use form. Many abbreviations have been included that are part of the bottle collector's language. The Tibbits' abbreviations appear throughout the book.

ABM means automatic bottle machine.
BIMAL means blown in mold, applied lip, open pontil.
FB means free-blown.
SC means sun-colored.
SCA means sun-colored amethyst.
OP means open pontil.
IP means iron pontil.
DUG means literally dug from the ground.

To make the descriptions of the bottles as complete as possible, an identification number has been added to the description in some categories. The serious collector knows the important books about a specialty, and these books have numbered lists of styles of bottles. Included in this book are identification numbers for milk glass from Belknap, flasks from McKearin and Watson, bitters from Watson and Ring, fruit jars from Creswick, and ink bottles from Covill. The full titles of the books used are included in the Bibliography and listed in the introductory paragraph for each category.

Medicine bottles include all medicine or drugstore bottles, except those under the more specific headings of bitters or sarsaparilla. Modern liquor bottles are listed under the brand name if more than five of the bottles are in the collectible series. If you are not a regular at bottle shows, it may take a few tries to become accustomed to the method of listing. If you cannot find a bottle, try several related headings. For instance, hair products are found under "Cosmetic." Many named bottles are found under "Medicine," "Food," "Fruit Jar," etc. If your fruit jar has several names, such as "Ball, Mason," look under "Fruit Jar, Ball" or "Fruit Jar, Mason." If no color is listed the bottle is clear.

The prices shown for old bottles are the actual prices asked for bottles during the past year. A few bottles have been included to complete a listing of new bottles. When this has been done, the prices are estimates based on known prices of the past two years. The estimated prices appear only for modern bottles in a series. Pre-World War I bottles are all listed at actual sale or auction prices.

Prices may vary in different parts of the country and if more than one bottle has been recorded a range is given. Because of the idiosyncrasies of the computer, it was impossible to place a range of prices on bottles that are illustrated. The price listed is an average.

Spelling is meant to help the collector. If the original bottle spelled "Catsup" as "Ketchup," that is the spelling that appears. The abbreviation "Dr." for doctor may appear on bottles as "Dr" (no period) or "Dr." (period). We have included a period each time to keep the computer alphabetizing more consistent. If a word is written "Kennedy's," "Kennedys,'" or "Kennedys," we have placed the apostrophe or omitted it as it appeared on the bottle. A few bottles are included that had errors in the original spelling in the bottle mold. These are listed under the category "Error," or the error is explained in the proper listing. Medicine, bitters, and other bottles sometimes use the term "Dr." and sometimes use just the last name of the doctor. We have used the wording as it appears on the bottle. "Whiskey" is used even if the bottle held Scotch or Canadian or was spelled "Whisky."

Every bottle illustrated in black and white is indicated by the word "Illus." in the text. Every bottle pictured in color is indicated by the word "Color" in the listing. There are a few color illustrated bottles shown without prices. These bottles were photographed in a display and no current price was available.

We welcome any information about clubs, prices, or content for future books, but cannot give appraisals by mail. We have tried to be accurate, but cannot be responsible for any errors in pricing or information that may appear.

Ralph M. Kovel, Life Member, Federation of Historical Bottle Clubs,
Senior Member, American Society of Appraisers

Terry H. Kovel, Life Member, Federation of Historical Bottle Clubs,
Senior Member, American Society of Appraisers
1982

Picture Acknowledgments

To the following companies and collectors, our thanks for their help in obtaining pictures: Amaretto, Avon Products, Ballantine, Paul Ballentine, James B. Beam Distilling Company (Nancy Walters), Beefeater, Mr. and Mrs. Werner Burker, Don and Glennie Burkett, Chip Cable, Coca-Cola Company, Cyrus Noble, Dant, Bill and Kathie Errera, Ezra Brooks, Famous Firsts (Richard E. Magid), Garnier, Sue and Bob Gilbert, Grenadier Spirits Company, Heaven Hill Distilling Company (Rudy F. Moeller, Sr.), Hoffman Distilling Company, Inc. (William Ukrainetz), Ernie Hurd, Jack Daniel Distillery, Jon-Sol, Inc., Butch and Gloria Kim, Kobrand Corporation (Roger J. Lee), Linda and Adam Koch, Kontinental Classics, Donna and Joe Krutzer, Lionstone, Luxardo, McCormick Distilling Co., Donald Maggie, Medley Distilling (Gerald F. Marco), Michters, Millville Art Glass, Elvin Moody, Old Commonwealth, Old Fitzgerald, Raintree, Therman Riggs, Anna Sadler, Ski Country, J. E. Swedberg, Al Vignon, Wheaton Village, Bill and Rose White, Wild Turkey.

Special thanks to Deena Caniff, Anna Sadler, and the Jefferson County Antique Bottle Club for permitting photographs to be taken at the 1981 Antique Bottle Show and Sale, Steubenville, Ohio, and to the Robert W. Skinner Gallery.

Bottle Clubs

There are hundreds of bottle clubs that welcome new members. This list is arranged by state and city so you can find the club nearest your home. If no club is listed nearby, we suggest you contact the national organizations (see below). New clubs are formed each month.

Any active bottle club that is not listed and wishes to be included in future editions of *The Kovels' Bottle Price List* should send the necessary information to the authors, c/o Crown Publishers, Inc., One Park Avenue, New York, New York 10016.

NATIONAL CLUBS

Most of these clubs have publications as well as meetings.
They have lists of local chapters and meetings.

AMERICAN COLLECTORS
OF INFANT FEEDERS
540 Croyden Road
Cheltenham, Pennsylvania
19012

BUD HASTIN'S NATIONAL
AVON CLUB
P.O. Box 12088
Overland Park, Kansas 66212

FEDERATION OF
HISTORICAL BOTTLE CLUBS
10118 Schuessler
St. Louis, Missouri 63128

INTERNATIONAL
ASSOCIATION OF JIM BEAM
BOTTLE AND SPECIALTIES
CLUB
c/o Mrs. Shirley Clark
5120 Belmont Road, Suite D
Downers Grove, Illinois 60515

INTERNATIONAL CHINESE
SNUFF BOTTLE SOCIETY
2601 North Charles Street
Baltimore, Maryland 21218

LIONSTONE BOTTLE
COLLECTORS OF AMERICA
P.O. Box 2418
Chicago, Illinois 60690

MICHTER'S NATIONAL
COLLECTORS SOCIETY
P.O. Box 481
Schaefferstown, Pennsylvania
17088

MILKBOTTLES ONLY
ORGANIZATION (MOO)
P.O. Box 5456
Newport News, Virginia 23605

NATIONAL EZRA BROOKS
BOTTLE AND SPECIALTIES
CLUB
420 West 1st Street
Kewanee, Illinois 61443

NATIONAL GRENADIER
BOTTLE CLUB
3108A West Meinecke
Avenue
Milwaukee, Wisconsin 53210

NATIONAL SKI COUNTRY
BOTTLE CLUB
1224 Washington Avenue
Golden, Colorado 80401

WESTERN WORLD AVON
CLUB
P.O. Box 27587
San Francisco, California
94127

WORLD WIDE AVON CLUB
44021 Seventh Street, East
Lancaster, California 93534

STATE CLUBS

Alabama

Alabama Bottle Collectors'
Society
2768 Hanover Circle
BIRMINGHAM, ALABAMA
35205

Avon Club
4264 Cleveland Avenue
MONTGOMERY, ALABAMA
36105

Montgomery Bottle & Insulator
Club
2021 Merrily Drive
MONTGOMERY, ALABAMA
36311

Mobile Bottle Collectors Club
6927 Historic Mobile Parkway
THEODORE, ALABAMA
36582

Alaska

Alaska Bottle Club
8510 E. 10th Street
ANCHORAGE, ALASKA
99504

Arizona

Pick & Shovel Antique Bottle
Club of Arizona
P.O. Box 7020
PHOENIX, ARIZONA 85011

Arizona Territory Antique
Bottle & Collectibles Club, Inc.
P.O. Box 26312
TUCSON, ARIZONA 85726

Southern Arizona Historical
Collectors' Association, Ltd.
6211 Piedra Sega
TUCSON, ARIZONA 85718

Arkansas

Fort Smith Area Bottle
Collectors Association
5809 Apache Trail
FORT SMITH, ARKANSAS
72904

Northeast Arkansas Antique
Bottle Club
529 N. Church
JONESBORO, ARKANSAS
72401

Arkansas Traveler Ezra
Brooks Club
2309 Ridge Park Drive
LITTLE ROCK, ARKANSAS
72204

Little Rock Antique Bottle Club
610 N. Polk
LITTLE ROCK, ARKANSAS
72205

California

Queen Mary Beam &
Specialties Club
Box 2081
ANAHEIM, CALIFORNIA
92804

Superior California Bottle Club
P.O. Box 555
ANDERSON, CALIFORNIA
96007

49er Historical Bottle
Association
Box 91, Station A
AUBURN, CALIFORNIA 95603

Kern County Antique Bottle
Club
P.O. Box 6724
BAKERSFIELD, CALIFORNIA
93306

Peninsula Bottle Club
P.O. Box 886
BELMONT, CALIFORNIA
94402

Golden Gate Historical Bottle
Society
P.O. Box 1234
BERKELEY, CALIFORNIA
94701

San Bernardino Historical
Bottle & Collectible Club
Box 127
BLOOMINGTON,
CALIFORNIA 92316

Orange County Miniature
Bottle Club
836 Carob Street
BREA, CALIFORNIA 92691

Bidwell Bottle Club
Box 546
CHICO, CALIFORNIA 95927

Original Sippin' Cousins
Brooks Specialties Club
5823 Bartmus Street
CITY OF COMMERCE,
CALIFORNIA 90040

Avon Bottle & Specialty
Collectors Club
P.O. Box 23
CLAREMONT, CALIFORNIA
91711

Tinseltown Beam Club
12205 Marshall Street
CULVER CITY, CALIFORNIA
90230

Mission Bells Jim Beam Bottle
Club, Inc.
P.O. Box 225
DOWNEY, CALIFORNIA
90241

Mt. Bottle Club
422 Orpheus
ENCINITAS, CALIFORNIA
92024

Orange County Avon Club
P.O. Box 505
GARDEN GROVE,
CALIFORNIA 92642

San Francisco Bay Area
Miniature Bottle Club
160 Lower Via Casitas #8
KENTFIELD, CALIFORNIA
94904

xi

San Jose Antique Bottle
Collectors Association
1231 Thurston
LOS ALTOS, CALIFORNIA
94022

Lilliputian Bottle Club
5626 Corning Avenue
LOS ANGELES, CALIFORNIA
90056

Los Angeles Historical Bottle
Club
P.O. Box 60762 Terminal
Annex
LOS ANGELES, CALIFORNIA
90060

Avon Collectors of San Diego
County
4660-91 N. River Road
OCEANSIDE, CALIFORNIA
92054

San Luis Obispo Bottle
Society (SLOBS)
124 21st Street
PASO ROBLES, CALIFORNIA
93446

Tehama Country Antique
Bottle Club
Route 1, Box 775
RED BLUFF, CALIFORNIA
96080

West Valley Avon Club
19331 Lorne Street
RESEDA, CALIFORNIA 91335

Morning Avon Club
10245 Bonita Avenue
RIVERSIDE, CALIFORNIA
92503

Riverside Avon Club
P.O. Box 8445
RIVERSIDE, CALIFORNIA
92505

Southern California Avon
Collectors
3603 Earle Street
ROSEMEAD, CALIFORNIA
91770

River City Avon Club
2814 Hyannis Way
SACRAMENTO, CALIFORNIA
95827

San Bernardino Avon &
Specialty Club
P.O. Box 622
SAN BERNARDINO,
CALIFORNIA 92402

Gold Panner Ezra Brooks Club
8808 Capricorn Way
SAN DIEGO, CALIFORNIA
92126

San Diego Antique Bottle Club
P.O. Box 5137
SAN DIEGO, CALIFORNIA
92105

San Diego Beam Club
8043 Hillandale Drive
SAN DIEGO, CALIFORNIA
92120

Golden Gate Ezra Brooks
Club
1337 Natoma Street
SAN FRANCISCO,
CALIFORNIA 94103

Golden Gate H.B.S.
2131 Via Murietta
SAN LORENZO, CALIFORNIA
94580

Antique Bottle Collectors of
Orange County
223 E. Ponona
SANTA ANA, CALIFORNIA
92707

Mission Trails Ezra Brooks
Club
1254 Crowley Avenue
SANTA CLARA, CALIFORNIA
95051

Avon Treasures Unlimited
P.O. Box 847
STANTON, CALIFORNIA
90680

Stockton Avon Club
3107 No. Eldorado Street
STOCKTON, CALIFORNIA
95204

Sequoia Antique Bottle
Society
Box 3695
VISALIA, CALIFORNIA 93277

Colorado

Avon Collectors of Colorado
Rt. 2
CALHAN, COLORADO 80808

Rocky Mountain Avon
Collectors
8612 W. Warren Lane
LAKEWOOD, COLORADO

Colorado Mile-Hi Ezra Brooks
Club
7401 Decatur Street
WESTMINSTER, COLORADO
80030

Connecticut

Greenwich Antique Bottle
Collectors Club
67 Church Street
GREENWICH, CONNECTICUT
06830

East Coast Mini Bottle Club
156 Hillfield Road
HAMDEN, CONNECTICUT
06514

Nutmeg State Ezra Brooks
Bottle Club
2330 South Main Street
MIDDLETOWN,
CONNECTICUT 06457

Antique Bottle Club of
Middletown
15 Elam Street, Apt. #10
NEW BRITAIN,
CONNECTICUT 06053

Connecticut Specialty Bottle
Club (Jim Beam)
P.O. Box 752
ORANGE, CONNECTICUT
06477

Southern Connecticut Antique
Bottle Collectors Association
186 Waverly Road
SHELTON, CONNECTICUT
06484

Somers Antique Bottle Club,
Inc.
Box 373
SOMERS, CONNECTICUT
06071

Central Connecticut Antique
Bottle Collectors
38 Village Road
SOUTHINGTON,
CONNECTICUT 06489

Delaware

Tri-State Bottle Collectors &
Diggers Club, Inc.
730 Papermill Road
NEWARK, DELAWARE 19711

Florida

M-T Bottle Collectors
Association
P.O. Box 1581
DELAND, FLORIDA 32720

Harbor City
1232 Causeway
EAU, FLORIDA 32935

Antique Bottle Collectors of
Florida, Inc.
2512 Davie Boulevard
FT. LAUDERDALE, FLORIDA
33112

Antique Bottle Club of North
Florida
Box 14796
JACKSONVILLE, FLORIDA
32210

Cross Arms Collectors Club
1756 N.W. 58th Avenue
LAUDERHILL, FLORIDA
33313

Mid-State Antique Bottle
Collectors, Inc.
88 Sweetbriar Branch
LONGWOOD, FLORIDA
32750

Antique Bottle Collectors of
Florida
5901 S.W. 16th Street
MIAMI, FLORIDA 33144

Canal Area Bottle Collectors
Association
PSC Box 3402
MIAMI, FLORIDA 34004

Pensacola Bottle & Relic
Collectors Association
1004 Fremont Avenue
PENSACOLA, FLORIDA
32505

Everglades Antique Bottle &
Collectors Club
6981 S.W. 19th Street
POMPANO BEACH, FLORIDA
33068

Suncoast Antique Bottle
Collectors Association
P.O. Box 12712
ST. PETERSBURG, FLORIDA
33733

Sanford Antique Bottle
Collectors Club
2656 Grandview Avenue
South
SANDFORD, FLORIDA 32771

Antique Bottle Collectors
Association
Route 1, Box 74-136
SARASOTA, FLORIDA 33583

Florida West Coast Ezra
Brooks Club
6583 Bluewater Avenue
SARASOTA, FLORIDA 33581

Tampa Antique Bottle
Collectors
P.O. Box 4232
TAMPA, FLORIDA 33607

Gold Coast Collector's Club
P.O. Box 10183
WILTON MANORS, FLORIDA

Georgia

Atlanta B.C.
6500 Cascade Road S.W.
ATLANTA, GEORGIA 30331

Southeastern Antique Bottle
Club
Box 441
FAIRBORN, GEORGIA 30213

Macon Antique Bottle Club
5532 Jan Ru Circle
MACON, GEORGIA 31206

Rome Antique Bottle Club
527 Broad Street
ROME, GEORGIA 30161

Coastal Empire Bottle Club
P.O. Box 3714 Station B
SAVANNAH, GEORGIA 31402

Hawaii

Hawaii Historical Bottle
Collectors Club
6770 Hawaii Kai Drive, Apt.
708
HONOLULU, HAWAII 96825

Idaho

Gem Antique Bottle Club, Inc.
1630 Londoner Avenue
BOISE, IDAHO 83706

Rock & Bottle Club
Route 1
FRUITLAND, IDAHO 83619

Em Tee Bottle Club
Box 62
JEROME, IDAHO 83338

Pocatello Antique Bottle
Collectors Association
4530 S. 5th Street
POCATELLO, IDAHO 83201

Illinois

Alton Area Bottle Club
2448 Alby Street
ALTON, ILLINOIS 52035

Metro-East Bottle & Jar
Association
309 Bellevue Park Drive
BELLEVILLE, ILLINOIS 62223

Chicago Ezra Brooks Club
13200 Baltimore
CHICAGO, ILLINOIS 60533

First Chicago Bottle Club
P.O. Box A3382
CHICAGO, ILLINOIS 60690

Midwest Miniature Bottle
Collectors
3510 South 52nd Court
CICERO, ILLINOIS 60650

Antique Bottle Club of North
Illinois
P.O. Box 23
INGLESIDE, ILLINOIS 60041

Pekin Bottle Collectors
Association
P.O. Box 372
PEKIN, ILLINOIS 61554

Indiana

Indiana Ezra Brooks Bottle
Club
58 North 13th
BEECH GROVE, INDIANA
46107

Kentuckian Antique Bottle &
Outhouse Society
554 Andalusia Avenue
CLARKSVILLE, INDIANA
47130

The Midwest Antique Fruit Jar
& Bottle Club
P.O. Box 38
FLAT ROCK, INDIANA 47234

Fort Wayne Historical Bottle
Club
5124 Roberta Drive
FORT WAYNE, INDIANA
46806

Hoosier Avon Collectors
Rt. 1
HARTFORD CITY, INDIANA
47348

Lafayette Antique Bottle Club
3664 Redondo Drive
LAFAYETTE, INDIANA 47905

Iowa

Iowa Antique Bottleers
935 West 145th Avenue
MARION, IOWA 52302

Kansas

Southeast Kansas Bottle &
Relic Club
121 North Lafayette
CHANUTE, KANSAS 66720

Kansas City Antique Bottle
Club Association
5528 Aberdeen
SHAWNEE MISSION,
KANSAS 66205

Air Capital City Jim Beam
Bottle & Specialty Club
3256 Euclid
WICHITA, KANSAS 67217

Happy Avoners Club of
Wichita
3401 Laura
WICHITA, KANSAS 57216

Kentucky

Kentuckiana Antique Bottle &
Outhouse Society
5801 River Knolls Drive
LOUISVILLE, KENTUCKY
40220

Louisiana

Celna Bottle Club
Route 1, Box 463
DRY PRONG, LOUISIANA
71423

Bayou Ezra Brooks Bottle
Club
733 Wright Avenue
GRETNA, LOUISIANA 70053

Northeast Louisiana Bottle &
Insulator Club
P.O. Box 4192
MONROE, LOUISIANA 71201

New Orleans Antique Bottle
Club
4336 Palmyra
NEW ORLEANS, LOUISIANA
70119

Shreveport Antique Bottle
Club
1157 Arncliffe Drive
SHREVEPORT, LOUISIANA
71107

Maine

New England Antique Bottle
Club
Box 246
ALFRED, MAINE 04002

Waldo County Bottlenecks
Club
Head-of-the-Tide
BELFAST, MAINE 04915

Dirigo Bottle Collectors' Club
24 Maple Street
DEXTER, MAINE 04930

Maryland

Baltimore Antique Bottle
Hounds
1014 Breezewick Road
TOWSON, MARYLAND 21204

Southern Maryland Bottle
Collectors
905 Stone Avenue
WALDORF, MARYLAND
20601

Massachusetts

Merrimack Valley Bottle Club
42 Donald Road
BURLINGTON,
MASSACHUSETTS 01803

New England Bottle Collectors
Association
7a Broad Street
LYNN, MASSACHUSETTS
01902

Berkshire Antique Bottle
Association
66 Wood Avenue
PITTSFIELD,
MASSACHUSETTS 01201

Satuit Bottle Club
3 Adam Street
SOUTH EASTON,
MASSACHUSETTS 02375

Cape Cod Antique Bottle Club
262 Setuket Road
YARMOUTH,
MASSACHUSETTS 02675

Michigan

Great Lakes Miniature Bottle
Club
P.O. Box 245
FAIRHAVEN, MICHIGAN
48023

Metro East Bottle & Jar
Association
309 Bellevue Park Drive
FAIRVIEW HEIGHTS,
MICHIGAN 48621

Flint Antique Bottle Club
450 Leta Avenue
FLINT, MICHIGAN 48507

Ye Old Corkers
P.O. Box 7
GAASTRA, MICHIGAN 49927

Central Michigan Krazy
Korkers Bottle Club
Mid-Michigan Community
College
Clare Avenue
HARRISON, MICHIGAN 48625

Huron Valley Bottle &
Insulator Club
6349 West Silver Lake Road
LINDEN, MICHIGAN 48451

Chief Pontiac Antique Bottle
Club
755 Scottwood
PONTIAC, MICHIGAN 48058

Metro Detroit Antique Bottle
Club
315 Dwight Street
TRENTON, MICHIGAN 48183

Minnesota

Minnesota's First Antique
Bottle Club
5001 Queen Avenue N
MINNEAPOLIS, MINNESOTA
55430

North Star Historical Bottle
Association
3308 32nd Avenue South
MINNEAPOLIS, MINNESOTA
55406

Mississippi

South Mississippi Historical
Bottle Club
165 Belvedere Drive
BILOXI, MISSISSIPPI 39530

The Magnolia State Bottle &
Specialties Club
2918 Larchmont
JACKSON, MISSISSIPPI
39209

Middle Mississippi Antique
Bottle Club
5528 Crepe Myrtle Drive
JACKSON, MISSISSIPPI
39206

Missouri

Antique Bottle & Relic Club of
Central Missouri
Route 1
FRANKLIN, MISSOURI 65274

St. Louis Antique Bottle
Collector Association
7316 Landi Court
HAZELWOOD, MISSOURI
63042

"64" Mustang Avon Club
432 Huntington Road
KANSAS CITY, MISSOURI
64113

Heart of America Ezra Brooks
Club
3839 Powers Drive
ST. JOSEPH, MISSOURI
64503

Pack Rats United
Route 6
WARDSVILLE, MISSOURI
65101

Montana

Hellgate Antique Bottle Club
P.O. Box 7411
MISSOULA, MONTANA 59807

Nebraska

1st Mid-Nebraska Avon Club
RR #, Box 11
GRAND ISLAND, NEBRASKA
68801

Nebraska Antique Bottle &
Collectors Club
P.O. Box 37021
OMAHA, NEBRASKA 68137

Nevada

Lincoln County Antique Bottle
Club
P.O. Box 191
CALIENTE, NEVADA 89008

Las Vegas Bottle Club
35555 East Cheyenne
Avenue, Sp. 56
NORTH LAS VEGAS,
NEVADA 89030

Reno-Sparks Antique Bottle
Collectors Association
P.O. Box 1061
VERDI, NEVADA 89439

New Hampshire

Yankee Bottle Club
P.O. Box 702
KEENE, NEW HAMPSHIRE
03431

New Jersey

Burlington Antique Bottle Club
38 Yorktown Road
BORDENTOWN, NEW
JERSEY 08505

New Jersey Ezra Brooks Club
Sayres Neck Road
CEDARVILLE, NEW JERSEY
08311

Lakeland Antique Bottle Club
18 Alan Lane, Mine Hill
DOVER, NEW JERSEY 07801

South Jersey's Heritage Bottle
& Glass Club
P.O. Box 122
GLASSBORO, NEW JERSEY
08028

Jersey Devil Bottle Club
14 Church Street
MT. HOLLY, NEW JERSEY
08042

The Jersey Shore Bottle Club
P.O. Box 995
TOMS RIVER, NEW JERSEY
08753

North New Jersey Antique
Bottle Collectors Association
560 Overlook Drive
WYCOFF, NEW JERSEY
07481

New York

Auburn Bottle Club
74 Capitol Street
AUBURN, NEW YORK 13026

Tonowanda Valley Glass and
Bottle Collectors Club
14 Franklin Street
BATAVIA, NEW YORK 14020

North County Bottle Collectors
Association
Road 1
CANTON, NEW YORK 13617

Twin Counties Old Bottle Club
R.D. #2 Box 342
CATSKILL, NEW YORK 12414

Empire State Bottle Collectors
Association
262 West 7th Street
FULTON, NEW YORK 13069

Long Island Antique Bottle
Association
Box 271
HUNTINGTON, LONG
ISLAND, NEW YORK 11743

Finger Lakes Bottle Collectors
Association
Box 815
ITHACA, NEW YORK 14850

Western New York Bottle
Collectors
62 Adams Street
JAMESTOWN, NEW YORK
14701

The Muscoot Bottle &
Insulator Collectors Club
Allison Road
KATONAH, NEW YORK
10536

West Valley Bottletique
Collectors Association
P.O. Box 204
KILLBUCK, NEW YORK
14748

The Greater Catskill Antique
Bottle Club
LOCH SHELDRAKE, NEW
YORK 12759

Hudson Valley Bottle Club
Mt. Zion Road
MARLBORO, NEW YORK
12542

Suffolk County Antique Bottle
Association of Long Island
Box 943
MELVILLE, NEW YORK
11746

Northeast Mini Bottle Club
420 Bayside Avenue
OCEANSIDE, NEW YORK
11572

The Genesee Valley Bottle
Collectors Association
P.O. Box 7528
West Ridge Station
ROCHESTER, NEW YORK
14615

Rensselaer County Antique
Bottle Club, Inc.
Box 792
TROY, NEW YORK 12181

Warwick Valley Bottle Club
Box 393
WARWICK, NEW YORK
10990

Upper Hudson Valley Club
Box 206
WEST COXSACKIE, NEW
YORK 12192

North Carolina

North Carolina Bottle
Collectors Club
Box 220031
CHARLOTTE, NORTH
CAROLINA 28222

LaFayette Avon Collectors
Club
4210 Isham Street
FAYETTEVILLE, NORTH
CAROLINA 28304

Goldsboro Bottle & Collectors
Club
2406 E. Ash Street
GOLDSBORO, NORTH
CAROLINA 27530

Avon Club
Rt. 4, Box 496
SPARTA, NORTH CAROLINA
28675

Wilson Bottle & Artifacts Club
Route 1, Box 59
WILSON, NORTH CAROLINA
27893

North Dakota

Red River Valley Ezra Brooks
Club
PARK RIVER, NORTH
DAKOTA 58270

Ohio

Ohio Bottle Club, Inc.
P.O. Box 585
BARBERTON, OHIO 44203

Central Ohio Bottle Club
6522 Hearthstone Avenue
COLUMBUS, OHIO 43229

Dayton Golden Slipper Avon
Club
159 East Apple Street
DAYTON, OHIO 45409

Jeep City Beamers
213 West Main
DELTA, OHIO 43515

Tri-State Historical Bottle Club
P.O. Box 609
EAST LIVERPOOL, OHIO
43920

Findlay Antique Bottle Club
P.O. Box 3129
FINDLAY, OHIO 45840

Greater Cleveland Jim Beam
Bottle Club
2381 Dale Brook Circle
HINCKLEY, OHIO 44233

First Capital Bottle Club
Route 1, Box 94
LAURELVILLE, OHIO 43135

Heart of Ohio Bottle Club
P.O. Box 353
NEW WASHINGTON, OHIO
44854

Southwestern Ohio Antique
Bottle & Jar Club
P.O. Box 53
NORTH HAMPTON, OHIO
45349

Lazarus Bottle Club
22000 Shaker Boulevard
SHAKER HEIGHTS, OHIO
44122

Fort Steuben Ezra Brooks
Bottle and Specialty Club
P.O. Box 491
STEUBENVILLE, OHIO 43952

Jefferson County Antique
Bottle Club
1223 Oak Grove Avenue
STEUBENVILLE, OHIO 43952

Buckeye Bottle Diggers Club
9236 Twp. Road 79 NW
THORNVILLE, OHIO 43076

Oklahoma

T-Town Bottle & Relic News
8921 S. 200th East Avenue
BROKEN ARROW,
OKLAHOMA 74012

Cherokee Strip Ezra Brooks
Club
214 N. 2nd Street
TONKAWA, OKLAHOMA
74653

Tulsa Antique Bottle & Relic
Club
P. O. Box 4278
TULSA, OKLAHOMA 74104

Oregon

Rogue Valley Avon Collectors
Club
366 Tudor Street
ASHLAND, OREGON 97520

Central Oregon Bottle & Relic
Club
671 N.E. Seward
BEND, OREGON 97701

Oregon Bottle Collectors
Association
3661 S.E. Nehalem Street
PORTLAND, OREGON 97202

Pennsylvania

Washington County Bottle
Club
Route 1
AVELLA, PENNSYLVANIA
15312

Bedford County Antique Bottle
Club
107 Seifert Street
BEDFORD, PENNSYLVANIA
15522

Classic Glass Bottle Collectors
R.D. #2
COGAN STATION,
PENNSYLVANIA 17728

Forks of the Delaware Bottle
Club
P.O. Box 693
EASTON, PENNSYLVANIA
18042

Kiski Mini Bottle Club
243 Maryland Drive
GLENSHAW, PENNSYLVANIA
15116

Camoset Bottle Club
Box 252
JOHNSTOWN,
PENNSYLVANIA 15907

Tri-State BC & DC
958 E. Baltimore Pike
KENNETT SQUARE,
PENNSYLVANIA 19380

The East Coast Ezra Brooks
Club
2815 Fiddlers Green Road
LANCASTER,
PENNSYLVANIA 17601

Laurel Valley Bottle Club
RD #4 Box 127A
LIGONIER, PENNSYLVANIA
15658

Middletown Area Bottle
Collectors Association
P.O. Box 1
MIDDLETOWN,
PENNSYLVANIA 17057

Delaware Valley Bottle Club
303 W. Walnut Street
NORTH WALES,
PENNSYLVANIA 19454

Pittsburgh Antique Bottle Club
209 Palomina Drive
OAKDALE, PENNSYLVANIA
15071

Del Val Miniature Bottle Club
Presidential Apts., Madison
Penthouse
PHILADELPHIA,
PENNSYLVANIA 19131

Philada Collectors' Club
P.O. Box 8302
PHILADELPHIA,
PENNSYLVANIA 19111

Philadelphia Bottle Club
8445 Walker Street
PHILADELPHIA,
PENNSYLVANIA 19136

Indiana Bottle Club
R.D. 1 Box 281
SHELOCTA, PENNSYLVANIA
15775

Classic Glass Bottle Club
1720 Memorial Avenue
WILLIAMSPORT,
PENNSYLVANIA 17701

Pennsylvania Bottle Collectors
Association
P.O. Box 156
YORK, PENNSYLVANIA
17371

Rhode Island

Little Rhody Bottle Club
3161 W. Shore Road
WARWICK, RHODE ISLAND
02992

South Carolina

South Carolina Bottle Club
330 Barnmount Drive
COLA, SOUTH CAROLINA
29210

Tennessee

Goodlettsville Antique Bottle
Club
128 E. Lawn Drive
GOODLETTSVILLE,
TENNESSEE 37072

Cotton Carnival Beam Club
P.O. Box 17951
MEMPHIS, TENNESSEE
38117

Memphis Bottle Collectors
Club
1373 Wrenwood
MEMPHIS, TENNESSEE
38122

Middle Tennessee Bottle
Collectors Club
P.O. Box 120083
NASHVILLE, TENNESSEE
37205

Texas

The Austin Bottle & Insulator
Collectors
1614 Ashberry Drive
AUSTIN, TEXAS 78723

Exploration Society
603 9th Street
CORPUS CHRISTI, TEXAS
78419

Texas Longhorn Bottle Club
P.O. Box 5346
IRVING, TEXAS 75062

Avon Collector's Corner
Rt. 6, Box 99
MARSHALL, TEXAS 75670

Gulf Coast Bottle & Jar Club
P.O. Box 1754
PASADENA, TEXAS 77501

Avon's Tip O Tex Chapter
818 N. Dowling
SAN BENITO, TEXAS 78586

Utah

Golden Spike A.B.C.
548 1st Street
OGDEN, UTAH 84404

Utah Antique Bottle & Relic
Club
3099 South 2078 East
SALT LAKE CITY, UTAH
84109

Virginia

Metro-Washington Bottle
Collectors
4305 Guinea Road
ANNANDALE, VIRGINIA
22003

Ye Old Bottle Club
P.O. Box 688
CLARKSVILLE, VIRGINIA
23987

Metropolitan Antique Bottle
Club
109 Howard Street
DUMFRIES, VIRGINIA 22026

Potomac Bottle Collectors
Club
6602 Orland Street
FALLS CHURCH, VIRGINIA
22043

Richmond Area Bottle
Collectors Association
16 Georgia Avenue
GLEN ALLEN, VIRGINIA
23060

Historical Bottle Diggers of
Virginia
Route 1, Box 8A
HINTON, VIRGINIA 22831

Hampton Roads Area Bottle
Collectors Association
4012 Winchester Drive
PORTSMOUTH, VIRGINIA
23707

Apple Valley Bottle Collectors
Club, Inc.
P.O. Box 2201
WINCHESTER, VIRGINIA
22601

Washington

Capitol Bottle Collectors &
Bottle Club
P.O. Box 202
OLYMPIA, WASHINGTON
98507

Washington Bottle Collectors
Association
P.O. Box 80045
SEATTLE, WASHINGTON
98108

Avon Club
18008 1/2 28th Avenue E.
TACOMA, WASHINGTON
98445

Northwest Mini Club of
Portland
38306 S.E. 10th Street
WASHOUGAL, WASHINGTON
98671

West Virginia

Nutmeg State Ezra Brooks
Club
1929 Penn Avenue
WEIRTON, WEST VIRGINIA
26062

Wild & Wonderful West
Virginia Ezra Brooks Bottle &
Specialty Club
3922 Hanlin Way
WEIRTON, WEST VIRGINIA
26062

Wisconsin

Avon Club
708 Ridge Street
STOUGHTON, WISCONSIN
53589

Milwaukee Antique Bottle
Club, Inc.
2343 Met-to-Wee Lane
WAUWATOSA, WISCONSIN
53226

Wyoming

Cheyenne Antique Bottle Club
4417 E. 8th Street
CHEYENNE, WYOMING
82001

CANADA

Wild Rose Antique Bottle
Collectors
P.O. Box 1471, Main Post
Office
EDMONTON, ALBERTA,
CANADA

Rangeland Collectors Club
P.O. Box 724
LETHBRIDGE, ALBERTA
T1J 3Z6, CANADA

Prince Rupert Olde Tyme
Bottle & Collectables Club
P.O. Box 622
PRINCE RUPERT, BRITISH
COLUMBIA, CANADA

The Old Time Bottle Club of
British Columbia
P.O. Box 77154, Postal
Station 5
VANCOUVER/6, BRITISH
COLUMBIA, CANADA

Avon Club
4088 Lochside Drive
VICTORIA, BRITISH
COLUMBIA V8X 2C8,
CANADA

The Saint John Antique Bottle
Club
25 Orange Street
SAINT JOHN, NEW
BRUNSWICK E2L 1L9,
CANADA

Land of Evangeline Antique
Bottle Club
Cambridge Station
KINGS COUNTY, NOVA
SCOTIA, CANADA

Quinte Bottle Collectors
637 Bridge Street
EAST BELLEVILLE,
ONTARIO, CANADA

Avon Club
RR1
WESTPORT, ONTARIO,
CANADA K0G 1X0

Essex County Antique Bottle &
Insulator Club
9767 Ridge Road
WINDSOR, ONTARIO N8R
1G5, CANADA

Club Mini Barman
c.p. 126 Rosemont
MONTREAL, QUEBEC H1X
3B6, CANADA

Bridge City Collectors' Club
111-115th Street East
SASKATOON,
SASKATCHEWAN 57N 2E1,
CANADA

ENGLAND

Old Bottle Club of Great
Britain
14 Derwent Crescent
WHITEHILL, KIDSGROVE,
ENGLAND

The Mini Bottle Club
42 Keats Way, W. Brayton
MIDDLESEX, ENGLAND

Publications of Interest to Bottle Collectors

NEWSPAPERS

The American Collector
Drawer C
Kermit, Texas 79745

Antique Trader Weekly
P.O. Box 1050
Dubuque, Iowa 52001

Collector's News
P.O. Box 156
Grundy Center, Iowa 50638

Maine Antique Digest
Box 358, Jefferson Street
Waldoboro, Maine 04572

Ohio Antique Review
72 East North Street
Worthington, Ohio 43085

Southeast Trader
P.O. Box 519
Lexington, South Carolina 29072

NEWSLETTERS

Fruit Jar Newsletter
7 Lowell Place
West Orange, New Jersey 07052

Kovels on Antiques and Collect-
ibles
P.O. Box 22200
Beachwood, Ohio 44122

Milk House Moosletter
The Time Travelers
P.O. Box 366
Bryn Mawr, California 92318

The Milk Route
4 Ox Bow Road
Westport, Connecticut 06880

Miniature Bottle Mart
24 Gertrude Lane
West Haven, Connecticut 06516

MAGAZINES

Antique Bottle Collecting
Chapel House Farm, Newport Road
Albrighton, North Wolverhampton
Staffs, England

Antique Bottle World
5003 West Berwyn
Chicago, Illinois 60630

Antiques Journal
P.O. Box 1046
Dubuque, Iowa 52001

The Miniature Bottle Collector
P.O. Box 2161
Palos Verdes Peninsula, California 90274

Old Bottle Magazine
P.O. Box 243
Bend, Oregon 97701

Pictorial Bottle Review
Brisco Publications
P.O. Box 2161
Palos Verdes Peninsula, California 90274

Most of the books not published privately and listed in the Bibliography can be obtained at local bookstores. Specialized shops that carry many books not normally stocked are:

Al Cembura
139 Arlington Avenue
Berkeley, California 94707

Antique Publications
Emmitsburg, Maryland 21727

Collector Books
P.O. Box 3009
Paducah, Kentucky 42001

Hotchkiss House
18 Hearthstone
Pittsford, New York 14534

Old Bottle Magazine
Box 243
Bend, Oregon 97701

Bibliography

This list includes most of the books about bottles available in bookstores or through the mail. Out-of-print books or price books published before 1979 are not included unless of importance as research tools.

GENERAL

Belknap, E. M. *Milk Glass*. New York: Crown Publishers, Inc., 1959.

Cleveland, Hugh. *Bottle Pricing Guide*. Revised 3rd Edition. Paducah, Kentucky: Collectors Books, 1980.

Ferson, Regis F. and Mary F. *Yesterday's Milk Glass Today*. Privately printed, 1981. (Order from authors, 122 Arden Rd., Pittsburgh, Pennsylvania 15216.)

Ketchum, William C., Jr. *A Treasury of American Bottles*. Indianapolis: The Bobbs-Merrill Company, 1975.

Klamkin, Marian. *The Collector's Book of Bottles*. New York: Dodd, Mead & Company, 1971.

Kovel, Ralph and Terry. *Kovels' Know Your Antiques*. Revised edition. New York: Crown Publishers, Inc., 1981.

———. *The Kovels' Antiques Price List*. Fourteenth edition. New York: Crown Publishers, Inc., 1981.

McKearin, George L. and Helen. *Two Hundred Years of American Blown Glass*. New York: Crown Publishers, Inc., 1950.

Munsey, Cecil. *The Illustrated Guide to Collecting Bottles*. New York: Hawthorn Books, Inc., 1970.

Neal, Nelson and Marna. *Common Bottles for the Average Collector*. Wolfe City, Texas: The University Press, 1975.

Ohio Bottle Club. *10th Anniversary Edition Ohio Bottles*. Barberton, Ohio: Ohio Bottle Club, 1978.

Potomac Bottle Collectors. *Washington D.C. Bottles*. 1976. (Order from Tom & Kaye Johnson, 7722 Woodstock St., Manassas, Virginia 22110.)

Sellari, Dot and Carlo. *The Official Price Guide to Bottles Old & New*. Fourth edition. Orlando, Florida: House of Collectibles, 1979.

Switzer, Ronald R. *The Bertrand Bottles: A Study of 19th Century Glass and Ceramic Containers*. Washington, D.C.: National Park Service, 1974.

Toulouse, Julian Harrison. *Bottle Makers and Their Marks*. Camden, New Jersey: Thomas Nelson, Inc., 1971.

BITTERS

Ring, Carlyn. *For Bitters Only*. Privately printed, 1980. (Order from author, 59 Livermore Rd., Wellesley, Massachusetts 02181.)

Watson, Richard. *Bitter Bottles*. Fort Davis, Texas: Thomas Nelson & Sons, 1965.

———. *Supplement to Bitters Bottles*. Camden, New Jersey: Thomas Nelson & Sons, 1968.

CANDY CONTAINERS

Eikelberner, George, and Agadjanian, Serge. *American Glass Containers.* Privately printed, 1967. (Order from authors, River Rd., Belle Mead, New Jersey 08502.)

──────. *More American Glass Candy Containers.* Privately printed, 1970. (Order from authors, River Rd., Belle Mead, New Jersey 08502.)

Long, Jennie D. *An Album of Candy Containers.* Privately printed, 1978. (Order from author, P.O. Box 552, Kingsburg, California 93631.)

FIGURAL

Revi, Albert Christian. *American Pressed Glass and Figure Bottles.* New York: Thomas Nelson & Sons, 1964.

Umberger, Jewel and Arthur L. *Collectible Character Bottles.* Privately printed, 1969. (Order from Corker Book Company, 819 W. Wilson, Tyler, Texas 75701.)

Wearin, Otha D. *Statues That Pour: The Story of Character Bottles.* Denver, Colorado: Sage Books (2679 South York St.), 1965.

FLASKS

McKearin, Helen, and Wilson, Kenneth M. *American Bottles & Flasks and Their Ancestry.* New York: Crown Publishers, Inc., 1978.

Roberts, Mike. *Price Guide to All the Flasks.* Privately printed, 1980. (Order from author, 840 Elm Court, Newark, Ohio 43055.)

Thomas, John L. *Picnics, Coffins, Shoo-Flies.* Privately printed, 1974. (Order from author, P.O. Box 446, Weaverville, California 96093.)

Van Rensselaer, Stephen. *Early American Bottles & Flasks—Revised.* Privately printed, 1969. (Order from J. Edmund Edwards, 61 Winton Place, Stratford, Connecticut 06497.)

FRUIT JARS

Brantley, William F. *A Collector's Guide to Ball Jars.* 1975. (Order from Ball Corporation, Consumer Publications, Muncie, Indiana 47302.)

Creswick, Alice. *The Red Book of Fruit Jars No. 3.* Privately printed, 1977. (Order from author, 0-8525 Kenowa SW, Grand Rapids, Michigan 49504.)

Toulouse, Julian Harrison. *Fruit Jars: A Collector's Manual.* Jointly published by Camden, New Jersey: Thomas Nelson & Sons and Hanover, Pennsylvania: Everybody's Press, 1969.

INKWELLS

Covill, William E., Jr. *Ink Bottles and Inkwells.* Taunton, Massachusetts: William S. Sullwold Publishing, 1971.

MEDICINE

Baldwin, Joseph K. *A Collector's Guide to Patent and Proprietary Medicine Bottles of the Nineteenth Century.* New York: Thomas Nelson, Inc., 1973.

Blasi, Betty. *A Bit About Balsams: A Chapter in the History of Nineteenth Century Medicine.* Privately printed, 1974. (Order from author, 5801 River Knolls Drive, Louisville, Kentucky 40222.)

MILK

Giarde, Jeffrey L. *Glass Milk Bottles: Their Makers and Marks.* Bryn Mawr, California: The Time Travelers Press (P.O. Box 366), 1980.

MINIATURES

Cembura, Al, and Avery, Constance. *A Guide to Miniature Bottles.* Vol. 1, sections 1–3. Privately printed, 1972 and 1973. (Order from authors, 139 Arlington Avenue, Berkeley, California 94708.)

Triffon, James A. *The Whiskey Miniature Bottle Collection, Scotch Whiskey.* Vol. 2. Privately printed, 1981. (Order from P.O. Box 1900, Garden Grove, California 92640.)

MODERN

Fred's Price Guide to Modern Bottles, July-August, 1981. Privately printed. (Order from P.O. Box 1423, Cheyenne, Wyoming 82001.)

Montague, H. F. *Montague's Modern Bottle Identification and Price Guide.* Privately printed, 1980. (Order from P.O. Box 4059, Overland Park, Kansas 66204.)

AVON

Hastin, Bud. *Bud Hastin's Avon Bottle Encyclopedia.* 1981 edition. Privately printed, 1980. (Order from author, P.O. Box 8400, Fort Lauderdale, Florida 33310.)

Western World. *Avon: Western World Handbook & Price Guide to Avon Bottles.* Privately printed, 1979. (Order from 511 Harrison St., San Francisco, California 94105.)

BEAM

Cembura, Al, and Avery, Constance. *Jim Beam Bottles, Identification and Price Guide.* 1981. 10th edition. Privately printed, 1981. (Order from authors, 139 Arlington Ave., Berkeley, California 94707.)

POISON BOTTLES

Durflinger, Roger L. *Poison Bottles Collectors Guide.* Vol. 1. Privately printed, 1972. (Order from author, 132 W. Oak St., Washington C.H., Ohio 43160.)

SARSAPARILLA

DeGrafft, Joan. *American Sarsaparilla Bottles.* Privately printed, 1980. (Order from author, 47 Ash St., North Attleboro, Massachusetts 02760.)

Shimko, Phyllis. *Sarsaparilla Bottle Encyclopedia.* Privately printed, 1969. (Order from author, Box 117, Aurora, Oregon 97002.)

SEAL

Morgan, Roy. *Sealed Bottles: Their History and Evolution (1630–1930).* Burton upon Trent, England: Midlands Antique Bottle Publishing, 1976.

SODA AND MINERAL WATER

Herr, J. A. *Breweries & Soda Works of St. Thomas Ont., 1833–1933: An Illustrated History for Bottle Collectors.* Vol. 1. Ontario Series. Privately printed, 1974. (Order from Canada West Publishing Company, 175 Alma St., St. Thomas, Ontario N5P 3B5.)
———. *The Ontario Soda Water Bottle Collector's Index and Price Guide.* Vol. 2. Ontario Series. Privately printed, 1975. (Order from Canada West Publishing Company.)
———. *The Ontario Stone Ginger Beer Collector's Index and Price Guide.* Vol. 3. Ontario Series. Privately printed, 1975. (Order from Canada West Publishing Company.)
Markota, Peck and Audia. *Western Blob Top Soda and Mineral Water Bottles.* Revised edition. Privately printed, 1972. (Order from authors, 8512 Pershing Ave., Fair Oaks, California 95628.)

SOFT DRINKS

Coca-Cola Company. *The Coca-Cola Company . . . An Illustrated Profile.* Atlanta, Georgia: The Coca Cola Company, 1974. (Order from P.O. Drawer 1734, Atlanta, Georgia 30301.)
Ellis, Harry E. *Dr Pepper, King of Beverages.* Dallas, Texas: Dr. Pepper Company, 1979. (Order from P.O. Box 225086, Dallas, Texas 75265.)
Goldstein, Shelly and Helen. *Coca-Cola Collectibles with Current Prices and Photographs in Full Color.* Vols. 1–4 and Index. Privately printed, 1971–1980. (Order from P.O. Box 301, Woodland Hills, California 91364.)
Munsey, Cecil. *The Illustrated Guide to the Collectibles of Coca-Cola.* New York: Hawthorn Books, Inc., 1972.
Munsey, Cecil, and Petretti, Allan. *Official Coca-Cola Collectibles Price Guide.* 1980–1981 edition. Hackensack, New Jersey: The Nostalgia Publishing Company, 1980.
Paul, John R., and Parmalee, Paul W. *Soft Drink Bottling: A History with Special Reference to Illinois.* Springfield, Illinois: Illinois State Museum Society, 1973.
Pitcock, Florene. *Soft Drink Bottle Guide.* Privately printed, 1975. (Order from author, 30 North Powell Ave., Columbus, Ohio 43204.)
Rawlingson, Fred. *Brad's Drink: A Primer for Pepsi-Cola Collectors.* Privately printed, 1976. (Order from FAR Publications, Box 5456, Newport News, Virginia 23605.)

WHISKEY AND BEER

Anderson, Sonja and Will. *Andersons' Turn-of-the-Century Brewery Dictionary.* Privately printed, 1968. (Order from authors, 1 Lindy St., Carmel, New York 10512.)

Anderson, Will. *The Beer Book: An Illustrated Guide to American Breweriana.* Princeton, New Jersey: The Pyne Press, 1973.

Barnett, R. E. *Pacific Coast Whiskey Bottles.* Privately printed, 1979. (Order from author, 729 North H, Lakeview, Oregon 97630.)

Kay, Robert E. *Miniature Beer Bottles & Go-Withs.* Privately printed, 1980. (Order from 216 N. Batavia Ave., Batavia, Illinois 60510.)

Kroll, Wayne L. *Badger Breweries, Past and Present.* Privately printed, 1976. (Order from author, Box 266, Jefferson, Wisconsin 53549.)

Triffon, James A. *The Whiskey Miniature Bottle Collection.* Vol. 1. Privately printed, 1979. (Order from author, P.O. Box 1900, Garden Grove, California 92640.)

AESTHETIC SPECIALTIES INC., Bing Crosby, 38th, 1978 .... 22.00 To 27.00
  Bing Crosby, 39th, 1979 .... 39.00
  Kentucky Derby, 1979 .... 17.00 To 42.00
  Model T, Ice Cream Truck, 1980 .... 35.00 To 65.00
  Model T, Telephone Truck, 1980 .... 57.00 To 65.00
  World's Greatest Golfer, 1979 .... 35.00 To 42.00
  World's Greatest Hunter, 1979 .... 35.00 To 42.00
  1903 Cadillac, Blue, 1979 .... 50.00
  1903 Cadillac, Gold, 1980 .... 402.00
  1903 Cadillac, White, 1979 .... 50.00
  1909 Stanley Steamer, 1978 .... 48.00 To 49.99
  1910 Oldsmobile, Black, 1980 .... 65.00
  1912 Chevrolet, Black, 1979 .... 50.00
  1912 Chevrolet, Gold 500.00
     ALPHA, see Lewis & Clark
     AUSTIN NICHOLS, see Wild Turkey

*Avon started in 1886 as the California Perfume Company. It was not
until 1929 that the name Avon was used. In 1939 it became Avon
Products, Inc. Each year Avon sells many figural bottles filled with
cosmetic products. Ceramic, plastic, and glass bottles are made in limited
editions.*

AVON, A Man's World, 1969, Gold Globe On Stand .... 5.00 To 9.00
  A Winner, Boxing Gloves, 1960, Hair Guard 20.00
  After Shave Caddy, Full & Boxed 12.00
  After Shower Sample, 1959-62, Black Glass, Red Cap, 1/2 Ounce 8.00
     AVON, AIRPLANE, see Avon, Spirit of St. Louis
  Aladdin's Lamp, 1971 .... 5.00 To 10.00
  Aladdin's Lamp, 1971, Full & Boxed 10.00
  Alaskan Moose, 1974, Full & Boxed .... 4.75 To 6.00
  Albee Award Figurine, 1978, No.1 .... 80.00 To 100.00
  Albee Award Figurine, 1979, No.2 .... 100.00
  Alpine Flask, 1966-67 .... 30.00 To 40.00
  Alpine Flask, 1968, Full & Boxed 50.00
  American Belle, 1976, Full & Boxed .... 5.00 To 8.00
  American Buffalo, 1975 .... 5.00
  American Eagle Bureau Organizer, 1972, Full & Boxed .... 17.50 To 30.00
  American Eagle Pipe, 1974-75 .... 5.00
  American Eagle, 1971, Amber, Full & Boxed 5.00
  American Ideal Perfume, 1911, California Perfume Co. 125.00
  American Schooner, 1972, Full & Boxed .... 5.00 To 8.00
  Andy Capp Figural, 1970, England 98.00
     AVON, ANGEL, see also Avon, Heavenly Angel Cologne
  Angel Song With Lyre, 1978-79 .... 6.00
  Angler, 1970, Full & Boxed .... 4.00 To 5.00
  Antiseptic, 1946, Black, Full, Round, 6 Ounce 40.00
  Apple Blossom Toilet Water, 1941-42 .... 40.00
  Ariane First Edition Cologne Spray, 1977, 1.8 Ounce .... 5.00 To 10.00
  Armoire, 1972, Full 4.00
  At Point, 1973, Full & Boxed 4.00
  Athena Bath Urn, 1974, Full & Boxed .... 2.00 To 10.00
  Atlantic, 4-4-2, 1972, Full & Boxed 11.00
     AVON, AUTO HORN, see Avon, It's A Blast
  Auto Lantern, 1973 .... 6.00
  Auto Lantern, 1973, Full & Boxed 12.00
  Autumn Harvest Pomander, 1979-80 .... 5.50
  Avon Calling, 1969-70, Phone, Wild Country 15.00
  Avon Calling, 1969, Phone .... 4.00 To 7.00
  Avon Calling, 1973, 1905 Phone, Full & Boxed .... 6.00 To 10.00
  Avon Lady Porcelain Figurine, Full & Boxed 49.00
  Avon Lady 1896, 1976 Club Bottle 50.00
  Avon Lady 1906, 1977 Club Bottle 35.00

Avon Lady 1916, 1978 Club Bottle 30.00
Avon Open, 1972-75, Golf Cart .... 3.00 To 5.00
Avon, Dueling Pistol II, 1974, Black Glass 9.00
Avonshire Blue Cologne, 1972, Full & Boxed 6.00
Baby Basset, 1978, Full & Boxed 2.50
Baby Grand Perfume Glace, 1971-72, Full & Boxed 9.50
Baby Hippo, 1977-80, Full & Boxed 3.00
Ballad Perfume, 1939, 3 Drams, 3/8 Ounce 100.00
    AVON, BARBER, see also Avon, Close Harmony
Barber Pole, Full & Boxed .... 3.00 To 4.00
    AVON, BAROMETER, see Avon, Weather-Or-Not
    AVON, BASEBALL MITT, see Avon, Fielder's Choice
Bath Bouquet, 1965, Full & Boxed 25.00
Bath Classic Cologne, Somewhere, 1962 .... 36.00
Bath Cruet Urn, 1963 .... 15.00
Bath Oil For Men, 1965, Full & Boxed 17.00
Bath Seasons, Lilac, 1967-68, Full & Boxed 5.00
Bath Treasure, 1973, Snail, Full & Boxed 4.50
Bath Urn, 1974, Green, Full 6.00
Bay Rum Jug, 1962 .... 8.00 To 15.00
Bay Rum Keg, 1965 .... 6.00
Bay Rum Keg, 1965, Full & Boxed 12.00
Beautiful Awakening, 1973, Clock 6.00
Beauty Basket, 1947, Full, In Basket 65.00
Beauty Bound Black Purse, 1964 .... 45.00
Beauty Mark, 1948 .... 28.00
Bell Jar Cologne, 1973, Full & Boxed .... 4.00 To 8.50
Benjamin Franklin, Bust, 1974, White, Full & Boxed 7.00
Betsy Ross Cologne, 1976, Full & Boxed .... 7.00 To 12.00
Big Bolt, 1976, Full & Boxed 1.50
Big Game Rhino, 1972-73, Full & Boxed .... 3.50 To 6.00
Big Mack, 1973, Full & Boxed 7.00
Big Whistle, 1972, Full & Boxed .... 3.00 To 4.00
Bird Of Paradise Cologne Decanter, 1969, Full & Boxed 9.00
Bird Of Paradise Cologne Mist, 1970 .... 3.50
Birdfeeder, 1969, Full & Boxed .... 7.00 To 11.00
Birdhouse Bubble Bath, 1969, Full & Boxed .... 7.00 To 9.00
Blacksmith's Anvil, 1972 .... 3.00
Bloodhound Pipe, 1975, Full & Boxed 4.00
Blue Blazer After Shave Lotion, 1964 .... 20.00
Blue Blazer Deluxe, 1965 .... 50.00
Blue Blossoms Cup & Saucer, 1974-75 .... 25.00
Blue Eyes, 1975, Cat 5.50
Blunderbuss Pistol, 1976 .... 7.50
Bold Eagle, 1976, Full & Boxed .... 4.00 To 4.50
Bon Bon, 1972, Black Poodle, Full & Boxed 2.00
Boot, Miss Lollypop, 1967, Full & Boxed 5.00
Boot, Western, 1973, Full & Boxed .... 3.00 To 4.00
Boot, 1965, Amber, Gold Top .... Illus   7.00
Boot, 1966, Gold Cap .... 3.00 To 4.00
Boot, 1976, Christmas Surprise, Green, Red Top 2.00
Boots & Saddle, 1968 .... 18.00
    AVON, BOWLING PIN, see Avon, King Pin
Bridal Moments, 1976-77, Full & Boxed .... 4.50 To 11.00
Bright Night Toilet Water, 1955-61, Full & Boxed 12.00
Bristol Blue Cologne, 1974 .... 10.00
Brocade Deluxe, 1967, Full & Boxed .... 27.50 To 30.00
Brocade Perfume Glace, 1968 .... 8.50
Brocade Perfume Oil, 1969, 1/2 Ounce 6.00
Bucking Bronco, 1971, Full & Boxed .... 4.50 To 9.00
Bugatti, 1974 .... 8.00 To 12.00
Bulldog Pipe, 1972, Full & Boxed .... 3.50 To 5.00

Avon, Boot, 1965, Amber, Gold Top

Bunny Candleholder, Ceramic 8.00
Bunny Ceramic Planter Candleholder, Brazil 20.00
Bureau Organizer, 1966-67 .... 30.00 To 50.00
Butter Dish, 1973, Clear, Covered 10.00
Butterfly Cologne, 1972 .... 5.00 To 6.50
Butterfly Fantasy Egg, 1974, First Issue 20.00
Butterfly Fantasy Egg, 1974, Full & Boxed 45.00
Buttons & Bows Cologne, 1960, Full & Boxed 7.00
Buttons & Bows Cream Lotion, 1962, 4 Ounce, Full & Boxed 5.00
Buttons & Bows Pretty Choice, 1962, Full & Boxed 18.00
Cable Car, 1974, Full & Boxed .... 6.00 To 8.00
Calabash Pipe, 1974, Full & Boxed 8.00
California Perfume Company, Face Lotion, Box ....*Color*
California Perfume Company, Factory Club Bottle, 1974 .... 50.00
California Perfume Company, Heliotrope Sachet, Contents 70.00
California Perfume Company, Heliotrope Sachet, Contents, 1898 .... 70.00
Cameo Set, 1965, Full & Boxed .... 27.50 To 30.00
Camper, 1972-74, Full & Boxed .... 6.00 To 10.00
Canada Goose, 1973, Full & Boxed .... 6.00 To 9.00
Candlestick Cologne, 1966 .... 3.00 To 10.00
Candlestick Cologne, 1972 .... 8.00
Cannon, Defender, 1966 .... 10.00 To 15.00
Cannon, Revolutionary, 1975 .... 7.00
Cannon, 1966 .... 18.00
Cannonball Express 4-6-0, 1976, Locomotive 6.00
Cape Cod Wine Decanter, 1977-80 .... 10.00
Capitol, 1970, Amber, Full & Boxed .... 3.00 To 3.50
Captain's Choice, 1964 .... 5.00 To 10.00
Captain's Choice, 1964, Full & Boxed 13.00
Captain's Lantern, 1975 .... 3.00
Captain's Pride, 1970, Full & Boxed .... 3.00 To 6.00
Car, Army Jeep, 1974-75 .... 3.00
Car, Big Rig, 1975-76, Full & Boxed 6.50
Car, Buick Skylark, 1953, Full & Boxed 9.00
Car, Cadillac, Gold, 1969, Full & Boxed .... 5.00 To 8.00
Car, Cement Mixer, 1979-80 .... 9.00
Car, Checker Cab, 1977-78, Full & Boxed 5.00
Car, Chevy, 1955, 1975 .... 7.00
Car, Chrysler, 1948 .... 8.00
Car, Cord, 1937, 1974 .... 5.00
Car, Country Vendor, 1973, Full & Boxed 8.00
Car, Duesenberg, Silver, 1970, Full & Boxed 6.00

Car, Electric Charger, 1970, Full & Boxed 3.00
Car, Ford, 1936, 1976 .... 10.00
Car, Highway King, 1977, Full & Boxed 7.00
Car, Jaguar, 1973, Full & Boxed 5.00
Car, Mustang, 1976, Full & Boxed .... 2.00 To 6.00
Car, Packard Roadster, 1970, Full & Boxed .... 5.00 To 6.00
Car, Pierce Arrow, 1933, 1975, Full & Boxed 6.00
Car, Red Depot Wagon, 1906, 1972, Full & Boxed 5.00
Car, Rolls-Royce, 1972, Full & Boxed 5.00
Car, Stanley Steamer, Dated May, 1978, Tai Winds 10.00
Car, Station Wagon, 1971, Full & Boxed .... 5.00 To 9.00
Car, Sterling Six, 1968, Ribbed Top, Full & Boxed .... 5.00 To 9.00
Car, Sterling Six, 1968, Smooth Top .... 40.00 To 45.00
Car, Straight Eight, 1969, Green .... 3.00 To 3.50
Car, Stutz Bearcat, 1974, Full & Boxed .... 4.00 To 5.00
Car, Sure Winner, 1972 .... 3.50
Car, Thomas Flyer, 1908, Full & Boxed, 1974 .... 4.00 To 10.00
Car, Thunderbird, 1955, Blue, 1974-75 .... 2.00 To 6.75
Car, Touring T, 1969 .... 5.00 To 9.00
Car, Volkswagen Bus, 1975, Full & Boxed 5.00
Car, Volkswagen, 1970, Black .... 4.00 To 5.00
Car, Volkswagen, 1972, Red 3.00
Car, Volkswagen, 1973, Blue 4.00
Casey Jones Jr., 1956, Soaps .... 40.00 To 45.00
Casey's Lantern, 1966, Amber, Full & Boxed 35.00
Casey's Lantern, 1966, Green 35.00
Casey's Lantern, 1966, Red .... 30.00 To 42.50
Castleford Bath Beads, 1974, Jar & Lid, Crystal 3.00
    AVON, CAT, see Avon, Blue Eyes; Avon, Tabatha; Avon, Kitten
    Little; Avon, Ming Cat
Catch-A-Fish, 1976, Full & Boxed .... 8.00 To 9.00
Centennial Express 1876, After Shave, 1978, Locomotive 9.00
Charisma Perfume Oil, 1969, 1/2 Ounce 6.00
Charmlight Lamp, 1975, Full & Boxed 5.00
Chick A Peek, Full & Boxed 3.00
Chief Pontiac, Car Ornament, 1976 .... 6.00
Chimney Lamp, 1973 .... 5.00 To 6.00
China Teapot, 1972 .... 10.00 To 20.00
Christmas Classic, 1962-63, Full & Boxed 15.00
Christmas Gift Perfume, 1963, Full & Boxed 30.00
Christmas Ornament, 1967, Gold 8.00
Christmas Ornament, 1967, Red 8.00
Christmas Ornament, 1967, Silver 8.00
Christmas Ornament, 1968, Purple 30.00
Christmas Tree Bubble Bath, 1968, Full & Boxed .... 3.00 To 6.50
Christmas Wreath, 1965, Full & Boxed 5.00
Church Mouse Bride, 1978-79 .... 4.50
Church Mouse Groom, 1979-80, Full & Boxed 6.00
Clancey The Clown, 1973-74, Full & Boxed 4.00
Classic Beauty, 1972-76, Full & Boxed 4.00
Classic Decanter, 1969 .... 6.00
Classic Lion, 1973-75, Full & Boxed 4.00
Clean As A Whistle, 1960 .... 6.00
    AVON, CLOCK, see Avon, Beautiful Awakening; Avon, Daylight
    Shaving Time; Avon, Enchanted Hours; Avon, Fragrance Hours;
    Avon, Leisure Hours
Close Harmony, 1963 .... 10.00 To 25.00
Cluck A Doo, 1971, Full & Boxed 6.00
Cockatoo Pomander, 1972 .... 5.00
    AVON, COFFEE MILL, see Avon, Country Store Coffee Mill
Coleman Lantern, 1977, Full & Boxed 4.00
Collector's Pipe, 1973, Full & Boxed 4.00
Collector's Stein, 1976, Full & Boxed, Stoneware 15.00

Cologne Elegante, Red Rose On Top, 1971-72 .... 8.00
Cologne Elegante, 1971, Full & Boxed .... 6.00 To 10.00
Cologne For Men, 1949, Full & Boxed 13.00
Cologne Gems, Set, 1967, Full & Boxed 10.00
Cologne Gems, 1967 .... 4.00
Cologne Royale, 1972 .... 2.00
Cologne Silk, 1966 .... 10.00
Cologne Trilogy, 1969-70 .... 15.00 To 20.00
Color Bar, 1958 .... 15.00
Color Garden, 1964, Full & Boxed 15.00
Concertina Bubble Bath, 1970, Full & Boxed 5.00
Corncob Pipe, 1974 .... 2.00 To 3.00
Corncob Pipe, 1974, Full & Boxed 4.00
Cornucopia, Skin So Soft Bath Oil, 1971, Full & Boxed 5.50
Cotillion Beauty Dust, With Puff, 1961, Full 5.00
Cotillion Body Powder, 1950, 5 Ounce, Full 10.00
Cotillion Cologne Mist, 1959 .... 20.00
Cotillion Perfume, 1937, 2 Dram, Gold Cap, Boxed 70.00
Cotillion Perfume, 1953, 3/8 Ounce 84.00
Country Charm Lamp, 1976, Full & Boxed 6.00
Country Charm, 1973, Butter Churn, Full & Boxed 4.00
Country Peaches, 1977, Soap Jar 7.00
Country Store Coffee Mill, 1972-76 .... 3.00 To 5.00
Courting Carriage, 1973, Crystal, Gold Cap .... 2.00 To 3.00
Courting Rose, 1974-77, Full & Boxed .... 6.00 To 13.00
Courtship Perfume, 1938 .... 40.00
Covered Wagon, 1970-71 .... 5.00
Covered Wagon, 1970-71, Full & Boxed 20.00
Cruet Cologne Set, 1973-74, Full & Boxed 6.00
Crystal Candelier, 1969, Full & Boxed 12.00
Crystal, Beauty Dust, 1966 .... 15.00
Crystalsong Bell, Mexican 10.00
Crystalsong Bell, 1975, Full & Boxed .... 3.00 To 6.00
Cupid's Bow, 1955, Full & Boxed .... 45.00 To 50.00
Dachshund, 1973, Full & Boxed 3.50
Daisy Bouquet, 1957, Full & Boxed 25.00
Daisy Darling, 1958, Set, Full & Boxed 35.00
Daylight Shaving Time, 1968, Full & Boxed .... 5.00 To 10.00
Dear Friends, 1973, Figurine Cologne, Full & Boxed 10.00
Decisions, 1965, Full & Boxed .... 18.00 To 20.00
Delft Blue Foaming Bath Oil, 1973, Full & Boxed 4.50
Deluxe Electric Pre-Shave, 1961-63, Wood Top 20.00
        AVON, DOG, see Avon, At Point; Avon, Bon Bon; Avon,
        Dachshund; Avon, Lady Spaniel; Avon, Old Faithful; Avon,
        Queen of Scots; Avon, Snoopy; Avon, Suzette
Dollars 'n Scents, 1966-67, Spicy After Shave .... 12.50 To 20.00
Dollars 'n Scents, 1966, Full & Boxed 20.00
Dolphin Decanter, 1968, Full & Boxed .... 3.00 To 6.00
Dolphin, Miniature, 1973, Full & Boxed 2.50
Doubly Yours, 1949, Set, Cologne 50.00
Dream Castle, 1964, Full & Boxed, Cologne & Cream Sachet 22.50
Dream Garden, 1972, Full & Boxed .... 8.00 To 12.00
        AVON, DUCK, see also Avon, Mallard
Duck Decoy Pomander, 1974 .... 5.00
Duck, Collector's Organizer, 1971, Full & Boxed .... 20.00 To 27.50
Duck, Collector's Organizer, 1971, 2 Bottles & Soap .... 17.50 To 25.00
        AVON, DUELING PISTOLS, see also Avon, Twenty Paces
Dueling Pistol 1760, 1973, Full & Boxed .... 11.00 To 12.00
        AVON, DUESENBERG, see Avon, Car, Duesenberg
Dutch Girl Cologne, 1973, Full & Boxed .... 5.00 To 8.00
Dutch Maid Cologne, 1977, Full & Boxed .... 5.00 To 6.00
Dutch Pipe, 1973, Full & Boxed .... 8.00 To 10.00
Eiffel Tower, 1970, Pressed Glass, Gold Cap .... 3.50 To 5.00

Eight Ball, 1973, Full & Boxed 2.00
El Toro, 1974, Full & Boxed, Mexican 9.00
    AVON, ELECTRIC CHARGER, see Avon, Car, Electric Charger
Electric Guitar, 1974-75, Full & Boxed .... 3.00 To 4.00
Electric Pre-Shave, 1957-58, Full & Boxed 8.00
Elegante Cologne, 4 Ounce, 1956-59 .... 17.00
Elegante Toilet Water, 1957, Full & Boxed 30.00
Elizabethan Fashion Figurine, 1972, Pink, Full & Boxed .... 7.00 To 15.00
Elusive Perfume Oil, 1969, 1/2 Ounce 6.00
Emerald Bell, 1978, Full & Boxed, Cologne 7.00
Enchanted Hours, Full 4.00
Enchanted Hours, 1973, Full & Boxed, Swiss Cuckoo Clock, Milk Glass 5.00
Evening Glow Perfume, 1974, Full & Boxed, Miniature Lamp .... 4.00 To 7.00
Excalibur Cologne, 1969, American, Full & Boxed .... 5.00 To 10.00
Fashion Boot Pin Cushion Cologne, 1976, Full & Boxed 6.00
Felina Fluffles, 1976, Full & Boxed 5.00
Fielder's Choice, 1971 .... 3.00 To 5.00
Fife, 1965 .... 14.00
Fire Alarm Box, 1975-76 .... 2.00
Firm Grip, 1977-78, Wrench, After Shave 3.00
First Avon Lady, 1972, Porcelain Figurine 125.00
First Class Male, 1970, Full & Boxed, Mail Box .... 2.50 To 5.00
First Down Football, 1963 .... 18.00
First Down Football, 1965 .... 10.00
First Edition, 1967, Full & Boxed, Book .... 5.00 To 10.00
First Volunteer, 1971, Fire Engine, Full & Boxed .... 5.00 To 9.00
    AVON, FISH, see Avon, Dolphin; Avon, Sea Spirit
Flaming Tulip Candle, 1973, Full & Boxed 5.00
Flight To Beauty, 1974, Boxed 4.00
Flower Maiden, 1974, Full & Boxed .... 5.00 To 7.00
Flowertime Talc, 1949-53 .... 25.00
Flowertime, 1942, Full & Boxed 75.00
Flowertime, 1943, Full & Boxed 65.00
Fly-A-Balloon Boy, 1975, Holding Red Balloon 10.00
    AVON, FOOTBALL, see Avon, First Down
    AVON, FOOTBALL HELMET, see Avon, Opening Play
Forever Spring Toilet Water, 1956, Full & Boxed 15.00
Four-A After Shave, 1964 .... 15.00
Fox Hunt, 1966, Full & Boxed .... 20.00 To 26.00
Fragrance & Frills, 1972, Full & Boxed 6.00
Fragrance Bell, 1965, Full & Boxed 16.00
Fragrance Bell, 1968, Full & Boxed 6.00
Fragrance Chest, 1966, Full & Boxed .... 25.00 To 27.00
Fragrance Duette, 1966, Set 11.00
Fragrance Fancy, 1972-75, Full & Boxed 4.00
Fragrance Favorites, 1965 .... 18.00
Fragrance Fling Trio, 1968, Full & Boxed 10.00
Fragrance Gold, 1964, Full & Boxed 18.00
Fragrance Hours, 1971-73, Grandfather Clock .... 3.00 To 4.00
Fragrance Jar, Frosted Stopper, 1949 .... 30.00
Fragrance Jar, Lavender, 1914-23 .... 110.00
Fragrance Jar, Pink Ceramic, White Leaves, 1946 .... 75.00
Fragrance Ornament, 1965, Full 11.00
Fragrance Ornament, 1965, Full & Boxed .... 37.50 To 40.00
Fragrance Rainbow, 1956, Set .... 45.00 To 75.00
Fragrance Splendor, 1971 .... 8.00
Fragrance Touch, 1969, Full & Boxed, Hand Holding Bottle 6.00
Fragrance Vanity Tray, 1966 .... 5.00
Freddy The Frog Mug, Bubble Bath, 1970, Full & Boxed 5.00
    AVON, FRENCH TELEPHONE, see Avon, Telephone, French
Fresh Aroma Smoker's Candle, 1979, Pipe 8.00
Frilly Duck, 1960, Soap 5.00
Futura, 1969, Full & Boxed .... 12.00 To 26.00

Garden Girl, 1975, Yellow .... 4.00 To 6.00
Garden Girl, 1978, Pink, Full & Boxed 6.00
Garden Of Love Perfume, 1940-44 .... 100.00
Gardenia Perfume, 1940-42, Full & Boxed 65.00
Gardenia Perfume, 1948, Full & Boxed 80.00
Garnet Bud Vase, 1973-76 .... 3.00
Gavel, 1967 .... 7.00 To 10.00
Gavel, 1967, Full & Boxed .... 15.00 To 17.50
Gay Nineties, 1974, Full & Boxed .... 6.00 To 15.00
General 4-4-0, 1972, Full & Boxed, Locomotive .... 4.50 To 9.00
Geni Butterfly Egg, Canada, Full & Boxed 2.00
Gentle Moments, 1975, Plate 12.00
Gentleman's Choice, 1969 .... 4.00
Gentlemen's Collection, 1968, Full & Boxed .... 15.00 To 20.00
George Washington Candleholder, 1976, Full & Boxed .... 9.00 To 10.00
Geranium Bath Oil, 1956-57 .... 10.00
Get The Message, 1978, Full & Boxed 4.00
Gift Of The Sea, 1972, Full & Boxed, Seashell Soaps & Dish 5.00
Gilroy The Ghost, 1976, Full & Boxed 2.50
Globe Bank, 1966 .... 6.00
Golden Apple, 1968, Candle 10.00
Golden Arch, 1964 .... 15.00
Golden Pine Cone Fragrance Candle, 1974 .... 2.00
Golden Promise Perfume, 1950-54 .... 100.00
Golden Thimble Cologne, 1972 .... 3.00
Golden Topaz, 1960-61 .... 15.00
Golden Vanity Compact, 1966 .... 25.00
    AVON, GOLF, see Avon, Avon Open; Avon, Perfect Drive; Avon,
    Swinger
Gone Fishing, 1973-74 .... 4.00 To 6.00
Good Fairy, 1978, Full & Boxed 5.00
Good Shot, 1976, Full & Boxed 1.50
Graceful Giraffe, 1975, Crystal, Gold Neck & Head 2.00
Grecian Pitcher, 1972, Full & Boxed .... 5.00 To 7.00
Greyhound, 1976, Full & Boxed, 1931 Bus 5.00
Handy Frog, 1975, Decanter 5.00
Hansel & Gretel, 1965, Soaps 20.00
Happy Hours Cologne, 1948 .... 23.00 To 30.00
Harvester Tractor, 1973, Full & Boxed 4.00
Hawaiian Delights, 1962, Full & Boxed, Nail Polish 9.00
    AVON, HEAD, see Avon, Warrior
Hearth Lamp, Full & Boxed .... 6.00 To 8.00
Hearth Lamp, 1973 .... 7.00
Heavenly Angel Cologne, 1974, Full & Boxed 2.00
    AVON, HELMET, see Avon, Opening Play
Here's My Heart Perfume, 1963, 1/2 Ounce 12.00
Hidden Treasure, 1972, Full & Boxed, Perfume Pearl In Soap Shell 7.00
Holiday Spice, 1965 .... 10.00
Hooty Tooty, 1973, Full & Boxed, Tugboat Soaps 2.00
Hospitality Bell, 1976, Full & Boxed .... 7.00 To 15.00
Hunter's Stein, 1972, Full & Boxed .... 9.00 To 20.00
Icicle Perfume, 1967-68 .... 2.50 To 5.00
Imperial Garden Cologne Mist, 1973 .... 6.00
Imperial Garden Ginger Jar, 1973, Bath Crystals 22.50
Imperial Garden Tea Set, 1973 .... 125.00
Indian Chieftain, 1972, Full & Boxed 2.00
Indian Head Penny, 1970, Full & Boxed .... 3.00 To 4.75
Indian Tepee, 1974, Full & Boxed 2.00
Inhalant Cologne, 1937 .... 27.00
Inkwell Decanter, 1969, Full & Boxed .... 4.00 To 7.00
Iron Horse Shaving Mug, 1974, Decal, Milk Glass 4.00
Iron Horse Shaving Mug, 1974, Full & Boxed, Decal, Milk Glass 8.00
Island Parakeet, 1977, Full & Boxed 3.00

It's A Blast, 1970-71, Full & Boxed .... 4.00 To 10.00
Jack-In-The-Box Baby Cream, 1974, Full & Boxed 3.00
Jewel Collection, 1964, Full & Boxed .... 24.50 To 50.00
Jewelry Case, 1977 .... 10.00
Jolly Holly Day, 1963, Full & Boxed 15.00
Jolly Santa, 1978 .... 5.00
Jolly Surprise Merriment Cologne, 1955 .... 24.00
Joyous Bell, 1978, Full & Boxed 4.00
Just A Twist, 1977, Full & Boxed 2.00
Just Two, 1965, Full & Boxed .... 40.00 To 85.00
Keepsake, 1971, Full & Boxed, Cream Sachet 3.00
Keepsakes, 1967, Full & Boxed, Set, Cologne & Rollette 12.00
Keynote Perfume, 1967, Full 5.00
Keynote Perfume, 1967, Full & Boxed .... 9.00 To 12.00
King For A Day, 1957, Full & Boxed 20.00
King Pin, 1969, Wild Country 3.00
Kitten Little Cologne, 1972, Milk Glass 4.00
Kitten's Hideaway, 1974, Full & Boxed 3.00
Kodiak Bear, 1977 .... 3.00 To 8.00
Koffee Klatch, 1971, Yellow Coffeepot 5.00
Lady Slipper, 1965 .... 25.00
Lady Spaniel, 1974, Full & Boxed .... 2.50 To 2.75
Ladybug Perfume, 1975-76, Full & Boxed .... 3.50 To 4.00
Lamp, Courting, 1970, Blue, White Shade, Full & Boxed .... 5.00 To 9.00
Lamp, Hurricane, 1973, Full & Boxed 7.00
Lamp, Library, 1976, Full & Boxed .... 4.00 To 8.00
Lamp, Ming Blue, 1974, Full & Boxed .... 5.00 To 8.00
Lamp, Parlor, 1971, Full & Boxed .... 4.00 To 10.00
Lamp, Tiffany, 1973, Full & Boxed .... 5.25 To 10.00
      AVON, LANTERN, see Avon, Casey's Lantern
Lavender & Lace Cologne, 1970, Full & Boxed 5.00
Leisure Hours Clock, 1970, Milk Glass, Bath Oil Decanter 3.00
Leisure Hours Clock, 1974, Milk Glass, Miniature Cologne 2.00
Liberty Bell, 1971, Amber 4.00
Liberty Dollar, 1970, Full & Boxed 5.00
Lights & Shadows, 1969, Full & Boxed 6.00
Little Bo Peep, 1976-78, Full & Boxed 4.50
Little Girl Blue, 1972, Full & Boxed .... 5.50 To 6.00
Little Jack Horner Decanter, 1979-80 .... 5.00
Little Kate, 1973-74, Full & Boxed .... 6.00 To 8.00
Little Miss Muffet Cologne, 1978 .... 4.00 To 8.00
Longhorn Steer, 1975, Full & Boxed 6.00
Looking Glass Cologne, 1970, Full & Boxed .... 5.00 To 8.00
Lovable Seal, 1976, Full & Boxed 2.00
Love Bird Perfume, 1969 .... 5.00
Love Bird Perfume, 1969, Full & Boxed .... 8.00 To 10.00
Loving Lion Decanter, 1978-79, Plastic 6.00
Lucy, 1970-72, Bubble Bath, Full & Boxed 3.50
Luscious Perfume, 1950, Suede Wrapper 15.00
Magic Pumpkin Coach, 1976 .... 1.50
Magic Pumpkin Coach, 1976, Petite, Crystal 3.00
Majestic Elephant Cologne, 1977, Full & Boxed .... 3.50 To 6.00
Mallard Duck, Organizer, 1978, Full & Boxed .... 14.00 To 15.00
Mallard Duck, 1967-68, Green Glass, Silver Head .... 6.00 To 8.00
Mallard In Flight, 1974-76, Full & Boxed, Amber Glass, Green Head 6.00
Mandolin, 1971-72, Boxed, Perfume Glace 9.50
Mansion Lamp, 1976, Full & Boxed .... 5.00 To 6.00
Marine Binoculars, 1973, Full & Boxed .... 6.00 To 9.00
Marionette Perfume, 1938 .... 40.00
Marionette Toilet Water, 1939-40 .... 30.00
Martha Washington Candleholder, 1976, Full & Boxed 10.00
Mary, Mary, 1977, Full & Boxed, Cologne Figurine .... 4.00 To 6.00
Master Organizer, 1970, Full & Boxed, Log .... 20.00 To 30.00

Meadow Bird Pomander, 1975, Full & Boxed 5.00
Men's Fragrance Wardrobe, 1965, Full & Boxed 17.50
Merry Elfkins, 1977, Full & Boxed, Guest Soaps 3.00
Mickey Mouse, 1969, Bubble Bath 6.00
Ming Cat, 1971, Cologne 7.00
Mini-Bike, 1972, Full & Boxed .... 3.00 To 4.00
Minuette Duet, 1973, Full & Boxed 5.00
Minuteman, 1975 .... 8.00
Moonwind Cologne Mist, 1971, Full & Boxed 25.00
Mothicide, 1942, 8 1/2 Ounce 16.00
Mrs.Quackles, 1979-80, Full & Boxed .... 5.00 To 7.00
Mt.Vernon Pitcher, 1977-79, Full & Boxed 10.00
Naughty-Less Submarine, 1961, Red Plastic 7.00
Nile Green Bath Urn, 1974 .... 6.00
Occur, Sophisticate, 1963, Full & Boxed, Set 32.00
Old Faithful, 1972, Full & Boxed .... 6.50 To 9.00
On The Avenue, 1979, Full & Boxed .... 6.00 To 8.00
On The Level, 1978, Full & Boxed 2.00
One Good Turn, 1976, Screwdriver 3.00
One, Two, Lace My Shoe, 1968-69, Bubble Bath, Full & Boxed 5.00
Opalique Candlestick, 1976, Full & Boxed 6.00
Opening Play, 1968, Football Helmet, Gold, Blue Stripe 9.00
Opening Play, 1968, Football Helmet, Gold, No Stripe 12.00
Opening Play, 1969, Football Helmet, Shiny Gold, No Stripe .... 20.00 To 25.00
Orchard Blossoms Cologne, 1941 .... 35.00
Oriental Figurine Pomander, 1973, Green 5.00
     AVON, ORNAMENT, see Avon, Christmas Ornament
     AVON, OWL, see also Avon, Precious Owl; Avon, Wise Choice
Owl Fancy, 1974, Full & Boxed 2.50
Packy Elephant, 1964 .... 6.50
Parisian Garden Perfume, Full & Boxed 6.00
Partridge Cologne, 1973, Milk Glass 1.00
Pass Play, 1973, Full & Boxed, Football Player Decanter 5.50
Patchwork Cologne Mist, 1973, Full & Boxed 6.00
Pawn, 1974-78, Full & Boxed 4.00
Peach Surprise, 1964, Full & Boxed, Set 20.00
Pepperbox Pistol, 1976 .... 3.00 To 8.00
Pepperbox, 1976, Full & Boxed 10.00
Perfect Drive, 1975, Golfer 5.00
Perfume Concentre, 1974-76, Crystal, Gold Cap 4.00
Perfume Oil Petites, 1966, Full & Boxed, Pincushion .... 20.00 To 55.00
Perfume Petite Mouse, 1970, Full & Boxed .... 9.00 To 17.00
Perfume Petite Piglet, 1972, Full & Boxed .... 4.00 To 7.00
Perfume Petite Snail, 1968, Full & Boxed .... 5.00 To 9.00
Perfumed Pair, 1969, Full & Boxed 7.00
Perfumed Pair, 1970, Full & Boxed 6.00
Perfumed Pair, 1974-75, Full & Boxed 4.00
Persian Pitcher, 1974, Blue 2.00
Persian Treasure, 1959-62, Full & Boxed 60.00
Persian Wood Cologne, 1959, Full & Boxed 6.00
Persian Wood Perfume Oil, 1965 .... 14.00
Persian Wood, 1960-62, 4 Ounce, Full & Boxed 18.00
Petite Mouse, 1970, Full & Boxed 17.00
Petti Fleur, 1969, Flower, Gold Cap .... 2.00 To 8.00
Petunia Piglet, 1973, Full & Boxed, Pink Soap 2.50
Pewter Award Cup, 1977 .... 40.00
Pheasant, 1972, Full & Boxed, Decanter .... 4.00 To 8.00
Piano Decanter, 1972, Full & Boxed .... 3.00 To 5.00
Pick-A-Berry, 1974, Strawberry Soap Dish & Soap 4.00
     AVON, PIN BOTTLE, see Avon, King Pin
Pine Bath Oil, 1944-45, Full & Boxed 28.50
Pineapple Cologne, Canada, Full & Boxed .... 5.00 To 7.00
Pink Roses Cup & Saucer, 1974 .... 25.00

AVON, PIPE, see also Avon, Pony Express Rider Pipe; Avon,
Uncle Sam Pipe; Avon, Wild Mustang Pipe

Pipe Dream, 1967, Full & Boxed	15.00 To 20.00
Pipe Full, 1971, Brown, Full & Boxed	2.00
Pipe Full, 1972, Green, Full & Boxed	2.00
AVON, PISTOLS, see Avon, Twenty Paces	
Plaid Thermos, 1978	4.00
Pony Express Rider Pipe, 1975, Full & Boxed	4.00
Pony Express, 1971, Full & Boxed	6.00 To 7.00
Pony Post Test Bottle, 1973, Mexican	60.00
Pony Post, 1972, Full & Boxed	5.00
Pony Post, 1972, Gold	3.00
Pony Post, 1973, Amber	5.00
Pool Paddlers, 1959, 3 Soaps	30.00
Potbelly Stove, 1970, Full & Boxed	5.00
Precious Doe, 1976, Full & Boxed	2.00
Precious Lamb, 1974, Full & Boxed	4.00
Precious Owl, 1972	5.00
Precious Pair, 1971-73, Full & Boxed	5.00
Precious Slipper, 1973, Full & Boxed	4.00 To 7.00
Precious Swan, 1974, Full & Boxed	5.50
President Lincoln Bust, 1973, White, Full & Boxed	8.00
President Lincoln Bust, 1979, Bronze, Full & Boxed	7.50 To 8.00
President Washington Bust, 1974, White, Full & Boxed	8.00
President Washington Bust, 1979, Bronze, Full & Boxed	7.50 To 8.00
Pretty Girl Pink, 1974, Figural Cologne	6.00
Pretty Me, 1968, Boxed	15.00
Pretty Peach Bubble Bath, 1972, Europe, Full & Boxed	5.00
Pretty Peach Talc, 1964, Full	5.00
Princess Of Yorkshire, 1976-78	3.00
Proud Groom Cologne, 1978	7.00
Proud Groom Cologne, 1978, Full & Boxed	8.00
Pump Decanter, 1968, Full & Boxed	5.00
Purse Petite, 1971	6.00
Pyramid Of Fragrance, 1969, Full & Boxed	10.00 To 25.00
Quail, 1973, Full & Boxed	6.00
Quaintance Cologne, 2 Ounce, Full & Boxed	9.00
Quaintance Cream Lotion	9.00
Queen Of Scots, 1973	3.00 To 5.00
Queen's Gold Cologne, 1975, Full & Boxed	6.00
Rainbow Trout, 1973, Full & Boxed	4.00 To 5.00
Rapture Deluxe, 1965	20.00 To 30.00
Rapture Rhapsody Set, 1964	30.00 To 50.00
Regal Peacock Blue, 1973, Full & Boxed	4.00 To 9.00
Regence Gift Set, 1966, Full & Boxed	24.50
Regence Perfume, 1966, 1 Ounce, Full & Boxed	25.00 To 32.50
Regence Perfume, 1966, 1/2 Ounce	18.00
Reginald G.Racoon III, 1970, Full & Boxed	7.00
Remember When Gas Pump, 1976	3.00 To 6.00
Remember When School Desk, 1973	4.00 To 7.00
Renaissance Trio, 1966-67, Full & Boxed	10.00
Right Connection, 1977, Full & Boxed	1.50
Road Runner, 1973-74, Motorcycle	4.00
Roaring 20s, 1972, Full & Boxed, Fashion Figurine	6.00 To 10.00
Robin Redbreast, 1974	4.00
Roll-A-Hoop Cologne, 1977, Full & Boxed	3.50 To 9.00
Rose Fragrance Jar, 1946, Pink Ceramic	60.00
Rose Fragrance Jar, 1948, Clear Top	30.00
Rose Fragrance Jar, 1949, Frosted Stopper	15.00
Rosepoint Bell, 1977, Full & Boxed	5.00
Roses, Roses Bowl, 1972	15.00
Royal Coach, 1972	3.00
Royal Orb, 1965, Full & Boxed	8.00 To 12.00

Royal Swan, 1971, Full & Boxed 2.50
Royal Vase, 1970, Full & Boxed 5.00
Safe Sam, 1965 .... 8.00
Santa's Chimney, 1964, Boxed 15.00
Santa's Team, 1964, Full & Boxed 15.00
Scent With Love, 1971-72, Full & Boxed .... 7.00 To 9.00
Schoolhouse, 1968, Full & Boxed 5.00
Scimitar, 1968-69, Full & Boxed .... 12.00 To 22.00
Scottish Lass, 1975, Full & Boxed .... 5.00 To 6.00
Sea Horse, 1970, Full & Boxed .... 7.00 To 8.00
Sea Maiden, 1971, Crystal, Gold Crown, Full & Boxed .... 3.00 To 5.00
Sea Spirit, 1973, Full & Boxed .... 5.00 To 7.00
Sea Trophy, 1972, Full & Boxed .... 5.00 To 9.00
Secretaire, 1972 .... 4.00
Side Wheeler, 1971 .... 3.00 To 10.00
Silk & Honey Milk Bath, 1970, Full & Boxed 5.50
Silver Dove Ornament, 1976, Cologne, Full & Boxed 4.00
Silver Fawn, 1978 .... 1.50
Silver Swirls, 1977, Full & Boxed 4.00
Sitting Pretty, 1971, Full & Boxed .... 3.00 To 4.00
Skater's Waltz, Blue, 1979-80 .... 5.00 To 7.00
Skater's Waltz, Red, 1977 .... 6.00 To 11.00
Skip-A-Rope, 1975, Full & Boxed 7.00
Small Wonder, 1972, Full & Boxed .... 6.00 To 7.00
Small World Heidi, 1970 .... 4.00
Small World Splash-U, 1970, Full & Boxed 6.00
Small World Wendy Cowgirl, 1971, Full & Boxed 6.00
Smart Move, 1967 .... 35.00
Smart Move, 1971 .... 8.00 To 10.00
Snoopy Come Home, 1973, Full & Boxed 4.00
Snoopy Surprise, 1969 .... 6.00
Snoopy's Ski Team, 1974 .... 5.00
Snowman Petite, 1973, Full & Boxed .... 5.00 To 8.00
Snowmobile, 1973 .... 3.00 To 8.00
    AVON, SOLID GOLD CADILLAC, see Avon, Car, Cadillac
Somewhere Scentiments, 1968-69, Full & Boxed 6.00
Song Bird, 1971, Full & Boxed .... 2.00 To 2.50
Sonnet Robe, 1972, President's Club Prize 35.00
Sonnet Treasure Chest, 1973, Full & Boxed 25.00
Sonnet Vanity, 1972 .... 16.00
Spanish Senorita, 1975, Full & Boxed .... 10.00 To 12.50
Spark Plug, 1975, Full & Boxed .... 1.50 To 2.00
Spice O' Life, 1966, Boxed 15.00
Spicy Treasure Set, Boxed, 1968 .... 10.00 To 14.00
Spirit Of St.Louis, 1970, Full & Boxed 10.00
Splash 'n Spray Set, 1968, Full & Boxed .... 14.00 To 30.00
Sport Of Kings Decanter, 1975, Full & Boxed .... 2.00 To 6.00
Sporting Stein, 1978 .... 19.50
Spring Tulips, 1970, Full & Boxed, Soaps 7.00
Stage Coach, 1960, Embossed, Indented Cap, 8 Ounce 10.00
Stage Coach, 1970, Full & Boxed 8.00
Stamp Decanter, 1970 .... 3.00 To 5.00
Steak Knife Set, 1972 .... 30.00
Stein, Silver, 1968, 6 Ounce, Silver Paint Over Glass .... *Illus* 8.00
Stein, 1965, 8 Ounce, Silver Paint Over Glass 6.50
Stop & Go, 1974, Green With Red, Yellow & Green For Lights 3.00
    AVON, STRAIGHT EIGHT CAR, see Avon, Car
Strawberries & Cream Bath Foam, 1969, Milk Glass Cruet 5.00
Strawberry Bath Foam Pitcher, 1971 .... 3.00 To 4.00
Strawberry Fair Perfume, 1974 .... 3.00
Structured For Men, 1969, Full & Boxed .... 10.00 To 12.00
Super Cycle, 1971, Full & Boxed 9.00
Suzette Poodle, 1973 .... 3.00

Avon, Stein, Silver, 1968, 6 Ounce,
Silver Paint Over Glass

(See Page 11)

Swan Lake Cologne, 1947	29.50
Sweet As Honey, Beehive, 1951	90.00 To 100.00
Sweet Dreams, 1974, Full & Boxed	6.00 To 20.00
Sweet Shoppe Pincushion, 1972-74, Full & Boxed	3.50 To 5.00
Swinger, 1969, Full & Boxed	5.00
AVON, SWORD, see Avon, Scimitar	
Tabatha, 1975, Full & Boxed	5.00
Tag-Along Set, 1967	10.00
Team Achievement Cup, 1978	10.00
Teatime, 1974, Full & Boxed	3.50 To 5.00
Teddy Bear, 1976	2.00
AVON, TELEPHONE, see also Avon, Avon Calling	
Telephone, French, 1971, Full & Boxed	25.00 To 30.00
Telephone, LaBelle, 1974, Full	4.50
Temple Of Love, 1960	12.00
Ten-Point Buck, 1973-74, Full & Boxed	4.50
Theodore Roosevelt Bust, 1975, White, Full & Boxed	7.00
Thomas Jefferson Bust, 1977, White, Full & Boxed	7.00
AVON, TO A WILD ROSE, see Avon, Wild Rose	
Tooth Tablet, 1936	50.00
Topaze Elegance, 1963	15.00
Topaze Gift Cologne, 1959-60, Full & Boxed	13.00
Topaze Perfume Oil, 1963, Full & Boxed	40.00
Topaze Perfume, 1959-63, Full & Boxed, 1 Ounce, Pillared Box	130.00
Topaze Spray Perfume, 1959, 2 Dram	6.00
Tortoise, 1970-71, Boxed	7.00
Touch Of Christmas Cologne, 1975, Full & Boxed	1.00
AVON, TOURING T CAR, see Avon, Car	
Trading Post, 1957, Full & Boxed	50.00
Trailing Arbutus Talc, 1914-17	60.00
AVON, TRAIN, see Avon, General 4-4-0	
Traveler, The, 1969, Full & Boxed	8.00 To 12.00
Treasure Chest, 1973, Full & Boxed	18.00
Tub Catch, 1968, Full & Boxed, Fishing Rod & Plastic Fish	7.00
Tug A Brella, 1979-80, Full & Boxed, Figural Cologne	9.00 To 12.00
Turn A Word Bubble Bath, 1972, Full & Boxed	3.50
AVON, TURTLE, see Avon, Tortoise	
Twenty Paces, Dueling Pistols, 1967-69, Blue Lined Box	100.00 To 150.00
Twenty Paces, Dueling Pistols, 1967-69, Red Lined Box	30.00 To 40.00
Twenty Paces, Dueling Pistols, 1967, Black Lined, Full & Boxed	105.00
Twice Spice, 1967, Full & Boxed	10.00
Two Loves, 1967, Full & Boxed	10.00
Uncle Sam Pipe, 1975, Full & Boxed	3.00 To 6.00
Unforgettable Heirloom Set, 1965	40.00 To 45.00
Unforgettable Heirloom Set, 1965-66, Full & Boxed	60.00
Unicorn, 1974	12.50
Venetian Pitcher, 1973, Full & Boxed	8.00

Victorian Bowl & Pitcher, Marbleized, Full & Boxed 25.00
Victorian Fashion Figurine, 1971, White 8.00
Victorian Fashion Figurine, 1971, White, Full & Boxed .... 12.00 To 13.00
Victorian Fashion Figurine, 1973, Aqua .... 25.00 To 35.00
Victorian Fashion Figurine, 1973, Aqua, Full & Boxed .... 20.00 To 25.00
Victorian Lady Foaming Bath Oil, 1972, Full & Boxed .... 5.00 To 6.00
Victorian Manor, 1972, Full & Boxed .... 5.00 To 7.00
Victorian Washstand, 1974, Full & Boxed .... 3.00 To 4.00
Viennese Waltz Pomander, 1978, Full & Boxed 6.00
Vigorate After Shave, 1960-62, Gold Cap 6.00
Viking Discoverer Ship, 1977, Full & Boxed 8.00
Viking Horn, 1966, Full & Boxed .... 10.00 To 15.00
Volcanic Repeating Pistol, 1979-80 .... 5.00
Warrior, 1967, Head, Blue, Full & Boxed 12.50
Warrior, 1968, Frosted 4.00
Weather-Or-Not, 1969 .... 3.00 To 8.00
Western Choice, 1967, Steer Horns .... 10.00 To 18.00
Western Saddle, 1971 .... 6.00 To 10.00
Whale Oil Lantern, 1974-75 .... 3.00
Whale Organizer, 1973, Full & Boxed .... 17.50 To 25.00
White Moire, 1945-46, 6 Ounce, Cologne 60.00
Wilbur The Whale, 1974, Full & Boxed 2.50
Wild Mustang Pipe, 1976, Full & Boxed 4.00
Wild Roses, 1964 .... 20.00
Wilderness Classic, 1976, Full & Boxed .... 4.50 To 6.00
Windjammer, 1969, Full & Boxed 4.00
Wise Choice, 1969, Owl 4.00
Wishing Toilet Water, 1952, Full & Boxed 28.50
Woodstock Brush & Comb, 1975 .... 4.00
World's Greatest Dad Trophy, 1971 .... 5.00
Yuletree Cologne, 1974-79, Full & Boxed 2.00

BALLANTINE, Charioteer, 1969 .... 5.00
Discus Thrower, 1969 .... 5.00
Duck, Mallard, 1969 .... 13.00 To 20.00
Fisherman, 1969 .... 12.00
Gladiator, 1969 .... 5.00
Golf Bag, 1969 .... 11.00 To 20.00
Knight, Silver, 1969 .... Illus 19.00
     BALLANTINE, MALLARD, see Ballantine, Duck
Mercury, 1969 .... 5.00
Zebra, 1970 .... Illus 15.00

Ballantine, Knight, Silver, 1969

Ballantine, Zebra, 1970

BAR, Athride Rye, W.S. & Co., Quilted, Fluted Shoulder 16.00
Bonfield Rye, Enameled 25.00
Brown, Forman Co., Distillers, Quilted, Bell Shape, Quart 14.00
Graef's Private Stock, Bell Shape, Quilted, Stopper, 1/2 Pint 35.00
Grommes & Ulrich, Bell Shape, Stopper, Quart 15.00
Kentucky Reserve, Enameled, Pinch Type 10.00
Paul Jones, Cut Stars Either Side, Enameled, Stopper 14.00
Paul Jones Whiskey, Enameled, Pinch Type 12.00
Royer's Bitters, In Wreath, Bell Shaped, Paneled, Clear 70.00

*Barber bottles were used either at the barbershop or in the home. They
held hair tonic. These special, fancy bottles were popular in the last half
of the 19th century.*

BARBER, Bay Rum, Milk Glass 26.50
Cobalt 23.00
Enamel Design, Open Pontil, Blue Green 75.00
Enamel Design, Open Pontil, Dark Blue 75.00
Enamel Flower Decoration, Orange, 7 In. ....*Color*
Enamel Overlay Flowers, Pontil, Reddish Purple, 8 In. 75.00
Enameled Flowers, Pontil, Cobalt Blue, Pair 195.00
Enameled Flowers, Red-Purple, Pontil, 8 In. 75.00
Flowered, Pontil, Lime Green, Pair 150.00
Footed, Cobalt Blue 75.00
Gold Long-Stem Bellflowers, Medium Green, Pontil, 8 In. 70.00
Heisey Type, Thumbprint Pattern Lower Body, Fluted Neck, 5 1/2 In. 14.00
Satin Glass, Pink, 7 1/2 In., Pair ....*Color* 150.00
Stars & Stripes, Cranberry 150.00
Stopper, Tan Ginger 20.00
Turn Mold, 8 1/2 In. Flared Round Base, Milk Glass, Stopper 85.00

*Beam bottles are made as containers for Kentucky Straight Bourbon made
by the James Beam Distilling Company. The Beam ceramics were first
made in 1953. Executive series bottles started in 1955. Regal china
specialties were started in 1955 and political figures in 1956. Customer
specialties were first made in 1956, trophy series in 1957, state series in
1958.*

BEAM, AC Spark Plug, 1977 .... 6.00 To 11.00
Ahepa, 1972 .... 6.00
Aida, Opera Series, 1978 .... 300.00
Alaska Purchase, Centennial, 1966 .... 10.00
Alaska Purchase, 1966 .... 9.00
Alaska Star, Reissue, 1964, State 63.00
Alaska Star, 1958, State .... 40.00 To 55.00
Amber Crystal, Glass Specialty, 1973 .... 5.00
Amvets, 1970 .... 6.00
Antioch, Centennial, 1967 .... 5.00 To 7.00
Antique Globe, 1980 .... 16.95 To 25.00
Antique Trader, 1968 .... 5.00 To 7.00
Arizona, 1968, State .... 4.00 To 8.00
Armadillo, 1981 .... 23.00
Armanetti Award, 1969 .... 6.00
Armanetti Shopper 5.00
Armanetti Shopper, 1971 .... 5.00
Armanetti Vase, 1968 .... 5.00 To 6.00
Australia, Galah Bird, 1979, Foreign Countries Series 18.00
Australia, Kangaroo, 1977, Foreign Countries Series 23.00
Australia, Koala Bear, 1973, Foreign Countries Series ....*Illus* 19.00
Australia, Magpie, 1977, Foreign Countries Series .... 12.00 To 18.00
Australia, Queensland, 1978, Foreign Countries Series .... 16.00 To 21.00
Australia, Swag Moon, 1979 .... 16.00
Australia, Sydney Opera House, 1977, Foreign Countries Series 25.00
Australia, Tiger, 1977, Foreign Countries Series 23.00
B.P.O.Does, 1971 .... 6.00

Bartenders Guild, 1973	5.00 To 8.00
Baseball, 1969	6.00 To 9.00
Bass, 1973, Trophy	12.00 To 14.00
Beam Pot, 1980	18.95 To 26.00
Beaver Valley Jim Beam Club, 1977	11.00 To 16.00
Bell's Scotch Bell, 1969	8.00
Bellringer No.I, Plaid, 1970	6.00 To 8.00
Bellringer No.2, Afore Ye Go, 1970	12.00
Big Apple, N.Y., 1979	10.00
Bing Crosby, 29th Pro-Am, 1970, Golf Series	7.00
Bing Crosby, 30th Pro-Am, 1971, Golf Series	10.00
Bing Crosby, 31st Pro-Am, 1972, Golf Series	33.00
Bing Crosby, 32nd Pro-Am, 1973, Golf Series	29.00
Bing Crosby, 33rd Pro-Am, 1974, Golf Series	32.00
Bing Crosby, 34th Pro-Am, 1975, Golf Series	89.00
Bing Crosby, 35th Pro-Am, 1976, Golf Series	30.00
Bing Crosby, 36th Pro-Am, 1977, Golf Series	30.00
Bing Crosby, 37th Pro-Am, 1978, Golf Series	33.00
Binion's Horse Shoe, 1970	8.00
Black Crystal, 1974	6.00
Blue Crystal, 1971	6.00
Blue Fox, 1967	115.00
Blue Gill, 1974, Trophy	9.00 To 11.00
Blue Goose Order, 1971	8.00
Blue Goose, 1979, Trophy	10.00 To 15.00
Blue Jay, 1969, Trophy	10.00 To 11.00
Bob Hope, 14th Desert Classic, 1973	14.00
Bob Hope, 15th Desert Classic, 1974	Illus 11.00
Bobby Unser, No.48, 1975	28.00 To 42.00
Bohemian Girl, 1974	Illus 18.00

Beam, Australia, Koala Bear, 1973,
Foreign Countries Series

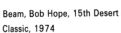

Beam, Bob Hope, 15th Desert
Classic, 1974

Beam, Bohemian Girl, 1974

Beam, Broadmoor Hotel, 1968

Beam, Cable Car, 1968

Bonded, Gold, 1975	6.00
Bonded, Mystic, 1979	13.00
Bonded, Silver, 1975	6.00
Bowling Proprietors, 1974	7.00 To 9.00
Broadmoor Hotel, 1968	*Illus* 5.00
Buffalo Bill, 1971	8.00
Bulldog, 1979, Trophy	23.00
C.P.O.Mess, 1974	12.00
Cable Car, 1968	*Illus* 5.00
Caboose, 1980	32.50 To 40.00
California Mission, 1970	22.00 To 24.00
Camellia City, 1979	30.00 To 35.00
Cameo Blue, Glass Specialty, 1965	4.00 To 5.00
Cannon, Glass Specialty, 1970	4.00
Canteen, 1979	9.00 To 16.00
Captain & Mate, 1980	17.95 To 21.00
Cardinal, Female, 1973, Trophy	*Illus* 21.00
Cardinal, Male, 1968, Trophy	47.00 To 50.00
Carmen, Opera Series, 1978	383.00
Cat, Burmese, 1967, Trophy	10.00
Cat, Siamese, 1967, Trophy	12.00
Catfish, 1981, Trohpy	22.00 To 24.00
Cedars Of Lebanon, 1971	6.00
Centennial, 1960, Santa Fe	226.00

Beam, Cardinal, Female, 1973, Trophy

Centennial, 1961, Civil War, North .... 27.00 To 33.00
Centennial, 1961, Civil War, South .... 57.00 To 65.00
Centennial, 1964, St.Louis Arch .... 22.00 To 25.00
Centennial, 1966, Alaska Purchase 10.00
Centennial, 1967, Antioch .... 5.00 To 7.00
Centennial, 1967, Cheyenne 6.00
Centennial, 1968, Laramie .... 5.00 To 6.00
Centennial, 1968, Reno 5.00
Centennial, 1968, San Diego .... 5.00 To 7.00
Centennial, 1969, Lombard 5.00
Centennial, 1971, Chicago Fire 15.00
Centennial, 1971, Indianapolis .... 4.00 To 5.00
Centennial, 1972, Colorado Springs .... 5.00 To 8.00
Centennial, 1972, Dodge City 8.00
Centennial, 1972, Key West 7.00
Centennial, 1972, Yellowstone Park 8.00
Centennial, 1973, Reidsville 8.00
Centennial, 1976, Colorado Centennial 19.00
Centennial, 1976, New Mexico Bicentennial 10.00
Centennial, 1976, Statue Of Liberty Bicentennial .... 6.00 To 9.00
Centennial, 1978, Hawaii Paradise 24.00
Centennial, 1979, Edison Light Bulb .... 6.00 To 13.00
Charlie McCarthy 31.00
Cherry Hills Country Club 6.00
Cheyenne, Centennial, 1967 .... 6.00
Chicago Bottle Show, 1977 .... 30.00 To 35.00
Chicago Fire, Centennial, 1971 .... 15.00
Chili Society, 1976 .... 10.00
Churchill Downs, 95th, 1969, Pink Roses 5.00
Churchill Downs, 95th, 1969, Red Roses 12.00
Churchill Downs, 96th, 1970, Double Rose 20.00
Churchill Downs, 97th, 1971 .... 5.00 To 7.00
Churchill Downs, 98th, 1972 .... 7.00 To 10.00
Churchill Downs, 100th, 1974 .... 8.00 To 10.00
Circus Wagon, 1979 .... 20.00 To 35.00
Civil War, North, Centennial, 1961 .... 27.00 To 33.00
Civil War, South, Centennial, 1961 .... 57.00 To 65.00
Cleopatra, 1962, Rust 4.00
Cleopatra, 1962, Yellow 15.00
Clint Eastwood, 1973 .... 10.00
Cocktail Shaker, 1953, Glass Specialty 13.00
Coffee Grinder, 1979 .... 9.00 To 20.00
Coffee Warmer, 1954, Glass Specialty 10.00
Coffee Warmer, 1956, Black Handle, Glass Specialty 5.00
Coffee Warmer, 1956, Gold Handle, Glass Specialty 5.00
Colorado Centennial, 1976 .... 19.00
Colorado Springs, Centennial, 1972 .... 5.00 To 8.00
Colorado, 1959, State .... 30.00 To 42.00
Convention, No.l, Denver, 1971 .... 12.00
Convention, No.2, Anaheim, 1972 .... 68.00 To 100.00
Convention, No.3, Detroit, 1973 .... 26.00
Convention, No.4, Lancaster, 1974 .... 80.00 To 112.00
Convention, No.5, Sacramento, 1975 .... 17.00
Convention, No.6, Hartford, 1976 .... 17.00
Convention, No.7, Louisville, 1977 .... 12.00 To 14.00
Convention, No.8, Chicago, 1978 .... 18.00 To 20.00
Convention, No.9, Houston, 1979 .... 75.00 To 85.00
Convention, No.10, Norfolk, 1980 .... 30.00
Convention, No.11, Las Vegas, 1981 .... 28.00 To 30.00
Cowboy, 1979 .... 347.00
Crappie, 1979, Trophy .... 9.00 To 14.00
Crispus Attucks, Glass Specialty, 1976 .... 5.00
CRLDA, 1973 .... 7.00

Dancing Scot Couple, Glass Specialty, 1964 .... 347.00
Dancing Scot, Glass Specialty, Short 109.00
Dancing Scot, Tall, Glass Specialty, 1964 .... 13.00
Delaware, 1972, State .... 6.00 To 8.00
Delft Blue, 1963 .... 3.00 To 5.00
Delft Rose, 1963 .... 3.00 To 6.00
Denver Club, 1970 .... 14.00 To 20.00
Dodge City, Centennial, 1972 .... 8.00
Doe, 1963, Trophy .... 28.00 To 35.00
Don Giovanni, Opera Series, 1980 .... 205.00
Donkey, Ashtray, Political, 1956 .... 16.00
Donkey, Boxer, Political, 1964 .... 16.00
Donkey, Campaigner, Political, 1960 .... 16.00
Donkey, Clown, Political, 1968 .... 8.00
Donkey, Drum, New York City, Political, 1976 .... 12.00
Donkey, Drum, Political, 1976 .... 12.00
Donkey, Football, Political, 1972 .... 7.00
Donkey, Superman, Political, 1980 .... 20.00 To 25.00
Duck, 1957, Trophy .... 33.00 To 35.00
Ducks & Geese, Glass Specialty, 1955 .... 6.00
Ducks Unlimited, No.I, Mallard, 1974 .... 38.00 To 40.00
Ducks Unlimited, No.2, Wood Duck, 1975 .... 28.00
Ducks Unlimited, No.3, 40th, 1977 .... 16.00 To 18.00
Ducks Unlimited, No.4, Head, 1978 .... 12.00 To 16.00
Ducks Unlimited, No.5, Canvasback, 1979 .... 19.00
Ducks Unlimited, No.6, Teal, 1980 .... 18.00 To 26.00
Ducks Unlimited, No.7, 1981 .... *Color*
Eagle, 1966, Trophy .... 11.00 To 15.00
Edison Light Bulb, Centennial, 1979 .... 6.00 To 13.00
Elephant, Agnew, Political, 1970 .... 1800.00 To 1876.00
Elephant, Ashtray, Political, 1956 .... 16.00
Elephant, Boxer, Political, 1964 .... 16.00
Elephant, Campaigner, Political, 1960 .... 16.00
Elephant, Clown, Political, 1968 .... 8.00
Elephant, Drum, Kansas City, Political, 1976 .... 12.00
Elephant, Drum, Political, 1976 .... 5.00 To 7.00
Elephant, Football, Miami Beach, Political, 1972 .... 800.00
Elephant, Football, Political, 1972 .... 7.00
Elephant, Football, San Diego, Political, 1972 .... 25.00
Elephant, Football, Washington, D.C., Political, 1972 .... 750.00
Elephant, Superman, Political, 1980 .... 20.00 To 25.00
Elks National Foundation, 1978 .... 9.00
Elks, 1968 .... 5.00
Elks, 1977 .... 14.00
Emerald Crystal, Glass Specialty, 1968 .... 6.00
Emmett Kelly, With Kansas Autograph, 1973 .... *Illus* 75.00
Emmett Kelly, 1973 .... 10.00 To 25.00
Ernie's Flower Cart, 1976 .... 18.00 To 30.00
Evergreen, 1974, Club Series .... *Illus* 17.00
Executive, 1955, Black Porcelain 421.00
Executive, 1956, Gold Round 131.00
Executive, 1957, Royal DiMonte 70.00
Executive, 1958, Gray Cherub .... 380.00 To 390.00
Executive, 1959, Tavern Scene 61.00
Executive, 1960, Blue Cherub 126.00
Executive, 1961, Golden Chalice .... 62.00 To 66.00
Executive, 1962, Flower Basket .... 40.00 To 50.00
Executive, 1963, Royal Rose 49.00
Executive, 1964, Gold Diamond .... 46.00 To 49.00
Executive, 1965, Marbled Fantasy .... 70.00 To 75.00
Executive, 1966, Majestic 34.00
Executive, 1967, Prestige .... 11.00 To 13.00

Beam, Emmett Kelly, With
Kansas Autograph, 1973

Beam, Evergreen, 1974, Club Series

Beam, Executive, 1975,
Reflections In Gold

Executive, 1968, Presidential .... 9.00 To 11.00
Executive, 1969, Sovereign .... 9.00 To 11.00
Executive, 1970, Charisma .... 5.00 To 12.00
Executive, 1971, Fantasia 12.00
Executive, 1972, Regency 12.00
Executive, 1973, Phoenician 11.00
Executive, 1974, Twin Cherubs 11.00
Executive, 1975, Reflections 10.00
Executive, 1975, Reflections In Gold ....Illus   12.00
Executive, 1976, Floro De Oro 15.00
Executive, 1977, Golden Jubilee 12.00
Executive, 1978, Yellow Rose Of Texas .... 16.00 To 20.00
Executive, 1979, Mother-Of-Pearl .... 14.00 To 22.99
Executive, 1980, Titian 22.50
Expo 74, 1974 .... 8.00
Falstaff, Opera Series, 1979 .... 200.00
Fiesta Bowl, 1973 .... 10.00 To 12.00
Figaro, Opera Series, 1977 .... 328.00
Fiji Island, 1971 .... 7.00
Fire Chief's Car, 1981 ....Color   55.00
Fire Engine, 1978 .... 35.00 To 55.00
First National Bank, 1964 .... 320.00
Five Seasons Club, 1980 .... 21.00 To 24.00
Fleet Reserve, 1974 .... 6.00 To 7.00
Florida, 1968, State .... 4.00 To 5.00
Florida, 1968, Weinkles Label, State 7.00
Football Hall Of Fame, 1972 .... 6.00 To 8.00
Fox On Dolphin, Florida Club Bottle, 1980 .... 15.00 To 35.00
Fox, Blue, 1967 .... 127.00
Fox, Gold, 1969 .... 78.00 To 85.00
Fox, Green, 1965, Trophy .... 33.00 To 36.00
Fox, Red, 1973 .... 1700.00 To 1900.00

Beam, Germany, Wiesbaden, 1973,
Foreign Countries Series

Beam, Fox, Renee, 1974

Fox, Renee, 1974 .... *Illus*	12.00
Fox, Uncle Sam, 1971	12.00
Fox, White, 1969	115.00
Franklin Mint, 1970 .... 6.00 To 9.00
General Stark, 1972 .... 10.00 To 16.00
George Washington Commemorative Plate, 1976 .... 9.00 To 15.00
Germany, Hansel & Gretel, 1971 .... 9.00 To 12.00
Germany, Pied Piper, 1974 .... 6.00
Germany, Wiesbaden, 1973, Foreign Countries Series .... *Illus* 7.00
Germany, 1970 .... 5.00 To 6.00
Glen Campbell, 1976 .... 7.00 To 12.00
Gold Choice, 1976 .... 4.00
Golden Gate, 1969 .... 40.00 To 50.00
Golden Gate, 1970 .... 15.00
Golden Nugget, 1969 .... 40.00
Grand Canyon, 1969 .... 8.00 To 11.00
Grant Locomotive, 1979 .... 39.99 To 44.00
Gray Slot Machine, 1968 .... 9.00
Great Dane, 1976, Trophy 10.00
Grecian, 1961, Glass Specialty .... 4.00 To 5.00
Hannah Dustin, 1973 .... 28.00
Harolds Club, Covered Wagon, 1969 .... 6.00
Harolds Club, Man In Barrel, No.I, 1957 .... 425.00 To 450.00
Harolds Club, Man In Barrel, No.2, 1958 .... 225.00 To 230.00
Harolds Club, Nevada Gray, 1963 .... 167.00 To 175.00
Harolds Club, Nevada Silver, 1964 .... 171.00 To 175.00
Harolds Club, Pinwheel, 1965 .... 60.00 To 64.00
Harolds Club, Silver Opal, 1957 .... 22.00
Harolds Club, Slot Machine, Blue, 1967 .... 14.00
Harolds Club, Slot Machine, Gray, 1968 .... 8.00
Harolds Club, V.I.P., 1967 .... 51.00
Harolds Club, V.I.P., 1968 .... 45.00 To 55.00
Harolds Club, V.I.P., 1969 .... 230.00 To 265.00
Harolds Club, V.I.P., 1970 .... 62.00
Harolds Club, V.I.P., 1971 .... 23.00 To 67.00
Harolds Club, V.I.P., 1972 .... 40.00
Harolds Club, V.I.P., 1973 .... 31.00
Harolds Club, V.I.P., 1974 .... 23.00 To 31.00
Harolds Club, V.I.P., 1975 .... 23.00 To 28.00
Harolds Club, V.I.P., 1976 .... 27.00
Harolds Club, V.I.P., 1977 .... 36.00
Harolds Club, V.I.P., 1978 .... 43.00
Harolds Club, V.I.P., 1979 .... 38.00

Harolds Club, V.I.P., 1980	35.00 To 38.00
Harrah's Club, Gray, 1963	807.00
Harrah's Club, Silver, 1963	1000.00 To 1171.00
Harvey's, 1969, Glass	10.00
Hatfield, 1973	23.00
Hawaii Aloha Club, 1971	27.00
Hawaii Aloha, 1971	7.00
Hawaii Paradise, Centennial, 1978	24.00
Hawaii Paradise, 1978	19.00
Hawaii, Reissue, 1967, State	30.00 To 34.00
Hawaii, With Medallion	22.00
Hawaii, 1959, State	45.00 To 51.00
Hawaiian Open, 1972, Pineapple	6.00 To 9.00
Hawaiian Open, 1973, Golf Ball	10.00
Hawaiian Open, 1974, Tiki God	6.00 To 9.00
Hawaiian Open, 1975, Emblem	12.00
Hawaiian Open, 1975, Menehune	13.00
Hawaiian Open, 1975, Outrigger	13.00
Homebuilders, 1978	27.00
Hongi Hika, 1980	151.00
Horse, Appaloosa, 1974, Trophy	12.00
Horse, Black, 1961, Trophy	19.00 To 25.00
Horseshoe, Reno, 1969	9.00
Hula Bowl, 1975	12.00
Humboldt County Fair, 1970, Glass Specialty	14.00
Hyatt House, Chicago, 1971, Customer Specialty	17.00
Hyatt Regency, New Orleans, 1976	20.00
Idaho, 1963, State	52.00 To 61.00
Illinois, 1968, State	5.00 To 10.00
Indian Chief, 1979	18.50 To 40.00
Indianapolis 500, 1970	4.00 To 6.00
Indianapolis, Centennial, 1971	4.00 To 5.00
International Petroleum, 1971	8.00
Italy, Boys Town, 1973	7.00
Jackelope, 1971, Trophy	12.00 To 15.00
Jaguar, 1981	Color 25.00
Jewel Tea Wagon, 1974	75.00 To 95.00
John Henry, 1972	49.00 To 58.00
Jug, Green, 1965	6.00
Jug, Turquoise, 1966	6.00
Kaiser International, 1971	4.00 To 5.00
Kansas, 1960, State	42.00 To 59.00
Katz, Black, 1968	11.00
Katz, Yellow, 1967	20.00 To 25.00
Kentucky Brown Horse	17.00
Kentucky Colonel, 1970	3.00 To 6.00
Kentucky, Black Head, 1967, State	12.00 To 16.00
Kentucky, Brown Head, 1967, State	16.00 To 26.00
Kentucky, White Head, 1967, State	19.00 To 23.00
Key West, Centennial, 1972	7.00
King Kong, 1976	14.00
Labrador Retriever, 1977, Collector's Edition, Vol.XII	Illus 3.00
Laramie, Centennial, 1968	5.00 To 6.00
Las Vegas, 1969	5.00
Legion Music	19.00
Lombard Lilac Festival, 1969	5.00
Lombard, Centennial, 1969	5.00
London Bridge, With Medallion, 1971	185.00
London Bridge, 1971	4.00 To 6.00
Louisiana Superdome, 1975	9.00
Louisville Downs, 1978	69.00 To 110.00
Madame Butterfly, Opera Series, 1977	750.00

Maine, 1970, State 6.00
Man In Barrel, No.1, 1957 .... 425.00 To 450.00
Man In Barrel, No.2, 1958 .... 225.00 To 230.00
Marbleized Crystal, Glass Specialty, 1972 .... 5.00
Marina City, 1962 .... 30.00 To 32.00
Marine Corps, 1975 .... 35.00 To 45.00
Mark Anthony, 1962, Glass Specialty 24.00
Martha Washington Commemorative Plate, 1975 .... 10.00
Mephistopheles, 1979 .... 242.00
Mexican Fighting Bull, 1981 .... 23.00
Michigan, 1972, State .... 6.00 To 8.00
Milwaukee Stein, 1972 .... 77.00
Mint 400, 3rd, 1970, Ceramic Stopper 56.00
Mint 400, 3rd, 1970, Metal Stopper .... 7.00 To 15.00
Mint 400, 4th, 1971, Motorcycle Stopper 8.00
Mint 400, 5th, 1972, Helmet Stopper .... 5.00 To 8.00
Mint 400, 6th, 1973, Gold 10.00
Mint 400, 7th, 1975, Triangle .... 7.00 To 11.00
Mint 400, 8th, 1976, Round 16.00
Model A Ford, 1903, 1978 .... 35.00
Model A Ford, 1928, 1980 .... 35.00 To 48.00
Model T Ford, Black, 1974, Automotive Series 55.00
Model T Ford, 1974 .... 55.00
Momence Gladiolas Festival, 1974 .... 8.00
Montana, 1963, State .... 70.00 To 80.00
Monterey Bay Club, 1977 .... 13.00 To 22.00
Mortimer Snerd, 1976, Fantasy Series .... *Illus* 40.00
Mr.Goodwrench, 1978 .... 9.00 To 16.00
Mt.St.Helens, 1980 .... 34.00 To 40.00
Musicians On Wine Cask, 1964 .... 7.00
Muskie, 1971, Trophy .... 23.00 To 25.00
Nebraska, 1967, State .... 4.00 To 8.00

Beam, Labrador Retriever, 1977,
Collector's Edition, Vol.XII

(See Page 21)

Beam, Mortimer Snerd,
1976, Fantasy Series

Beam, New Zealand, Kiwi, 1974

Beam, Ohio State Fair, 1973

Nevada, 1963, State .... 40.00 To 47.00
New Hampshire Gold Eagle, 1971 .... 35.00 To 42.00
New Hampshire, 1967, State 7.00
New Jersey, Blue, 1963, State .... 60.00 To 65.00
New Jersey, Yellow, 1963, State 55.00
New Mexico Bicentennial, 1976 .... 10.00
New Mexico, 1972, State .... 15.00 To 18.00
New York World's Fair, 1964 .... 12.00 To 18.00
New Zealand, Kiwi, Wrong Way 22.00
New Zealand, Kiwi, 1974 ....*Illus* 9.00
North Dakota, 1964, State 84.00
Northern Pike, 1978, Trophy .... 12.00 To 14.00
Nutcracker, Opera Series, 1978 .... 195.00 To 280.00
Ohio State Fair, 1973 ....*Illus* 8.00
Ohio, 1966, State 10.00
Oldsmobile, 1972 .... 80.00 To 110.00
Olympian, 1960, Glass Specialty 7.00
Olympic, 1971, Glass Specialty 5.00
Opaline Crystal, 1969, Glass Specialty 8.00
Oregon, 1959, State .... 35.00 To 43.00
Oriental Jade, 1972, Glass Specialty .... 3.00 To 5.00
Owl, Gray, 1979 .... 18.00 To 19.00
Owl, Red, 1979 .... 18.00 To 19.00
Owl, 1979, Trophy .... 18.00 To 19.00
P.G.A., 1971 .... 6.00
Panda, 1980, Trophy .... 15.00 To 17.00
Passenger Car, 1981 .... 48.00
Paul Bunyan, 1970 .... 9.00 To 11.00
Pearl Harbor, 1972 .... 21.00 To 25.00
Pearl Harbor, 1976 .... 9.00 To 11.00
Pennsylvania Dutch, 1974 .... 17.00 To 19.00
Pennsylvania, 1967, State .... 4.00 To 7.00
Perch, 1980, Trophy .... 16.00 To 17.00
Permian Basin Oil Show, 1972 .... 7.00
Pheasant, 1960, Trophy .... 22.00 To 27.00
Pheasant, 1967, Trophy 17.00
Phi Sigma Kappa, 1973 .... 6.00
Pin, Gold Top, Amber, Glass Specialty 22.00
Political, Donkey, 1956, Ashtray 16.00
Political, Donkey, 1960, Çampaigner 16.00
Political, Donkey, 1964, Boxer 16.00
Political, Donkey, 1968, Clown 8.00
Political, Donkey, 1972, Football 7.00
Political, Donkey, 1976, Drum 12.00
Political, Donkey, 1976, Drum, New York City 12.00
Political, Donkey, 1980, Superman .... 20.00 To 25.00
Political, Elephant, 1956, Ashtray 16.00
Political, Elephant, 1960, Campaigner 16.00
Political, Elephant, 1964, Boxer 16.00
Political, Elephant, 1968, Clown 8.00
Political, Elephant, 1970, Agnew .... 1800.00 To 1876.00
Political, Elephant, 1972, Football 7.00
Political, Elephant, 1972, Football, Miami Beach 800.00
Political, Elephant, 1972, Football, San Diego 25.00
Political, Elephant, 1972, Football, Washington, D.C. 750.00
Political, Elephant, 1976, Drum .... 5.00 To 7.00
Political, Elephant, 1976, Drum, Kansas City 12.00
Political, Elephant, 1980, Superman .... 20.00 To 25.00
Ponderosa, 1969 .... 6.00
Pony Express, 1968 .... 6.00
Poodle, Tiffany, 1973 .... 22.00
Portland Rose Festival, 1972 .... 8.00

(See Page 26)

Beam, Trophy, 1970, Poodle

Poulan Chain Saw, 1979	20.00 To 25.00
Powell, Expedition, 1969	8.00
Preakness, 1970	5.00 To 7.00
Preakness, 1975	7.00
Pretty Perch, 1980	16.00
Prima Donna, 1969	8.00
Rabbit, 1971, Trophy	9.00 To 11.00
Rainbow Trout, 1975, Trophy	11.00
Ram, 1958, Trophy	110.00 To 140.00
Ramada Inn, 1976	8.00
Red Mile Race, 1975	9.00
Redwood, 1967	6.00 To 8.00
Reidsville, Centennial, 1973	8.00
Reno, Centennial, 1968	5.00
Reno, 1968	4.00 To 5.00
Republic Of Texas Club, 1980	35.00 To 50.00
Riverside, Centennial, 1970	12.00
Robin, 1969, Trophy	7.00 To 10.00
Rocky Marciano, 1973	12.00
Royal Crystal, 1959, Glass Specialty	5.00
Royal Emperor, 1958, Glass Specialty	4.00 To 6.00
Royal Opal, 1957, Glass Specialty	5.00 To 8.00
Royal Reserve, 1953, Glass Specialty	5.00
Royal Rose, 1963	40.00 To 50.00
Rubber Capitol Club, 1973	25.00
Ruby Crystal, 1967, Glass Specialty	7.00 To 11.00
Ruidosa Downs, Pointed Ears, 1968	23.00
Ruidosa Downs, 1968	4.00 To 5.00
Sahara Invitational, 1971	7.00
Sailfish, 1957, Trophy	28.00 To 31.00
Salmon, Coho, 1976, Trophy	7.00 To 15.00
Samoa, 1973	8.00
San Diego, Centennial, 1968	5.00 To 7.00
San Francisco Cable Car, 1968	3.00 To 5.00
Santa Fe, Centennial, 1960	226.00
Scotch Bell, 1970	8.00
Seafair, 1972	10.00
Seattle World's Fair, 1962	15.00 To 20.00
Setter, 1958, Trophy	50.00 To 55.00
Sheraton Hotel, 1975	7.00
Short Timer, 1975	28.00 To 30.00
Shriners, 1970, Indiana	3.00 To 6.00
Shriners, 1972, Moila No.1, With Sword	33.00
Shriners, 1975, El Kahir Temple	15.00
Shriners, 1975, Moila No.2, With Camel	18.00
Shriners, 1975, Rajah Temple	25.00
Shriners, 1980, Western Association	35.00
Sigma Nu	9.00 To 10.00

Smith's North Shore Club, 1972 .... 15.00
Snow Goose, 1979 .... 10.00 To 15.00
South Carolina, 1970, State .... 4.00 To 6.00
South Dakota, Mt.Rushmore, 1969, State .... 4.00 To 8.00
Speckled Beauty, 1956 .... 550.00
Sports Car Club, 1976 .... 10.00
St.Bernard, 1979, Trophy .... 44.00 To 75.00
St.Louis Arch, Centennial, 1964 .... 22.00 To 25.00
St.Louis Club, 1972 .... 17.00
State, Alaska Star, Reissue, 1964 .... 63.00
State, Alaska Star, 1958 .... 40.00 To 55.00
State, Arizona, 1968 .... 4.00 To 8.00
State, Colorado, 1959 .... 30.00 To 42.00
State, Delaware, 1972 .... 6.00 To 8.00
State, Florida, 1968 .... 4.00 To 5.00
State, Florida, 1968, Weinkles Label 7.00
State, Hawaii, Reissue, 1967 .... 30.00 To 34.00
State, Hawaii, 1959 .... 45.00 To 51.00
State, Idaho, 1963 .... 52.00 To 61.00
State, Illinois, 1968 .... 5.00 To 10.00
State, Kansas, 1960 .... 42.00 To 59.00
State, Kentucky, Black Head, 1967 .... 12.00 To 16.00
State, Kentucky, Brown Head, 1967 .... 16.00 To 26.00
State, Kentucky, White Head, 1967 .... 19.00 To 23.00
State, Maine, 1970 .... 6.00
State, Michigan, 1972 .... 6.00 To 8.00
State, Montana, 1963 .... 70.00 To 80.00
State, Nebraska, 1967 .... 4.00 To 8.00
State, Nevada, 1963 .... 40.00 To 47.00
State, New Hampshire, 1967 .... 7.00
State, New Jersey, Blue, 1963 .... 60.00 To 65.00
State, New Jersey, Yellow, 1963 .... 55.00
State, New Mexico, 1972 .... 15.00 To 18.00
State, North Dakota, 1964 .... 84.00
State, Ohio, 1966 .... 10.00
State, Oregon, 1959 .... 35.00 To 43.00
State, Pennsylvania, 1967 .... 4.00 To 7.00
State, South Carolina, 1970 .... 4.00 To 6.00
State, South Dakota, Mt.Rushmore, 1969 .... 4.00 To 8.00
State, Washington, 1975 .... 12.00 To 13.00
State, Washington, 1976 .... 12.00 To 16.00
State, West Virginia, 1963 .... 225.00 To 250.00
State, Wyoming, 1965 .... 55.00 To 63.00
Statue Of Liberty, Bicentennial, 1976 .... 6.00 To 9.00
Stone Mountain, 1974 .... 5.00 To 7.00
Sturgeon, 1980 .... 32.00 To 35.00
Stutz Bearcat, 1977 .... 32.00 To 49.99
Submarine, Redfin, 1970 .... 6.00
Telephone, Coin, 1981 .... *Color*
Telephone, French Cradle, 1979 .... 12.95 To 22.00
Telephone, 1897, 1978 .... 23.00
Telephone, 1907, 1975 .... 34.00
Telephone, 1919 Dial, 1980 .... 19.00 To 22.00
Texas Hemisfair, 1968, Regal China .... *Illus*   9.00
Thailand, 1969 .... 3.00 To 7.00
Thomas Flyer, 1977, Automotive Series, Blue or Cream .... *Illus*   44.00
Tobacco Festival, 1973 .... 10.00 To 12.00
Tombstone, Arizona, 1970 .... 4.00 To 6.00
Treasure Chest, 1979 .... 10.00 To 23.99
Trophy, 1957, Duck .... 33.00 To 35.00
Trophy, 1957, Sailfish .... 28.00 To 31.00
Trophy, 1958, Ram .... 110.00 To 140.00
Trophy, 1958, Setter .... 50.00 To 55.00
Trophy, 1960, Pheasant .... 22.00 To 27.00

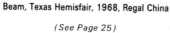

Beam, Texas Hemisfair, 1968, Regal China

(See Page 25)

Beam, Thomas Flyer, 1977, Automotive
Series, Blue Or Cream

Trophy, 1961, Horse, Black	19.00 To 25.00
Trophy, 1963, Doe	28.00 To 35.00
Trophy, 1965, Fox, Green	33.00 To 36.00
Trophy, 1966, Eagle	11.00 To 15.00
Trophy, 1967, Cat, Burmese	10.00
Trophy, 1967, Cat, Siamese	12.00
Trophy, 1967, Pheasant	17.00
Trophy, 1968, Cardinal, Male	47.00 To 50.00
Trophy, 1969, Blue Jay	10.00 To 11.00
Trophy, 1969, Robin	7.00 To 10.00
Trophy, 1969, Woodpecker	10.00
Trophy, 1970, Poodle	*Illus* 11.00
Trophy, 1971, Jackelope	12.00 To 15.00
Trophy, 1971, Muskie	23.00 To 25.00
Trophy, 1971, Rabbit	9.00 To 11.00
Trophy, 1973, Bass	12.00 To 14.00
Trophy, 1973, Cardinal, Female	21.00
Trophy, 1974, Blue Gill	9.00 To 11.00
Trophy, 1974, Horse, Appaloosa	12.00
Trophy, 1975, Rainbow Trout	11.00
Trophy, 1976, Great Dane	10.00
Trophy, 1976, Salmon, Coho	7.00 To 15.00
Trophy, 1977, Walleye Pike	*Illus* 10.00
Trophy, 1978, Northern Pike	12.00 To 14.00
Trophy, 1979, Blue Goose	10.00 To 15.00
Trophy, 1979, Bulldog	23.00
Trophy, 1979, Crappie	9.00 To 14.00
Trophy, 1979, Owl	18.00 To 19.00
Trophy, 1979, St.Bernard	44.00 To 75.00
Trophy, 1980, Panda	15.00 To 17.00
Trophy, 1980, Perch	16.00 To 17.00
Trophy, 1981, Catfish	22.00 To 24.00
Trout Unlimited, 1977	14.00
Truth Or Consequences, 1974	8.00
Turtle, Long Neck, 1975	26.00
Turtle, Short Neck, 1975	15.00 To 18.00
Twin Bridges, 1971, Club Series	50.00 To 55.00
U.S.Open, 1972	15.00
V.F.W., 1971	15.00
Vendome Drummer's Wagon, 1975	49.00 To 75.00
Viking, 1973	12.00
Volkswagen, Blue, 1973	23.00
Volkswagen, Red, 1973	23.00 To 27.00
Walleye Pike, 1977, Trophy	10.00
Washington, 1975, State	12.00 To 13.00
Washington, 1976, State	12.00 To 16.00
Waterman, Pair, 1980	400.00

Beer, Dosequis, Brown, 9 1/2 In.

Beam, Trophy, 1977, Walleye Pike

Beam, Zimmerman Z, 1970

Waterman, Yellow, 1980	200.00
West Virginia, 1963, State	225.00 To 250.00
Wolverine Club, 1975	16.00 To 19.00
Woodpecker, 1969, Trophy	10.00
Wyoming, 1965, State	55.00 To 63.00
Yellowstone Park, Centennial, 1972	8.00
Yosemite, 1967	6.00
Yuma Rifle Club, 1968	20.00 To 28.00
Zimmerman Bell, Light Blue, 1976	9.00
Zimmerman Blue Beauty, 1969	12.00
Zimmerman Peddler, 1971	15.00
Zimmerman Z, 1970 *Illus*	10.00
Zimmerman, Cherub, 1968	8.00
Zimmerman, Chicago Art Institute, 1972	11.00 To 15.00

Beer was bottled in all parts of the United States by the time of the Civil War. Stoneware and the standard beer bottle shape of the 1870s are included in this category.

BEER, A.Hain, Lebanon, Pa., Squat, Green	45.00
A.P.Hotaling Co.Wholesale Liquors, Portland, Or., Brandy Style, Amber	25.00
A.R.Cox, Norristown, Pa., Squat, Green	40.00
A.R.Peru, Indiana, Light Orange, Pint	10.00
Altoona W.S.R.Brewing Co., Crown Top, BIM, Amber, 9 1/2 In.	2.00
Anheuser-Busch, Eagle Inside A, Bale & Stopper, Aqua	23.00
Anheuser-Busch, Monogram, Aqua, 7 1/2 In.	8.00
Anheuser-Busch, Pictorial Blob	20.00
Birch Mead, John Kelsey & Co., N.Y., Embossed, Woman, Trees, Eagle, Quart	65.00
Blumerick & Co., Batavia, N.Y., Crown Top, BIM, Amber, 9 In.	3.00
Boss Lager, Saranac Lake, N.Y., BIM, Blob Top, 9 In.	3.00
Brookville Distilling Co.Distillers, Cincinnati, O., Clear, Quart	10.00
Buffalo Brewing, S.K.Agency, Green, Quart	75.00
C.Conrad & Co., Original Budweiser, Aqua, Quart	5.00 To 16.00
C.Norsheim, Newark, N.Y., Crown Top, BIM, Amber, 8 In.	2.00
Carry S.Bacon, Albion, N.Y., Crown Top, BIM, Amber, 8 In.	3.00
Charles Capito, West Virginia, Blob Top, Amber	20.00
Charleston Brewing Co., Amber	4.00
Cincinnati Beer, Wm.Schausten, Bloomington, 266, Amber, Quart	15.00
Columbia Brewing Co., Shenandoah, Pa., Weiss Beer, Aqua	10.00
Columbia Weiss, St.Louis, Emerald Green, Pint	18.00
Crescent Brewing Co., Aurora, Ind., Crescent, Amber, Pint	18.00
Crown Embossed, Black Glass, Paint	5.00
Dennis & Co., Mt.Morris, N.Y., Crown Top, BIM, Amber, 9 1/2 In.	2.00
Dobler Brewery, Embossed D With Mug & Hand, Clear	4.00
Dobler Brewery, Trademark, Metal Stopper, BIM, 9 In.	6.00
Dosequis, Brown, 9 1/2 In. *Illus*	1.00

Dotterweich Brewing Co., Olean, N.Y., Crown Top, BIM, Amber, 9 1/4 In. 2.00
Dumpe & Glitz, S.Jasper, Mo., Wire Top, 1888, Large Embossing, Brown 10.00
Dutch Porter, 18th Century 54.50
E.Froelich, Potsdam, Green, Porcelain Stopper & Bail 15.00
E.Martin & Son Bottlers, Utica, N.Y., Crown Top, BIM, Amber, 9 1/4 In. 3.00
Eagar & Co., Batavia, N.Y., BIM, Amber, 9 1/2 In. .... 2.00 To 3.00
Eagle Bottling Wks., Auburn, N.Y., Crown Top, BIM, Amber 2.00
Earl Newton, New Jersey, Amber 6.00
Elgin Eagle Brewing Co., Elgin, Ill., Embossed Eagle, Brown 3.50
Emmerling, Crown Top, BIM, Amber, 9 1/2 In. 2.00
Evans Ale, Husdon, N.Y., ABM, Amber 2.00
Excelsior Lager, Aqua 6.00
F.R. & J.F., Slatington, Pa., Green, Pony 55.00
F.Seitz, Easton, Pa., Squat, Green 65.00
Frank Brewery, Eagle In Horseshoe, Aqua, Brooklyn, N.Y. 8.00
G.Breght Brewing Co., Franklin, Pa., Crown Top, BIM, Amber, 9 In. 2.00
G.Hausburg, Blue Island, Illinois, Amber, Quart 10.00
G.Rothfuss & Co., Boston, Stopper, Blob Top, Aqua 3.00
Gahm & Son, Embossed Mug, Clear, Boston, Mass. 4.00
George Fraun Bottler, Pine Street, San Francisco, GB In Shield 35.00
Gold Narragansett Lager Beer, Copyright 1959, Crown Top 18.00
Golden Gate Bottling Works, Chas.Roschmann, S.F., Blob Top, Amber 45.00
Grand Rapids Brewing Co., Silver Foam, Embossed Eagle On Barrel, Aqua 8.00
Grumman's Bottling Works, Norwalk, Ct. 25.00
H.Flotos, Reading, Pennsylvania, Aqua 22.00
Hamm's 1973 Bears 20.00
Hanson & Kaher, Oakland, Quart 6.00
Henry Duensing, Chicago Heights, Ill., Amber 7.00
Herancourt Brg.Co., Cincinnati, Crown Top, BIM, Amber, 8 1/4 In. 2.00
Herman Minehart, Olive Green 20.00
Hohmann & Bartlett, Schlitz, 1903, Clear 8.00
Home Brewing Co., Aqua 12.00
Honolulu Brewing & Malting, Honolulu, Hawaii, Aqua 25.00
Hoster, Columbus, O., Wiener Beer, BIM, Amber, 10 In. 3.00
Hoster, Columbus, Ohio, Globe Trademark, Large H & Wings, Aqua 6.00
Huebner Toledo Breweries Co., Crown Top, Yellow-Green 5.00
Indianapolis Brewing Co., Crown Top, Dancing Lady, Amber 8.00
Indianapolis Brewing Co., Embossed Women, Amber, 7 1/4 In. 8.00
International Brewing Co., Buffalo, N.Y., Crown Top, BIM, Amber 2.00
J.A.Seitz, Easton, Pa., Green 25.00
J.C.Buffum Co., Pioneer Bottlers, Pittsburgh, Pa., Quart 18.00
J.Obermann & Co., Milwaukee, Golden Amber 40.00
J.T.Martin, 558 Thames St., Newport, R.I., Aqua, Pint 5.00
Jackson Brewing Co., San Francisco, JBCo Monogram, Stopper & Wire 10.00
James Kane, Wilkes Barre Hill, Pa., Not To Be Sold, Cobalt Blue 375.00
Japan Brewing Co., San Francisco, Aqua, Quart 10.00
Johann Hoff, Embossed On Shoulder, Olive Green 3.00
John Dewey, Johnstown, N.Y., BIM, Aqua, 9 1/4 In. 5.00
John Dietz, River Road & Union St., Pavonia, N.J., Aqua 5.00
John Lyon & Co., Applied Blob Top, Deep Green, White Highlights, 9 In. 20.00
John McMahon Bottler, Fort Edward, N.Y., Crown Top, BIM, Aqua 2.00
John Stanton Brewing Co., Troy, N.Y., Monogrammed, Green 25.00
Jos.Schlitz Brewing Co., Partial Label, Turnmold, Green 15.00
Jos.Schlitz, Script & Etched, Table, 1890-1900, Brass Handle, Amber 125.00
Julius Fahrenvack, Chicago, Il., Quart 20.00
Kitscher Bros., Bridgeport, Conn., Stubby, BIMAL, Aqua 15.00
L.B.Bassett, Norwich, N.Y., Stopper, BIM, Amber, 9 In. 5.00
Labue & Co., Buffalo, N.Y., Crown Top, BIM, Amber, 8 1/4 In. 3.00
Lake City Brewery, Dunkirk, N.Y., BIM, Amber, 9 1/4 In. 4.00
Los Angeles Brewing Co., Slug Eagle On Crest, Red Amber 35.00
M.Duheme, Northville, N.Y., Blob Top, BIM, Aqua 3.00
M.H.Swift & Co.White Beer, Cobalt Blob Top, Incised Shoulder, Quart 53.00
M.Keane XXX Ale, Louisville, Ky., Cobalt 600.00

McAvoy Brewing Co., Chicago, Amber	3.00
McManue & Meade Bottlers, Nasonville, R.I., Crown Top, Amber	5.00
BEER, MINIATURE, see Miniature, Beer	
National Bottling Co., San Francisco, Embossed Eagle Clutching Arrow	30.00
Nelson's Bottling Wks., Hornell, N.Y., Crown Top, BIM, 9 1/2 In.	2.00
Norris Beer, Heavy Paneled, Iron Pontil, Aqua	475.00
North Star Bottling Works, San Francisco, Embossed Star, Amber, Quart	20.00
Northern Brewing Co., West Superior, Wisc., Balto Loop, Aqua, Quart	10.00
Northwestern Bottling Works, J.H.Schlueter, Washington, D.C., Aqua	6.50
Old Style Lager, LaCrosse, Wis., Crown Top, Aqua	7.00
Olden Time Matz Beer, Brown, 9 1/2 In. .... *Illus*	2.00

Beer, Olden Time Matz Beer, Brown, 9 1/2 In.

Olean Brewing Co., N.Y., Crown Top, BIM, 9 1/2 In.	2.00
Pabst Brewing Co. Of Milwaukee, Red Amber, Quart	18.00
Pabst Brewing Co., Clyde Glass Works, Embossed Leaf, Amber	12.00
Pabst Brewing Co., Winona, Minn., Aqua, Pint	20.00
Peasle Ale, Dubuque, Squat, Black, Red, Amber, Quart	65.00
People's Brewing Company, Embossed Eagle, Quart	6.00
Philadelphia XXX Porter Ale, Homesdale, Reverse P, Iron Pontil	55.00
Phoenix Beverage, Buffalo, N.Y., Crown Top, ABM, Aqua, 9 1/2 In.	2.00
Piel Bros., East N.Y. Brewery, Crown, Amber	5.00
Quandt Brewing Co., Troy, N.Y., Mercury, Green	35.00
Reinhart & Co., Salvador, Toronto, Aqua	22.00
Reno, Blob Top, Golden Amber	25.00
Reymann Brewing Co., Wheeling, W.Va., Crown Top, Metal Stopper, Amber	2.00
Rochester Brewing Co., New York Branch, Amber	10.00
Rock Island Brewing Co., Lightning Stopper	12.00
Ruby Red	7.00 To 13.00
Rudolph Sherf, San Jose, Quart	5.50
S.F.Swan Brewing Co. XXX Ale, Swan In Front, Green	250.00
S.Stringer, Rochester, N.Y., Aqua	5.00
San Miguel Brewery, Manila, P.I., Applied Blob, Green, Pint	45.00
Santa Fe Bottling Co., C.V. & Co., San Francisco	15.00
Schroeder's Berliner Weiss, St.Louis, Emerald Green, Pint	15.00
Schwarzenbach Brewing Co., Hornell, N.Y., Crown Top, BIM, SCA	1.50
Seitz & Bros., Easton, Pa., Squat, Iron Pontil, Cobalt Blue	50.00
Standard Brewery, Trademark, Chicago, Eagle, Aqua	8.00
Star Lager, Miniature Wooden Shoes	20.00
T.F.Donahue Co., Providence, R.I., Stopper, 9 3/4 In.	3.00
Tacoma Bottling Co., San Francisco	10.00
Tenant, Pale, Pure Blob	15.00
Tiger Whiskey	3.50
Toohey's Beer, Deer, Sydney, Olive Green	15.00

W.F.Crickler, Batavia, N.Y., Crown Top, BIM, Amber, 9 1/2 In. 2.00
Wagner, Manchester, N.H., Golden Amber 6.00
Wall & Heverin, Auburn, N.Y., Crown Top, BIM, Amber, 9 1/2 In. 2.50
Wellville Bottling Co., N.Y., Crown Top, BIM, Amber, 9 1/2 In. 3.00
Wetz & Zerweck High Ground Brewery, Embossed King, Aqua 6.00

BENNINGTON, Coachman, Marked, Pottery, Mottled Tan & Brown Glaze, 11 1/4 In. 200.00

BININGER, A.M.& Co., Cannon, Label, Wooden Carriage, Amber 495.00
Barrel, Amber, 9 1/2 In. 95.00
Barrel, Open Pontil, 2/3 Quart, Medium Amber 140.00
Barrel, Orange Amber, Pontil, 9 1/4 In. 140.00
Bitters, No.375, Broadway, Citron To Yellow, Green, Quart 59.50
Bourbon, Barrel, Medium Amber, 3/4 Quart 140.00
Cannon, Light Amber 295.00
Great Gun Bourbon, Cannon, Label, Amber 325.00
London Dock Gin, Amber, Small 30.00
Old Kentucky Bourbon, Barrel, Amber, 3/4 Quart .... 65.00 To 90.00
Old Kentucky Bourbon, Barrel, Open Pontil, Amber, Quart 170.00
Old Kentucky Bourbon, Barrel, Open Pontil, Quart .... 110.00 To 155.00
Old London Dock Gin, Fleur De Lis, Variant Full, Mint, Label 75.00
Regulator, Amber 225.00
Urn With Handle, Yellow Amber 900.00
Urn, Light Yellow Amber 695.00
Whiskey, Apricot, 10 In. 60.00
Whiskey, N.Y., Barrel, Ribbed Bands, Amber, 7 3/4 In. 95.00

Bischoff Company has made fancy decanters since it was founded in 1777 in Trieste, Italy. The modern collectible Bischoff bottles have been imported to the United States since about 1950. Glass, porcelain, and stoneware decanters and figurals are made.

BISCHOFF, African Head, 1962 .... 130.00
Alpine Pitcher, 1969 .... 18.00
Amber Leaf, 1952 .... 33.00
Amphora, 1 Handle, 1950 .... 24.00
Amphora, 2 Handle, 1950 .... 24.00
Antique Candlestick, 1958 .... 23.00
Bell House, 1960 .... 37.00
Bell Tower, 1959 .... 20.00
Black Cat, 1969 .... 13.00
Blue Gold, 1956 .... 48.00
Cameo Pitcher, 1962 .... 19.00
Canteen, Floral, 1969 .... 14.00
Canteen, Fruit, 1969 .... 16.00
Chariot Urn, 1966 .... 23.00
Chinese Boy, 1962 .... 36.00
Chinese Girl, 1962 .... 36.00
Christmas Tree, 1957 .... 48.00
Clown, Candlestick 8.00
Coronet Crystal, 1952 .... 33.00
Dachshund, 1966 .... 39.00
Deer, 1969 .... 11.00
Duck, 1964 .... 47.00
Egyptian Ashtray, 1961 .... 16.00
Egyptian Dancers, 1961 .... 13.00
Egyptian Musical Trio, 1959 .... 22.00
Egyptian Musicians, 1963 .... 15.00
Egyptian Tall Vase, 1961 .... 17.00
Emerald Rose, 1952 .... 48.00
Festival, 1957 .... 48.00
Fish Ashtray, 1961 .... 19.00
Fish, Golden, 1964 .... 46.00
Fish, Ruby, 1969 .... 16.00

Fruit Bowl, 1966	29.00
Gold Aqua, 1956	30.00
Gold Candlestick, 1958	27.00
Gold Dust, 1958	37.00
Gold Flower, 1956	48.00
Gold Rose, 1952	28.00
Gold Topaz, 1955	24.00
Gold Vase	19.00
Gold Violet, 1954	23.00
Grecian Vase, 1969	15.00
Green Rose, 1954	33.00
Green Striped, 1958	33.00
Jungle Scene, Ruby, 1952	25.00
Jungle Scene, Topaz, 1952	28.00
Mask, Colombian, 1963	18.00
Mask, Nigerian	19.00
Modern Vase, 1959	33.00
Opaline, 1957	48.00
Pageantry Vase, 1962	14.00
Pink Rose, 1953	33.00
Pirate	20.00
Porcelain Cameo, 1953	15.00
Red Bell, 1957	43.00
Red Rose, 1957	48.00
Red Striped, 1958	33.00
Rooster Ashtray, 1962	20.00
Ruby Etched, Czech, 1952	37.00
Ruby Etched, Germany, 1953	37.00
Ruby Flowers, 1953	37.00
Ruby Grapes, 1953	37.00
Silver Aqua, 1954	33.00
Silver Blue, 1954	43.00
Silver Green, 1954	33.00
Silver Spotted, 1958	33.00
Silver Topaz, 1955	38.00
Silver Violet, 1954	31.00
Spanish Boy, 1961	30.00
Spanish Girl, 1961	34.00
Topaz Basket, 1958	33.00
Tower Of Fruit	18.00
Venetian Blue, 1953	28.00
Watchtower, 1960	9.00
White Pitcher, 1960	17.00
Wild Geese Pitcher, 1951	17.00
Wild Geese, Ruby, 1952	28.00
Yellow Vase, 1959	23.00

Bitters bottles held the famous 19th century medicine called bitters. It was often of such a high alcohol content that the user felt healthier with each sip. The word bitters must be embossed on the glass or a paper label must be affixed for the collector to call the bottle a bitters bottle. Most date from 1840 to 1900. The numbers used in the entries in the form W-0 or W-L-0 refer to the books "Bitters Bottles" and "Supplement to Bitters Bottles" by Richard Watson. Numbers in the form R-00 refer to the book "For Bitters Only" by Carlyn Ring.

BITTERS, A.L.Heintz, Famous Tonic Wine, Gallon Crockery, R-H76	175.00
Abbott's Aromatic, Complete Label, Amber, W-L3, R-A5	25.00
Abbott's, Amber, Label, Sealed, Contents, Sample	10.00
Abbott's, Baltimore, Embossed, 3 5/8 In., R-A2	2.50
African Stomach, Amber, W-3b, R-A16	30.00 To 60.00
African Stomach, Cylinder, Light To Yellow Amber, W-3b, R-A16	49.50
Alpine Herb, Amber, Square, W-6, R-A37	114.00 To 120.00
Angelica Tonic, Jos. Trinet, Chicago, Ill., Amber, Flask, 9 1/2 In.	25.00

Angostura Bark, Amber, W-11, R-A68 .... 45.00 To 50.00
Angostura Miniature, Embossed, Dug, BIMAL 11.00
Angostura, Trinidad, 5 In. 1.50
Appetine, George Benz & Sons, Black Amethyst, W-L8, R-A77 .... 550.00
Arp's Stomach, Aqua, Quart, W-L153, R-A96 .... 30.00
Arron Extract Co., Detroit, No.60867, 90 Proof 2.50
Arron Liqueur Corp, N.Y.C.Branch, Orange 2.00
Asparagine, Fluted Shoulder Asparagus Tips, Clear, R-A104 .... 22.00
Atwood's Genuine, Aqua, W-15, R-A109 .... 40.00
Atwood's Jaundice, Aqua, 6 In., W-16, R-A111 .... *Illus* 6.00
Atwood's Jaundice, 12-Sided, Open Pontil, Aqua, W-17, R-A118 .... 55.00
Atwood's Jaundice, 37 1/2 Cents, Full Label 9.50
Atwood's Quinine Tonic, Aqua, W-18, R-A129 .... 40.00 To 50.00
Atwood's Quinine Tonic, Sealed Contents, W-18, R-A129 .... 50.00
Atwood's, Miniature, ABM, W-17h 8.00
Augauer, Both Labels, Green, W-21, R-A134 .... 75.00
Augauer, Rectangle, Emerald Green, 8 In., W-21, R-A134 .... 35.00 To 50.00
B & L Invigorator, Ohio, Contents, 1/2 Pint, R-B3 .... 10.00
Baker's Orange Grove, Apricot, W-23, R-B9 .... 150.00
Baker's Orange Grove, Light Amber, W-23, R-B9 .... 100.00
Baldwin's Celery Pepsin Dandelion Tonic, Yellow Amber 45.00
Begg's Dandelion, Square, Amber, W-30, R-B31 .... 30.00 To 70.00
Bell's Cocktail, James M.Bell & Co., New York, Lady's Leg, Amber 235.00
Bell's Cocktail, Lady's Leg, Golden Amber, W-32, R-B58 .... 375.00
Ben-Hur, Amber, Square, Contents, W-36, R-B69 .... 30.00
Bennet's Celebrated Stomach, San Francisco, R-B73 .... 175.00 To 210.00
Berkshire, Pig, Amber, 9 1/2 In., W-38, R-B81 .... 975.00
Berlin Magen, Rothenburg, Square, Milk Glass, W-L112, R-B82 .... 45.00
Berliner Magen Co., Square, Amber, W-39, R-886 .... 30.00
Big Bill Best, Amber, W-41, R-B95 .... 55.00
Big Bill Best, Red Amber, 3/4 Quart, W-41, R-B95 .... 50.00
Bird, Food For Song Since 1882, Box, Contents, 5 In., W-L15 .... 9.00
Bischoff's Stomach 400.00
     BITTERS, BOONEKAMP, see Bitters, Underberg
Botanic, Herzberg Bros., Near Yellow, W-50, R-B165 .... 69.00
Bourbon Whiskey, Label, Red Amber, W-52, R-B171 .... 295.00
Bourbon Whiskey, Puce, W-52, R-B171 .... 180.00 To 235.00
Brand Bros.Co., Eigenthumer, Gesetzlich, Geschutzi, W-L160, R-B201 .... 60.00
Brown's Boston Sarsaparilla & Tomato, Pontil, Aqua, W-58, R-S36 .... 115.00
Brown's Celebrated Indian Herb, Pat.1867, Amber, W-57a 180.00
Brown's Celebrated Indian Herb, Pat.1867, Light Amber, W-57a 275.00
Brown's Celebrated Indian Herb, Pat.1868, Amber, W-57 .... 160.00 To 300.00

Bitters, Atwood's Jaundice, Aqua, 6 In., W-16, R-A111

Brown's Celebrated Indian Herb, Pat.1868, W-57c 225.00
Brown's Celebrated Indian Herb, Yellow, W-57a 410.00
Brown's Iron, Quinine, Burlington, Vermont, 16 Ounce, R-I28 .... 60.00
Brown's Iron, R-B231 .... 3.00 To 18.00
Burdock Blood, Aqua, W-60, R-B262 .... 9.00
Burdock Blood, Clear, W-60, R-B262 .... 8.00 To 12.00
Burgurden Wein, Green 25.00
BITTERS, BYRNE, see Bitters, Professor Geo. J. Byrne
C.Gates & Co., Life Of Man, Rectangle, Aqua, W-214, R-G .... 25.00 To 35.00
C.H.Swains Bourbon, Square, Amber, W-326, R-S228 .... 80.00
C.K.Wilson Wa-Hoo, Label & Contents, W-L147, R-W127 .... 20.00
BITTERS, C.W. ROBACK'S, see Bitters, Dr. C.W. Roback's
C.W.Weston & Co., New York, Olive Green, Pint 38.00
BITTERS, CABIN, see Bitters, Drake's Plantation; Bitters, Edw.
Wilder's Stomach; Bitters, Golden; Bitters, Grave's & Son;
Bitters, H.P. Herb Wild Cherry; Bitters, Kelly's Old Cabin
Caldwell's Herb, Dark Amber, W-65a, R-C9 .... 145.00 To 165.00
Caldwell's Herb, Iron Pontil, Amber, W-65a, R-C9 .... 190.00
Caldwell's Herb, Iron Pontil, Honey Amber, W-65a, R-C9 .... 225.00 To 250.00
California Fig & Herb, San Francisco, Light Amber, W-66, R-C15 .... 50.00
Campana, Mexico 2.50
Capitol, Clear, W-L166, R-C39 .... 25.00
Capitol, J.F.L., Pineapple, Iron Pontil, R-C40 .... 975.00
Carmeliter Stomach Bitters Co., New York, Amber, W-71a, R-C52 .... 45.00
Carmeliter Stomach, Green, W-71a, R-C54 .... 60.00
Caroni, Round, Amber, W-72, R-C59 .... 9.00
Caroni, Round, Dark Green, W-72a, R-C60 .... 25.00
Carpathian Herb, Square, Amber, W-73a, R-C62 .... 30.00
Carter's Liver, New York, Amber, W-75, R-C67 .... 25.00
Celebrated Crown, Yellow, W-80, R-C93 .... 120.00
Chafee's Tonic .... 360.00 To 400.00
Clark's California Cherry Cordial, Amber 28.00
Clark's Giant, Philadelphia, Pa., Label, W-412, R-C166 .... 75.00
Clarke's Compound Mandrake, Oval, Aqua, W-85, R-C151 .... 30.00
Clarke's Vegetable Sherry Wine, Aqua, 11 1/2 In., W-88d 55.00
Clarke's Vegetable Sherry Wine, Sharon, Aqua, 1 Gal., W-88h, R-C155 .... 235.00
Clober, Full Label, Aqua, W-L34, R-C177 .... 50.00
Cobalt Blue, 12 In. ....Color 350.00
Coburn & Land & Co., XX Boston, Cobalt Blue 85.00
Cole Bros.Vegetable, Aqua, W-413, R-C189 .... 20.00 To 26.00
Colleton, Plain Base .... 50.00 To 75.00
Colleton, Pontil Base, W-91, R-C195 .... 75.00
Columbo Peptic, L.E.Jung, New Orleans, Amber, W-93, R-C200 .... 20.00
Columbo Peptic, New Orleans, Square, Red Amber, 9 In., W-93, R-C200 .... 30.00
Comus Stomach, Cierc Bros. & Co., New Orleans, La., R-C212 .... 75.00
Congress, Rectangular, Amber, R-C216 .... 125.00
Constitution, Seward & Bentley, Chocolate Amber, W-95, R-C222 .... 325.00
Constitution, Seward & Bentley, Olive Amber, W-95, R-C222 .... 275.00
Constitution, Seward & Bentley, Orange Amber, W-95, R-C222 .... 300.00
Corwitz Stomach, Square, Indented Panels, Aqua, 7 1/2 In., R-C236 .... 40.00
Cunderango, Dr.Place, Aqua, W-L98, R-P106 .... 29.00 To 35.00
Cunderango, Dr.Place, Green, W-L98, R-P106 .... 290.00
Curtis & Perkins Wild Cherry, Aqua, W-102, R-C262 .... 75.00 To 85.00
Damiana, Baja, California, Aqua, Fifth, W-103, R-D4 .... 32.00 To 38.00
Damiana, Baja, California, Blob Top, W-103, R-D4 .... 19.00
Damiana, Baja, California, Stretched Neck, Aqua, W-103, R-D4 .... 38.00
Damiana, Clear, R-D4.5 .... 22.00 To 29.50
Davis Drug Co., Green 50.00
Delight's Spanish Mixture, Open Pontil, Aqua 36.00
Demuth's Stomach, Philadelphia, Amber, W-106, R-D46 .... 60.00
Devil-Cert Stomach, Quart, W-425, R-D59 .... 45.00
DeWitt's Stomach, Amber, Flask, Label, Pint, R-D65 .... 20.00 To 45.00
DeWitt's Stomach, Chicago, Amber, Rectangle, W-426, R-D64 .... 40.00

Didier's, Front & Back Labels, Amber, Pint, R-D72 .... 75.00 To 110.00
Digestine, Amber 300.00
Digestine, P.J.Bowlin Liquor Co., St.Paul, Amber 150.00
Digestine, Sample, Amber, R-D74 .... 275.00
Doctor Fisch's, Golden Amber, W-124, R-F44 .... 125.00 To 135.00
Doctor Fisch's, W-124, R-F44 .... 120.00 To 140.00
Domingo, Amber 50.00
Doyle's Hop, Amber, W-110, R-D93 .... 20.00 To 40.00
Doyle's Hop, Olive Green, Oversized, W-110, R-D93 .... 200.00 To 250.00
Doyle's Hop, Red Amber, W-110, R-D93 .... 22.50
Doyle's Hop, Yellow, W-110, R-D93 .... 34.50
Dr. Baxter's Mandrake, Label, Aqua, W-29, R-B36 .... 15.00
Dr.A.S.Hopkins Union Stomach, Honey Amber, W-177a, R-H180 .... 50.00
Dr.A.S.Hopkins Union Stomach, 4 3/4 In., R-H183 .... 70.00
Dr.Ball's Vegetable Stomachic, Northboro, OP, Aqua, W-25, R-B14 .... 120.00
Dr.Baxter's Mandrake, Burlington, 12 Panels, Dark Aqua, W-29, R-B36 .... 8.00
Dr.Blake's Aromatic, OP, Aqua, W-45, R-B120 .... 85.00 To 90.00
Dr.Boyce's Tonic, Aqua, W-53, R-B175 .... 28.00 To 45.00
Dr.C.D.Warner's German Hop, 1880, Square, Amber, W-355, R-W32 .... 90.00
Dr.C.W.Roback's Stomach, Light Amber, 10 In., W-280, R-R73 .... 185.00
Dr.C.W.Roback's Stomach, Light Amber, 9 3/8 In., R-R74 .... 115.00
Dr.C.W.Roback's Stomach, Pontil, Amber, 10 In., W-280, R-R73 .... 275.00
Dr.Caldwell's Herb, The Great Tonic, Amber, W-65a, R-C9 .... 145.00
Dr.D.S.Perry & Co.Excelsior Aromatic, New York, Olive Amber 200.00
Dr.Fisch's, 1866, Amber, Original Cork, W-125a, R-F45 .... 375.00
Dr.Fisch's, 1866, Dark Amber, 11 In., W-124, R-F44 .... 185.00
Dr.Fisch's, 1866, Light Amber, W-124, R-F44 .... 120.00
Dr.Fisch's, 1866, Near Yellow, W-124, R-F44 .... 330.00
Dr.Fisch's, 1866, Seed Bubbles, Dark Amber, W-124, R-F44 .... 95.00
Dr.Flint's Quaker, Providence, R.I., Aqua, W-126, R-F58 .... 20.00 To 25.00
Dr.George Pierce's Indian Restorative, W-258a, R-P95 .... 30.00 To 40.00
Dr.Gillmore's Laxative, Kidney, & Liver, Amber, Large, W-436, R-G43 .... 55.00
Dr.Gruessie-Altherr's Krauter, Lady's Leg, Amber, W-157, R-G122 .... 25.00
Dr.H.C.Stewart's Tonic, Columbus, Amber, 9 1/2 In., W-500a, R-S194 .... 30.00
Dr.Harter's Wild Cherry, Dayton, O., Amber, Sample, W-158, R-H49 .... 35.00
Dr.Harter's Wild Cherry, Dayton, O., Rectangle, Amber, W-158, R-H50 .... 35.00
Dr.Harter's, St.Louis, Large, R-H51 .... 20.00
Dr.Harter's, St.Louis, No Bottom Embossing, 7 1/2 In., W-158, R-H50 .... 27.00
Dr.Hartshorn's Jaundice, Embossed, Label, Aqua, W-L59, R-H62 .... 20.00
Dr.Henley's California, Square, Aqua, W-444, R-H81 .... 300.00
Dr.Henley's IXL, Aqua, 12 3/4 In., W-164, R-H84 .... 50.00
Dr.Henley's IXL, Light Strike, Aqua, 12 In., W-163, R-H83 .... 35.00
Dr.Henley's IXL, Lime Green 150.00
Dr.Henley's IXL, Wild Grape Root, Medium Green, W-164, R-H85 .... 250.00
Dr.Henley's Wild Grape Root, Aqua, W-164, R-H85 .... 30.00
Dr.Hoofland's German, Aqua, W-178, R-H168 .... 25.00 To 65.00
Dr.Hoofland's German, Open Pontil, Aqua, W-174, R-H168 .... 50.00 To 70.00
Dr.Hopkins Union Stomach, ABM, Amber, W-177b, R-H182 .... 19.00
Dr.Hopkins Union Stomach, Amber, BIMAL, W-177, R-H180 .... 28.00
Dr.Hopkins Union Stomach, Contents, 95% Label, W-177, R-H180 .... 75.00
     BITTERS, DR. HOSTETTER'S, see Bitters, Dr. J. Hostetter's
Dr.Huntington's Golden Tonic, Portland, Maine, W-182, R-H213 .... 145.00
Dr.J.Hostetter's Stomach, A.G.W.T.On Base, Amber, R-H195 .... 15.00
Dr.J.Hostetter's Stomach, Black Glass 55.00
Dr.J.Hostetter's Stomachic, W-179b, R-H198 .... 29.00
Dr.J.Hostetter's, Honey Amber, R-H199 .... 110.00
Dr.J.Hostetter's, L & W On Base, Amber, R-H195 .... 25.00
Dr.J.Hostetter's, Old Variant, I On Base, Deep Dark Leaf Green 90.00
Dr.J.Hostetter's, Olive Green, W-179, R-H194 .... 75.00
Dr.J.Hostetter's, Yellow, W-179, R-H194 .... 15.00 To 38.00
Dr.J.Sweet's Strengthening, Aqua, W-328, R-S234 .... 35.00
Dr.Jacob's, New Haven, Ct., W-190a, R-J11 .... 55.00
Dr.Jewett's Celebrated Health Restoring, Aqua, W-193, R-J37 .... 19.50

Dr.John Bull Compound Cedron, Louisville, Ky., Amber, R-B254 .... 100.00
Dr.Kaufmann's Sulphur, Label & Contents, Booklet, W-L77, P-K15 .... 18.00
Dr.Kaufmann's Sulphur, Original Label, Aqua, 10 In. 17.50
Dr.Langley's Root & Herb, Boston, Light Green, 7 In., W-206o, R-L22 .... 37.00
Dr.Langley's Root & Herb, Boston, Partial Label, Aqua, W-206b, R-L21 .... 52.00
Dr.Langley's Root & Herb, Golden Amber, 1/2 Pint, W-206f, R-L20 .... 30.00
Dr.Langley's Root & Herb, 76 Union St., Boston, Small, W-206, R-L26 .... 45.00
Dr.Langley's Root & Herb, 99 Union St., Boston, W-206b, R-L21 .... 20.00
Dr.Langley's, Backwards 9's, Aqua, W-206e, R-L24 .... 65.00
Dr.Loew's Celebrated Stomach, Emerald Green, R-L113 .... 70.00 To 100.00
Dr.Mampe's Herb Stomach, Rectangular, Aqua, W-225, R-M26 .... 30.00
Dr.Manly Hardy's Genuine Jaundice, Bangor, Me., Pontil, R-H34 .... 115.00
Dr.Petzold's Genuine German, Great Elixir Of Life, Amber, R-P77 .... 110.00
Dr.Petzold's German, Medium Amber, W-256, R-P75 .... 95.00
Dr.Pierce's Indian Restorative, Lowell, W-258a, R-P95 .... 20.00 To 36.00
Dr.Renz's, Apple Green, W-273, R-R36 .... 165.00
    BITTERS, DR. RUSSELL'S, see Bitters, Pepsin Calisaya
Dr.Sawen's Life Invigorating, Amber, W-295, R-S40 .... 50.00
Dr.Sawen's Life Invigorating, Utica, N.Y., Clear, W-295a, R-S41 .... 45.00
Dr.Soule Hop, Bubbles, Deep Amber, R-S145 .... 60.00
Dr.Soule Hop, 1872, Golden Amber, Thick, R-S147 .... 120.00
Dr.Stanley's South American Herb, Amber, W-314, R-S174 .... 65.00
Dr.Stanley's South American Indian, Aqua, W-314, R-S174 .... 75.00
Dr.Stephen Jewett's Celebrated Health Restoring, Pontil, Aqua 120.00
Dr.Stephen Jewett's Celebrated, Rindge, N.H., Open Pontil 105.00
Dr.Stoever's, Est. 1837, Amber, Kryder & Co., W-320 .... 60.00
Dr.Stoever's, Yellow Amber, 3/4 Quart, W-320 .... 60.00
Dr.Thos. Hall's, Applied Top 140.00
Dr.Van Dyke's, Holland, Clear 30.00
Dr.Von Hopf's Curacao, Amber, Label, W-343, R-V28 .... 50.00
Dr.Von Hopf's Curacao, Partial Label 45.00
Dr.Von Hopf's, Flask Shape, Des Moines, W-343, R-V27 .... 20.00 To 33.00
Dr.Warren's Bilious, Aqua, W-513b, R-W45 .... 40.00
Dr.Wilson's Herbine, Brayley Drug Co., Aqua, W-368, R-W125 .... 38.00
Dr.Wood's Sarsaparilla & Wild Cherry, Pontil, W-372, R-W151 .... 175.00
Dr.Young's Wild Cherry, Amber, R-Y11 .... 80.00
Drake's Plantation, 4 Log, W-111b, R-D110 .... 55.00 To 65.00
Drake's Plantation, 4 Log, Gold Amber, W-111b, R-D110 .... 35.00 To 55.00
Drake's Plantation, 4 Log, Medium Amber, W-111b, R-D110 .... 110.00
Drake's Plantation, 4 Log, Orange Amber, W-111b, R-D110 .... 75.00
Drake's Plantation, 5 Log, Honey Amber, W-111d, R-D109 .... 185.00
Drake's Plantation, 5 Log, Light Amber, W-111d, R-D109 .... 160.00
Drake's Plantation, 6 Log, Amber, W-111, R-D105 .... 45.00 To 65.00
Drake's Plantation, 6 Log, Bluish Red, W-111, R-D105 .... 200.00
Drake's Plantation, 6 Log, Brown Amber, W-111, R-D105 .... 70.00
Drake's Plantation, 6 Log, Claret, W-111, R-D105 .... 125.00
Drake's Plantation, 6 Log, Deep Red, W-111, R-D105 .... 100.00
Drake's Plantation, 6 Log, Golden Amber, W-111, R-D105 .... 50.00 To 68.00
Drake's Plantation, 6 Log, Greenish Yellow, W-111, R-D105 .... 150.00
Drake's Plantation, 6 Log, Honey Amber, W-111c, R-D102 .... 55.00
Drake's Plantation, 6 Log, Light Amber, W-111, R-D105 .... 65.00 To 75.00
Drake's Plantation, 6 Log, Light Citron Yellow, W-111e, R-D104 .... 925.00
Drake's Plantation, 6 Log, Light Puce, W-111, R-D105 .... 350.00
Drake's Plantation, 6 Log, Medium Amber, W-111, R-D105 .... 48.00
Drake's Plantation, 6 Log, Medium Olive, W-111, R-D105 .... 475.00
Drake's Plantation, 6 Log, Part Label, Yellow Green, W-111, R-D105 .... 350.00
Drake's Plantation, 6 Log, Pink, W-111, R-D105 .... 800.00
Drake's Plantation, 6 Log, Red, W-111, R-D105 .... 75.00 To 110.00
Drake's Plantation, 6 Log, Yellow, W-111, R-D105 .... 75.00
E.A.Smith, Brandon, Vermont 5.00
E.L.Arpkiel Pepsin, Clear 35.00
E.R.Clarke's Sarsaparilla, Pontil, Aqua, W-86, R-C154 .... 150.00
Eagle Angostura Bark, Amber, W-11, R-E2 .... 50.00

BITTERS, EAR OF CORN, see Bitters, National, Ear of Corn

Ear Of Corn Shape, Molded Kernels, Amber, 9 3/4 In.	75.00
Edw.Wilder's Stomach, Cabin, Clear, W-366, R-W116	375.00
Edw.Wilder's Stomach, Louisville, Ky., W-366, R-W116	120.00 To 150.00
Egon Braun, Hamburg, 8-Sided, Olive Green	70.00
EJB, Round, Amber	1.00
Electric Brand, Amber, 10 In., W-115, R-E31	10.00 To 25.00
Electric Brand, Amber, 8 5/8 In., R-E33	15.00
Electric, Amber, Label, W-114, R-E29	12.50
Electric, Honey Color, Square, 8 3/4 In., W-114, R-E29	17.00
Emerson's Excelsior Botanic, Full Label, Aqua, R-E41	18.00 To 25.00
Erso Anti Bilious, Label, Contents, R-E49	18.00
Excelsior, Applied Top, Amber, W-119, R-E64	325.00
F.Brown, Boston, Sarsaparilla & Tomato, W-58, R-S36	80.00
F.Chevalier Co.	45.00
Faith Whitcomb's, Aqua, W-362, R-W90	30.00
Fernet Branca Co., N.Y., Original Label, Green, 10 In., R-F16	10.00
Ferro-China Bisleri Iron & Cinchona, Dark Green, Label	30.00
Ferro-China, Olive Amber, Labeled, Quart, R-F31	25.00 To 35.00
Ferro-China, Triangular Shape, Embossed Lion, R-F31	75.00
Ferro-Quina Blood Maker, Amber, W-123, R-F40	65.00
Fish, W.H.Ware, Amber, W-125a, R-F45	95.00 To 130.00
Fish, W.H.Ware, Black-Amber, W-125a, R-F45	625.00
Fish, W.H.Ware, Citron, W-125a, R-P45	1150.00
Fish, W.H.Ware, Clear, W-125, R-F46	695.00 To 850.00
Fish, W.H.Ware, Dark Amber, W-125a, R-F45	125.00
Fish, W.H.Ware, Smoky Clear, W-125, R-F46	1350.00
Fish, W.H.Ware, Yellow-Green, W-125a, R-F45	1600.00
Gates, Life Of Man, Clear, Label, W-214, R-G7	36.00 To 60.00
Genuine Turkish Rhubarb, Label, Lady's Leg, ABM, Green, R-G17l	59.50
German Balsam, Milk Glass, W-129, R-G18	375.00
German Hop, Reading, Mich., Light Yellowish Amber, W-130, R-G24	75.00
Germania Peppermint Schnapps, 6-Sided, Clear	6.00 To 8.00
Globe Tonic, Clear	175.00
Globe Tonic, Dark Amber, W-134, R-G49	35.00
Globe Tonic, Golden Amber, W-134, R-G49	56.00
Goff's Herb, Camden, N.J., Aqua, 5 5/8 In., W-137, R-G55	5.00 To 12.00
Goff's, ABM, Amethyst, 5 1/4 In., R-G56	10.00
Golden, Geo.C.Hubbell Co., Cabin, Aqua, W-138, R-G63	50.00 To 195.00
Gorman's, Jersey City	1.50
Grand Prize, Etched, W-142, R-G89	195.00 To 200.00
Grave's & Son, Louisville, Ky., Cabin Shape, Aqua, W-438a, R-G96	350.00
Greeley's Bourbon Whiskey, Cranberry Amethyst, W-145, R-G102	290.00
Greeley's Bourbon Whiskey, Wine, 3/4 Quart, W-145, R-G102	160.00
Greeley's Bourbon, Cranberry Amethyst, W-144, R-G101	310.00 To 325.00
Greeley's Bourbon, Gray Green, W-144, R-G101	300.00
Greeley's Bourbon, Green, W-144, R-G101	340.00
Greeley's Bourbon, Olive Amber, W-144, R-G101	210.00 To 220.00
Greeley's Bourbon, Olive Green, W-144, R-G101	270.00
Greeley's Bourbon, Puce, Label, W-144, R-G101	350.00
Greeley's Bourbon, Smoky Amber, W-144, R-G101	145.00
Greeley's Bourbon, Smoky Olive, W-144, R-G101	265.00
Greeley's Bourbon, Smoky Puce, W-144, R-G101	70.00
Greeley's, Vertical, Cranberry Amethyst, W-145, R-G102	325.00
Greeley's, Vertical, Light Copper Puce, W-145, R-G102	175.00
Greeley's, Vertical, Topaz, W-145, R-G102	235.00
Green Mountain Cider, W-146, R-G103	100.00
Greer's Eclipse, Amber, W-147, R-G112	48.00
H.G.Leisenring & Co., Celebrated Cordial, Square, Amber	45.00
H.Klass' Oregon Peach, R-K60	90.00
H.P.Herb Wild Cherry, Cabin, Amber, W-148, R-H93	125.00 To 180.00
H.P.Herb Wild Cherry, Reading, Pa., Honey Amber, W-148, R-H93	170.00
H.Theilmann's, Aqua, R-T19	45.00

BITTERS, HUA, see Bitters, Underberg

Hall's, E.E.Hall New Haven, 1842, Honey Amber, W-151, R-H10 .... 110.00
Hall's, E.E.Hall, Golden Amber, 3/4 Quart, W-151, R-H10 .... 50.00 To 70.00
Hansard's Genuine Hop, Tan Stone, R-H25 .... 70.00
Henley's IXL, Heavy Strike, Aqua, W-164a, R-H84 .... 50.00
Henley's IXL, Light Strike, Aqua, W-164a, R-H84 .... 32.00
Hi-Hi, Rock Island, Ill., Amber, Embossed, W-167, R-H118 .... 65.00
Hiawatha Liver & Kidney, Label, Amber, W-L61, R-H107 .... 25.00
Hibernia, Applied Top, W-446, R-H113 .... 122.00 To 150.00
Highland & Scotch Tonic, Barrel, Orange Amber, W-170, R-H117 .... 675.00
Highland Bitters & Scotch Tonic, Amber To Orange, W-170, R-H117 .... 975.00
Holtzermann's Patent Stomach, 2-Sided Roof, Amber, W-172a, R-H155 .... 395.00
Holtzermann's Patent Stomach, 4-Sided Roof, Amber, W-172, R-H154 .... 125.00
Holtzermann's Stomach, 4-Sided Roof, Label, Amber, W-172, R-H154 .... 200.00
Home Bitters Co., St.Louis, Amber, W-173, R-H156 .... 45.00
Hoofland's German, Liver Complaint, Phila., Aqua, W-174, R-H168 .... 28.00
Hop & Iron, W-175, R-H172 .... 25.00
Hopkin's Union Stomach, Labels, Contents, R-H178 .... 50.00
Hops & Malt, Amber, W-176, R-H186 .... 35.00 To 85.00
    BITTERS, HOSTETTER'S, see Bitters, Dr. J. Hostetter's
    BITTERS, HUBBELL CO., see Bitters, Golden
Humphries Cooling, Aqua 32.00
Hutching's Dyspepsia, New York, Open Pontil, Aqua, W-184, R-H218 .... 40.00
    BITTERS, INDIAN QUEEN, see Bitters, Brown's Celebrated Indian
    Herb
    BITTERS, INDIAN RESTORATIVE, see Bitters, Dr.George Pierce's
    BITTERS, IRON, see Bitters, Brown's Iron
J.H.Henke's Schnapps Aromatic, Green, Quart 18.00
J.M.Leonard, Bangor, Maine, Wild Cherry & Blood Jaundice, Aqua 15.00
JNO Moffat, New York, Price, $1.00, Olive Amber, W-257a, R-M111 .... 325.00
JNO Moffat, Price, $1.00, Phoenix, Olive Amber, W-257b, R-M110 .... 240.00
J.T.Higby Tonic, Square, Amber, W-331, R-T40 .... 50.00
J.Triner, Chicago, American Elixir, Amber, Quart 20.00
John Moffat, Phoenix, Aqua, W-257c, R-M112 .... 38.00
John Moffat, Phoenix, Price, $1.00, N.Y., Green, W-257, R-M113 .... 52.00
John Moffat, Price, $1.00, N.Y., Phoenix, Pontil, Aqua, W-257c, R-M112 .... 150.00
Johnson's Calisaya, Amber, W-194, R-J45 .... 60.00
Kaiser Wilhelm Bitters Co., Clear, W-197, R-K5 .... 30.00 To 50.00
Kaiser Wilhelm, Amber, W-197, R-K5 .... 135.00
Kaufmanns, Label, Contents, Boxed 25.00
Kelly's Old Cabin, Amber, W-199, R-K21 .... 300.00 To 550.00
Kelly's Old Cabin, Black-Olive Green, W-199, R-K21 ....2500.00
Kelly's Old Cabin, March, 1870, Olive Green, R-K22 .... 300.00 To 400.00
Kennedy's East India, W-200, R-K26 .... 17.00
Keystone, Barrel, Amber, W-201, R-K36 .... 275.00
Keystone, Honey Amber, W-201, R-K36 .... 450.00
Keystone, Light Honey Amber, W-201, R-K36 .... 285.00
Kimball's Jaundice, Pontil, Olive Amber, W-202, R-K42 .... 275.00 To 340.00
Kimball's Jaundice, Troy, N.H., Amber, W-202, R-K42 .... 325.00
King Solomon's, Amber, 4 1/2 In., R-K50 .... 21.00
King Solomon's, Seattle, Wash., Amber, W-457, R-K49 .... 58.00 To 60.00
Landsberg, Chicago Centennial 1776-1876, Yellow Amber, R-L14 .... 525.00
Lash's Kidney & Liver, Cathartic & Blood, Amber, W-208, R-L34 .... 15.00
Lash's Kidney & Liver, Indented Panels, Amber, W-208, R-L38 .... 20.00
Lash's, Amber, Label & Contents, W-207, R-L32 .... 25.00
Lash's, Back Bar, Amber, Quart, W-208, R-L41 .... 60.00
Lash's, Cap, Amber 3.00
Lash's, New York, San Francisco, Chicago, Amber, R-L43 .... 20.00
Lash's, San Francisco, California, Round, Amber, R-L47 .... 10.00 To 20.00
Leak's Kidney & Liver, Amber, W-210, R-L53 .... 35.00
Leipziger Burgunder Wein, Embossed Bottom, Dark Green, W-212, R-L69 .... 45.00
Lippman's, New York & Savannah, R-L99 .... 75.00
Litthauer Stomach, Clear, W-216a, R-L101 .... 70.00
Litthauer Stomach, Misspelled Invented, Clear, 7 In., W-216, R-L103 .... 30.00
Litthauer, Hartwig Kantorowicz Posen, Green, 11 1/4 In., W-216 .... 450.00

Litthauer, Hartwig Kantorowicz Posen, Milk Glass, W-216, R-L106 .... 37.00
Litthauer, Hartwig Kantorowicz Posen, Milk Glass, 3 1/2 In., W-216 .... 125.00
Litthauer, Hartwig Kantorowicz, N.Y., Milk Glass, W-216, R-L106 .... 60.00
Litthauer, Hartwig Kantorowicz, Onion Shape, Embossed Trees, Clear 65.00
Litthauer, Hartwig Kantorowicz, Star & Fish, Amber, W-216, R-L104 .... 80.00
Litthauer, Hartwig Kantorowicz, Vertical Embossed, Milk Glass 60.00
Malakoff, N.Kieffer, Patented Sept.18th, 1866 .... 250.00
Malt, Boston, Green, W-224, R-M20 .... 40.00
Mampe, Carl Srampe Berlin, Elephant In Circle, Contents, Dark Green 55.00
BITTERS,MANDRAKE, see Bitters, Dr. Baxter's
McKeevers, Army, Amber, W-228, R-M58 .... 1750.00 To 2700.00
BITTERS, MINIATURE, see Miniature, Bitters
Mishler's Herb Bitters, Square, Amber, W-229, R-M99 .... 25.00 To 32.00
Mishler's Herb, Light Citron, W-229, R-M99 .... 28.00
Mock's Hop, Green 25.00
Molt, Boston, Embossed On Bottom, Green, Quart 9.00
Morning Inceptum, Light Amber, W-232, R-M135 .... 140.00 To 160.00
Morse's Celebrated Syrup, Iron Pontil 55.00
Mouquin Orange, Round, Green, Label 15.00
Mrs.Leonard's Dock & Dandelion, Label, Box & Contents, R-L74 .... 100.00
N.K.Brown Iron Quinine, Burlington, Vt., Aqua, Pint, R-I29 .... 75.00
National Bitters, Label, Amber, W-236, R-N8 .... 220.00
National Friedrichshall Bitter Water, Olive Green 38.00
National, Ear Of Corn, Amber, W-236, R-N8 .... 175.00 To 200.00
National, Ear Of Corn, Aqua, W-236, R-N8 .... 1800.00
National, Ear Of Corn, Black Amber, Label, W-236, R-N8 .... 1000.00
National, Ear Of Corn, Deep Claret, W-236, R-N8 .... 1000.00
National, Ear Of Corn, Orange Amber, W-236, R-N8 .... 220.00
National, Ear Of Corn, Yellow, W-236, R-N8 .... 275.00 To 375.00
Neuropin Stomach, ABM, Clear, W-L209, R-N19I 50.00
New York Hop Bitters Co., Embossed U.S.Flag, Light Green, W-472 .... 210.00
Old Dr.Solomon's Great Indian, Amber, W-311, R-S137 .... 50.00
Orange, Label 8.00
Oregon Grape Root, Amethyst, W-246, R-O77 .... 165.00
Original Pocahontas, Barrel, Aqua, W-259, R-O86 .... 1600.00
Orruro, Green, 10 5/8 In., W-248, R-O90 .... 22.00
Osgood's India Chologogue 3.00
Oxygenated, Aqua, W-248, R-O100 .... 35.00 To 45.00
Oxygenated, W-249b, R-099 .... 75.00
Parker's Celebrated Stomach, Monogram, Amber, W-480, R-P22 .... 45.00
Pawnee Indian, Amber, W-482, R-P34 .... 7.50
Pepsin Calisaya, Dr.Russell's, Emerald Green, W-253, R-P50 .... 60.00
Pepsin Calisaya, Dr.Russell's, Green, W-253, R-P50 .... 25.00 To 30.00
Peruvian Bark, Dr.M.Perl & Co., New Orleans, La., R-P70 .... 150.00
Peruvian, Monogram On Front, Square, Brown, 9 1/2 In., W-254b, R-P67 .... 27.00
Petzold's, Genuine German, W-256b, R-P74 .... 100.00
Peychaud's American Aromatic, New Orleans, Amber, R-P81 .... 37.50
Peychaud's Aromatic Cordial, Label, Embossed, Content, R-P81I 30.00
BITTERS, PIG, see Bitters, Berkshire; Bitters, Suffolk
Pineapple, Amber, 9 In. 118.00
Pineapple, Honey Amber, 9 In. 130.00
Pineapple, Light Amber, 9 In. 85.00
Pipifax, Square, Amber, R-P104 .... 55.00
Polo Club Stomach, 2 Paper Labels, Amber, W-260, R-P117 .... 120.00
Polo Club, Amber 60.00
Pond's Kidney & Liver, Partial Labels, Contents, W-487, R-P121 .... 25.00
Pond's, ABM, Rectangle, Amber, W-487, R-P121 .... 10.00
Poor Man's Family, Aqua, W-262, R-P123 .... 18.00 To 20.00
Poor Man's Family, Contents, Yellow Label, W-262, R-P123 .... 35.00
Prickley Ash Co. .... 10.00 To 22.50
Prickly Ash Bitters Co., Amber, W-263 .... 25.00 To 40.00
Professor George J.Byrne, Amber 400.00
Professor George J.Byrne, Honey Amber, W-63, R-B280 .... 1000.00

Prune Stomach & Liver, Best Cathartic, Square, Amber, W-264, B-P151 .... 45.00
Pure Hop, Tan & White, Threads, Clear 30.00
BITTERS, QUAKER, see Bitters, Dr. Flint's
R.J.Holtzermann's Patent Stomach, Cabin, Amber, W-172, R-H154 .... 145.00
Ramsey's Trinidad, Olive Amber, W-268, R-R8 .... 25.00 To 30.00
Red Star Stomach, Fluted Base, Golden Amber, R-R25 .... 150.00 To 185.00
Reed's, Lady's Leg, Amber, 3/4 Quart, W-272, R-R28 .... 140.00 To 150.00
Reed's, Lady's Leg, Honey Amber, W-272, R-R28 .... 210.00
Renault, Amber, Label, Pewter Top, W-L105, R-R33 .... 10.00
Rex Kidney & Liver, Rectangular, Amber, W-274, R-R43 .... 10.00
Rex, Round, Amber, Quart, R-R41 .... 20.00 To 25.00
Rice's, Milford, Mass. 13.00
Rising Sun, John Hurst, Burnt Orange Amber, W-277, R-R66 .... 65.00
Rising Sun, John Hurst, Honey Amber, W-277, R-R66 .... 75.00
Rohrer's Expectoral Wild Cherry Tonic, Lancaster, Amber, R-R85 .... 110.00
Rohrer's, Eastern, Light Honey Amber 160.00
Romaine's Crimean, Square, Amber, W-282, R-R87 .... 75.00
Romany Wine, Rectangle, Aqua, 6 7/8 In., W-283, R-R88 .... 60.00
Royal Italian, Amethyst, 13 1/2 In., W-286, R-R111 .... 375.00
Royal Pepsin Stomach, Amber, W-287, R-R113 .... 55.00 To 85.00
Rush's, A.H.Flanders, M.D., N.Y., Amber, W-289, R-R124 .... 20.00 To 45.00
Russ' St.Domingo, Amber, 9 7/8 In., W-290, R-R125 .... 42.00 To 50.00
S.O.Richardson, Rectangular, Pontil, Aqua, 6 7/8 In., W-275, R-R57 .... 35.00
BITTERS, S.T. DRAKE'S, see Bitters, Drake's
Saint Jacobs, Square, Amber, W-453 .... 42.00 To 55.00
Sanborn's Kidney & Liver Vegetable Laxative, Fluted Neck, Amber 68.00
Sanborn's Kidney & Liver Vegetable Laxative, W-293, R-S28 .... 55.00
Sarasina Stomach, Square, Amber, W-294, R-S22 .... 35.00 To 50.00
Sarracenia Life, Tucker, 3 Legs, Amber, Quart, W-496, R-S3 .... 100.00 To 150.00
Sazerac, Lady's Leg, Milk Glass, W-296, R-S47 .... 300.00 To 325.00
Schroeder's, Vertical Embossing, 10 1/2 In., R-S73 .... 125.00
Seaworth, Lighthouse, Amber, 6 1/2 In., W-299a, R-S82 .... 1495.00
Sechsomterlropfer Magenbitter, Germany 1.50
Secrestat, Applied Seal, Olive Green 85.00
Simon's Centennial, Washington, Aqua, W-304, R-S110 .... 525.00 To 700.00
Smith's Green Mountain Renovator, Iron Pontil, Bubbles 650.00
Smith's, Barrel, Medium Amber, 9 In., W-308, R-S124 .... 480.00
Solomon's Strengthening & Invigorating, Cobalt, W-313, R-S140 .... 225.00
Star Anchor, Portsmouth, Ohio, Amber, W-499, R-S176 .... 55.00
Star Kidney & Liver, Square, Amber, W-315, R-S178 .... 33.00
Suffolk, Pig, Boston, Amber, W-322, R-S217 .... 275.00 To 425.00
Suffolk, Pig, Double Ring Lip, Amber, W-322, R-S217 .... 475.00 To 500.00
Sumter, Square, Amber, 9 7/8 In., W-323, R-S221 .... 300.00
Sun Kidney & Liver, Contents, Square, Amber, W-324, R-S222 .... 25.00
Sunny Castle Stomach, Milwaukee, Square, Amber, 9 In., W-324, R-S223 .... 50.00
Tigero Medicinal Wine, Label Front & Back, Clear, 1 Quart 15.00
Tippecanoe, H.H.Warner & Co., Canoe, Amber, 9 1/8 In. .... 65.00 To 85.00
Tippecanoe, H.H.Warner & Co., Canoe, Light Amber, 9 In. .... 68.00 To 75.00
Tippecanoe, H.H.Warner & Co., Canoe, Olive Green 1200.00
Tippecanoe, Rocheter & Rochestr, Misspelled 74.50
Toneco Stomach, Clear, 9 In., W-330, R-T38 .... 20.00
Triner's American Elixir, Amber 20.00
Triner's, Chicago, Label & Neckband, Wrapper, Czech Writing 6.00
Turner Bros., Green 100.00
Turner Brothers, N.Y., Golden Amber With Olive Color, R-T67I 125.00
Tyler's Standard American, Golden Amber, 9 1/4 In., W-337, R-T72 .... 30.00
Tyree's Chamomile, 1880, Square, Amber, 9 1/2 In., W-338, R-T75 .... 50.00
Udolpho Wolfe's Aromatic Schnapps, Amber, Pint 40.00
Udolpho Wolfe's Aromatic Schnapps, Amber, Quart .... 10.00 To 30.00
Udolpho Wolfe's Aromatic Schnapps, Dark Olive Amber, Pint 32.50
Udolpho Wolfe's Aromatic Schnapps, Iron Pontil, Amber, Pint 35.00
Udolpho Wolfe's Aromatic Schnapps, Pontil, Olive .... 35.00 To 58.00
Underberg Boonekamp, Lady's Leg, HUA, Label, Amber, W-L17, R-B141 .... 24.00

Underberg Boonekamp, Lady's Leg, HUA, Label, W-L134 .... 30.00
Underberg Boonekamp, Lady's Leg, Label, Red Amber, W-L17, R-B141 .... 45.00
Underberg, Lady's Leg, HUA, Red Amber, W-L134, R-U6 .... 17.00
Van Bibber, Labeled, St.Paul, Minn. 45.00
Vaughn's Vegetable Mixture, Aqua, 6 1/4 In. 60.00
Vermo Stomach, Clear, Square, W-342, R-V15 .... 5.00 To 10.00
Voldner's Aromatic Schnapps, Green 25.00
Von Hopf's Curacao, Amber, W-344, R-V27 .... 40.00
W.C., Barrel, Dark Amber 385.00
W.C., Honey Amber 290.00
W.McC & Co., Base Embossed, McCully, Golden Amber, 3/4 Quart 35.00
Wahoo & Calisaya, Square, Golden Amber, W-349, R-W3 .... 170.00
Wait's Kidney & Liver, Square, Amber, 9 In., W-350, R-W .... 30.00 To 38.00
Wakefield's Strengthening, Aqua, 8 In., W-510, R-W7 .... 35.00
Walker's Tonic, Lady's Leg, 11 3/4 In., W-351, R-W13 .... 450.00
Warner's Safe Tonic, Amber, W-512, R-W39 .... 200.00
West India Stomach, Square, Amber, W-359, R-W79 .... 32.00 To 35.00
Whitwell's Temperance, Boston, Pontil, Green, W-364, R-W105 .... 125.00
Whitwell's Temperance, Open Pontil, Aqua, W-364, R-W105 .... 95.00
Wiggs Bros.& Co., Memphis, Tenn., Cabin Shape, Embossed 2500.00
Wild Cherry & Blood Root Jaundice, Round, Aqua, R-W113I 15.00
William Allen's Congress, Aqua, W-4, R-A29 .... 125.00
William Allen's Congress, Yellow Olive, 3/4 Quart, W-4a, R-A29 .... 490.00
Wilson's Herbine, Oval, Aqua, R-W123 .... 15.00
Wishart's Pine Tree Tar Cordial, Patent 1859, Green .... 50.00 To 68.00
Woodcock Pepsin, Rectangular, Amber, W-374, R-W158 .... 40.00 To 55.00
Yerba Buena, S.F., Cal., Amber, 8 1/4 In., W-375, R-Y3 .... 45.00 To 48.00
Yerba Buena, San Francisco, Flask Shape, Amber, W-375, R-Y4 .... 45.00
Yochim Bros.Celebrated Stomach, Square, Amber, W-376, R-Y5 .... 55.00
Zingari, Lady's Leg, Amber, 12 In., W-377, R-Z4 .... 230.00
Zingari, Lady's Leg, Medium Amber, W-377, R-Z4 .... 210.00
Zubrownik Medicinal Wine, Amber 12.00

BLACK GLASS, Ale, English, Dense Red Amber, 19 1/2 In. 140.00
Ale, Shoulder Emblem, J.Evans, Galena, Ill., 3-Mold 145.00
Ale, 3-Mold, Olive Green 8.00
Arden, Embossed On Bottom, Cobalt Blue Stopper 10.00
Dutch Onion, Matte, 6 1/2 In. 70.00
English, C.1750, Cylinder, 7 X 4 In. 135.00
Gin, A.Miller Bros., & Co. 22.50
Gin, African 15.00
Gin, E.Kiderlien 20.00
Gin, Forward 30.00
Gin, J.J.W.Peters, Dog Holding Bird In Mouth 35.00
Gin, V.Haytema & Co. 15.00
Gin, V.Marken & Co. 15.00
Jos.Risdon, 1818, Applied Seal, McK Plate 221, No.11, 10 In. 450.00
Mallet-Shaped Onion, 2 Stars, Green, 6 1/4 In. 95.00
Porter, Small Stars, C.1800, 11 1/2 In. 25.00
Rectangle, Paneled Sides, Dark Olive Green, 7 In. 100.00
Soda, Doneraile House, Star In Seal, C.1850 .... 65.00
Whiskey, Patent On Shoulder, Ricketts, Bristol On Bottom, Quart 7.00
3-Mold, Squat 6.00
    BLACKING, see Shoe Polish

BLOWN, Applied Lip, Olive Amber, 7 3/8 In. 175.00
Chestnut, Aqua, 6 In. 35.00
Chestnut, Bulbous Shape, Olive Amber, 8 1/4 In. 65.00
Chestnut, Kent, 20 Broken Vertical Ribs, Iron Pontil, 7 5/8 In. 35.00
Chestnut, Ludlow, Deep Clear Green, 9 3/4 In. 65.00
Chestnut, Ludlow, Swirls Of Bubbles Encircling, Light Olive Green 89.50
Chestnut, Mantua, 16 Swirled Ribs, Pale Green, 6 1/4 In. 120.00

Medicine, King's Royal Patent, 2½ In.

**Soda, Utopia Grape,
Amber, 8 In.**

**Fruit Jar, Bostwick Perfect Sealer,
Clear, Pint, C-487**

Fruit Jar, Almy, Aqua, 6 In.

Ink, Felt Stationer's Hall,
N.Y., Pottery, 4½ In.

Ink, Davids Black Ink,
Open Pontil, Aqua, 5½ In.

Medicine, Dr. Harter's Dixie Tonic,
Dayton, Brown, 7½ In.

Mineral Water, The Emancipator, Clear, 9 In.

Food, Mustard, Golden Eagle, Battleship, Maine, SCA, 5 In.

Fruit Jar, Leader, Amber, Quart

Figural, Barrel, Brown, 5 In.

Mineral Water, Hiram Ricker, Facsimile, 1st Poland, Amber

Fruit Jar, Mason's Patent Nov. 30th, 1858, Amethyst, ½ Gallon

Figural, Ear of Corn, Carnival
Glass, 5 In.

Cathedral, Aqua, 9½ In.

Pickle, Heinz, Clear, 7½ In.

Fruit Jar, Open Pontil,
Blue, 8 In.

**Target Ball, New
Brunswick Glass
Works, 2½ In.**

**Tobacco Jar,
Globe Tobacco,
Amber, 8 In.**

**Mineral Water, Setters Vichy,
L. Cohen & Son, Pitts., 6½ In.**

**Milk, Sun Valley Dairy, Green,
Yellow Pyro, ½ Gallon**

Ink, Wood Case, Clear Ink, 4½ In.

Ezra Brooks, Clown Bust, No. 4, Keystone Cop, 1980

Bitters, Cobalt Blue,
12 In.

Figural, John Bull, Amber, 12 In.

Figural, Success To
Reform Derby, New
Brown, 8 In.

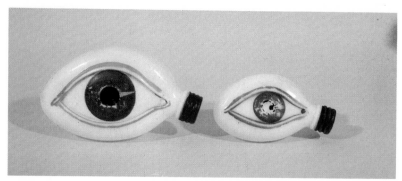

Figural, Eye Opener, Milk Glass, 5 In.

Mineral Water, Blue Lick, Olive, 8 In.

Food, Catsup, Paper Label, Aqua, 9 In.

Chestnut, Midwestern, Aqua, 1/2 Pint 50.00
Chestnut, New England, Olive Amber, 5 3/4 In. 60.00
Chestnut, Pontil, Applied Collared Lip, Amber 6 3/8 In. .... 75.00 To 105.00
Chestnut, Pontil, Applied Collared Lip, Dark Green, 9 3/8 In. 140.00
Chestnut, Pontil, Applied Collared Lip, Green, 5 1/4 In. 95.00
Chestnut, Pontil, Applied Collared Lip, Olive Amber, 4 7/8 In. 95.00
Chestnut, Pontil, Applied Collared Lip, Olive Yellow, 5 1/4 In. 90.00
Chestnut, Zanesville, 24 Vertical Ribs, Aqua, 4 1/2 In. 85.00
Chestnut, 24 Swirled Ribs, Flared Lip, Aqua, 6 1/4 In. 185.00
Chestnut, 30 Vertical Ribs, Terminal Ring, Bluish Tint, 5 3/4 In. 20.00
Club, Aqua, 9 5/8 In. 20.00
Club, Light Green, 8 1/8 In. 50.00
Club, Light Green, 8 3/4 In. 55.00
Club, Pale Aqua, 9 7/8 In. 35.00
Club, Zanesville, 24 Crooked Vertical Ribs, Aqua, 8 1/4 In. 55.00
Covered Mug, Aqua, 9 1/2 In. 55.00
Ludlow, Olive Green, 5 In. 65.00
Olive Amber, 9 In. 45.00
Polychrome Enameled Figures & Flowers, Cobalt Blue, 6 In. 105.00

BRANDY, Homer's California Ginger Brandy, Amber, 1/5 Quart 25.00
      BROOKS, see Ezra Brooks
      C.P.C., CALIFORNIA PERFUME COMPANY, see Avon
      CABIN STILL, see Old Fitzgerald
      CALABASH, see Flask

Candy containers of glass were very popular after World War I. Small glass figural bottles held dime-store candy. Today many of the same shapes hold modern candy in plastic bottles.

CANDY CONTAINER, Airplane, Spirit Of Goodwill 27.00
    Army Hat 6.00
    Automobile Trinket, E & A No.55, Cobalt 20.00
    Battleship .... 12.00 To 15.00
    Bulldog, Screw-On Tin Base 65.00
    Bureau 60.00
    Chamberstick, Clear 9.00
    Chamberstick, Opalescent 12.00
    Charlie Chaplin, Clear, 3 1/2 In. .... *Illus* 70.00
    Charlie Chaplin, L.E.Smith Co. On Base, 1 1/2 Ounce 48.00
    Duck Family, Swimming 60.00
    Electric Car 45.00
    Fedora, Milk Glass 40.00
    Fire Engine, Embossed Fire Dept, In Circle, Filled 15.00

Candy Container, Charlie Chaplin, Clear, 3 1/2 In.

Candy Container, Scotty, Clear, 3 In.

Candy Container, Santa
In Chimney, Clear, 5 In.

Candy Container, Telephone,
Clear, 4 In.

Franklin Auto, E & A No.55, Blue	20.00
Gayhead Lighthouse	30.00
Hen On Nest	16.00
Jeep, Embossed J.H.Millstein Co.	10.00
Limousine	60.00
Locomotive & Lithograph, E & A No.496	60.00
Military Hat, Mirror Lid	18.00
Motorboat	6.00
Mule Pulling Barrel	20.00
Pistol, Original Cap, Clear	12.50
Pump	50.00
Rabbit Eating Carrot	12.00
Rabbit Emerging From Cracked Egg	45.00
Rabbit, Ears Back, Pewter Top, Green	15.00
Rabbit, Left Ear Up, Screw-On Tin Base	65.00
Rabbit, Sitting, Embossed Millstein	10.00
Railroad Lantern, With Lightbulb, Battery Operated	5.00
Revolver, Mercury Flashed	10.00
Revolver, Original Cap, Amber	25.00
Revolver, West Bros.Co., Grapeville, Pa., Metal Cap, 7 In.	30.00
Santa In Chimney, Clear, 5 In. ....*Illus*	65.00
Scotty, Clear, 3 In. ....*Illus*	17.00
Sedan, Candy, Cardboard Closure	12.00
Spark Plug, E & A No.699	25.00
Spirit Of Goodwill Airplane, Paint Complete	65.00
Station Wagon	10.00
Streamlined Auto, Cardboard Closure	10.00
Suitcase, Clear	10.00
Suitcase, Metal Slide Base Closure	25.00
Tank, 2 Large Gun Barrels	18.00
Telephone, Candy, Cardboard Closure, Wooden Receiver	12.00
Telephone, Clear, 4 In. ....*Illus*	8.00
Tot Telephone, 2 1/2 In. ....*Color*	22.50
Train, Candy, Cardboard Closure	15.00
Umbrella	15.00

CANNING JAR, see Fruit Jar

CHEMICAL, Brown Chemical, Top Embossed Kepler	5.00
Chemical Industrial Co., Providence, Embossed, Dark Cobalt Blue	10.00
Dayson & Hewitts Chemical Extracts, London, Dark Green, 7 In.	12.00
Dickeys Pioneer 1850 Chemists, S.F., On Mortar & Pestle, Blue	15.00
Eastman Kodak, Tested Chemicals, Amber, 7 1/2 In.	15.00
Espy's Embalming Fluid, Springfield, Ohio, Ounce Measurements	75.00
Frigid Fluid Co., I.C.Co.Embalming Fluid, Amethyst, 1/2 Gallon	10.00
Rumford Chemical Works, Label, Teal Green	13.00

CLEVENGER, Apollo 9 .... 14.00
  Bismark, North Dakota 6.00
  Bunker Hill 7.00
  C & O Canal 9.00
  Capt.Cook, Hawaii 11.00
  Charles Gardner 9.00
  Corvette, 25th Anniversary 10.00
  Cowpens 7.00
  Delaware 10.00
  East Clay Grange 9.00
  Freedom Train 28.00
  Hubert Humphrey, Light Blue 14.00
  Hubert Humphrey, Light Green 90.00
  Independence Hall 10.00
  Israel, 25th Anniversary 10.00
  Jersey Devil 9.00
  John F. Kennedy, 10 Yr. Memorial, Light Blue .... 25.00 To 27.00
  King Mountain 7.00
  Lexington 7.00
  New Castle Ferry 8.00
  New Jersey 11.00
  Pennsylvania 11.00
  Robert F.Kennedy 10.00
  SS Charles S.Price 10.00
  SS Columbus 10.00
  SS Eastland 10.00
  SS Stewart Cort 10.00
  Walt Whitman 8.00
  Washington City 9.00
  Watergate, Amethyst 550.00
  Watergate, Topaz 10.00
  Western Maryland Railroad 9.00
  Wright Brothers 12.00

*Coca-Cola was first made in 1886. Since that time the drink has been
sold in all parts of the world in a variety of bottles. The "waisted"
bottle was first used in 1916.*

COCA-COLA, AAR Convention, Red & White 40.00
  Albuquerque, 75th 7.00
  Amelia Earhart 15.00
  Baltimore, Md., Slug Plate, Amber 25.00
  Bicentennial 5.00
  Biedenharn, Hutchinson 90.00
  Biedenharn, Registered, Coca-Cola In Script 50.00
  Biedenharn, Straight-Sided 30.00
  Blue Grass, 75th 7.00
  Bottling Works, Roth Bros., Glens Falls, Sky Blue 5.00
  Brunswick, Ga., Hutchinson 400.00
  Canton, Ohio, Amber 40.00
  Christmas, Aqua, 20 In. 100.00
  Christmas, Dayton, Tenn. 8.00
  Christmas, Embossed, Dec.25, 1923 .... Illus 5.00
  Christmas, Las Vegas 10.00
  Christmas, McMinnville, Tenn. 6.00
  Christmas, Waynesboro, Ga., Clear 10.00
  Cincinnati, Ohio, Amber 27.00
  Cincinnati, Ohio, Aqua 6.00
  Cleveland, Ohio, Amber .... 20.00 To 25.00
  Cleveland, Ohio, With Arrows, Amber 35.00
  Cleveland, Tn., Black 4.00
  Cleveland, Tn., Red 7.00
  Coca-Cola Bottling Co., Birmingham, Hutchinson .... Illus 140.00

(See Page 43)

Coca-Cola, Christmas, Embossed,
Dec.25, 1923

Coca-Cola, Coca-Cola Bottling Co.,
Birmingham, Hutchinson

Cola Clan, 1976	8.00
Cola Clan, 1978	6.00
Cola Clan, 1979, Houston	6.00
Columbus, Ohio, Amber	20.00 To 25.00
Columbus, Ohio, BIMAL, Amber	9.50
Danville, Va., Straight-Sided	10.00
Elizabethtown Convention	8.00
Farmville, Va., 1915, Green	10.00
Florida, 1975, ACL	13.00
Georgia Bulldogs	9.00
Gold, Reading, Pa., 6 Fluid Ounce	30.00
Harry A.Tully	6.00
Hartford, Conn., Sky Blue, 7 Fluid Ounces	5.00
Hobble Skirt, Chinese Letters, 6 1/2 Ounce, Green	4.50
Houston, 75th	7.00
Huntsville, Alabama, 75th	8.00
Hutchinson, Script	450.00
Israel Expo, 1975	4.00
Jackson, Tn., 75th	8.00
Johnstown, Pa., 1915	4.00
Knoxville, Arrow, Amber	16.00
Las Vegas, Nev.	75.00
Lexington, Kentucky, Amber	8.00
Lexington, Ky., Amber	20.00
Louisville, Ky., Amber	15.00 To 25.00
Louisville, Ky., Circle Arrow Around Coca-Cola, Amber	35.00
Lynchburg, Va., Straight-Sided, Blue	7.50
Memphis, Tenn., Amber	20.00
Monroe, La.	25.00
Morgantown	3.00
Nashville, Tenn., Amber	15.00
Painesville Mineral Springs, Painesville, Ohio, Amber	35.00
Pittsburgh, Pa., Amber	16.00 To 35.00
Savannah, Ga., Crown Top, BIM, Aqua	7.50
Toledo, Lima Scott On Base, Amber	25.00
Toledo, Ohio, In Diamond	25.00
Turkey Trot	6.00
Vandalia, Illinois, Clear	10.00
Vernon Springs	25.00
Washington, C.H., Ohio, Aqua	6.00
Winter Olympics	6.00

1923, Aqua, 7 1/2 In. .... *Illus*   3.50
50th Anniversary, Western 50.00
75th Anniversary 3.00
75th Anniversary, 1975, Atlanta, Ga., Contents 12.00

CODD, Embossed Cow 7.00
   Leigh Co.Salford, Embossed Globe, Yellow 65.00

COLLECTORS ART, Brahma Bull 39.00
   Charolais Bull 36.00
   Corvette Stingray 24.00
   Flower Child 4.00
   Hereford 42.00
   Mexican Fighting Bull 37.00
      COLLECTORS ART, MINIATURE, see Miniature, Collectors Art
   Texas Longhorn 40.00

     COLOGNE, see also Perfume; Scent
COLOGNE, Ball Stopper, Worn Gilding, Opaque Blue, 5 1/4 In. 60.00
   Basket Weave, Open Pontil 20.00
   Bass Fiddle, Pontil, Clear .... 48.00 To 55.00
   Beaded Rib, Milk Glass, 9 1/2 In. 90.00
   Blown, 16 Vertical Ribs, Iron Pontil, Amethystine Tint, 6 In. 17.50
   Blown, 3 Mold, Blown Stopper, 5 7/8 In. 22.50
   Bunker Hill, Clear 30.00
   Cathedral, Embossed Knight 30.00
   Cathedral, McK Plate 109, No.10 .... 45.00
   Cathedral, McK Plate 109, No.9 .... 30.00
   Cut Stopper, Traces Of Gilding, Purple, 5 3/4 In. 55.00
   Dancing Indian, McK Plate 244, No.5, Aqua, 4 3/4 In. 78.00
   Eddy Jamaica Ginger, Brattleboro, Vt., Clear, Pumpkinseed, 4 In. 15.00
   Fancy, Bellows Shape, McK Plate 108, No.7, Aqua, 6 In. 45.00
   French Blown, 4 Mold, Deep Amethyst, 5 In. 80.00
   Indian On Side Panel, Aqua, 4 In. 3.00
   J.M.Farina, Emerald Green, BIMAL 8.50
   J.M.Farina, Open Pontil, Clear, 5 In. 18.00
   J.M.Farina, 6-Sided, Open Pontil 12.00
   L.M., Barrel, 4 Rings Top & Bottom, Floral Embossing, 3 3/4 In. 42.00
   Larsen, Diamond Pattern, Amethyst, 5 1/4 In. 90.00
   Larsen, Diamond Pattern, Red, 1/2 Pint 310.00
   Larsen, Hexagonal & Dot Design, Amethyst, 1/2 Pint 90.00
   Larsen, Swirled To Right, Electric Blue, 5 In. 140.00
   Larsen, Swirled To Right, Orange Amber, 5 3/4 In. 290.00
   Larsen, Vertically Ribbed, Deep Amethyst, 5 In. 160.00

Coca-Cola, 1923, Aqua, 7 1/2 In.

McK Plate 111, No.3, Sapphire Blue, 5 1/2 In. 250.00
Monument, Sandwich, Clear Brickwork, Hexagonal, Cobalt Blue 27.50
Monument, Sandwich, Milk Glass 59.00
Octagon, Amethyst, 5 7/8 In. 20.00
Paneled Sandwich, Cobalt Blue, 3 In. 75.00
Pocahontas, BIM, C.1830, 2 1/4 In. .... *Illus* 500.00
Ribbed, Amethyst, 4 In. 90.00
Round, Cobalt Blue, 10 1/2 In. 80.00
Shedd's German, 25 Size, Clear 10.00
Square, 4 Stars On 3 Sides, Roped Corners, Milk Glass, 7 1/2 In. 80.00
Stiegel Type, Amber, Blue & White Painted Floral, 6 1/2 In. 210.00
Two Dancing Indians, Triangle, Open Pontil, Aqua 128.00
Two Indians In Panels, Pontiled, Aqua, 4 7/8 In. 50.00
Vantine Lotus Flower, Original Wicker, Tax Stamp 18.00
W.T.Co., Rectangle, Figural Acorn Stopper, Milk Glass, 6 In. 10.00

CORDIAL, B.Toscotts, Anodyne, Embossed, OP, Aqua, 4 3/4 In. 35.00
Charles, London, Emerald Green, Pint 44.00
Clark's California Cherry Cordial, Amber 28.00
Dr.Eaton's Infantile, Church & Dupont, Clear, Set 325.00
Dr.Ford's Tonic, Cazenovia, N.Y., Rectangular, 5 In. 87.00
Dr.Green's Anodyne, Aqua, Oval, 4 1/2 In. 165.00
Dr.Morse's Invigorating, C.H.Ring Proprietor, Oval, Aqua, 7 3/4 In. 150.00
Dunbar & Co., Wormwood, Boston, Olive Amber, 9 1/2 In. 85.00
Fosgate's Anodyne, Aqua .... 20.00 To 25.00
Jacob's Cholera & Dysentery, Box & Ad 50.00
Mrs.Kidder's Dysentery, Boston, Aqua, 8 In. 90.00
Mrs.Kidder's Dysentery, Open Pontil 55.00
Smith's Worm 3.00
Wisharts, Pine Tree Tar, Amber, Fifth 35.00

COSMETIC, A.H.Brown, Hair Specialist, Cobalt Blue 45.00
Ayer's Hair Vigor, Original Contents, Paper Label, Aqua, 7 3/8 In. 22.50
Ayer's Hair Vigor, Peacock Blue .... 22.50 To 30.00
Ayer's Hair Vigor, Stopper, Rectangular, Cobalt, 6 1/2 In. 15.00
Bachelors Liquid Hair Dye No.2, Embossed, 4 Panels, OP, Aqua 12.00
Ballard's Hair Dye, Open Pontil, Aqua, 3 5/8 In. 30.00
Barry's Tricopherous For Skin & Hair, Open Pontil, 5 In. 12.00
Barry's Tricopherous For Skin & Hair, 6 In. 19.00
Bartine's Lotion, Open Pontil, Aqua 95.00
Batchelor's Hair Dye, Open Pontil 6.00
Batchelor's Liquid Hair Dye No.1 & No.2, Small, Set 39.00
Batchelor's Liquid Hair Dye No.2, Small 10.00
Bogle's Electric Hair Dye, Boston, No.2, Open Pontil, Aqua 35.00
Bogle's Hyperion Fluid For The Hair, Aqua, 7 In. 110.00
Bruceline Hair Restorer, Amber 22.00
Buchan Hungarian Balsam, Open Pontil, Sheared Lip 20.00
Bush's Argentine Hair Dye, Lowell, Mass., Pontil, 5 In. 200.00
C.S.Emerson's American Hair Restorative, Cleveland, Ohio 135.00
Canitian For The Hair, Swan & Co., Fall River, Mass., Embossed, Aqua 75.00
Chadwick's Hair Renewer, Aqua, Snap Case 24.00
Coke Dandruff Cure, Rectangular, Amethyst, 6 3/8 In. 4.50
Crimpline Hair Curling Fluid, Cornflower Blue 12.00
Cristadoro No.1 Hair Dye, Open Pontil, Aqua, 3 1/4 In. 15.00
Crock-Crem, Day Cream For Skin, Richard Hudnut, Blue, 2 3/4 In. 25.00
Dr.Campbell's Hair Invigorator, Aurora, N.Y., Pontil, 6 1/2 In. 22.00
Dr.Tebbett's Hair Regenerator, Medium To Dark Amethyst 100.00
Dr.Tebbett's Physiological Hair Regenerator, Puce, 6 1/2 In. 100.00
Ely's Cream Balm, Amber 2.00
Emerson's American Hair Restorative, Cleveland, Ohio, Deep Aqua 150.00
Famo Retards Grayness, Label, Clear 5.00
Fitch's Ideal Dandruff Cure 6.00

Cologne, Pocahontas, BIM, C.1830, 2 1/4 In.   Cosmetic, Hair Tonic, Paper Label, Clear, 6 3/4 In.

G.E.Haye's Hair Dye, Aqua, 4 1/2 In.Square	30.00
G.W.Laird, Perfumer, Broadway, N.Y., Milk Glass	15.00
George's Hair Dye	35.00
Hagan's Magnolia Balm, Milk Glass	12.00
Hair Restorer, Cobalt Blue	24.00
Hair Tonic, Paper Label, Clear, 6 3/4 In. ....*Illus*	4.00
Hay's Hair Health, Rectangular, Amber, 7 1/4 In.	4.00
Hill's Hair Dye No.1, Open Pontil	10.00
Hill's Hair Dye No.2	10.00
Hover's Hair Dye, 6-Sided	45.00
Hover's Hair Dye, 8-Sided, Aqua	25.00
Jenny Lind Hair Glass	32.00
Kelly's Petroline Hair Cream, Cobalt Blue	26.50 To 35.00
Kromer's Hair Dye No.1	6.00
L.Miller's Hair Invigorator, N.Y., Pontil, Oval, 5 1/2 In.	125.00
Lyon's Kathairon For The Hair, New York, Aqua	12.00 To 15.00
Lyon's Kathairon For The Hair, Open Pontil, Aqua	10.00 To 25.00
Lyon's Powder, B.P., New York, Open Pontil, Puce	50.00 To 85.00
McCombie's Compound Restorative	20.00
Mexican Hair Renewer, Cobalt Blue	34.50
Mme.Campbell's Tooth Powder	6.00
Mrs.Allen's World Hair Restorer, Amber	4.00 To 7.00
Mrs.S.A.Allen's World Hair Balsam, Broome Street, New York, Aqua	35.00
Mrs.S.A.Allen's World Hair Restorer, Honey Amber	12.00
Murgittroyd's Cuticine, Spokane, Wash., 6 In.	4.00
Owl Theatrical Cold Cream	20.00
Parisian Sage Hair Tonic, SCA	3.00
Parker's Hair Balsam, Amber, Large	3.00
Parker's Hair Balsam, Amber, Small	3.00
Phalon's Chemical Hair Invigorator	28.00
Phalon's Chemical Hair Restorer Invigorator, Open Pontil	15.00
Phalon's Magic Hair Dye	10.00
Professor Wood's Hair Restorative, St.Louis & N.Y.	25.00 To 110.00
Rhode's Hair Rejuvenator, Amber, 6 In.	15.00
Ridgway's Acme Liniment, Pleasantville, Pa.	17.00
Rowland's Macassar Oil For Hair, Open Pontil, Flared Lip, Clear	22.00
Rowland's Macassar Oil For The Hair, Open Pontil, 3 1/2 In.	25.00
Sanitol For The Teeth, Stopper, Milk Glass	18.00
Seven Sutherland Sisters' Hair Grower, Lockport, N.Y.	5.00
Shaker Hair Restorer, Embossed, Light Golden Amber, 7 1/2 In.	110.00
Silkodono For The Hair & Scalp, Milk Glass	19.00 To 42.50
Storr's Hair Invigorator, Philada., Open Pontil, Aqua	50.00
Swayne's London Hair Color Restorer, Philada.	50.00
T.Jones Coral Hair Restorative, Pontil	85.00
Terriff's Medicated Hair Tonic, Portland, Metal Crown Stopper	12.00
W.C.Montgomery's Hair Restorer, Amber	10.00

W.C.Montgomery's Hair Restorer, Philada., Chocolate 25.00

CURE, see also Medicine
CURE, Calcura Solvent, Amber, 4 Peaked Panels 65.00
Dr.Kilmer's Indian Cough Cure, Consumption Oil, 5 3/4 In. 12.00
Elipizone Certain Cure For Fits & Epilepsy, Dr.H.G.Root, N.Y. 40.00
Frog Pond Chill & Fever Cure, Amber 75.00
Graham's Dyspepsia Cure 4.00
Magic Cure Liniment, Aqua, Partial Label 18.00
Microbe Killer Cures All Diseases, Amber 60.00
Spohn's Distemper Cure 5.00
Stewart D.Howes Arabian Milk Cure, N.Y., Aqua 15.00
Tussand Cures Coughs & Colds 30.00
Warner's Safe Cure, Concentrated, Amber 33.00
Warner's Safe Cure, 3 Cities, Pint 40.00
Warner's Safe Cure, 4 Cities, Double Collar, Pint 75.00
Warner's Safe Diabetes Cure 45.00
Warner's Safe Rheumatic Cure, Amber 50.00

CYRUS NOBLE, Animals, Set Of 6 .... 280.00
Assayer, 1972 .... 135.00 To 185.00
Bartender, 1971 .... 120.00 To 175.00
Bear & Cubs, 1978, 1st Edition .... 132.00 To 137.00
Bear & Cubs, 1978, 2nd Edition .... 60.00 To 75.00
Beaver & Kit, 1978, 1st Edition 113.00
Beaver & Kit, 1978, 2nd Edition .... 54.00 To 65.00
Big Horn Sheep, 1978, 1st Edition .... 100.00 To 136.00
Big Horn, 1978, 2nd Edition 64.00
Blacksmith, 1974 .... 10.00 To 59.99
Buffalo Cow And Calf, 1977 ....*Illus* 130.00
Buffalo Cow And Calf, 1977, 2nd Edition 94.00
Burro, 1973 .... 60.00 To 85.00
Carousel Pipe Organ, 1980 .... 53.00
Carousel, Set Of 4 .... 150.00
Carousel, Tiger .... 31.00 To 33.00
Deer, White Tail Buck, 1979 .... 53.00 To 57.00
Dolphin, 1979 .... 49.00
Elk, Bull, 1980 .... 59.00
Gambler, 1974 .... 10.00 To 60.00
Gambler's Lady, 1976 .... 30.00 To 50.00
Gold Miner, 1970 .... 550.00 To 643.00
Harp Seal, 1979 .... 50.00
Horse, Black Flyer, 1979 .... 39.00 To 42.00
Horse, White Charger, 1979 .... 22.00 To 39.00
Landlady, 1977 .... 22.00 To 34.00
Lion, 1979 .... 22.00 To 39.00

Cyrus Noble, Buffalo Cow And Calf, 1977

Middle Of Piano, Trumpeter, 1978 .... 51.00
Mine, 1978 .... 48.00
Miner, 1970 .... 400.00 To 600.00
Miner's Daughter, 1975 .... 56.00
       CYRUS NOBLE, MINIATURE, see Miniature, Cyrus Noble
Moose & Calf, 1977, 2nd Edition .... 75.00 To 91.00
Moose, 1977, 1st Edition 113.00
Mountain Lion, 1977, 1st Edition 122.00
Mountain Lion, 1977, 2nd Edition 112.00
Music Man, 1977 .... 14.00 To 39.00
Oklahoma Dancers, 1978 .... 33.00 To 45.00
Olympic Skater, 1980 .... 46.00
Owl, 1980 .... 35.00 To 42.00
Penguins, 1978 .... 47.00
Sea Turtle, 1979 .... 50.00
Seal Family, 1978 .... 37.00
Snowshow Thomson, 1972 .... 180.00 To 350.00
South Of The Border, 1978 .... *Illus* 50.00
Tonopah, Milk Glass, Octagonal, 1972 .... *Illus* 300.00
U.S.C.Trojan, 1980 .... 58.00
Violinist, 1976 .... 35.00 To 40.00
Walrus Family, 1978 .... 30.00 To 52.00
Whiskey Drummer, 1975 .... 50.00

Dant figural bottles were first released in 1968 to hold J. W. Dant alcoholic products. The company has made the Americana series, field birds, special bottlings, and ceramic bottles.

DANT, Alamo, 1969 .... 5.00
    American Legion, 1969 .... *Illus* 6.00
    Atlantic City, 1969 .... 5.00
    Boeing 747 .... 10.00
    Boston Tea Party, Eagle Left, 1968 .... 4.00
    Boston Tea Party, Eagle Right, 1968 .... 5.00
    Burr-Hamilton Duel 8.00
    Clear Tip Pinch, 1953 .... 8.00
    Constitution & Guerriere, 1969 .... 6.00
    Field Bird, Pheasant, 1969 .... 7.00
    Field Bird, Prairie Chicken, 1969 .... 7.00

Cyrus Noble, South Of The Border, 1978

Cyrus Noble, Tonopah, Milk
Glass, Octagonal, 1972

Dant, American Legion, 1969

Dant, Fort Sill, Oklahoma, 1969

Dant, Indy 500, 1969

Field Bird, Ruffed Grouse, 1969	7.00
Field Bird, Woodcock, 1969	7.00
Fort Sill, Oklahoma, 1969 *Illus*	12.00
Indy 500, 1969 *Illus*	6.00
Mountain Quail, 1969	7.00
Mt.Rushmore, 1969 4.00 To	6.00
Patrick Henry, 1969	6.00
Paul Bunyan	5.00
Potbelly Stove, 1966	8.00
San Diego Harbor, 1969	5.00
Washington At Delaware	6.00

Decanters were first used to hold the alcoholic beverages that had been stored in kegs. At first a necessity, the decanter later was merely an attractive serving vessel.

DECANTER, see also Beam; Bischoff; Kord; etc.

DECANTER, Blown & Cut, 3 Rings, Star Base, Stopper, 8 1/8 In.	115.00
Blown & Ribbed, Copper Wheel Engraved Vintage, 8 1/2 In.	32.50
Blown, Applied Lip, Polished Pontil, 8 1/4 In.	5.00
Blown, 2 Rings, Cut Design, With Whiskey, Faceted Stopper	40.00
Blown, 3 Applied Rings, Faceted Stopper, 7 1/2 In.	10.00
Blown, 3 Mold, Replaced Wheel Stopper, 6 3/4 In. 50.00 To	55.00
Blown, 3 Mold, Shoulder Embossed Gin Stopper, 8 1/2 In.	165.00
Blown, 3 Rings, Copper Wheel Cut Floral Band, 8 3/4 In.	10.00
Figural, Madonna, Applied Handle, Cobalt Blue, 9 1/2 In.	2.00
Flint, Flat Diamond & Panel, Original Stopper, 10 1/2 In.	65.00
Geometric, Round, Open Pontil, Olive Green, 3 X 7 In.	375.00
McK G II-006, Blown, 3 Mold, Bulbous, Aqua, Quart	750.00
McK G II-018, Blown, 3 Mold, 3 Applied Rings, Pint	95.00
McK G II-018, Blown, 3 Mold, 3 Rings, Stopper, Quart	125.00
McK G III-006, Blown, 3 Mold, Clear, 1/2 Pint	310.00
McK G III-012, Blown, 3 Mold, Stopper, Clear, 3 In.	525.00
McK G III-016, Keene, Blown, 3 Mold, Olive Amber, Pint	250.00
Pillar Mold, Pewter Insert, Green Marble Stopper, 12 1/2 In.	40.00
Pineapple & Sawtooth, Flint, Applied Lip, 11 In.	50.00
Pittsburgh, Flint Pillar Mold, Applied Lip & Collar, 11 In.	20.00
Pittsburgh, Flint Pillar Mold, Hollow Ear Handle, 9 1/2 In.	25.00
Pittsburgh, Pillar Mold, Amethystine Tint, 11 3/8 In.	30.00
Pittsburgh, Pillar Mold, Applied Handle, 9 In.	22.50
Pittsburgh, Pillar Mold, Applied Lip & Ring, 10 1/4 In.	40.00
Silver Script Rye, Shield, 3 Engraved Initials, Red Amber	170.00
Wheel Cut, Stopper, Flamingos, Palm Trees, Lead Glass, Pint	35.00

DEMIJOHN, Amber, Gallon	10.00
Boley Mfg.Co., Bottles & Demijohns, Aqua	13.00
Deep Red Amber, 1/2 Gallon	14.00
Embalming Fluid, Wraparound Band On Neck, Olive Green, 26 In.	275.00
Emerald Green, Open Pontil, 15 1/4 In.	45.00
Kidney Shape, Black, 16 1/4 X 18 In.	179.50
Kidney, 3-Piece Mold, Spanish, EBRA De La Llave, Emerald Green	150.00
Light Olive Green, 3-Part Mold, Open Pontil, 18 1/2 X 10 1/2 In.	79.50
Olive To Emerald, Pumpkin Shape, Swirls, 16 X 14 In.	99.50
Stoddard Type, Light Green, 1 1/2 Gallon	24.50
Stoddard, Iron Pontil, Red Amber, 1/2 Gallon	29.50
Stoddard, Open Pontil, Amber, 12 In.	45.00
DICKEL, Gold Club, 1/5 Quart	5.00
Powder Horn	5.00
DOUBLE SPRINGS, Bentley, 1972	34.00
Buick, 1972	69.00
Bull, Red, 1969	18.00
Cadillac, 1971	30.00 To 52.00
Cale Yarborough, 1974	12.00 To 21.00
Cord, 1978	26.00
Coyote, Gold, 1971	12.00
Duesenburg SJ, 1931	17.00 To 22.00
Excaliber Phaeton, 1975	19.00 To 22.00
Georgia Bulldog, 1971	6.00 To 10.00
Kentucky Derby, With Glass, 1964	10.00
Matador, 1969	13.00
Mercedes Benz, 1975	26.00
Mercer, 1972	29.00
Milwaukee Buck, 1971	11.00
Model T Ford, 1970	37.00
Owl, Brown, 1968	20.00
Peasant Boy, 1968	7.00
Peasant Girl, 1968	7.00
Pierce Arrow, 1970	32.50 To 33.00
Rolls-Royce, 1971	32.00
Stanley Steamer, 1971	38.00
Stutz Bearcat, 1970	37.00
Tiger On Football	12.00
Watertower	14.00
DRIOLI, African	26.00
Cat, Teardrops Cherry Wine, Italy, 1969, Green, 5 1/2 In.	12.50
Cherry Log	8.00
Coffeepot	10.00
Duck, Teardrops Cherry Wine, Italy, 1969, Green, 6 In.	12.50
Egyptian Vase, Black	12.00
Egyptian Vase, Yellow	12.00
DRIOLI, MINIATURE, see Miniature, Drioli	
DRUG, Anaconda, North Dakota	5.00
Apothecary, Cylinder Label & Stopper, 1/2 Gallon	34.50
B.P.Lyon's Powders, Puce	70.00
B.Ward Druggist, Mobile, Ala., Fancy Monogram, Amber	12.00
Bear's Oil, Horizontal Embossing, OP	35.00
Bear's Oil, Recessed Panels, OP	40.00
BO & GC Wilson, Botanic Druggist, Boston, Open Pontil, Aqua	80.00
Burnett Cocaine, Boston, Aqua	10.00
Caswell Hazard Co., Chemists, New York, Cobalt Blue	35.00
Central Drug Co., Flared Lip, Cobalt Blue, 6 In.	5.00
Christie's Magnetic Fluid, Label, Aqua	48.00

Clear Extract, 7 In. 5.00
Cook, Everett, & Pennell, Druggists, Portland, Maine, Strap-Sided, Amber 15.00
Corner Drug Store, Bellows Falls, Vt., Amber, 5 In. 20.00
Dickey Pioneer Chemist, 1850, San Francisco, 5 1/2 In. .... 6.00 To 9.00
Dolley Madison, Addison, Wisconsin, War Slogan 2.00
Dover Drug, Dover, N.H., Amber, 4 1/2 In. .... 11.00 To 12.00
Dyottville Glass Works, Philadelphia, Cylinder, Olive Yellow 18.00
F.Frown, Philadelphia, Open Pontil, Aqua 18.00
F.McKinney, Philadelphia, Pa., Aqua 3.00
Fairbanks, Alaska, Pair 90.00
G.W.Merchant Chemist, Round Iron Pontil, Green 85.00
Geo.E.Fairbanks Druggist, Worcester, Amber, 1/5 Quart 40.00
H.J.O'Connor, Corner Drug Store, Whitewater, Wisc., Amber, 4 In. 35.00
H.L. & J.W.Brown, Hartford, Connecticut, Squat, Olive Green 100.00
Harry Elwood Prescription Druggist, Ellensburg, Wash., Quart 8.00
Holderness Leading Druggist, Fordyce, Ark. 4.00
J.B.Marchisi, M.D., Utica, N.Y., Embossed, Oval, Aqua 5.00
Kanawha, Jug, Gallon 25.00
Kneeland, Homeopathic Pharmacy, Topeka, Kansas, Amber, 2 3/4 In. 20.00
Laughlins & Bushfield Druggists, Wheeling, Va., OP, Deep Aqua 125.00
Maebbe The Druggist, Baker, Ore., Emerald Green, 8 In. 25.00
Maxham Pharmacy, Johnstown, Pa., Amber, 4 1/4 In. .... 13.00 To 16.00
McMunn's Elixir Of Opium 10.00
Morse's Celebrated Syrup, Providence, R.I., Green, 9 1/2 In. 40.00
New York Pharmacal Assoc., Cobalt Blue, 8 In. 18.00
New York Pharmacal Association, Pharmacy Bottle, 12 In., Blue, Gallon 30.00
North Dakota 5.00
Osgood's Tooth Powder 8.00
Owl Drug Co., Amber, 4 3/8 In. 30.00
Owl Drug Co., Amber, 8 In. 125.00
Owl Drug Co., Clear, 4 In. 5.00
Owl Drug Co., Crown Top, Green 10.00
Owl Drug Co., Ear, Ulcer Syringe In Box 8.00
Owl Drug Co., Embossed, Mortar & Pestle, Milk Glass Pot Lid 25.00
Owl Drug Co., Epsom Salt Container, Owl Embossed On Lid 8.00
Owl Drug Co., Horseshoe 100.00
Owl Drug Co., One Wing, Blob Top, Teal 35.00
Owl Drug Co., Palmer, Soda, Green 40.00
Owl Drug Co., Peroxide, Amber, 8 In. 30.00
Owl Drug Co., Solution Citrate Magnesia, Embossed 12.00
Owl Drug Co., Square, Embossed, Cobalt Blue, Quart 100.00
Owl Drug Co., Square, Two Wing, Clear, 8 1/8 In. 15.00
Owl Drug Co., Sunken Oval Panel, Smoky Aqua, 10 In. 75.00
Owl Drug Co., Two Wing, Teal 50.00
Paine Druggist & Apothecary, Windsor, Vt., Milk Glass 80.00
Porter's Cure Of Pain, Bundysburg, Ohio, Iron Pontil, Aqua, 7 In. 200.00
Price & Son, London, Light Green, 8 In. 245.00
R.W.Davis Drug Co., Chicago, Milk Glass 100.00
Reserrer's, Druggist, Pittsburgh, Aqua 20.00
Rexall Store, Leadville, Colo., Amber, 3 In. 15.00
Russian Bear's Grease, Scented As Improved, Large Bear, Black & White 225.00
Samuel Simes, Phila., Open Pontil, Aqua, 9 In. 115.00
Shaker Syrup No.I, Canterbury, N.H., Partial Label, Aqua 100.00
Sutcliffe McAllister & Co., Louisville, Light Green 320.00
Tarrant Druggist, N.Y., Open Pontil, Clear 18.00
Taylor & Myers, Druggist, St.Paul, Minn., Glass Stopper, Square 7.50
Trade Mark, Embossed, Owl On Mortar & Pestle, Cobalt Blue, 6 In. 20.00
Will H.Murgittroyd, Marysville, Mont., Clear, 7 In. 15.00
Wilson Botanic Druggists 20.00
Wolff Wilson Drug Co., St.Louis, Mo., Cobalt Blue, 2 1/4 In. 15.00
Wyeth, Dose, Cap, Cobalt Blue 5.00

DUG'S NEVADA BROTHELS, Barbara's My Place 20.00

Billie's Day N Nite .... 25.00 To 35.00
Carol's Stardust 20.00
Chicken Ranch .... 25.00 To 35.00
Club Mona Lisa 20.00
Fran's Ranch .... 21.00 To 25.00
LaBelle's Ranch .... 21.00 To 25.00
Lucky Strike .... 20.00 To 25.00
Moonlight Ranch 125.00
Mustang Bridge Ranch .... 30.00 To 38.00
Patricia's Hacienda .... 20.00 To 25.00
Shamrock Ranch 38.00

DUTCH PORTERS, Long Neck 49.50
    EMBALMING FLUID, see Chemical

ERROR, Bitter, Tippecanoe, Rochester 65.00
    Flask, Backward S, Clear, 8 In. .... *Illus* 8.00

EVAN WILLIAMS, Kentucky's 1st Distillery .... *Illus* 30.00

Ezra Brooks fancy bottles were first made in 1964. The Ezra Brooks
Distilling Company is in Frankfort, Kentucky.

EZRA BROOKS, African Lion, 1980 .... 46.00 To 50.00
    Alabama Bicentennial, 1976 .... 30.00
    American Legion, Chicago, No.2, 1972 .... 78.00
    American Legion, Denver, 1977 .... 18.00 To 20.00
    American Legion, Hawaii, No.3, 1973 .... 9.00 To 15.00
    American Legion, Houston, No.1, 1971 .... 22.00 To 54.00
    American Legion, Miami Beach, No.4, 1974 .... 5.00 To 15.00
    Amvets, 1973 .... 9.00
    Amvets, 1974 .... 18.00
    Antique Cannon, 1969 .... 5.00 To 16.00
    Antique Phonograph, 1970 .... 15.00 To 30.00
    Arizona Desert Scene, 1969 .... 7.00 To 13.00
    Auburn Boat Tail 1932, 1978 .... 25.00 To 32.00
    Baltimore Oriole, 1979 .... 25.00 To 36.00
    Bareknuckle Fighter, 1972 .... 8.00 To 12.00
    Basketball Players, 1974 .... *Illus* 12.00
    Beaver, 1973 .... 6.00 To 15.00

Error, Flask, Backward
S, Clear, 8 In.

Evan Williams, Kentucky's 1st Distillery

Ezra Brooks, Basketball Players, 1974

Ezra Brooks, Bengal Tiger, Wildlife, 1979

Ezra Brooks, Bowler, 1973

Bengal Tiger, Wildlife, 1979	*Illus*	46.00
Bentley		40.00
Betsy Ross, 1975		9.00 To 15.00
Big Bertha Elephant, 1970		12.00 To 22.00
Big Daddy Lounges, Florida, 1969		6.00 To 18.00
Bird Dog, 1971		9.00 To 20.00
Birthday Cake Club No.2, 1972		20.00
Bordertown, Nevada, 1970		6.00 To 20.00
Bowler, 1973	*Illus*	6.00
Brahma Bull, 1971	*Illus*	18.00
Bucket Of Blood, 1970		7.00 To 15.00
Bucking Bronco, 1974		12.00 To 20.00
Bucky Badger, No.1, Boxer, 1974		10.00 To 25.00
Bucky Badger, No.2, Football, 1975		16.00 To 25.00
Bucky Badger, No.3, Hockey, 1975		15.00 To 22.00
Buffalo Hunt, 1971	*Illus*	9.00
Bull Dog, Georgia, 1972		18.00 To 24.00
C.B.Convoy Radio, 1976		9.00 To 20.00
California Quail, 1970		9.00 To 12.00
Canadian Honker, 1975		18.00 To 25.00
Canadian Loon		25.00 To 40.00
Casey At Bat, 1973		12.00

Ezra Brooks, Brahma Bull, 1971

Ezra Brooks, Buffalo Hunt, 1971

Ceremonial Indian, 1970	18.00 To 35.00
Charolais, 1973	9.00 To 18.00
Cheyenne Shootout, 1970	8.00 To 20.00
Chicago Fire, 1975	20.00 To 25.00
Chicago Water Tower, 1969	9.00 To 22.00
Christmas Tree, 1979	25.00 To 45.00
Cigar Store Indian, 1968	5.00 To 12.00
Clown Bust, No.1, Smiley, 1979	30.00 To 40.00
Clown Bust, No.2, Cowboy, 1979	31.00 To 40.00
Clown Bust, No.3, Pagliacci, 1979	35.00 To 40.00
Clown Bust, No.4, Keystone Cop, 1980	*Color* 35.00
Clown With Accordion, 1972	14.00 To 18.00
Clown With Balloons, 1974	21.00
Clown, Imperial Shrine, 1978	22.00 To 25.00
Clown, No.5, Cuddles, 1980	36.00
Clown, No.6, Tramp, 1980	36.00
Clydesdale, 1974	12.00 To 15.00
Conquistadors Drum & Bugle, 1972	6.00 To 18.00
Corvette Mako Shark I, 1979	25.00 To 45.00
Corvette Pace Car 1978, 1978	40.00
Corvette 1957, 1977	25.00 To 47.00
Court Jester, 1972	9.00 To 28.00
Creensboro Open No.2, 1973	75.00
Creighton Blue Jay, 1976	18.00 To 25.00
Dakota Cowboy, 1975	45.00 To 50.00
Dakota Cowgirl, 1976	20.00 To 45.00
Dakota Grain Elevator, 1978	25.00 To 75.00
Dakota Shotgun Express, 1977	100.00
Deadwagon, Nevada, 1970	8.00 To 20.00
Delta Belle, 1969	9.00 To 20.00
Democratic Convention '76, 1976	16.00
Dirt Bike, 1973	9.00 To 16.00
Distillery No.I Club Bottle, 1970	45.00 To 50.00
Duesenberg Model SJ, 1971	20.00 To 28.00
Elk, 1973	*Illus* 25.00
Equestrienne, 1974	*Illus* 12.00
EZ Jug, No.1, Old Time, 1 3/4 Liter, 1977	20.00
EZ Jug, No.2, 1 3/4 Liter, 1980	80.00
F.O.E. Eagle, 1978	18.00 To 22.00
F.O.E. Eagle, 1979	*Illus* 30.00
F.O.E. Eagle, 1980	39.00
Farthington Bike, 1972	8.00 To 9.00
Fire Engine, 1971	10.00 To 20.00

Ezra Brooks, Elk, 1973

Ezra Brooks, Equestrienne, 1974

Ezra Brooks, F.O.E. Eagle, 1979

(See Page 55)

Fireman, 1975	15.00 To 24.00
Fisherman, 1974	*Illus* 10.00
Flintlock Dueling Pistol, 1968	6.00 To 29.00
Florida Gator, No.1, Passing, 1972	18.00 To 25.00
Florida Gator, No.2, Running, 1973	21.00
Florida Gator, No.3, Blocker, 1975	23.00 To 32.00
Football Player, 1974	9.00 To 12.00
Ford Thunderbird, 1956, Blue, 1977	46.00
Ford Thunderbird, 1956, Yellow, 1977	28.00
Fordson Tractor	13.00
Foremost Astronaut, 1970	5.00 To 15.00
Foremost Dancing Man, 1969	9.00 To 10.00
Fresno Grape, 1970	8.00 To 25.00
Gamecock, So.Carolina, 1970	11.00 To 35.00
Go Big Red No.1, 1970	20.00 To 50.00
Go Big Red No.2, 1971	15.00 To 30.00
Go Big Red No.3, 1972	15.00 To 20.00
Go Tiger Go, 1973	12.00 To 17.00
Gold Eagle, 1971	15.00 To 28.00
Gold Horseshoe, Reno, 1970	9.00 To 20.00
Gold Prospector, 1970	5.00 To 10.00
Gold Rooster, 1969	40.00 To 75.00
Gold Seal, 1972	9.00 To 15.00
Gold Turkey	55.00
Golden Grizzly Bear, 1968	6.00 To 10.00

Ezra Brooks, Fisherman, 1974

Goose, 1974 .... 9.00 To 12.00
Grandfather's Clock, 1970 .... 9.00 To 22.00
Great White Shark, 1977 .... 9.00
Greater Greensboro Open, 1972, Gold .... 19.00 To 39.00
Greater Greensboro Open, 1973, Golfer 25.00
Greater Greensboro Open, 1974, Map .... 40.00 To 43.00
Greater Greensboro Open, 1975, Cup .... 40.00 To 80.00
Greater Greensboro Open, 1977, Club & Ball .... 30.00 To 43.00
Groucho Marx Bust, 1977 .... 22.00 To 27.00
Gun Series, Set Of 4, 1969 .... 30.00
Hambletonian, 1971 .... 9.00 To 17.00
Harold's Club Dice No.7, 1968 .... 6.00 To 10.00
Hereford, 1972 .... 12.00 To 15.00
Historical Flask 4.00
Historical Flask, Set Of 6, 1970 .... 20.00
Hollywood Cops, 1972 .... 14.00 To 16.00
Idaho Potato, 1973 .... 23.00
Idaho Skier, 1972 .... 12.00
Indiana Elephant, 1973 .... 22.00
Indy Pace Car, Mustang, 1979 .... 37.00 To 45.00
Indy Pace Car, Pontiac, 1980 .... 43.00
Indy Racer No.21, 1970 .... 24.00 To 35.00
Indy Sprint Car, 1971 .... 23.00
Iowa Farmer, 1977 .... 45.00 To 55.00
Iowa Farmer's Elevator, 1978 ....Illus   32.00
Iron Horse Engine, 1969 .... 8.00 To 16.00
Jack Of Diamonds, 1969 .... 8.00 To 12.00
Jug, Owl, 1/2 Gallon 15.00
Kachina Doll, No.1, Morning Singer, 1971 .... 125.00 To 170.00
Kachina Doll, No.2, Hummingbird, 1973 .... 65.00 To 85.00
Kachina Doll, No.3, Antelope, 1974 .... 60.00 To 70.00
Kachina Doll, No.4, Maiden, 1975 .... 25.00 To 60.00
Kachina Doll, No.5, Longhair, 1976 .... 28.00 To 30.00
Kachina Doll, No.6, White Buffalo, 1977 .... 27.00 To 40.00
Kachina Doll, No.7, Mud Head, 1978 .... 35.00 To 45.00
Kachina Doll, No.8, Hopata Drummer, 1979 .... 43.00
Kachina Doll, No.9, Rattlesnake, Watermelon, 1980 .... 32.00 To 35.00
Kansas Jayhawk, 1969 .... 5.00 To 20.00
Katz Cat, Gray, 1969 ....Illus   12.00
Katz Cat, Philharmonic, 1970 .... 8.00 To 15.00
Katz Cat, Tan, 1969 .... 9.00 To 22.00
King Of Clubs, 1969 .... 8.00 To 12.00
King Tut Tomb Guard, Shrine, 1979 ....Illus   33.00

Ezra Brooks, Iowa Farmer's
Elevator, 1978

Ezra Brooks, Katz Cat, Gray, 1969

Ezra Brooks, King Tut Tomb Guard, Shrine, 1979

Kitten On Pillow, 1975	9.00 To 15.00
Liberty Bell, 1970	6.00 To 15.00
Lighthouse	20.00
Lincoln Continental 1941, 1979	25.00 To 35.00
Lion On The Rock, 1971	5.00 To 12.00
Liquor Square, 1972	6.00 To 24.00
Loon	25.00 To 33.00
Macaw, 1980	Color 49.00
Maine Lighthouse, 1971	24.00 To 35.00
Maine Lobster, 1970	26.00 To 45.00
Maine Potato, 1973	8.00 To 20.00
Man O' War, Gold	45.00
Man O' War, Horse, 1969	8.00 To 25.00
Map Club Bottle, 1973	17.00
Masonic Shrine Fez, 1976	15.00
Max The Hat Zimmerman, 1976	28.00
Michigan-Minnesota Brown Jug, 1975	23.00 To 25.00
Military Tank, 1972	22.00 To 30.00
Minnesota Hockey Player, 1975	19.00 To 22.00
Minuteman, 1975	9.00 To 15.00
Missouri Mule, 1972	11.00 To 20.00
Moose, 1973	25.00
Motorcycle, 1972	18.00
Mr.Foremost, 1969	25.00
Mr.Merchant, 1970	10.00 To 25.00
New Hampshire State House, 1969	25.00
North Carolina	9.00 To 11.00
North Carolina Bicentennial, 1975	27.00
Northern Raccoon Wild Life, 1978	30.00 To 44.00
Nugget Classic, 1970	11.00 To 15.00
Oil Gusher, 1969	4.00 To 10.00
Old Capitol, Iowa, 1971	35.00 To 38.00
Old EZ, No.1, Barn Owl, 1977	50.00 To 60.00
Old EZ, No.2, Eagle Owl, 1978	45.00 To 75.00
Old EZ, No.3, Snow Owl, 1979	Color 42.00
Old EZ, No.4, Scops Owl, 1980	52.00
Old Man Of The Mountain, 1970	14.00 To 20.00
Oliver Hardy Bust, 1976	9.00 To 23.00
Ontario Race Car, 1970	14.00 To 23.00
Overland Express Stagecoach, 1969	8.00 To 25.00
Pagliacci, 1979	Illus 41.00
Panda, 1972	18.00 To 20.00
Penguin, 1973	9.00 To 22.00
Penny Farthington, 1973	12.00
Phoenix Bird, 1971	27.00 To 60.00
Pirate, 1971	5.00 To 12.00
Polish Legion Amvets, 1978	16.00 To 19.00
Pontiac Firebird, Black Special, 1980	40.00 To 45.00
Potbellied Stove, 1968	5.00 To 15.00
Queen Of Hearts, 1969	5.00 To 12.00
Ram, 1973	16.00 To 20.00
Razorback Hog, 1970	16.00
Razorback Hog, 1979	18.00 To 39.00
Razorback Hog, 1981	39.00
Red Fox	25.00 To 45.00
Reno Arch, 1969	4.00 To 8.00
Republican Convention, 1976	16.00
Sailfish, 1971	9.00 To 18.00
Salmon, Washington, 1971	20.00 To 50.00
San Francisco Cable Car, 1968	5.00 To 10.00
Sea Captain, 1971	Illus 12.00
Seal, Gold	11.00

Ezra Brooks, Pagliacci, 1979   Ezra Brooks, Sea Captain, 1971

Senator	10.00 To 14.00
Senator, Gold	25.00
Senator, 1972	20.00
Setter, 1974	18.00
Shriner Clown, 1978	22.00 To 25.00
Shriner Sphinx	36.00
Silver Dollar, 1804, 1970	7.00 To 20.00
Silver Saddle, 1972	30.00
Silver Saddle, 1973	20.00 To 42.00
Silver Spur, 1971	5.00 To 25.00
Ski Boot, 1972	9.00 To 15.00
Slot Machine, Liberty Bell, 1971	30.00
Snow Leopard, 1980	*Color* 47.00
Snowmobile, 1972	9.00 To 15.00
Snowy Egret, 1980	55.00
So. California Trojan, 1974	18.00 To 25.00
South Dakota Air National Guard, 1976	22.00 To 26.00
Spirit Of '76, 1974	6.00 To 18.00
Spirit Of St.Louis 50th, 1977	11.00 To 18.00
Stan Laurel Bust, 1976	23.00
Stock Market Ticker Tape, 1970	9.00 To 12.00
Stonewall Jackson, 1974	15.00 To 30.00
Strongman, 1974	9.00 To 18.00
Sturgeon, 1975	25.00 To 30.00
Tecumseh, 1969	6.00 To 15.00
Telephone, 1971	13.00 To 22.00
Tennis Player, 1973	9.00 To 12.00
Terrapin Maryland, 1974	15.00
Texas Longhorn Steer, 1971	21.00 To 30.00
Tonopah, 1972	15.00 To 20.00
Totem Pole No.1, 1973	10.00 To 22.00
Totem Pole No.2, 1973	9.00 To 15.00
Tractor, Fordson, 1971	13.00 To 35.00
Train, Casey Jones, No.1, 1980	*Color* 45.00
Trojan Horse, 1974	18.00
Trout & Fly, 1970	9.00 To 14.00
Truckin 'n Vannin, 1977	10.00 To 20.00
U.S.Map, Club Bottle, 1973	17.00
V.F.W., White, Gold, 1975	8.00 To 15.00
V.F.W., 75th, Blue, 1973	7.00 To 15.00
Vermont Skier, 1973	12.00 To 24.00
Virginia Cardinal, 1973	20.00
Walgreen Drugs, 1974	18.00 To 21.00

Weirton Steel, 1974 .... 18.00 To 20.00
West Virginia Mountain Lady, 1972 .... *Illus* 20.00
West Virginia Mountaineer, 1971 .... 92.00 To 100.00
Whale, 1973 .... 14.00 To 22.00
Wheat Shocker, Kansas, 1971 .... 9.00 To 20.00
White Tail Deer, 1974 .... 15.00 To 22.00
White Turkey, 1971 .... 18.00 To 35.00
Whooping Crane, 1981 .... 55.00
Wichita Centennial, 1970 .... 35.00
Winston Churchill, 1969 .... 5.00 To 10.00
Zimmerman's Hat, 1968 .... 5.00 To 20.00
100th Bottle Award, 1972 .... 10.00
    FACE CREAM, see Cosmetic; Medicine

FAMOUS FIRSTS, Alpine Bell, 1970 .... 18.00
Baby Hippo, 1980 .... 58.00
Baby Panda, 1981 ....*Color* 65.00
Balloon, 1971 .... 62.00
Bennie Bow Wow, 1973 .... 20.00
Bersaglieri, 1969 .... 20.00
Butterfly, 1971 .... 34.00
Cable Car, 1973 .... 53.00
Centurian, 1969 .... 20.00
China Clipper, 1979 ....*Color* 132.00
Circus Tiger, 1979 .... 28.00
Coffee Mill, 1971 .... 42.00
Don Sympatico, 1973 .... 18.00
Egg House, 1975 .... 38.00
Filomena Hen, 1973 .... 20.00
Fireman, 1981 ....*Color* 68.00
Garibaldi, 1969 .... 20.00
Golfer, He, 1973 .... 31.00
Golfer, She, 1973 .... 31.00
Honda, 1975 .... 33.00 To 39.00
Hurdy Gurdy, 1971 .... 30.00
Indy Racer, No.11, 1971 ....*Illus* 35.00
Johnny Reb Telephone, 1973 .... 30.00
Leopard, 1975 ....*Illus* 15.00
Lion, 1975 ....*Illus* 23.00
Lockheed C-130 .... 60.00
Locomotive, 1969 .... 49.00
Lombardy Scale, 1970 ....*Illus* 32.00
Lotus Race, No.2, 1971 .... 83.00
Marmon, Gold, 1971 .... 14.00 To 17.00
    FAMOUS FIRSTS, MINIATURE, see Miniature, Famous Firsts
Minnie Meow, 1973 .... 21.00
Napoleon, 1969 .... 20.00
Natchez Mail Packet, 1975 .... 37.00
National Race, No.8, 1972 .... 60.00
Pepper Mill, 1978 .... 35.00
Phonograph, 1969 .... 38.00
Porsche Targa, 1979 .... 45.00 To 47.00
Renault Racer, No.3a, 1969 .... 35.00 To 43.00
Richard Rooster, 1973 .... 20.00
Robert E.Lee Steamboat, 1971 .... 63.00
Sea Witch Clipper Ship, 1976 .... 83.00
Sea Witch Clipper Ship, 200 Ml., 1980 .... 19.00 To 25.00
Sewing Machine, 200 Ml. 22.00
Skier, He Sportster, 1973 .... 31.00
Skier, Jack, 1975 .... 31.00
Skier, Jill, 1975 .... 31.00
Skier, She Sportster, 1973 .... 31.00
St.Pol Bell, 1970 .... 19.00

Ezra Brooks, West Virginia
Mountain Lady, 1972

Famous Firsts, Indy Racer, No.11, 1971

Famous Firsts, Zebra, Leopard, Lion, Tiger, 1975

Famous Firsts, Lombardy Scale, 1970

Famous Firsts, Yacht America 13, 1970

Swiss Chalet Barometer, 1974	33.00
T-Bird, 1956	75.00
Telephone, Floral, 1975	30.00
Tennis, He, 1973	31.00
Tennis, She, 1973	31.00
Tiger, 1975 .... *Illus*	15.00
Winnie Mae, Airplane, 1972	90.00
Yacht America 13, 1970 .... *Illus*	36.00
Yankee Clipper, 1975	15.00
Yankee Doodle Telephone, 1973	32.00
Zebra, 1975 .... *Illus*	15.00

1931 Bugatti, 1974 .... 150.00 To 208.00
1953 Corvette, 1975 .... 40.00

Figural bottles are specially named by the collectors of bottles. Any bottle that is of a recognizable shape, such as a human head, or a pretzel, or a clock, is considered to be a figural. There is no restriction as to date or material.

FIGURAL, see also Bitters; Cologne; Perfume
FIGURAL, Acrobat, Lady, On Ball, Frosted, Pontil 75.00
   Acrobat, Upside Down On Ball, Frosted, 13 1/2 In. 125.00
   Amaretto Di Saronno, Guard Of The Tower, 1970 .... *Illus* 18.00
   Apple, White House Vinegar, Pint 5.00
   Baby, Crying, Patent 1874 .... 100.00
   Ballet Dancer, Clear, 14 1/2 In. 50.00
   Banjo, Amethyst 25.00
   Barrel, Brown, 5 In. ....*Color* 22.00
   Base Fiddle, Cologne, Clear 55.00
   Bather On The Rocks, Clear, 12 In. .... 85.00 To 115.00
   Bear, Bank 10.00
   Bear, Kummel, Milk Glass, Label 135.00
   Bear, Muzzled, Amethyst, C.1845, 3 3/4 In. .... *Illus* 200.00
   Bear, 4 1/2 In. 2.00
   Beefeater, Yeoman, Ceramic ....*Color* 50.00
   Bell, Dr.Bell's Peptonized Port, Honey Amber, 10 In. 95.00
   Billy Club, Tin Cap, Amber, 10 1/2 In. 10.00
   Bird, 3 1/2 In. 20.00
   Boot, Laced, With Stocking, 12 1/4 In. 9.00
   Buddha, Amber Lid, 6 3/4 In. 15.00
   Buddha, Contents, Amber Turban Cap 25.00
   Bulldog, Blue, Small 40.00
   Bulldog, Ink, Yellow Amber, 4 In. 40.00
   Bunker Hill, Cologne, Clear 30.00
   Bunker Hill, Milk Glass, 9 1/8 In. 105.00
   Bust Of Man With Metal, 12 1/4 In. 5.00
   Bust Of Man, Granger, Patented June 2nd, 1874, 6 3/8 In. 5.00
   Bust, Embossed Beecher, 6 1/2 In. 85.00
   Bust, Embossed Granger, 6 1/2 In. 40.00
   Bust, Garibaldi, 12 In. 35.00
   Bust, Granger, BIMAL, Clear, 7 In. 40.00
   Bust, Grover Cleveland, Frosted Glass, 10 In. 100.00
   Bust, Lincoln, Syrup & Bank .... 7.00 To 10.00
   Bust, Robert E.Lee, 11 In. .... 450.00 To 500.00
   Carrie Nation, Clear, 9 In. 10.00
   Cat, Sitting & Grinning, Necktie, 3 Mold, Clear 37.00
   Cat, Sitting & Grinning, Necktie, 4 Mold, Sapphire Blue 40.00
   Cat, 11 1/4 In. 4.00
   Charlie Chaplin, 12 3/4 In. .... 80.00 To 100.00
   Cherub, Holding Clock 12.00
   Chicken, Dressed, Tin Cap, Amber, 4 1/2 In. 22.50
   Chicken, 3-Mold, Patented, 9 1/2 In. ....*Color* 45.00
   Cigar, Amber, Pocket Size, 5 In. 35.00
   Cigar, Shows Leaf Wrappings, Amber, 5 In. 30.00
   Cigar, Whiskey Nip, Golden Amber 26.00
   Cigars, Ground Screw Top, Amber, 5 In. 37.50
   Clam, Ground Top, Closure, Clear 25.00
   Clam, Ground Top, Original Screw Cap, Amber .... 150.00 To 200.00
   Clam, Whiskey, Zinc Cap, Ground Lip 24.50
   Claw Holding Egg, 14 In. 5.00
   Claw, Clear, 14 1/2 In. ....*Illus* 8.00
   Clock Corker, Embossed Face Of Clock, Star On Back, 6 1/2 In. 50.00
   Clock, Star Pendulum, Pontil .... 75.00 To 80.00
   Clown On Rocking Horse 150.00
   Clown, Bank 10.00
   Coachman, Van Dunck's, Amber, 3/4 Quart .... 25.00 To 40.00

Figural, Amaretto Di Saronno,
Guard Of The Tower, 1970

Figural, Bear, Muzzled, Amethyst,
C.1845, 3 3/4 In.

Figural, Claw, Clear, 14 1/2 In.

Coachman, Van Dunck's, Olive Amber	75.00
Coachman, Van Dunck's, Puce	225.00 To 250.00
Court Jester With Little Dog, BIMAL, Clear, 7 1/2 In.	50.00
Cupid Holding Portrait, 13 3/4 In.	8.00
Dog, Sad Hound, Clear	18.00
Dog, Sitting & Crying, 4-Mold, Clear, 10 1/2 In.	45.00
Dog, Two Children Climbing Tree, 13 1/2 In.	6.00
Dolphins, Three, In Base With Bottle Top, 12 1/4 In.	6.00
Eagle, Amber	12.00
Ear Of Corn, Carnival Glass, 5 In. ....Color	175.00
Ear Of Corn, Citron, 11 In.	130.00
Ear Of Corn, Whiskey, Citron, 11 In.	130.00
Eiffel Tower, 13 1/2 In.	3.00
Elephant, Old Sol, Amber, Pint	17.00
Eye Opener, Milk Glass, 5 In. ....Color	100.00
Face, Happy & Sad, 11 7/8 In.	17.50
Fantasia, Clear, 14 In.	30.00
Fish, Amber, 6 1/4 In.	5.00
Fish, Amber, 9 3/4 In.	10.00
Fish, Clear, 9 In. ....Illus	22.50

Figural, Fish, Clear, 9 In.

Fish, Clear, 13 3/4 In.	5.00
Fish, Emerald Green, 14 1/2 In.	20.00
Fish, Screw Top, Cap, Aqua	35.00
Football, Meier's Sherry, Old Oblong Label, Ohio	7.50
Fox, Learned, Cap, Clear	70.00
Fox, Learned, No Cap, 4 1/2 In.	6.00 To 12.50
Fuzzy, Face, 2 3/4 In.	17.00
Fuzzy, Face, 4 3/4 In.	35.00
Gen.All'Roe Gallino, Bust, Clear	50.00
George Washington, Bust, Screw Top, Cobalt Blue, 4 In.	10.00
George Washington, Mini-Whiskey, Embossed Chas.Jacquin, Blue	20.00
George Washington, Standing, Corker, Embossed Washington On Base	20.00
George Washington, 10 In.	8.00
Girl With Muff, 6 1/4 In.	8.00
Glad Hand, Blue	50.00
Grapes, Smoky Gray, 6 3/8 In.	5.00
Gun, Clear	25.00
Gun, Purple	25.00
Gun, Rockingham Glaze	150.00
Gun, Screw Cap, Clear, 7 In.	22.00
Gun, Silver & Black, Ground Lip, 8 In.	20.00
Gun, Yellow Amber, No Cap, 5 1/4 In.	5.00
Half Barrel, Clear, 1/2 Pint	22.00
Hand Holding Bottle, Frosted, Open Pontil, Clear	15.00
Hand Holding Dagger	12.00
Hand Holding Gun, Frosted Glass, Clear Gun, Ground Pontil, 12 In.	55.00
Hand, Satin, Holding BIMAL Bottle, Cobalt Blue	200.00
Hercules Holding Clear Glass World, Metal	200.00
Hessian Soldier, Clear, 7 1/4 In.	50.00
Hobo, Hands In Pockets, Clear, 12 1/2 In.	35.00
Horseshoe, Ground Screw Top, Light Amber, 4 In.	12.00
FIGURAL, INDIAN QUEEN, see Bitters, Brown's Indian Queen	
Indian, Standing, Cologne, Open Pontil, Aqua	30.00
Ink, Carter, Light Amber, Master, 1/4 Pint	18.00
Jar, Potbelly Stove, Screw Top, 6 In.	8.00
Jester, Clear, 7 In.	40.00 To 50.00
Jester, Seated, Holding Round Bottle	155.00
Jester, Seated, Holding Round Bottle, Flared Lip	135.00
John Bull, Amber, 12 In.	*Color* 135.00
Jolly Man, Colored	50.00
Jolly Man, Ground Lip, Clear	25.00
Jolly Man, SCA	55.00
Jolly Man, Sun-Colored Amethyst	65.00
Kummel Bear, Black Glass	35.00
Kummel Bear, Dense Olive Amber, 11 1/4 In.	20.00
Lady's Shape, Clear, 6 1/2 In.	*Illus* 35.00
Lady's Torso, SCA	70.00
Liberty Bell, Embossed, Green, 3 1/2 In.	20.00 To 22.00
Lighthouse, Wood Closure, Clear, 7 1/2 In.	20.00
Little Guard, Clear, 7 In.	*Illus* 40.00
Lobster, SCA	50.00 To 55.00
Madonna, Embossed Stars, Open Pontil, Glass Stopper, 8 7/8 In.	60.00
Mailbox, Rheinstrom Bros., Patent 1891, Label, Rye	100.00
Man On Barrel, Crew Cap, Embossed, Clear	30.00 To 35.00
Man On Barrel, Rockingham	55.00 To 60.00
Man On Barrel, Viarengo, Painted, Labels	35.00
Man On Barrel, Yellow	50.00
Man On Barrel, 11 1/2 In.	20.00
Man With Beard, Clear, 9 In.	*Illus* 120.00
Man With Potbelly, 9 In.	75.00
Man With Potbelly, 10 In.	15.00
Mermaid, Rockingham Glaze	40.00 To 70.00
Mermaid, Rockingham, 7 5/8 In.	75.00

Figural, Lady's Shape, Clear, 6 1/2 In.

Figural, Little Guard, Clear, 7 In.

Figural, Man With Beard, Clear, 9 In.

Midget In Uniform, 7 1/8 In.	10.00
Moses, Hiram Ricker & Sons Liquor, Amber, Quart	15.00
Moses, 1925, Green, 6 In.	300.00 To 400.00
Mr.Pickwick, 9 In.	*Color* 12.00
Mrs.Buttersworth, Original Screw Cap, Amber	4.00
Napoleon, Clear, Removable Hat, 12 In.	45.00
Napoleon, Depose, Some Paint	60.00
Negro Waiter, Black Head, Clear & Frosted, 13 1/2 In.	30.00
Old Tom, Rockingham Glaze	200.00
Owl, Cobalt Blue	42.50
Owl, Milk Glass	46.00
Owl, Pink Glass, 10 In.	45.00
Oyster, Ground Screw Top, Clear, 6 In.	25.00 To 32.50
Peacock, Ground Glass Stopper Of Butterfly, Clear, 13 1/2 In.	40.00
Pickle, Green, 4 1/2 In.	40.00
Pig, Duffy's Saloon, Clear	545.00
Pig, Good Old Rye In A Hog's Head, Milk Glass	850.00
Pig, Something Good In A Hog's, He Won't Squeal, 4 1/4 In.	35.00
Poodle, Sitting Up With Paws Front, Clear, 7 In.	85.00 To 95.00
Potato, Ground Top, Original Closure, Clear	25.00
Potato, Screw Top, Aqua	25.00
Potato, Square, Screw Top	25.00
Potato, World's Fair 1893, Original Paint, Milk Glass, 5 In.	35.00
Potato, Zinc Cap, Aqua	25.00
Potbellied Stove, 11 1/2 In.	3.00
Potter's, Dog Sled	29.99
Powder Horn, Cap, Clear	25.00
Powder Horn, Flat, Tin Screw Lid	14.00
Powder Horn, Tin Cap, 8 1/2 In.	3.00
Queen Victoria, Rockingham Glaze	190.00
Rabbit Emerging From Egg	65.00
Rebecca At The Well, Clear & Frosted, Pontil	55.00
Rolling Pin, Free Blown, Milk Glass, 13 In.	50.00
Russian Peasant, Clear, 12 1/2 In.	40.00 To 140.00
Sailor At Attention, 12 7/8 In.	6.00
Santa Claus, Clear, 12 1/2 In.	40.00 To 140.00

Santa Claus, Husted, Sun-Colored Amethyst .... 95.00 To 105.00
Santa Claus, Leaving Chimney 65.00
Shampoodle, Cobalt Blue 18.00
Shoe, Zinc Cap, 5 3/4 In. 13.00
Smiling Jack, Original Paint 75.00
Spanish Matador & Senorita, Pair 60.00
Statue Of Liberty, Milk Glass, Metal Cap 150.00
Success To Reform Derby, New Brown, 8 In. ....*Color* 18.00
Suitcase, Metal Handle & Slide, Painted, Troy, N.Y. 25.00
Taxi, French 65.00
Trunk, Corded, Clear, 4 3/4 In. 45.00
Turk, Seated, Clear 80.00
Turk, Seated, Flint 100.00
Turkey Claw, Amber, 11 In. 20.00
Turkey, Whiskey, Amber 40.00
Turtle, Amber, 4 In. 27.50
Turtle, Cap, Clear 35.00
Turtle, Whimsy, Pale Green, 6 3/8 In. 65.00
U.S.N.Dreadnaught, Tin Cap, 5 3/4 In. 25.00
Uncle Sam, Ground Screw Top, Clear, 9 1/2 In. 35.00
Violin, Clear, 8 In. 2.00
Violin, Metal Stand, Amber, 9 1/2 In. 30.00
Violin, Original Stand & Bow, Amber, 10 1/2 In. 30.00
Violin, Purple, 10 In. 10.00
Washington Monument, 1880 Sesquicentennial, Deep Amber, 9 3/8 In. 525.00
Washington, Standing, Clear, 9 1/2 In. .... 15.00 To 20.00
Whisk Broom, Crooked Neck, Amethyst 15.00
White Lion Man, Japan 29.00
World's Fair, 1939, Milk Glass ....*Color* 22.00
FIRE GRENADE, Dri-Gas, Chattanooga, Diamond-Quilted Pattern, 11 In. 30.00
Dri-Gas Fire Extinguisher Co., Contents, 11 3/4 In. 35.00
Harden's Footed, Blue 65.00
Harden's Star, Blue 50.00
Hayward's Hand, Patented Aug.8, 1871, Honey Amber 100.00
Korbeline, Amber 90.00
Light Bulb Shape, Sealed Shur-Stop, Bracket 10.00
Lion Heads At Feet, Aqua, Quart 15.00
Lion Heads At Feet, Milk Glass, Quart 35.00
      FITZGERALD, see Old Fitzgerald

Flasks have been made since the 18th century in America. The free-blown, mold-blown, and decorated flasks are all popular with collectors. The numbers used in the entries in the form McK G I-0 refer to the book "American Bottles and Flasks" by Helen McKearin and Kenneth M. Wilson.

FLASK, Adolph Harris, San Francisco, AHCo Monogram, Amber Thread Top 20.00
Banjo, Blue, 6 X 10 In. 25.00
Cap Embossed U.S., Metal Screw, Clear 28.00
Carrol Rye Monogram, L.T. & Co., Amber, 7 1/4 In. 5.00
Ceramic, Embossed Flowers, Ribbed Shoulders, Tan & Cream, Pint 75.00
Chestnut, Blown, Deep Red Amber, 4 3/4 In. 10.00
Chestnut, Elongated Blown, Amber, 6 1/4 In. 20.00
Chestnut, Elongated, 14 Vertical Ribs, Green 125.00
Chestnut, Embossed Monkey, Clear 35.00
Chestnut, Grove Whiskey, Amber 95.00
Chestnut, Light Yellowish Olive Green, 11 In. 65.00
Chestnut, Open Pontil, Light Yellow Amber, 9 In. 85.00
Chestnut, Open Pontil, Yellow Amber, 9 In. 90.00
Chestnut, Swirled To Left, Golden Amber, 1/2 Pint ....*Illus* 250.00
Chestnut, Swirled, Midwestern, Golden Amber, 1/2 Pint ....*Illus* 250.00
Chestnut, Vertically Ribbed, Aqua, 1/2 Pint ....*Illus* 35.00

Flask, Chestnut, Vertically Ribbed,
Aqua, 1/2 Pint

Flask, Chestnut, Swirled To Left,
Golden Amber, 1/2 Pint

Flask, Chestnut, Swirled, Midwestern,
Golden Amber, 1/2 Pint

Flask, Chestnut, Vertically Ribbed,
Golden Amber, 1/2 Pint

Flask, Chestnut, Vertically Ribbed,
Golden Yellow, 1/2 Pint

Flask, Chestnut, Vertically Ribbed,
Yellow Olive, 1/2 Pint

Chestnut, Vertically Ribbed, Golden Amber, 1/2 Pint .... *Illus* 250.00
Chestnut, Vertically Ribbed, Golden Yellow, 1/2 Pint .... *Illus* 450.00
Chestnut, Vertically Ribbed, Yellow Olive, 1/2 Pint .... *Illus* 425.00

Flask, Chestnut, 10 Diamond,
Deep Aqua, 1/2 Pint

Flask, Chestnut, 10 Diamond, Midwestern,
Golden Amber, 1/2 Pint

Chestnut, Zanesville, 24 Rib, Flattened, Orange To Yellow Amber 289.00
Chestnut, 10 Diamond, Deep Aqua, 1/2 Pint .... *Illus* 525.00
Chestnut, 10 Diamond, Midwestern, Golden Amber, 1/2 Pint .... *Illus* 400.00
Chestnut, 14 Vertical Ribs, Sheared Lip, Open Pontil, Green 125.00
Chestnut, 16 Vertical Ribs, Sheared Lip, Open Pontil, Deep Puce 400.00
Civil War Travelers, Leather & Metal Cover, Screw Cap, 1/2 Pint 24.50
Clam, Original Closure, Amber 135.00
Clock, Milk Glass, 4 1/2 In. .... *Color* 125.00
Corn, Urn Shape, Olive Green, Pint 55.00
Corn, Urn Shape, Open Pontil, 1/2 Pint 55.00
Crown, Stars, & Wreath, Pumpkinseed 12.00
Cunningham & Ihmsen, Glassmakers, Pittsburgh, Strap-Sided, Aqua, Pint 35.00
D.Doherty, Boston, Amber Strap, Pint 16.00
D.F., Violin Shaped, Aqua, Leather Holder 5.00
Diamond Patterned, Poison, Open Pontil, Clear, 4 In. 65.00
Dragoon & Hound, Aqua, Quart 100.00
E.C.Smith & Son, E.Fayette St., Syracuse, N.Y., Deep Green, Pint 15.00
Eagle & J.Shepard & Co., Deep Red Amber, 6 3/4 In. 420.00
Eagle, In Slug Plate, Clear, Pint 27.00
Ebner Bros., Sacramento, Coffin, Clear, 1/2 Pint 15.00
Elk's Head, Light Aqua, Pint 40.00
Ellenville Glass Works, Large X On Both Sides, Olive Amber 500.00
Embossed Anchor & Rope On Front, Strap Sided, Aqua, Quart 8.00
Embossed Safe, Strap Sided, Aqua, 6 1/4 In. 42.50
Embossed Star, Pewter Cap, Amber, Pint 18.00
English, Onion, Virginia, 1690-1720 .... 249.50
Farmville Dispensary, Farmville, Va., Clear, 1/2 Pint 25.00
Four Roses, Metal Shot Cap, Label, Prohibition, Amber 5.00
Frank X.Oster, Utica, N.Y., Amber, Strap-Sided 20.00
Fred Harding, Utica, N.Y., Aqua, Quart 5.00
G.G.Meyer, Third & Bryant Sts., Clear, Coffin 35.00
G.W.Chesley, Importer, Sacramento, Picnic, Amethyst, 1/2 Pint 20.00
Globular, Swirled, Midwestern, Citron, Quart .... *Illus* 425.00
Goffin, D.Chesney, Clear, Pint 25.00
H.Brickwedel & Co., Wholesale, San Francisco, Medium Amber, 1 Pint 85.00
Harwell & Clark, Dadeville, Ala., Strap-Sided, Yellow Amber, Quart 50.00
Hero Of Manila, Dewey Bust Embossed, Screw Top, 1/2 Pint 35.00
Hoyt Brothers, Lynn, Mass., Pumpkinseed, Clear, 1/2 Pint 10.00
Hoyt Brothers, Tooled Top, Light Sun-Colored Amethyst, Pint 10.00
J.Angeli & Co., San Francisco, C.1860, Amber, Green Tint 1300.00

Flask, Globular, Swirled, Midwestern,
Citron, Quart

McK G I-001, Washington & Eagle,
Blue-Green, Pint

McK G I-001, Washington & Eagle,
Deep Aqua, Pint

McK G I-003, Washington & Eagle,
Deep Aqua, Pint

Jenny Lind, Calabash, Aqua, 10 1/4 In.	35.00
J.F.Meenehan, Washington, D.C., Strap-Sided, Clear, Pint	12.00
J.H.Cutter Old Bourbon, C.P.Moorman Mfg., Amber	155.00
Jimmie Durkin, Strap-Sided, 8 Ounce	6.00
Jimmie Durkin, Strap-Sided, 16 Ounce	12.00
Jno.F.Horne, Knoxville, Tennessee, Anchor, Amber Strap Side, Fifth	40.00
John Naumanns & Sons, Cleveland, Ohio, Light Amethyst, 1/2 Pint	18.00
John Naumanns & Sons, Ontario St., Cleveland, Ohio, Aqua, 1/2 Pint	20.00
John P.Cooney, Prov., R.I., Amber	95.00
Knickerbocker Wine Co., New York, Strap Sided, Turning Purple	10.00
Lady Pictured Under Glass, 5 1/2 In. *Color*	40.00
Landregan & White, Wholesale, Oakland, Coffin, Clear, 1/2 Pint	15.00
Lilianthal Coffin, Medium Light Amber	400.00
Lyndeboro, Embossed L.G.Co., Aqua, 7 1/2 In.	45.00
McK G I-001, Washington & Eagle, Blue-Green, Pint *Illus*	1200.00
McK G I-001, Washington & Eagle, Deep Aqua, Pint *Illus*	500.00
McK G I-001, Washington & Eagle, Dark Greenish Aqua, Pint	1100.00
McK G I-002, Washington & Eagle, Aqua, Pint	395.00 To 450.00
McK G I-002, Washington & Eagle, Light Green, Pint	375.00 To 425.00
McK G I-003, Washington & Eagle, Aqua, Pint	700.00
McK G I-003, Washington & Eagle, Deep Aqua, Pint *Illus*	500.00

McK G I-003, Washington & Eagle, Golden Amber, Pint .... *Illus* 6250.00
McK G I-005, Washington & Eagle, Aqua, Pint .... *Illus* 6400.00
McK G I-006, Washington & Eagle, Amethyst Tint, Pint .... *Illus* 2100.00
McK G I-006, Washington & J.R.Eagle, Pint .... *Illus* 2100.00
McK G I-007, Washington & Eagle, Aqua, Pint .... *Illus* 300.00
McK G I-009, Washington & Eagle, Pale Green, Pint .... *Illus* 1400.00
McK G I-009, Washington & Eagle, Yellow Green, Pint .... *Illus* 4750.00
McK G I-010, Washington & Eagle, Deep Aqua, Pint .... *Illus* 325.00
McK G I-011, Washington & Eagle, Aqua, Pint .... *Illus* 750.00
McK G I-011, Washington & Eagle, Light Green, Pint .... *Illus* 650.00
McK G I-014, Washington & Eagle, Aqua, Pint .... 350.00 To 400.00
McK G I-014, Washington & Eagle, Clear, Pint 450.00
McK G I-014, Washington & Eagle, Emerald Green, Pint .... *Illus* 500.00

McK G I-003, Washington & Eagle,
Golden Amber, Pint

McK G I-005, Washington & Eagle,
Aqua, Pint

McK G I-006, Washington & Eagle,
Amethyst Tint, Pint

McK G I-007, Washington & Eagle,
Aqua, Pint

McK G I-006, Washington
& J.R.Eagle, Pint

McK G I-009, Washington & Eagle,
Pale Green, Pint

McK G I-009, Washington & Eagle,
Yellow Green, Pint

McK G I-010, Washington & Eagle,
Deep Aqua, Pint

McK G I-011, Washington & Eagle,
Aqua, Pint

McK G I-014, Washington & Eagle,
Emerald Green, Pint

McK G I-011, Washington & Eagle,
Light Green, Pint

McK G I-014, Washington & Eagle,
Sapphire Blue, Pint

McK G I-017, Washington & Taylor,
Yellow Amber, Pint

McK G I-018, Washington,
Cornflower Blue, Pint

McK G I-020, Washington &
Monument, Lavender, Pint

McK G I-018, Washington,
Yellow Green, Pint

McK G I-014, Washington & Eagle, Pale Green, Pint 145.00
McK G I-014, Washington & Eagle, Sapphire Blue, Pint .... *Illus* 9000.00
McK G I-016, Washington & Eagle, Aqua, Pint 175.00
McK G I-017, Washington & Taylor, Yellow Amber, Pint .... *Illus* 1500.00
McK G I-018, Washington, Cornflower Blue, Pint .... *Illus* 900.00
McK G I-018, Washington, Yellow Green, Pint .... *Illus* 1300.00
McK G I-020, Washington & Monument, Amethyst, Pint 1200.00
McK G I-020, Washington & Monument, Aqua, Pint .... 90.00 To 115.00
McK G I-020, Washington & Monument, Lavender, Pint .... *Illus* 800.00

McK G I-020, Washington & Monument, Sapphire, Pint .... *Illus* 5500.00
McK G I-020, Washington & Monument, Vaseline, Pint 225.00
McK G I-021, Washington & Monument, Amethyst, Quart .... *Illus* 2600.00
McK G I-021, Washington & Monument, Aqua, Quart .... 165.00 To 170.00
McK G I-023, Washington & Bust, Topaz, Quart .... *Illus* 500.00
McK G I-024, Washington & Taylor, Aqua, Pint 125.00
McK G I-024, Washington & Taylor, Golden Amber, Pint .... *Illus* 1100.00
McK G I-024, Washington & Taylor, Peacock Green, Pint .... *Illus* 650.00
McK G I-025, Washington, Bridgetown, Deep Wine, Quart .... *Illus* 2300.00
McK G I-026, Washington & Eagle, Aqua, Quart .... 85.00 To 110.00

McK G I-020, Washington &
Monument, Sapphire, Pint

McK G I-021, Washington &
Monument, Amethyst, Quart

McK G I-023, Washington &
Bust, Topaz, Quart

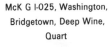

McK G I-025, Washington,
Bridgetown, Deep Wine,
Quart

McK G I-024, Washington &
Taylor, Golden Amber, Pint

McK G I-024, Washington &
Taylor, Peacock Green, Pint

McK G I-026, Washington & Eagle, Emerald Green, Quart .... *Illus* 1200.00
McK G I-026, Washington & Eagle, Medium Green, Quart 1200.00
McK G I-028, Albany Glass Works, Golden Amber 50.00
McK G I-028, Washington & Ship, Aqua, Pint 285.00
McK G I-028, Washington & Ship, Sapphire Blue, Pint .... *Illus* 2500.00
McK G I-031, Washington & Jackson, Amber, Pint 150.00
McK G I-031, Washington & Jackson, Olive Amber, Pint 85.00
McK G I-031, Washington & Jackson, Olive Green, Pint 185.00
McK G I-031, Washington & Jackson, Yellow Amber, Pint .... *Illus* 120.00
McK G I-032, Washington & Jackson, Olive Amber, Pint 100.00
McK G I-033, Washington & Jackson, Golden Amber, Pint 135.00
McK G I-033, Washington & Jackson, Olive Amber, Pint .... 75.00 To 120.00
McK G I-034, Washington & Jackson, Olive Amber, 1/2 Pint 150.00
McK G I-034, Washington & Jackson, Olive Green, 1/2 Pint 150.00
McK G I-035, Washington & Tree, Aqua, Quart 55.00
McK G I-036, Washington & Tree, Aqua, Quart 35.00
McK G I-037, Washington & Taylor, Amethyst, Quart .... *Illus* 800.00
McK G I-037, Washington & Taylor, Deep Claret 1600.00
McK G I-037, Washington & Taylor, Red-Puce, Quart .... 900.00 To 1400.00
McK G I-037, Washington & Taylor, Sapphire, Quart .... *Illus* 1300.00
McK G I-038, Washington & Taylor, Deep Amethyst, Pint .... 675.00 To 1295.00
McK G I-038, Washington & Taylor, Deep Aqua, Pint 50.00
McK G I-038, Washington & Taylor, Purple-Puce, Pint 1100.00
McK G I-038, Washington & Taylor, Yellow Green, Pint 575.00
McK G I-039, Washington & Taylor, Aqua, Quart .... 60.00 To 80.00
McK G I-039, Washington & Taylor, Deep Emerald, Quart .... 475.00 To 850.00
McK G I-039, Washington & Taylor, Medium Emerald, Quart 345.00
McK G I-040, Washington & Taylor, Aqua, Pint 25.00
McK G I-040a, Washington & Taylor, Aqua, Pint 40.00
McK G I-040a, Washington & Taylor, Moss Green, Pint 450.00
McK G I-040b, Washington & Taylor, Deep Sapphire Blue, Pint 1550.00
McK G I-041, Washington & Taylor, Aqua, 1/2 Pint .... *Illus* 60.00
McK G I-042, Washington & Taylor, Aqua, Quart .... 35.00 To 100.00
McK G I-042, Washington & Taylor, Dark Sapphire Blue, Quart 2500.00
McK G I-043, Washington & Taylor, Olive Yellow, Quart 700.00
McK G I-044, Washington & Taylor, Emerald Green, Pint 225.00
McK G I-044, Washington & Taylor, Shaded Citron, Pint 710.00
McK G I-045, Washington & Taylor, Aqua, Quart .... 180.00 To 200.00
McK G I-046, Washington & Taylor, Medium Green, Quart 180.00
McK G I-047, Washington, Blue Green, Quart 300.00
McK G I-047, Washington, Emerald Green, Quart .... 210.00 To 300.00

McK G I-026, Washington & Eagle,
Emerald Green, Quart

McK G I-028, Washington & Ship,
Sapphire Blue, Pint

McK G I-031, Washington & Jackson,
Yellow Amber, Pint

McK G I-037, Washington & Taylor,
Amethyst, Quart

McK G I-037, Washington & Taylor,
Sapphire, Quart

McK G I-041, Washington & Taylor,
Aqua, 1/2 Pint

McK G I-054, Washington & Taylor, Emerald, Quart

McK G I-048, Washington, Emerald Green, Pint .... 300.00 To 350.00
McK G I-049, Washington & Taylor, Aqua, Pint 45.00
McK G I-050, Washington & Taylor, Clear Green, Pint 110.00
McK G I-051, Washington & Taylor, Shaded Amber, Quart 825.00
McK G I-052, Washington & Taylor, Lime Green, Pint 595.00
McK G I-054, Washington & Taylor, Aqua, Quart 50.00
McK G I-054, Washington & Taylor, Clear Green, Pint 145.00
McK G I-054, Washington & Taylor, Dark Emerald Green, Pint 500.00
McK G I-054, Washington & Taylor, Emerald, Quart ....*Illus* 300.00
McK G I-054, Washington & Taylor, Olive Amber, Quart 270.00
McK G I-055, Washington & Taylor, Aqua, Pint 150.00

McK G I-068, Jackson & Floral, Aqua, Pint

McK G I-068, Jackson & Floral,
Yellow Olive, Pint

McK G I-071, Taylor & Ringgold,
Lavender, Pint

McK G I-055c, Washington & Taylor, Emerald Green, Pint 750.00
McK G I-057, Washington & Sheaf, Aqua, Quart .... 33.00 To 42.50
McK G I-059, Washington & Sheaf, Aqua, 1/2 Pint .... 55.00 To 95.00
McK G I-068, Jackson & Floral, Aqua, Pint .... *Illus* 1800.00
McK G I-068, Jackson & Floral, Yellow Olive, Pint .... *Illus* 7500.00
McK G I-071, Taylor & Ringgold, Amethyst, Pint 850.00
McK G I-071, Taylor & Ringgold, Aqua, Pint .... 110.00 To 125.00
McK G I-071, Taylor & Ringgold, Lavender, Pint .... *Illus* 1000.00
McK G I-073, Taylor & Monument, Amethyst, Pint .... *Illus* 2700.00
McK G I-074, Taylor & Cornstalk, Burgundy, Pint .... *Illus* 3200.00
McK G I-074, Taylor & Cornstalk, Topaz, Repaired Top, Pint 975.00
McK G I-076, Taylor & Eagle, Light Yellow Green, Pint .... *Illus* 4750.00

McK G I-073, Taylor & Monument,
Amethyst, Pint

McK G I-074, Taylor & Cornstalk,
Burgundy, Pint

McK G I-076, Taylor & Eagle,
Light Yellow Green, Pint

McK G I-077, Taylor & Eagle,
Aqua, Quart

McK G I-088, Lafayette & Masonic,
Olive Amber, Pint

McK G I-077, Taylor & Eagle, Aqua, Quart .... *Illus* 1100.00
McK G I-079, Grant & Eagle, Aqua, Pint 40.00
McK G I-085, Lafayette & Liberty Cap, Amber, Pint 450.00
McK G I-085, Lafayette & Liberty Cap, Olive Amber, Pint 525.00
McK G I-086, Lafayette & Liberty Cap, Olive Amber, 1/2 Pint 300.00
McK G I-086, Lafayette & Liberty Cap, Yellow Amber, 1/2 Pint 475.00
McK G I-088, Lafayette & Masonic, Olive Amber, Pint .... *Illus* 2100.00
McK G I-090, Lafayette & Eagle, Aqua, Pint .... *Illus* 400.00
McK G I-094, Franklin & Dyott, Aqua, Pint .... 190.00 To 300.00
McK G I-094, Franklin & Dyott, Pale Green, Pint 150.00
McK G I-096, Franklin & Dyott, Aqua, Quart 135.00
McK G I-096, Franklin & T.W.Dyott, M.D., Quart .... *Illus* 475.00

McK G I-090, Lafayette & Eagle,
Aqua, Pint

McK G I-096, Franklin & T.W.
Dyott, M.D., Quart

McK G I-099, Jenny Lind & Huffsey, Blue-Green, Quart .... *Illus* 650.00
McK G I-099, Jenny Lind & Huffsey, Deep Emerald Green, Quart 1100.00
McK G I-102, Jenny Lind & Factory, Aqua, Quart 60.00
McK G I-104, Jenny Lind & Factory, Sapphire, Quart .... *Illus* 900.00
McK G I-104, Jenny Lind, IP, Sapphire Blue, Quart .... *Illus* 1300.00
McK G I-105, Jenny Lind & Factory, Sapphire, Quart 450.00
McK G I-107, Jenny Lind & Fislerville, Aqua, Quart 55.00
McK G I-108, Jenny Lind & Lyre, Aqua, Pint .... *Illus* 800.00
McK G I-110, Jenny Lind & Lyre, Aqua, Quart .... *Illus* 950.00
McK G I-112, Kossuth & Frigate, Aqua, Quart .... 215.00 To 325.00
McK G I-112, Kossuth & Frigate, Calabash, IP, Aqua, Quart 135.00
McK G I-112, Kossuth & Frigate, Emerald Green, Quart 720.00
McK G I-112, Kossuth & Frigate, Golden Amber, Quart .... *Illus* 1500.00
McK G I-113, Kossuth & Tree, Aqua, Quart 55.00
McK G I-113, Kossuth & Tree, Light Green, Quart 195.00
McK G I-114, Byron & Scott, Olive Amber, 1/2 Pint .... *Illus* 120.00
McK G I-115, Wheat Price, Short Hair, Deep Aqua, Pint .... *Illus* 5500.00
McK G I-117, Columbia & Eagle, Aqua, Pint 275.00
McK G I-118, Columbia & Eagle, Faint Aqua, Pint 3600.00
McK G I-118, Columbia & Eagle, Lavender, 1/2 Pint .... *Illus* 5500.00
McK G I-118, Columbia & Eagle, Medium Green, Pint 295.00
McK G I-118, Columbia & Eagle, Yellow Green, 1/2 Pint .... *Illus* 2000.00
McK G I-118, Columbia & Eagle, Yellow Olive, 1/2 Pint .... *Illus* 1500.00

McK G I-099, Jenny Lind & Huffsey,
Blue Green, Quart

McK G I-104, Jenny Lind & Factory,
Sapphire, Quart

McK G I-104, Jenny Lind, IP,
Sapphire Blue, Quart

McK G I-108, Jenny Lind & Lyre, Aqua, Pint

McK G I-110, Jenny Lind & Lyre,
Aqua, Quart

McK G I-112, Kossuth & Frigate,
Golden Amber, Quart

McK G I-115, Wheat Price,
Short Hair, Deep Aqua, Pint

McK G I-114, Byron & Scott,
Olive Amber, 1/2 Pint

McK G I-118, Columbia & Eagle,
Lavender, 1/2 Pint

McK G I-118, Columbia & Eagle,
Yellow Green, 1/2 Pint

McK G I-118, Columbia & Eagle, Yellow Olive, 1/2 Pint

McK G I-119, Columbia & Eagle, Cobalt Blue, Pint *Illus*4000.00
McK G I-121, Columbia & Eagle, Aqua, Pint .... 275.00 To 355.00
McK G II-001, Eagle, Aqua, Pint 475.00
McK G II-008, Eagle & Medallion, Clear, Pint *Illus*6500.00
McK G II-011, Eagle & Cornucopia, Aqua, 1/2 Pint ....*Illus* 400.00
McK G II-016, Eagle & Cornucopia, Aqua, Pontil 400.00
McK G II-016, Eagle, Sapphire Blue, 1/2 Pint *Illus*3100.00
McK G II-017, Urn & Cornucopia, Emerald Green, 7 In. 205.00
McK G II-019, Eagle & Morning Glory, Aqua, Pint ....*Illus* 550.00
McK G II-022, Eagle & Lyre, Aqua, Pint ....*Illus* 750.00
McK G II-023, Eagle & Floral Medallion, Aqua, Pint 1100.00
McK G II-024, Double Eagle, Aqua, Pint ....*Illus* 105.00
McK G II-024, Double Eagle, Medium Yellow Green, Pint 325.00
McK G II-024, Double Eagle, Sapphire Blue, Pint *Illus*1600.00
McK G II-025, Double Eagle, Aqua, Pint 30.00
McK G II-026, Double Eagle & Banner, Bluish Aqua, Quart 90.00
McK G II-026, Double Eagle, Amber, Quart 950.00
McK G II-026, Double Eagle, Iron Pontil, Aqua, Quart 75.00
McK G II-026, Double Eagle, Light Yellow Green, Quart 600.00
McK G II-031, Double Eagle, Aqua, Quart 80.00
McK G II-032a, Double Eagle, OP, Aqua, Pint 300.00
McK G II-033, Eagle & Louisville, Ky., Amber, 1/2 Pint 120.00
McK G II-033, Eagle & Louisville, Ky., Olive Amber, 1/2 Pint 185.00
McK G II-037, Eagle & Ravenna Glass Co., Aqua, Pint 105.00
McK G II-039, Eagle, Amber, 1/2 Pint 65.00
McK G II-040, Double Eagle, Aqua, Pint 110.00
McK G II-040, Double Eagle, Light Yellow Green, Pint 225.00
McK G II-041, Eagle & Tree, Aqua, Pint 130.00
McK G II-042, Eagle & T.W.D., Frigate, Aqua, Pint 170.00
McK G II-042, Eagle & T.W.D., Frigate, Light Aqua, Pint 85.00
McK G II-043, Eagle & T.W.D., Amethyst, 1/2 Pint *Illus*3400.00
McK G II-043, Eagle & T.W.D., Cornucopia, Aqua, Pint 400.00

McK G I-119, Columbia & Eagle,
Cobalt Blue, Pint

McK G II-008, Eagle & Medallion,
Clear, Pint

McK G II-011, Eagle & Cornucopia,
Aqua, 1/2 Pint

McK G II-016, Eagle, Sapphire
Blue, 1/2 Pint

McK G II-019, Eagle & Morning Glory,
Aqua, Pint

McK G II-022, Eagle & Lyre,
Aqua, Pint

McK G II-024, Double Eagle,
Aqua, Pint

McK G II-024, Double Eagle,
Sapphire Blue, Pint

McK G II-043, Eagle & T.W.D.,
Amethyst, 1/2 Pint

McK G II-048, Eagle & Flag, Yellow Amber, Quart ....*Illus* 900.00
McK G II-052, Eagle & Flag, Deep Golden Amber, Pint ....*Illus* 1700.00
McK G II-053, Eagle & Flag, Light Olive Green, Pint ....*Illus* 2600.00
McK G II-053, Eagle & Flag, For Our Country, Aqua 140.00
McK G II-054, Eagle & Flag, For Our Country, Aqua 115.00
McK G II-054, Eagle & Flag, Olive Amber, Open Pontil, Pint 2000.00
McK G II-055, Eagle & Grapes, Aqua, Quart ....*Illus* 125.00
McK G II-055, Eagle & Grapes, Emerald Green, Quart 950.00
McK G II-055, Eagle & Grapes, Golden Amber, Quart ....*Illus* 850.00

McK G II-048, Eagle & Flag,
Yellow Amber, Quart

McK G II-052, Eagle & Flag,
Deep Golden Amber, Pint

McK G II-053, Eagle & Flag,
Light Olive Green, Pint

McK G II-055, Eagle & Grapes,
Golden Amber, Quart

McK G II-055, Eagle & Grapes,
Aqua, Quart

McK G II-056, Eagle & Grapes,
Amber, 1/2 Pint

McK G II-056, Eagle & Grapes,
Aqua, 1/2 Pint

McK G II-069, Eagle & Cornucopia,
Aqua, 1/2 Pint

McK G II-072, Eagle & Cornucopia,
Dark Green, Pint

McK G II-073, Eagle & Cornucopia,
Olive Amber, Pint

McK G II-056, Eagle & Grapes, Amber, 1/2 Pint ....*Illus* 2300.00
McK G II-056, Eagle & Grapes, Aqua, 1/2 Pint ....*Illus* 250.00
McK G II-060, Eagle & Charter Oak, Amber, 1/2 Pint 1125.00
McK G II-060, Eagle & Charter Oak, Aqua, 1/2 Pint 450.00
McK G II-062, Eagle & Liberty, Willington, Deep Green, Pint 155.00
McK G II-062, Eagle & Liberty, Willington, Olive Green, Pint 175.00
McK G II-063, Eagle & Liberty, Willington, Olive Amber, 1/2 Pint 80.00
McK G II-064, Eagle & Willington, Clear, Pint 160.00
McK G II-064, Eagle & Willington, Olive Green, Pint .... 65.00 To 175.00
McK G II-065, Liberty & Eagle, Westford, Olive Amber, 1/2 Pint 60.00
McK G II-069, Eagle & Cornucopia, Aqua, 1/2 Pint ....*Illus* 600.00
McK G II-070, Double Eagle, Lengthwise, Olive Amber, Pontil, Pint 139.00
McK G II-071, Double Eagle, Light Olive, 1/2 Pint 135.00
McK G II-071, Double Eagle, Olive Amber, 1/2 Pint 110.00
McK G II-071, Double Eagle, Olive Green, 1/2 Pint .... 130.00 To 175.00
McK G II-072, Eagle & Cornucopia, Dark Green, Pint ....*Illus* 125.00
McK G II-072, Eagle & Cornucopia, Olive Amber, Pint .... 35.00 To 55.00
McK G II-073, Eagle & Cornucopia, Deep Forest Green, Pint 150.00
McK G II-073, Eagle & Cornucopia, Deep Olive, Pint 80.00
McK G II-073, Eagle & Cornucopia, Golden Amber, Pint 150.00
McK G II-073, Eagle & Cornucopia, Olive Amber, Pint ....*Illus* 65.00

McK G II-076, Concentric
Ring Eagle, Green, Pint

McK G II-076a, Concentric
Ring Eagle, Green, Pint

McK G II-082, Double Eagle,
Stoddard, Amber, Pint

McK G II-087, Double Eagle,
Olive Amber, 1/2 Pint

McK G II-073, Eagle & Cornucopia, Yellow Amber, Pint 250.00
McK G II-074, Eagle & Cornucopia, OP, Deep Aqua, Pint 225.00
McK G II-076, Concentric Ring Eagle, Green, Pint .... *Illus* 4800.00
McK G II-076a, Concentric Ring Eagle, Green, Pint .... *Illus* 7200.00
McK G II-078, Double Eagle, Olive Amber, Quart 100.00
McK G II-081, Double Eagle, Stoddard, Olive Amber, Pint 90.00
McK G II-082, Double Eagle, Stoddard, Amber, Pint .... *Illus*   65.00
McK G II-082, Double Eagle, Stoddard, Olive Amber, Pint 95.00
McK G II-083, Double Eagle, Amber, Pint 40.00
McK G II-084, Double Eagle, Olive Amber, Pint 50.00
McK G II-086, Double Eagle, Stoddard, Olive Amber, 1/2 Pint 60.00
McK G II-086, Double Eagle, Stoddard, Open Pontil, Honey, 1/2 Pint 85.00
McK G II-086a, Double Eagle, Stoddard, Olive Amber, 1/2 Pint 70.00
McK G II-087, Double Eagle, Olive Amber, 1/2 Pint .... *Illus*   55.00
McK G II-088, Double Eagle, Golden Amber, 1/2 Pint 65.00
McK G II-088, Double Eagle, Yellow Amber, 1/2 Pint 160.00
McK G II-093, Double Eagle, Aqua, Pint 35.00
McK G II-093, Double Eagle, Ringed Top, IP, Sapphire Blue 1400.00
McK G II-098, Double Eagle, Geo.A.Berry & Co., In Oval, Aqua, Quart 55.00
McK G II-101, Double Eagle, Pittsburgh, Light Green, Quart 195.00
McK G II-104, Double Eagle, Pittsburgh, Black Glass 175.00
McK G II-105, Double Eagle, Pittsburgh, Golden Amber, Pint 50.00
McK G II-106, Double Eagle, Pittsburgh, Aqua, Pint 35.00
McK G II-106, Double Eagle, Pittsburgh, Black, Pint 165.00
McK G II-106, Double Eagle, Pittsburgh, Golden Amber, Pint 125.00
McK G II-109, Double Eagle, Pittsburgh, In Oval, Aqua, 1/2 Pint 35.00
McK G II-113, Double Eagle With Banner, Amber, Pint 50.00
McK G II-118, Double Eagle With Banner, Aqua, Pint .... 25.00 To 27.50

McK G II-122, Double Eagle With Banner, Aqua, 1/2 Pint	22.50
McK G II-125, Double Eagle With Banner, Aqua, 1/2 Pint	22.50
McK G II-126, Double Eagle With Wreath, Aqua, 1/2 Pint	22.50
McK G II-126, Double Eagle With Wreath, IP, Ice Blue, 1/2 Pint	90.00
McK G II-127, Double Eagle & C & I, Aqua, 1/2 Pint	25.00
McK G II-128, Double Eagle, Aqua, 1/2 Pint	75.00
McK G II-130, Double Eagle, Aqua, Pint	25.00
McK G II-139, Eagle, Amber, 1/2 Pint	60.00
McK G II-141, Eagle & Indian Shooting Bird, Aqua, Quart	90.00
McK G II-142, Eagle & Indian Shooting Bird, Aqua, Quart	130.00
McK G II-143, Eagle & Banner, Calabash, Emerald Green, Quart	130.00
McK G II-143, Eagle & Banner, Calabash, IP, Grass Green, Quart	80.00
McK G III-004, Cornucopia & Urn, Amber, Pint	105.00
McK G III-004, Cornucopia & Urn, Bright Green, Pint ....*Illus*	160.00
McK G III-004, Cornucopia & Urn, Open Pontil, Green, Pint	65.00
McK G III-004, Cornucopia & Urn, Open Pontil, Olive Green, Pint	60.00
McK G III-004, Cornucopia & Urn, Olive Amber, Pint ....*Illus*	40.00
McK G III-007, Cornucopia & Urn, Green, 1/2 Pint ....*Illus*	175.00
McK G III-007, Cornucopia & Urn, Yellow Amber, 1/2 Pint	75.00
McK G III-007, Cornucopia & Urn, Pontil, Aqua, 1/2 Pint	130.00
McK G III-007, Cornucopia & Urn, Pontil, Olive Amber, 1/2 Pint	85.00
McK G III-007, Cornucopia & Urn, Pontil, Olive Green, 1/2 Pint	110.00
McK G III-010, Cornucopia & Urn, Amber, 1/2 Pint	55.00
McK G III-011, Cornucopia & Urn, Olive Amber, 1/2 Pint	49.50
McK G III-011, Cornucopia & Urn, Bubbles, Olive Green, 1/2 Pint	70.00
McK G III-012, Cornucopia & Urn, Olive Amber, 1/2 Pint	80.00
McK G III-017, Cornucopia & Urn, Emerald, Pint ....*Illus*	200.00
McK G IV-001, Masonic & Eagle, Blue Aqua, Pint	310.00

McK G III-004, Cornucopia &
Urn, Olive Amber, Pint

McK G III-004, Cornucopia &
Urn, Bright Green, Pint

McK G III-007, Cornucopia &
Urn, Green, 1/2 Pint

McK G III-017, Cornucopia &
Urn, Emerald, Pint

McK G IV-001, Masonic & Eagle, Light Emerald Green, Pint 170.00
McK G IV-001, Masonic & Eagle, Light Green, Pint .... *Illus* 225.00
McK G IV-001, Masonic & Eagle, Purple, Pint .... *Illus* 7500.00
McK G IV-001, Masonic & Eagle, Pontil, Clear Green 275.00
McK G IV-001, Masonic & Eagle, Pontil, Crystal Clear 1400.00
McK G IV-003, Masonic & Eagle, Yellow Olive, Pint .... *Illus* 2250.00
McK G IV-007, Masonic, Amethyst Striations, Pint .... *Illus* 3500.00
McK G IV-008, Masonic & Eagle, Yellow Green, Pint .... *Illus* 950.00
McK G IV-008a, Masonic & Eagle, Clear, Pint 1800.00
McK G IV-014, Masonic & Eagle, Aqua, 1/2 Pint 800.00
McK G IV-017, Masonic & Eagle, Keene, Dark Olive Green, Pint 139.00
McK G IV-017, Masonic & Eagle, Olive Amber, Pint .... *Illus* 110.00
McK G IV-018, Masonic & Eagle, Keene, Dark Olive Amber, Pint 75.00
McK G IV-019, Masonic & Eagle, Olive Amber, Pint .... 80.00 To 110.00
McK G IV-019, Masonic & Eagle, Keene, Olive Green, Pint 175.00
McK G IV-020, Masonic & Eagle, Keene, Amber, Pint 125.00
McK G IV-020, Masonic & Eagle, Keene, Olive Amber, Pint 110.00
McK G IV-020, Masonic & Eagle, Keene, Olive Green, Pint 145.00
McK G IV-020, Masonic & Eagle, Keene, Yellow Olive Amber, Pint 170.00
McK G IV-021, Sunburst, Deep Emerald, Pint 225.00
McK G IV-024, Masonic & Eagle, 1/2 Pint .... 150.00 To 195.00
McK G IV-024, Masonic & Eagle, Olive Amber, 1/2 Pint 120.00
McK G IV-024, Masonic & Eagle, Olive Green, 1/2 Pint 155.00
McK G IV-024, Masonic & Eagle, Olive Green, Pint 170.00
McK G IV-024, Masonic & Eagle, Open Pontil, Olive Green, Pint 175.00
McK G IV-027, Masonic & Eagle, NEG, Aqua, Pint 325.00
McK G IV-028, Masonic Decoration, Deep Aqua, Pint 125.00
McK G IV-030, Crossed Keys, Compass, Amber, Pint .... *Illus* 500.00
McK G IV-032, Farmer's Arms & Zanesville, Red Amber, Pint 600.00
McK G IV-032, Farmer's Arms & Zanesville, Shaded Amber, Pint 600.00
McK G IV-032, Masonic & Eagle, Amber, Pint 375.00
McK G IV-032, Masonic & Eagle, Aqua, Pint .... 200.00 To 250.00
McK G IV-032, Masonic & Eagle, Bluish Aqua, Pint 175.00
McK G IV-032, Masonic & Eagle, Golden Amber, Pint .... *Illus* 375.00
McK G IV-032, Masonic & Eagle, Light Green, Pint 525.00
McK G IV-032, Masonic & Eagle, Puce, Pint 650.00

McK G IV-001, Masonic & Eagle,
Light Green, Pint

McK G IV-001, Masonic & Eagle,
Purple, Pint

McK G IV-003, Masonic & Eagle, Yellow Olive, Pint

McK G IV-007, Masonic, Amethyst
Striations, Pint

McK G IV-008, Masonic & Eagle,
Yellow Green, Pint

McK G IV-017, Masonic & Eagle,
Olive Amber, Pint

McK G IV-030, Crossed Keys,
Compass, Amber, Pint

McK G IV-032, Masonic & Eagle,
Golden Amber, Pint

McK G IV-032, Masonic & Eagle, Red Amber, Pint	285.00 To 600.00
McK G IV-032, Masonic & Eagle, OP, Flared Lip, Deep Aqua, Pint	700.00
McK G IV-034, Masonic & Franklin, Aqua, Pint	250.00
McK G IV-037, Farmer's Arms & Eagle T.W.D., Aqua, Pint	250.00
McK G IV-037, Farmer's Arms & Eagle T.W.D., Clear, Pint	187.50
McK G IV-042, Union & Clasped Hands, Eagle, Calabash, Citron, Quart	325.00
McK G IV-042, Union & Clasped Hands, Eagle, OP, Aqua, Quart	50.00
McK G IV-042, Union & Clasped Hands, Eagle, Yellow-Green, Quart	195.00
McK G V-001, Success To The Railroad, Aqua, Pint	1500.00
McK G V-001, Success To The Railroad, Clear Green, Pint	650.00
McK G V-001, Success To The Railroad, OP, Deep Aqua, Pint	450.00
McK G V-001, Success To The Railroad, Yellow, Pint	1300.00
McK G V-001, Success To The Railroad, Yellow Amber, Pint	80.00
McK G V-003, Success To The Railroad, Pontil, Dark Olive Green	190.00
McK G V-003, Success To The Railroad, Olive Amber, Pint	190.00
McK G V-003, Success To The Railroad, OP, Yellow Amber, Pint	175.00
McK G V-004, Success To The Railroad, Olive Amber, Pint	350.00

McK G V-009, Railroad & Eagle,
Deep Olive Amber, Pint

McK G VI-002, Monument,
Sloop, Topaz, 1/2 Pint

McK G VI-003, Baltimore Liberty
& Union, Aqua, Pint

McK G VI-004, Baltimore,
Corn, Olive, Quart

McK G V-005, Success To The Railroad, Aqua 300.00
McK G V-005, Success To The Railroad, Deep Amber, Pint 129.00
McK G V-005, Success To The Railroad, Olive Amber, Pint 65.00
McK G V-005, Success To The Railroad, Olive Green, Pint 200.00
McK G V-006, Success To The Railroad, Golden Amber, Pontil, Pint 175.00
McK G V-006, Success To The Railroad, Olive Green, Pint 120.00
McK G V-007, Cart & Horse, Green, Pint 750.00
McK G V-008, Success To The Railroad, Eagle, Olive Green, Pint 200.00
McK G V-009, Railroad & Eagle, Deep Olive Amber, Pint ....*Illus* 120.00
McK G V-010, Lowell Railroad & Eagle, Olive Amber, 1/2 Pint 130.00
McK G VI-002, Monument, Sloop, Deep Amethyst, Pontil, 1/2 Pint 1700.00
McK G VI-002, Monument, Sloop, Medium-Light Puce, 1/2 Pint 450.00
McK G VI-002, Monument, Sloop, Topaz, 1/2 Pint ....*Illus* 1300.00
McK G VI-003, Baltimore Liberty & Union, Aqua, Pint ....*Illus* 300.00
McK G VI-004, Baltimore & Corn For World, Aqua, Quart 120.00
McK G VI-004, Baltimore & Corn For World, Golden Amber, Quart 450.00
McK G VI-004, Baltimore & Corn For World, Pale Blue, Quart 85.00
McK G VI-004, Baltimore & Corn For World, Yellow, Quart 775.00
McK G VI-004, Baltimore, Corn For World, Yellow Olive Green, Quart 850.00
McK G VI-004, Baltimore, Corn, Olive, Quart ....*Illus* 700.00
McK G VI-004, Baltimore, Corn, Peacock Blue ....*Illus* 2300.00
McK G VI-006, Baltimore, Corn For World, Aqua, Pint .... 220.00 To 250.00
McK G VI-007, Baltimore, Corn For World, Aqua, 1/2 Pint 45.00
McK G VI-007, Corn For World, Green, 1/2 Pint ....*Illus* 1200.00

McK G VI-004, Baltimore,
Corn, Peacock Blue

McK G VI-007, Corn For World,
Green, 1/2 Pint

McK G VIII-002, Sunburst,
Clear Green, Pint

McK G VIII-002, Sunburst,
Light Green, Pint

McK G VIII-002, Sunburst, Clear Green, Pint ....*Illus* 400.00
McK G VIII-002, Sunburst, Light Emerald Green, Pint 300.00
McK G VIII-002, Sunburst, Light Green, Pint ....*Illus* 325.00
McK G VIII-002, Sunburst, Medium Green, Pint 475.00
McK G VIII-002, Sunburst, Puce, Pint 400.00
McK G VIII-003, Sunburst, Olive Amber, Pint .... 95.00 To 350.00
McK G VIII-003, Sunburst, Olive Green, Pint 575.00
McK G VIII-003, Sunburst, OP, Light Olive Green, Pint 425.00
McK G VIII-003, Sunburst, Yellow Amber, Pint 165.00
McK G VIII-003, Sunburst, Yellow Green, Pint 500.00
McK G VIII-005, Sunburst, Pontil, Deep Green, Pint 250.00
McK G VIII-005, Sunburst, Forest Green, Pint 495.00
McK G VIII-005, Sunburst, Olive Green, Pint .... 550.00 To 600.00
McK G VIII-007, Sunburst, Olive Amber, Pint 675.00
McK G VIII-007, Sunburst, OP, Golden Amber, Pint 1400.00
McK G VIII-008, Sunburst & Keen In Oval, Olive Amber, 1/2 Pint 95.00
McK G VIII-008, Sunburst & Keen, P & W, Olive Amber, Pint 550.00
McK G VIII-008, Sunburst & Keen, P & W, Olive Amber, Pint 210.00
McK G VIII-008, Sunburst & Keen, P & W, Pontil, Olive Green, Pint 350.00
McK G VIII-009, Sunburst & Keen, P & W, Golden Amber, 1/2 Pint 425.00
McK G VIII-009, Sunburst & Keen, P & W, Olive Amber, 1/2 Pint 200.00
McK G VIII-009, Sunburst & Keen, P & W, Olive Green, Pint 275.00
McK G VIII-010, Sunburst & Keen, Olive, 1/2 Pint 285.00
McK G VIII-010, Sunburst & Keen, Olive Amber, 1/2 Pint 395.00

McK G VIII-010, Sunburst & Keen, Olive Green, 1/2 Pint 300.00
McK G VIII-011, Sunburst, Green, 1/2 Pint 1750.00
McK G VIII-014, Sunburst, Emerald Green, 1/2 Pint 1070.00
McK G VIII-014, Sunburst, Green, 1/2 Pint 1000.00
McK G VIII-014, Sunburst, Yellow Green, 1/2 Pint 900.00
McK G VIII-016, Sunburst, Clear Olive Green, 1/2 Pint 305.00
McK G VIII-016, Sunburst, Light Olive Amber, 1/2 Pint 100.00
McK G VIII-016, Sunburst, Olive Amber, 1/2 Pint 205.00
McK G VIII-018, Sunburst, Light Olive Amber, 1/2 Pint 110.00
McK G VIII-018, Sunburst, Olive Amber, 1/2 Pint .... 85.00 To 350.00
McK G VIII-018, Sunburst, Olive Green, 1/2 Pint 375.00
McK G VIII-018, Sunburst, Yellow Amber, 1/2 Pint 425.00
McK G VIII-024, Sunburst, Aqua, 1/2 Pint 325.00
McK G VIII-028, Sunburst, Aqua, 1/2 Pint 260.00
McK G VIII-029, Sunburst, Aqua, 3/4 Pint 70.00
McK G VIII-020, Sunburst, Aqua, Pint 250.00
McK G VIII-029, Sunburst, Dark Aqua, 3/4 Pint 325.00
McK G VIII-029, Sunburst, Deep Aqua, Pint 105.00
McK G VIII-029, Sunburst, Deep Teal, 3/4 Pint 245.00
McK G IX-001, Scroll, Aqua, Quart 90.00
McK G IX-001, Scroll, Bluish Aqua, Quart 45.00
McK G IX-002, Scroll, Amber, Quart 825.00
McK G IX-002, Scroll, Aqua, Quart .... 90.00 To 95.00
McK G IX-002, Scroll, Deep Aqua, Quart 50.00
McK G IX-002, Scroll, Emerald Green, Double Collar, Quart 475.00
McK G IX-002, Scroll, Sapphire Blue, Quart .... *Illus* 750.00
McK G IX-003, Scroll, Aqua, Quart .... 58.00 To 90.00

McK G IX-002, Scroll,
Sapphire Blue, Quart

McK G IX-010, Scroll,
Cobalt Blue, Pint

McK G IX-010, Scroll,
Light Greenish Blue, Pint

McK G IX-010, Scroll, Amber, Pint 285.00
McK G IX-010, Scroll, Blue Aqua, Pint 75.00
McK G IX-010, Scroll, Cobalt Blue, Pint .... *Illus* 1000.00
McK G IX-010, Scroll, Light Greenish Blue, Pint .... *Illus* 175.00
McK G IX-010, Scroll, Open Pontil, Golden Amber, Pint 125.00
McK G IX-010a, Scroll, Aqua, Pint 55.00
McK G IX-011, Scroll, Collar, Amber, Pint 395.00
McK G IX-011, Scroll, Double Collar, Aqua, Pint 65.00
McK G IX-011, Scroll, Deep Olive Amber, Pint 500.00
McK G IX-011, Scroll, Light Green, Pint 105.00
McK G IX-011, Scroll, Iron Pontil, Aqua, Pint .... 55.00 To 85.00
McK G IX-011, Scroll, Iron Pontil, Bluish Aqua, Pint 45.00
McK G IX-011, Scroll, IP, Deep Bluish Green, Pint .... *Illus* 400.00
McK G IX-011, Scroll, IP, Deep Golden Amber, Pint .... *Illus* 400.00
McK G IX-013, Scroll, Yellow Amber, Pint 485.00
McK G IX-014, Scroll, Lime Green, Pint .... 445.00 To 500.00
McK G IX-016, Scroll, Iron Pontil, Deep Blue Aqua, Pint 375.00
McK G IX-020, Scroll, Light Green, Pint 255.00
McK G IX-020, Scroll, Olive Yellow, Pint .... *Illus* 550.00
McK G IX-025, Scroll, With C, Aqua, Pint .... 75.00 To 150.00
McK G IX-029, Scroll, Aqua, 2 Quart, 11 1/2 In. .... 300.00 To 425.00
McK G IX-031, Scroll, Aqua, Open Pontil, 1/2 Pint .... 40.00 To 45.00
McK G IX-031, Scroll, Iron Pontil, Bluish Aqua, 1/2 Pint 75.00
McK G IX-033, Scroll, Iron Pontil, Aqua, 1/2 Pint 65.00
McK G IX-034, Scroll, Pontil, Aqua, 1/2 Pint 60.00
McK G IX-036, Scroll, Fleur-De-Lis, Open Pontil, Aqua, 1/2 Pint 129.50
McK G IX-036, Scroll, Light Green, 1/2 Pint 200.00

McK G IX-020, Scroll,
Olive Yellow, Pint

McK G IX-011, Scroll,
IP, Deep Golden Amber, Pint

McK G IX-011, Scroll,
IP, Deep Bluish Green, Pint

McK G IX-037, Scroll,
Sapphire Blue, 1/2 Pint

McK G IX-041, Scroll,
Anchor, Deep Yellow, 1/2 Pint

McK G X-002, Good Game & Stag,
Willow, Aqua, 1/2 Pint

McK G X-003, Sheaf Of Rye, Grapes,
Aqua, 1/2 Pint

McK G IX-037, Scroll, Fleur-De-Lis, Pontil, Aqua, 1/2 Pint 95.00
McK G IX-037, Scroll, Sapphire Blue, 1/2 Pint .... *Illus* 1700.00
McK G IX-038, Scroll, B P & B, Aqua, 1/2 Pint 205.00
McK G IX-039, Scroll, B P & B, Aqua, 1/2 Pint 300.00
McK G IX-041, Scroll With Anchor, Aqua, 1/2 Pint .... 235.00 To 450.00
McK G IX-041, Scroll, Anchor, Deep Yellow, 1/2 Pint .... *Illus* 3000.00
McK G IX-043, Scroll, J R & Son, Aqua, Pint 650.00
McK G IX-044, Scroll, J R & Son, Deep Aqua, Pint 950.00
McK G IX-045, Scroll, Aqua, Pint .... 425.00 To 735.00
McK G IX-045, Scroll, OP, Green Aqua, Pint 800.00
McK G X-001, Good Game & Stag, Willow, Aqua, Pint .... 180.00 To 310.00
McK G X-002, Good Game & Stag, Willow, Aqua, 1/2 Pint .... *Illus* 650.00
McK G X-003, Sheaf Of Rye, Grapes, Aqua, 1/2 Pint .... *Illus* 140.00
McK G X-008, Sailing Ship & Star, OP, Aqua, 1/2 Pint .... 120.00 To 135.00
McK G X-014, Murdock & Cassel, Zanesville, Light Green, Pint 1200.00
McK G X-014, Murdock And Cassel, Zanesville, Aqua, Pint 185.00
McK G X-015, Summer & Winter, Aqua, Pint 50.00
McK G X-015, Summer & Winter, Light Green, Pint 90.00

McK G X-018, Spring,
Summer Tree,
Light Green, Quart

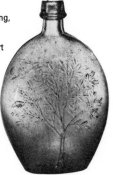

McK G X-018, Spring,
Summer Tree,
Sapphire Blue, Quart

McK G X-021, Steamboat, Rye Sheaf,
Deep Yellow Olive

McK G X-022, Cabin, Cider
& Barrel, Aqua, Pint

McK G X-024, Jared Spencer,
Light Olive Amber, Pint

McK G X-025, Jared Spencer,
Olive Amber, Pint

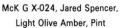

McK G X-018, Spring, Summer Tree, Light Green, Quart .... *Illus* 340.00
McK G X-018, Spring, Summer Tree, Sapphire Blue, Quart .... *Illus* 450.00
McK G X-019, Fall, Winter Tree, Pale Blue, Quart 200.00
McK G X-021, Steamboat, Rye Sheaf, Deep Yellow Olive .... *Illus* 7000.00
McK G X-022, Cabin, Cider & Barrel, Aqua, Pint .... *Illus* 3200.00
McK G X-024, Jared Spencer, Light Olive Amber, Pint .... *Illus* 4000.00
McK G X-025, Jared Spencer, Olive Amber, Pint .... *Illus* 6000.00
McK G XI-001, For Pikes Peak, Aqua, Quart 30.00
McK G XI-008, For Pikes Peak, Pittsburgh, Pa., Blue Aqua, Quart 55.00

McK G XI-031, For Pikes Peak,

Eagle, Aqua, Pint

McK G XI-031, For Pikes Peak, Eagle, Aqua, Pint .... *Illus* 60.00
McK G XI-041, For Pikes Peak, Eagle, Aqua, Pint 27.50
McK G XI-046, For Pikes Peak, Hunter, Olive Green, Pint 725.00
McK G XI-046, For Pikes Peak, Hunter, Pale Aqua, Quart 70.00
McK G XI-052, For Pikes Peak, Hunter, Aqua, 1/2 Pint 70.00
McK G XI-052, For Pikes Peak, Hunter, Aqua, Pint 69.00
McK G XII-002, Waterford Eagle, Aqua, Quart 64.00
McK G XII-006, Clasped Hands & Eagle, Citron, Quart 280.00
McK G XII-006, Clasped Hands & Eagle, Pale Green 55.00
McK G XII-009, Old Rye, Eagle, Aqua, Quart .... 55.00 To 60.00
McK G XII-013, Clasped Hands & Eagle, Pale Blue, Quart 90.00
McK G XII-022, Clasped Hands, Eagle A & Co., Yellow Green, Pint 135.00
McK G XII-030, Union, Eagle & Banner, Amber, 1/2 Pint 85.00
McK G XII-031, Clasped Hands, Eagle, Amber, 1/2 Pint 75.00
McK G XII-031, Clasped Hands, Eagle, Aqua, 1/2 Pint 25.00
McK G XII-036, Clasped Hands, Oval Frame, Pale Green, 1/2 Pint 105.00
McK G XII-037, Double Union, Clasped Hands, Pale Aqua, Quart 45.00
McK G XII-039, Clasped Hands, Cannon, Aqua, Pint .... 65.00 To 135.00
McK G XII-039, Clasped Hands, Cannon, Deep Aqua, Pint 90.00
McK G XII-040, Clasped Hands, Cannon, F.A.& Co., Aqua, Pint 88.00
McK G XII-043, Clasped Hands, Eagle, Amber, Quart 190.00
McK G XII-043, Clasped Hands, Eagle, IP, Bluish Aqua, Quart 25.00
McK G XIII-002, Not For Joe, Aqua, Pint 245.00
McK G XIII-004, Hunter & Fisherman, Amber, Quart .... 195.00 To 250.00
McK G XIII-004, Hunter & Fisherman, Aqua, Quart 75.00
McK G XIII-004, Hunter & Fisherman, Copper, Quart 200.00
McK G XIII-004, Hunter & Fisherman, Puce, Quart 135.00
McK G XIII-004, Hunter & Fisherman, IP, Golden Amber, Quart 225.00
McK G XIII-004, Hunter & Fisherman, IP, Red Amber, Quart 250.00
McK G XIII-005, Hunter & Fisherman, Aqua, Quart 20.00
McK G XIII-006, Hunter & Fisherman, Aqua, Quart 30.00
McK G XIII-011, Soldier & Dancer, Pale Yellow Green, Pint 210.00
McK G XIII-016, U.S.Army Dragoon, Hound, OP, Citron, Quart 650.00
McK G XIII-017, Horseman & Hound, Aqua, Pint 150.00
McK G XIII-017, Horseman & Hound, Olive Yellow, Pint 350.00
McK G XIII-019, Flora Temple, Smoky Amber, Quart 250.00
McK G XIII-021, Flora Temple, Amber, Pint .... 250.00 To 275.00
McK G XIII-021, Flora Temple, Smoky Amber, Pint .... 150.00 To 250.00
McK G XIII-027, Duck & Motto, Aqua, Quart 140.00
McK G XIII-035, Sheaf Of Grain, Westford, Conn., Dark Puce, Pint 110.00
McK G XIII-035, Sheaf Of Grain, Westford, Conn., Olive Amber, Pint 40.00
McK G XIII-035, Sheaf Of Grain, Westford, Conn., Olive Green, Pint 89.50
McK G XIII-036, Sheaf Of Grain, Westford, Amber, Pint 90.00
McK G XIII-036, Sheaf Of Grain, Westford, Honey-Red Amber 129.00

McK G XIII-037, Sheaf Of Grain, Westford, Olive Amber, 1/2 Pint 125.00
McK G XIII-036, Sheaf Of Grain, Westford, Olive Amber, Pint 65.00
McK G XIII-037, Sheaf Of Grain, Westford, Red Amber, 1/2 Pint 85.00
McK G XIII-038, Sheaf Of Grain, Star, Iron Pontil, Aqua, Quart 95.00
McK G XIII-038, Sheaf Of Grain, Westford, Olive Amber, Pint 45.00
McK G XIII-043, Sheaf Of Grain, Aqua, Quart 35.00
McK G XIII-044, Sheaf Of Grain, Star, Deep Puce Amber, Quart 195.00
McK G XIII-044, Sheaf Of Grain, Star, IP, Deep Amber, Quart 160.00
McK G XIII-052, Anchor, Sheaf Of Grain, Sapphire Blue, Quart 1375.00
McK G XIII-053, Anchor & Phoenix, Aqua, Pint .... 50.00 To 85.00
McK G XIII-053, Anchor & Phoenix, Deep Yellow-Green, Pint 375.00
McK G XIII-053, Anchor & Phoenix, Golden Amber, Pint 350.00
McK G XIII-054, Anchor & Phoenix, Golden Amber, Pint 350.00
McK G XIII-058, Anchor & Glasshouse, OP, Aqua, 1/2 Pint 110.00
McK G XIII-059, Anchor & Glasshouse, Aqua, Pint 75.00
McK G XIII-061, Spring Garden Glassworks, Citron, 1/2 Pint 475.00
McK G XIII-075, Key, Embossed, Aqua, Pint 20.00
McK G XIII-079, Safe, Embossed, Aqua, Pint 35.00
McK G XIII-087, Bininger's Regulator, Clock Dial, Amber, Pint 295.00
McK G XIII-090, C.C.Goodale, Rochester, Aqua, 1/2 Pint 45.00
McK G XIV-001, Traveler's Companion & Sheaf, Amber, Quart 100.00
McK G XIV-001, Traveler's Companion & Sheaf, Olive Amber, Quart 40.00
McK G XIV-003, Traveler's Companion, Golden Amber, Pint 360.00
McK G XIV-003, Traveler's Companion, Ravenna Glass Co., Aqua, Pin 135.00
McK G XV-007, Granite Glass Co., Light Golden Amber, Pint 155.00
McK G XV-007, Granite Glass Co., Open Pontil, Olive Amber, Pint 150.00
McK G XV-008, Granite Glass Co., Light Yellow Olive Amber, Pint 145.00
McK G XV-015, Newburgh Glass Co., Dark Olive Amber, Pint 400.00
McK G XV-018, Geo.Robinson, W.Va., Aqua, Quart 125.00
McK G XV-020, Geo.W.Robinson, W.Va., Aqua, Quart 125.00
McK G XV-034, J.H.B., Embossed, Aqua, Quart 45.00
McK Plate 100, No.1, Chestnut, Light Green 200.00
McK Plate 234, No.5, Ribbed, Golden Amber, Quart .... *Illus* 500.00
Merry Christmas & Happy New Year, In Wreath, Picnic, Clear, 4 3/4 In. 25.00
Merry Christmas & Happy New Year, In Wreath, Pumpkinseed, 1/4 Pint 30.00
Merry Christmas, Happy New Year 10.00
Midwestern Pitkin, German Half-Post, Sheared Lip, Open Pontil, Green 325.00
Midwestern, Broken Swirl, Deep Golden Amber, Pint .... *Illus* 575.00
Midwestern, Pitkin, Green 325.00

Flask, Midwestern, Broken Swirl,
Deep Golden Amber, Pint

McK Plate 234, No.5, Ribbed,
Golden Amber, Quart

Flask, Midwestern, Swirled
To Left, Citron, Pint

Midwestern, Swirled To Left, Citron, Pint .... *Illus* 475.00
Midwestern, 10 Diamond Pattern, Golden Amber, 5 In. 525.00
Midwestern, 17 Diamond, Light Aqua 40.00
Midwestern, 19 Swirls, Open Pontil, Aqua, Quart 89.50
Midwestern, 24 Swirls To Right, Amber 395.00
Midwestern, 24 Vertical Ribs, Aqua, 1/2 Pint 225.00
Miller's, Trade Mark Monogram, Medium Amber, Potstone On Back, 1 Pint 65.00
Nailsea Gemel, Clear With White Stripes, 7 1/2 In. 35.00
Old Bourbon Castle Whiskey, Double Ring, Blob Top, Light Amber 875.00
Old Gilt Edge Whiskey, Slug Plate, Straight Sided, Amber, 1/2 Pint 12.00
Old Phoenix, Picture Of Bird, Coffin, Light Amber, 1/2 Pint 125.00
Oval, D.F. Embossed, Open Pontil, Pewter Cap, Light Green 75.00
P.W.Benjamin & Co., Natchez, Miss., 1/2 Pint 55.00
Pap's Picnic's Pumpkinseed, Golden Amber, 4 In. 55.00
Patrician Bourbon Whiskey, New York, Label, Clear, 1/2 Pint 15.00
Pebbleford Kentucky Bourbon, Paper Label, Clear, Tapered 18.00
Persian Saddle, Applied Mouth, Neck Threading, Deep Green, Quart 20.00
Phoenix Bourbon Whiskey, Embossed Phoenix Bird, Coffin, Clear 95.00
Picnic, Open Pontil, Deep Aqua 20.00
Pitkin Type, Midwestern, Green 325.00
Pitkin Type, Midwestern, Ribs Swirled To Right, Deep Yellow Olive 280.00
Pitkin Type, New England, Light Olive Amber, 1/2 Pint .... *Illus* 125.00
Pitkin Type, New England, Swirled To Left, Olive Amber, 1/2 Pint 150.00
Pitkin Type, New England, Swirled To Right, Olive Amber .... *Illus* 140.00
Pitkin Type, Ribs Swirled To Left, Golden Amber, Pint .... *Illus* 300.00
Pitkin Type, Ribs Swirled To Left, Pontil, Golden Amber, Pint 525.00
Pitkin Type, Ribs Swirled To Left, Pontil, Light Yellow Green, Pint 295.00
Pitkin Type, Ribs Swirled To Left, Pontil, Olive Amber, Pint 350.00
Pitkin Type, Ribs Swirled To Left, Pontil, Olive Green, 1/2 Pint 295.00
Pitkin Type, Ribs Swirled To Left, Pontil, Olive Green, Pint 375.00
Pitkin Type, Ribs Swirled To Left, Pontil, Olive Yellow, Pint 350.00
Pitkin Type, Ribs Swirled To Right, Aqua, 1/2 Pint .... *Illus* 40.00
Pitkin Type, Ribs Swirled To Right, Light Olive Amber, Pint 180.00
Pitkin Type, Ribs Swirled To Right, Olive Amber, 1/2 Pint 150.00
Pitkin Type, Ribs Swirled To Right, Olive Green, Pint .... *Illus* 90.00
Pitkin Type, Ribs Swirled To Right, Pontil, Dark Olive Green 320.00
Pitkin Type, Ribs Swirled To Right, Pontil, Yellow Green, Pint 375.00
Pitkin Type, Swirled To Right, Olive Amber, Pint 130.00
Pitkin, Open Pontil, Light Olive Green, 1/2 Pint 225.00

Pitkin, Open Pontil, Light Olive Green, Pint 235.00
Pitkin, 30 Ribs, Broken Swirl, Olive Green, 6 1/2 In. 145.00
Pitkin, 30 Ribs, Broken Swirl, Pale Olive Green, 6 3/8 In. 145.00
Pitkin, 31 Ribs, Broken Swirl, Olive Green, 6 1/4 In. 160.00
Pocket, Bead & Diamond Design, Clambroth, 1/2 Pint, 5 1/4 In. 375.00
Pocket, Original Zinc Threaded Cap, Amber, 6 In. 20.00
Pocket, Wharton's Whiskey, Cobalt Blue 200.00
Poison, Flattened Pattern, Cobalt Blue, 1/2 Pint ....*Illus* 220.00
Polo Player, Ceramic, Lore On Bottom, 5 1/2 X 4 1/2 In. 10.00
Pottery, Decorated, Dogs, Humans, & Ferns, Brown Glaze, Quart 120.00
Pumpkinseed, A.Colburn & Co., Clear 16.00
Pumpkinseed, Life Preserver, Clear 35.00
Pumpkinseed, Oval, 1/2 Pint .... 4.00 To 10.00
Pumpkinseed, Spiderweb Design, Aqua 9.00
Queen, Tooled Top, Golden Amber 450.00
Ring Collar, Strap-Sided, Emerald Green, Pint 10.00
Roth & Co., Pine Street, San Francisco, Strap-Sided 185.00
S.F.Rose Straight Goods, Vallejo, Pumpkinseed, Embossed, 1/2 Pint 40.00
Saddle, Open Pontil, Teal, Large 40.00

Flask, Pitkin Type, New England,
Light Olive Amber, 1/2 Pint

Flask, Pitkin Type, New England,
Swirled To Right, Olive Amber

Flask, Pitkin Type, Ribs Swirled To
Left, Golden Amber, Pint

Flask, Pitkin Type, Ribs Swirled
To Right, Aqua, 1/2 Pint

Flask, Pitkin Type, Ribs Swirled To
Right, Olive Green, Pint

Flask, Poison, Flattened Pattern,
Cobalt Blue, 1/2 Pint

Scroll, Aqua, 1/2 Pint 45.00
Scroll, Aqua, Pint .... 52.00 To 65.00
Scroll, Aqua, Quart 35.00
Scroll, Iron Pontil, Amber, 7 1/8 In. 385.00
Scroll, Iron Pontil, Aqua, Pint 55.00
Scroll, Iron Pontil, Aqua, Quart 40.00
Scroll, Iron Pontil, Aqua, 8 1/2 In. 35.00
Scroll, Iron Pontil, Bluish Aqua, Pint 59.50
Scroll, Iron Pontil, Light Emerald Green, Quart 265.00
Scroll, Iron Pontil, Olive Green, 8 3/8 In. 960.00
Scroll, Iron Pontil, Plain Lip, Aqua, Quart 50.00
Scroll, Iron Pontil, Sapphire Blue, 8 3/4 In. 215.00
Scroll, Open Pontil, Bluish Aqua, Pint 64.50
Scroll, Stars, Open Pontil, Aqua, Original Stopper 155.00
St.Joseph's Assures Purity 3.00
Stoddard, Black Glass 30.00
T.J.Carty, Port Jervis, N.J., Amber Strap Side, Fifth 20.00
Teardrop Shape, Screw Top, Star On Cap, Amber, 1/2 Pint 20.00
Vertically Ribbed, Cobalt Blue, Pint ....*Illus* 400.00
    FLASK, VIOLIN, see also Flask, Scroll
Violin Shaped, Leather Holder, Aqua 35.00
W.B.Bond & Co., Newark, N.J., Amber Strap Side, Fifth 20.00
Wharton's Whiskey, Chestnut Grove, Pocket, Amber 115.00
Wheat Price & Co., Wheeling, Va., Fairview Works, Deep Aqua, 6 5/8 In. 3950.00
Whisk Broom, Button & Daisy, Clear, 1/2 Pint 25.00
Whiskey, Embossed C.C.G., Rochester, N.Y., Amber, Pint 45.00
Whiskey, Senate Leadville, Colo., Ground Top 20.00
Whiskey, Walter Moise Co., Distillers, Omaha, Nebraska, 1/2 Pint 30.00
Whitney Glass Works, Pale Yellow Green 35.00
Willington Eagle, Olive Green, 1/2 Pint 56.00
Winchell & Davis, Albany, N.Y., Strap Sided, Amber, Quart 20.00
Winchell & Davis, Utica, N.Y., Strap-Sided, Amber, Pint 20.00
Yosemite Rebmann & Reinke, Fillmore St., Clear, Threaded Top 15.00
    FLASK, ZANESVILLE, see Flask, Chestnut, Zanesville
16 Vertical Ribs, Deep Puce 400.00
20 Pronounced Vertical Ribs, Olive Green, 7 1/4 In. 85.00
24 Swirls, Pewter Screw Top, Cobalt 250.00

Food bottles include all of the many grocery store containers, such as those
for catsup, horseradish, jelly, and other foodstuffs. A few special bottles,
such as those for vinegar, are listed under their own headings.

FOOD, Aroostock Condensed Milk Co., Maine, Embossed Baby On Lid 12.00
B.& L., Mustard Barrel, Embossed, 5 In. 18.00
Baker's Flavoring Extracts, Rectangular, 3 1/2 In. 2.00
Berry, Fluted Vertical Panels, Green Aqua, Quart 135.00
Blanke's Aerial Globe Pure Spice, Shaped Like Globe, 4 In. 45.00
Blueberry, Paneled, Aqua 35.00
Bunker Hill Pickles, Monument, Amber, Round, 6 In. 7.00
    FOOD, CALIFORNIA PERFUME CO., see Avon, California Perfume Co.
California Fig Syrup Co., Wheeling, W.Virginia 4.00
Catsup, Paper Label, Aqua, 9 In. ....*Color* 10.00
Catsup, W.K.Lewis Bros., Boston, Label, Tomato & Wine, Aqua, 9 1/2 In. 25.00
Cloverleaf, Wells, Mill, & Provost, Dark, Pint 170.00
Condiment, Free-Blown, Square, Light Green 75.00
Condiment, Western Spice Mills, St.Louis, Aqua, 4 In. 25.00
Cumberland Sauce, Loren J.Wicks, Bridgeton, N.J., BIMAL, 7 1/2 In. 15.00
Cylinder, 19th Century, Open Pontil, Olive Green, 8 In. 250.00
DePaus Flavor Extracts, Open Pontil, Clear 20.00
Dodge & Olcott Co., Oil Spearmint, Partial Contents, Cobalt, 3 1/4 In. 6.00
Dr.Gunn's Onion Syrup 6.00
Edward J.Moor Syrup, North Carolina, Rectangular, Aqua 5.00
F. & J.McKee, Pittsburgh, Pa., Open Pontil 365.00

Flask, Vertically Ribbed, Cobalt Blue, Pint   Food, Heinz, H.J.Co., Vinegar, Barrel, Sampling

G.C.Giessen Mustard, New York, Open Pontil	32.00
Giessen Union, New York, Open Pontil, Clear	35.00
Gilletts High Grade Extract, Owl On Moon, Embossed, Sun Color	10.00
Gorton's H.P.Sauce, Aqua	7.00
Green And Clark Missouri Cider, Aug.27, 1878, Amber	20.00 To 30.00
Heinz, Catsup, Pat.June 17, 1890, 8-Sided, Sample, Clear	6.00
Heinz, H.J.Co., Vinegar, Barrel, Sampling ....*Illus*	150.00
Homer's Cooking Extract, Open Pontil	32.00
Hope's Flavoring Extract, 1870s, Aqua, 5 In.	3.00
I.B.Smith Co., Philadelphia, Pontil	140.00
J & K W Harvey, Porter Ale & Cider, Norwich, Ct., Pontil, Squat, Green	125.00
J.Laufer's Horse Radish, Buffalo, N.Y., Clear, 4 In. ....*Illus*	10.00
Jelly, Milk Glass, Square, 1/2 Pint	13.00
John Wyeth & Bro.Liq.Ext.Malt, Phil.	10.00
Jumbo, Peanut Butter, Clear, 5 In. ....*Illus*	10.00
Jumbo, Peanut Butter, 3 Ounce	5.00
Lahaina Ice Co., Ltd., Lahaina, Maui, Hutchinson, 4-Part Mold	25.00
Lemon Extract, Open Pontil, 5 1/2 In. ....*Color*	17.50
Log Cabin Extract, Corkscrew, Carton, Literature, Small	55.00
McK G II-013, Blown, 3 Mold, Brass Shaker Top, 4 1/2 In.	35.00
McK G III-004, Blown, 3 Mold, Folded Rim, 3 3/4 In.	40.00

Food, J.Laufer's Horse Radish,
Buffalo, N.Y., Clear, 4 In.

Food, Jumbo, Peanut Butter, Clear, 5 In.

Merchants Drug Corp.Blue Flag Extract, Rectangular 2.00
Merten, Moffitt & Co., San Francisco, Jamaica Ginger, Aqua, 6 In. 4.00
Mitchell's Flavoring Extract, Open Pontil, Smoky Clear .... 30.00 To 35.00
Moutarde PMM, Mustard, Pear Shape, 5 In. 5.00
Moxie Nerve Food, Trademark, Crown Top, Quart 12.00
Mustard Barrel, Fancy Design, Pontil 5.00
Mustard Barrel, Giessen Union, N.Y., Eagle, Clear 59.50
Mustard Barrel, Open Pontil, Aqua, 4 In. 18.00
Mustard, Golden Eagle, Battleship Maine, SCA, 5 In. ....*Color* 120.00
Mustard, London, Pottery Crock, Tan & White 5.00
Mustard, Square, Green Aqua, Open Pontil 10.00
National Butter, Gallon 200.00
Our Crown Jewel Pure Extract, Rectangular, 5 7/8 In. 2.00
Our Leader, Extract Of Vanilla & Tonka, Rectangular, 5 7/8 In. 2.00
Parker's Extract Of Lemon, Rectangular, 6 3/4 In. 2.00
Parker's Extract Of Peppermint, Rectangular, 4 3/4 In. 2.00
Parker's Extract Of Vanilla & Tonka, Rectangular, 4 3/4 In. 2.00
Penn Cress Buttermilk, Award, Pa.Farm Show, Gallon 8.00
    FOOD, PEPPER SAUCE, see Pepper Sauce
Pepper, Beveled Corners, Rectangular, Aqua, 6 In. 5.00
Pettingill's Pure Horse Radish, Aqua, 6 In. 7.50
    FOOD, PICKLE, see Pickle
Preserve, Shaped, Blown Amber 8.00
Pure Concentrate Extract Of Lemon, Rectangular, Clear 2.00
Red Frant Borand Pure Vanilla Extract, Rectangular, Aqua 2.00
Royal Mint Sauce, Detroit, Bulbous, Emerald Green, 6 In. 7.00
Royce's Topical Fruit Flavors, Rectangular, Aqua, 4 1/4 In. 2.00
Sanford's Ginger, Full Label 2.50
Sauce Bottle, Lyneboro, Aqua 20.00
Shrewsbury Brand, E.C.Hazard & Co., Aqua, 9 In. ....*Color*
Sinclair's Pickled Pigsfeet, Clear, 6 1/2 In. ....*Color* 8.00
Soy Sauce, Teapot Shape, 5 1/2 In. 4.00
Stoddard, Clover-Shaped, Amber 400.00
Strittmatter, Honey Jar 37.50
Sunshine Brand Coffee, Embossed Sun & Lion, Zinc Lid, 1 Lb. 2.50
Target Ball, Embossed Shooter, Quilted, Amethyst 110.00
Towle Maple Syrup Company, BIMAL, 11 In., Quart 10.00
True Lemon Syrup, W.K.Lewis & Co., Boston, Aqua, Quart 29.50
True Lemon Syrup, W.K.Lewis & Co., Boston, OP, Aqua, Quart 59.50
Upham's Fresh Meat Cure, Pat.Feb.12, 1867, Aqua 10.00
W.M. & P., N.Y., Traphite Pontil 120.00
Wallace & Gregory Bros., Apple Juice Vinegar, Paducah, Ky., 3 In. 26.00
Western Spice Mills, Mustard, Barrel, Aqua, 5 In. 25.00
Winslows Syrup, Amber 17.00
Wm.Jones, Boston, Embossed Bear In Shield, Pint 12.00
Wm.K.Lewis & Co., 8-Panel, Embossed, Aqua, 1/2 Gallon 160.00
Wm.Shotten, Open Pontil 9.00
Wm.Underwood & Co., Boston, Embossed, 1/2 Pint 10.00

> *Fruit jars made of glass have been used in the United States since the 1850s. Over one thousand different jars have been found with varieties of closures, embossing, and colors. The date 1858 on many jars refers to a patent, not the age of the bottle. Be sure to look in this listing under any name or initial that appears on your jar. If not otherwise indicated the jar is clear glass, quart size. The numbers used in the entries in the form C-O refer to the book "Red Book of Fruit Jars Number 3" by Alice Creswick.*

FRUIT JAR, A R & S, Script, A.Kline Stopper, Aqua, Quart, C-94 .... 50.00
  A.& D.H.Chambers, Embossed, Wax Sealer, Aqua, 1/2 Gallon, C-582 .... 20.00
  A.& D.H.Chambers, Pittsburgh, Pa., Aqua, Quart, C-582 .... 13.00
  A.H.Bullard, New York, Safety Valve Type, 1/2 Gallon, C-532 .... 12.00
  A.Kline, Pat'd. Oct. 27, 1863, Aqua, 7 3/4 In. 10.00

A.Stone & Co., Cunningham & Co., Dark Aqua, C-2753 .... 1500.00
A.Stone & Co., Philadelphia, Tapered Stopper, Aqua, Pint 100.00
A, Base Embossed, Groove Ring, Wax Sealer, Aqua, Quart, C-1 .... 3.00
ABC, Ground Lip, Iron Yoke Clamp, Pint, C-4 .... 295.00
Acme, Shield, Stars, Stripes, Square, Pint, C-12 .... 2.50
Acme, Shield, Stars, Stripes, Square, Quart, C-12 .... 3.00
Adlams' Patent, Original Metal Lid, 1/2 Gallon, C-21 .... 30.00
Agnew & Co., Pittsburgh, Pat'd.Apl.For, 1887, 1/2 Gallon, C-44 .... 65.00
Airtight, Barrel, Iron Pontil, Aqua, Quart, C-51 .... 350.00
Airtight, Cunningham & Co., Deep Aqua, Quart 850.00
Airtight, Open Pontil, Quart 475.00
Alart & McGuire 24.00
All Right, Aqua, Paid Jan 28th 1868, Error, Quart, C-62 .... 85.00
All Right, Dudley Closure, Aqua, Quart 85.00
All Right, Pat'd Jan 26th 1868, Aqua, Quart, C-59 .... 65.00
All Right, Pat'd Jan 28th 1868, Aqua, Quart, C-61 .... 75.00 To 85.00
Allen's Patent, June 1871, Repro.Clamp, Quart, C-57 .... 150.00
Almy, Aqua, 6 In. ....*Color* 175.00
Amazon Swift Seal, Blue, Quart, C-69 .... 5.00
Amazon Swift Seal, In Circle, Blue, Pint, C-69 .... 7.00
American, Eagle, Flag, Light Green, 1/2 Gallon, C-73 .... 125.00
American, Porcelain-Lined, N.A.G.Co., Aqua, 1/2 Gallon, C-75 .... 19.00
American, The, N.A.G.Co., Porcelain-Lined, Aqua, 1/2 Gallon, C-75 .... 25.00
Anchor Hocking Mason, H Over Anchor, Pint, C-82 .... 1.00
Arthur's Patent Jan.3rd, 1855, Yellow Ware Pottery, Wax Sealer 295.00
Atlas E-Z Seal, Amber, Quart, C-114 .... 25.00 To 30.00
Atlas E-Z Seal, Aqua, Pint, C-116 .... 2.00
Atlas E-Z Seal, Aqua, Squatty, Pint 4.00
Atlas E-Z Seal, Aqua, 1/2 Gallon 6.00
Atlas E-Z Seal, Blue, 1/2 Pint 7.00
Atlas E-Z Seal, Cornflower Blue, Quart 20.00
Atlas E-Z Seal, Light Green, Quart 18.00
Atlas E-Z Seal, Light Olive, Pint 8.50
Atlas E-Z Seal, Milk Glass Lid, Wire Closure, Amber, 7 3/4 In. 20.00
Atlas E-Z Seal, Quart 30.00
Atlas E-Z Seal, 1/2 Gallon 3.00
Atlas E-Z Seal, 1/2 Pint 2.00
Atlas Good Luck, Lightning Seal, Short, 1/2 Pint, C-131 .... 10.00
Atlas Good Luck, With Clover, Quart, C-130 .... 3.00
Atlas Good Luck, 1/2 Gallon, C-129 .... 8.00
Atlas Good Luck, 1/2 Pint, C-130 .... 10.00
Atlas HA Mason, Quart, C-133 .... 1.00
Atlas HA Mason, Stippled Circle, 1/2 Gallon, C-134 .... 2.50
Atlas HA Mason, 1/2 Gallon, C-136 .... 2.50
Atlas HA Mason, 1/2 Pint, C-133 .... 2.00
Atlas HA Mason, 1/2 Pint, C-141 .... 2.00
Atlas Junior Mason, Metal Lid, Insert Embossed, 1/2 Pint, C-139 .... 7.00
Atlas Mason Improved, Aqua, Quart, C-146 .... 3.50
Atlas Mason Improved, Pat'd., Aqua, Quart, C-148 .... 3.50
Atlas Mason Improved, Pat'd., Olive Green, Pint, C-148 .... 16.00
Atlas Mason, Round, Beaded Neck, 1/2 Pint, C-40 .... 2.00
Atlas Mason's Patent Nov.30th, 1858, Aqua, 1/2 Gallon, C-151 .... 5.50
Atlas Mason's Patent, Apple Green, Pint, C-154 .... 15.00
Atlas Mason's Patent, Aqua, Quart, C-150 .... 3.00
Atlas Mason's Patent, No Hyphens, Aqua, Quart, C-151 .... 2.00
Atlas Mason's Patent, SCA, Pint, C-150 .... 4.00
Atlas Special Mason, Embossed, Widemouth, Green, Quart, C-157 .... 12.50
Atlas Strong Shoulder Mason, Apple & Olive Green, Pint, C-164 .... 18.00
Atlas Strong Shoulder Mason, Aqua, Quart, C-164 .... .75
Atlas Strong Shoulder Mason, Olive Green, Pint, C-164 .... 13.00
Atlas Strong Shoulder, Olive Green, Quart, C-164 .... 14.00
Atlas Strong Shoulder, Olive Green, Quart, C-165 .... 23.00

Atlas Wholefruit Jar, Widemouth, Pint, C-170	4.00
Atlas Wholefruit Jar, Widemouth, Quart, C-170	3.00
Atlas Wholefruit, Glass Lid, Wire Bail, Pint, C-171	2.00
Automatic Sealer, The, Clayton Bottle Wks., N.J., Aqua, Qt., C-177	85.00
B B G M Co., Monogram, Aqua, Quart, C-194	27.00
B B G M Co., Monogram, 1/2 Gallon, C-195	29.50
B.B.Wilcox, Pat'd March 26th 1867, Aqua, Quart, C-3000	65.00
Baker Bros.& Co., Baltimore, Md., No Base, Aqua, 7 1/4 In., C-186	20.00
Baker Bros., Wax Sealer, Baltimore, 1/2 Gallon, C-186	22.00
Ball Eclipse, Quart, C-201	3.00
Ball Eclipse, Widemouth, Glass Lid, Wire Bail, 1/2 Gallon, C-202	1.75
Ball Eclipse, Widemouth, Pint, C-202	1.50
Ball Eclipse, Widemouth, Quart, C-202	3.00
Ball Freezer Jar, Pint, C-364	1.00
Ball Ideal, Beaded Neck, Aqua, 1/2 Pint, C-217	20.00
Ball Ideal, Bicentennial, Blue, 1/2 Pint, C-241	6.00
Ball Ideal, Centennial Jar On Reverse, Aqua, Quart	2.50
Ball Ideal, Glass Lid, Wire Bail, Aqua, Quart, C-216	.95
Ball Ideal, Glass Lid, Wire Bail, Quart, C-216	.75
Ball Ideal, Lightning Closure, 1/2 Pint, C-216	3.00
Ball Ideal, Made In U.S.A., Quart, C-212	.95
Ball Ideal, Made In Usa, Aqua, 1/2 Gallon, C-211	3.00
Ball Ideal, New Centennial, Aqua, 1/2 Pint	5.00
Ball Ideal, Pat'd.July 14, 1908, Lid, Bail, Aqua, 1/2 Gal., C-222	5.00
Ball Ideal, Pat'd.July 14, 1908, Lid, Bail, Quart, C-223	2.00
Ball Ideal, Pat'd.July 14, 1908, Lid, Wire Bail, Aqua, Qt., C-222	2.50
Ball Ideal, Pat'd.July 14, 1908, Pint, C-223	2.50
Ball Ideal, Round, B In Circle, Pint, C-208	1.50
Ball Ideal, Square, Glass Lid, Bail, Quart, C-212	.95
Ball Ideal, Square, Pint, C-212	2.00
Ball Improved, Aqua, Quart, C-250	1.00
Ball Improved, GIZB, Aqua, Pint	4.00
Ball Improved, Tapered Shoulders, Aqua, Quart, C-250	3.00
Ball Improved, Zinc Lid, Aqua, Quart	5.00
Ball Improved, 3 L Loop, Aqua, Pint, C-248	4.00
Ball Improved, 3 L Loop, Aqua, Quart, C-248	6.00
Ball Mason, Amber Streaks, Olive Green	35.00
Ball Mason, Aqua, Quart	1.00 To 1.50
Ball Mason, Bead Seal, Olive Green, 1/2 Gallon	15.00
Ball Mason, Glass Lid, Wire Bail, Patent 1908, Blue, 1/2 Pint	25.00
Ball Mason, Olive Green, Quart	10.00
Ball Mason, 3 L Loop, Aqua, 1/2 Gallon, C-297	20.00
Ball Mason's Patent Nov.30th, 1858, Aqua, Quart, C-316	3.00
Ball Mason's Patent Nov.30th, 1858, Script, Aqua, 1/2 Gallon	3.50
Ball Mason's Patent 1858, Aqua, Quart, C-306	4.00
Ball Mason's Patent 1858, Ball In Script, Aqua, Pint	2.50
Ball Mason's Patent 1858, Script, Underlined, Aqua, 1/2 Gallon	6.00
Ball Mason's Patent 1858, 3 L Ball Underline, Aqua, Quart	3.00
Ball Mason's Patent, Arched, Clear, Quart	5.00
Ball Mason's Patent, Arched, 1/2 Gallon	5.00
Ball Perfect Mason, Amber, Quart, C-345	15.00
Ball Perfect Mason, Amber, 1/2 Gallon, C-345	12.00 To 23.00
Ball Perfect Mason, Aqua, Pint, C-339	.50
Ball Perfect Mason, Aqua, 1/2 Pint, C-339	18.00 To 20.00
Ball Perfect Mason, Ball Not Underlined, 1/2 Pint, C-342	2.00
Ball Perfect Mason, Ball Over Boyd, Aqua, Quart, C-335	3.00
Ball Perfect Mason, Block Print, Aqua, Quart	10.00
Ball Perfect Mason, Green, Quart, C-339	25.00 To 27.00
Ball Perfect Mason, Gripper Ribs On Sides, Yellow Green, Pint	20.00
Ball Perfect Mason, Light Olive Green, Quart, C-339	18.00
Ball Perfect Mason, Olive Amber, 1/2 Gallon, C-399	41.00
Ball Perfect Mason, Olive Green, Pint, C-339	45.00
Ball Perfect Mason, Squat, 1/2 Gallon	20.00

Ball Perfect Mason, Yellow Amber, Pint, C-339	65.00
Ball Perfect Mason, 1/2 Gallon, C-332	3.50
Ball Perfection, SCA, 1/2 Pint, C-329	35.00
Ball Sanitary Sure Seal, Bead Neck Lightning, Aqua, Qt., C-367	4.00
Ball Sanitary Sure Seal, Dimple Neck, Aqua, Quart, C	4.00 To 5.00
Ball Special Mason, Aqua, Quart	3.50
Ball Square Mason, Pint, C-383	4.00
Ball Standard, Wax Seal, Aqua, Quart, C-386	2.00
Ball Standard, Wax Sealer, Aqua, 1/2 Gallon, C-386	3.00
Ball Standard, Wax Sealer, Original Lid, Aqua, 1/2 Gallon, C-386	8.00
Ball Standard, 3 L Loop, Aqua, 1/2 Gallon, C-386	2.00
Ball, The, Mason, Aqua, Quart	4.00
Ball, The, Mason, Aqua, 1/2 Gallon	6.00
Ball, The, Mason's Patent Nov.30th, 1858, Aqua, Quart	4.00
Baltimore Glass Works, Laid-On Ring, Aqua, Quart, C-399	145.00
Banner, Patent 1864, Aqua, 1/2 Gallon, C-403	58.00
Banner, Widemouth, Trademark, Aqua, Pint, C-408	4.50
BBGM Co., Bicentennial Repro., Amber, Quart, C-197	20.00
Beaver, Animal Embossed On Side, Aqua, Imperial Quart, C-424	12.50
Beaver, Clear, Imperial Pint, C-425	45.00
Beaver, Embossed, Amber, Imperial Quart, C-424	550.00
Beaver, Facing Right, Stippled Tail, Green, Imperial Quart, C-425	32.00
Beaver, Midget, C-424	48.00
Bee, Aqua, Quart, C-429	105.00 To 125.00
Beech Nut Trade Mark, Pat.In U.S.Oct.23, 1900, Pint, C-430	5.00
Beech Nut Trade Mark, Pint, C-431	4.00
Bennett's No.1, Laid-On Ring, Aqua, Quart, C-443	185.00
Berry, Vertical Flutes, Pontil, Deep Greenish Aqua, 8 1/4 In.	120.00
Best Fruit Keeper, The, Aqua, Quart, C-460	27.00 To 35.00
Best, D In Diamond, Quart, C-456	5.50
Best, Widemouth, Amber, Quart, C-453	200.00 To 350.00
Best, Widemouth, Aqua, Quart, C-453	35.00
Blown, Teal Green, Applied Wax Seal Rim, 6 In.	110.00
Bodine & Bros., Original Glass Lid, Aqua, Quart	795.00
Boldt Mason, Aqua, Quart, C-480	15.00
Boldt Mason, Aqua, 1/2 Gallon, C-480	18.00 To 20.00
Bostwick Perfect Sealer, Clear, Pint, C-487	Color 45.00
Bowers Three Thistles, Glass Lid, Metal Band, Amber, Quart, C-488	20.00
Boyd Perfect Mason, Aqua, Pint, C-500	2.50
Boyd Perfect Mason, Aqua, Quart, C-500	3.00
Boyd Perfect Mason, Light Green, Quart, C-500	3.00
Boyds Perfect Mason, Aqua, Quart, C-501	2.00
Boyds Perfect Mason, Aqua, 1/2 Gallon, C-501	3.00
Brighton, Embossed, Original Clamp, Aqua, Quart, C-512	55.00
Brockway Clear Vu Mason, Quart, C-514	2.00
FRUIT JAR, C. F. J. CO., see Fruit Jar, Mason's C. F. J. Co.	
C.F.Spencer's Patent, Repro Lid, Aqua, Quart, C-2682	65.00
C.F.Spencer's Patent, Rochester, N.Y., Aqua, 1/2 Gal., C-2682	55.00
C.K.Halle & Co., Cleveland, Kline Stopper, Aqua, Quart, C-1176	195.00
Calloway's Everlasting Jar, Pottery	30.00
Canadian Jewel, Made In Canada, Quart, C-1331	2.50
Candy Bros.Mfg, Co., St.Louis, 1/2 Gallon, C-559	12.00
Candy Products Co., Springfield, Mass., Original Label, 2 Quart	15.00
Canton Domestic Jar, 1/2 Gallon, C-566	45.00 To 65.00
Canton Domestic, Quart, C-565	60.00
Canton Domestic, Repro Clamp, Quart, C-565	47.00
Canton Electric, Clear Lid, Cobalt Blue, C-586	2500.00
Canton, The, Screw Lid, 1/2 Gallon, C-561	90.00
Champion Syrup And Refining Co., Aqua, Quart, C-584	20.00
Champion, Patent 1869, Original Clamp, Quart, C-583	145.00
Champion, The, Pat.Aug.31, 1861, Aqua, Quart, C-583	70.00 To 125.00
Chattanooga Mason, 1/2 Gallon, C-587	6.00
Chef, Berdan & Co., Beaded Neck, Pint, C-590	5.00

Fruit Jar, Cohansey, Aqua, Pint

Chef, Berdan & Co., Beaded Neck, Quart, C-590 .... 5.00
Chef, Berdan & Co., Toledo, Old Style Seal, Pint, C-589 .... 8.00
Clark's Peerless, Aqua, Pint, C-605 .... 6.75
Clark's Peerless, Aqua, 1/2 Gallon, C-605 .... 10.00
Clark's Peerless, Ground Lip, Aqua, Quart, C-605 .... 7.00 To 10.00
Clark's Peerless, Pint, C-605 .... 6.50
Clark's Peerless, Smooth Lip, Aqua, Quart, C-606 .... 8.00
Clarke And White, Black, Pint, C-607 .... 500.00
Clarke Fruit Jar Co., Cleveland, Closure, Aqua, Quart, C-603 .... 50.00
Clarke, Cleveland, Ohio, Aqua, Quart, C-603 .... 40.00 To 55.00
Clarke's, Cam Lever 1350.00
Cleveland Fruit Juice Co., Cleveland, Ohio, 1/2 Gallon, C-608 .... 15.00
Climax Trademark Registered, In Circle, Blue, Quart, C-613 .... 5.00
Climax, Trademark Registered, Aqua, Quart, C-610 .... 5.00
Climax, Trademark Registered, Blue, Pint, C-611 .... 5.00
Clyde, The, Embossed In Script, Quart, C-619 .... 7.00
Clyde, The, Ground Lip, Pint, C-619 .... 7.00
Cohansey Glass Mfg.Co., Barrel, 1 1/2 Quart, C-633 .... 130.00
Cohansey Glass Mfg.Co., Philadelphia, Honey Amber, Pint, C-626 .... 15.00
Cohansey Glass, Lorillard, Wire Closure, Amber, 6 1/2 In. 12.50
Cohansey, Aqua, Pint .... *Illus* 30.00
Cohansey, Aqua, Pint, C-628 .... 20.00
Cohansey, Aqua, Quart, C-628 .... 13.00 To 18.00
Cohansey, Aqua, 1/2 Gallon .... 12.00 To 20.00
Cohansey, Barrel, Aqua, Quart, C-633 .... 98.00
Cohansey, May 20 77, Barrel Shape, Aqua, Quart, C-633 .... *Illus* 100.00

Fruit Jar, Cohansey, May 20 77, Barrel
Shape, Aqua, Quart, C-633

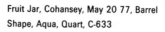

Figural, Mr. Pickwick, 9 In.

Flask, Clock, Milk Glass, 4½ In.

Figural, Chicken, 3-
Mold, Patented, 9½ In.

Ink, Mr. & Mrs. Carters, Pat.
Jan. 6, 1914, Germany,
C-1619

Flask, Lady Pictured Under Glass, 5½ In.

Seltzer, Larvex, Cobalt Blue, 7½ In.

Barber, Satin Glass, Pink, 7½ In., Pair

Snuff, Jar, Lorillard's,
Brown, 6½ In.

Food, Shrewsbury Brand,
E. C. Hazard & Co., Aqua,
9 In.

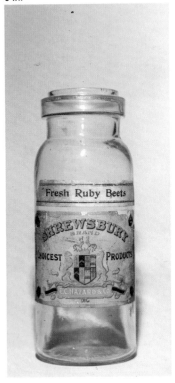

Medicine, Ingram's White
Pine Cough Balsam,
Aqua, 8 In.

**Whiskey, Hotchkiss,
Fenner, & Bennett, Dew Drop, 8½ In.**

**Food, Sinclair's Pickled Pigsfeet,
Clear, 6½ In.**

**Whiskey, Glass Label,
Clear, 6 In.**

**Food, Lemon Extract,
Open Pontil, 5½ In.**

**Wine, Zeller
Schwarze Katz,
Green, 13 In.**

**Household, C. C.
Parsons Ammonia,
Aqua, 10 In.**

Avon, California Perfume
Company, Face Lotion, Box

Figural, Beefeater, Yeoman,
Ceramic; Gin, Burroughs,
Paper Label

Figural, World's Fair,
1939, Milk Glass

Planters Peanut Jars

Bottles, G. W. Meredith Co., East Liverpool, Ohio

Pickle Jars

Flaccus Jars

Wheaton Commemorative, Democrat, 1972, Shriver, McGovern *(top row)*
Democrat, 1972, Eagleton, McGovern *(bottom row, first and third bottles)*
Republican, 1972 *(bottom row, center)*

Conserve, Double Canner, Copper Bottom, 1/2 Gallon 25.00
Conserve, Ground Lip, Pint, C-652 .... 6.00
Conserve, Ground Lip, Quart, C-652 .... 8.00
Corona, Made In Canada, Smooth Lip, Quart, C-655 .... 2.50 To 3.00
Crown Cordial & Extract Co., 1/2 Gallon, C-671 .... 10.00
Crown Mason, 1/2 Gallon, C-704 .... 1.00
Crown, Imperial, Aqua, Quart, C-694 .... 4.00
Crown, Imperial, 1/2 Pint, C-694 .... 4.00
Crown, T.Eaton Co.Limited, The, On Reverse, Midget, C-693 .... 75.00
Crown, With Picture, Aqua, Quart, C-679 .... 1.50
Crown, With Picture, Midget, C-676 .... 9.50
Crystal Jar, Pat., Twin Post Lid, Lavender, 1/2 Gal., C-706 .... 45.00
Crystal Jar, Twin Post Lid, Midget, C-706 .... 65.00
Crystal, Patent Dec.17, 1878, On Lid, Midget, C-709 .... 75.00
Cum Hoc Signo Cognitus Est, 1 1/2 In.Mouth Opening, Pint 16.00
Cunningham & Co., Pittsburgh, Iron Pontil, Quart, C-721 .... 95.00
Cunningham & Co., Pittsburgh, Pa., Aqua, Quart, C-722 .... 125.00
Cunningham & Ihmsen, Patent, 3 Mold, Amber, Quart, C-726 .... 10.00
Cunningham & Ihmsen, Pittsburgh, Aqua, 1/2 Gallon, C-727 .... 20.00
Curtis & Moore, Trademark, Boston, Mass., 1/2 Gallon, C-733 .... 20.00
D.C.G.Co., On Base, Wax Sealer, Aqua, Quart 12.00
Daisy, Clear, Quart 8.00
Daisy, In Circle, Glass Lid, Bale, Light SCA, Pint, C-742 .... 12.00
Daisy, The, F.E.Ward & Co., Aqua, Pint, C-744 .... 6.00 To 12.00
Daisy, The, 1/2 Gallon 95.00
Daisy, 1 Line, Pint, C-741 .... 7.00
Dandy, The, Trademark, Amber, C-751 .... 80.00
Dandy, The, Trademark, C-751 .... 25.00
Defiance Baking Powder, Around Edge Base, Aqua, Pint 4.00
Dexter Improved, Circle Of Fruits, 1/2 Gallon, C-775 .... 55.00
Dexter, Ground Lip, C-772 .... 6.00
Dexter, Wreath Of Fruit, Midget, C-775 .... 325.00
Diamond Fruit Jar Improved Trademark, On Base, Pint, C-778 .... 4.00
Diamond Fruit Jar Improved Trademark, On Base, Quart, C-778 .... 3.00
Dictator D, Pat.D.I.Holcomb, Aqua, Quart, C-786 .... 50.00 To 62.00
Dictator, Pat.D.I.Holcomb, Aqua, 1/2 Gallon, C-786 .... 80.00
Dillon G Co., Fairmont, Ind., Wax Sealer, Aqua, 1/2 Gallon, C-790 .... 12.00
Doolittle, Embossed, Aqua, 1/2 Gallon, C-809 .... 20.00
Doolittle, Embossed, Lid Embossed & Dated 1900, Quart, C-809 .... 32.00
Doolittle, Script, Wire Ear Clamps, Clear, Pint, C-811 .... 30.00
Double Safety, Old Style Seal, Pint, C-822 .... 4.00
Double Safety, Smalley, Kivlan & Onthank, Pint, C-817 .... 3.00
Double Safety, Smalley, Kivlan & Onthank, Quart, C-817 .... 3.00
Drey Improved Everseal, Lightning Seal, Pint, C-837 .... 1.25
Drey Improved Everseal, Quart, C-837 .... 1.25
Drey Mason, Aqua, Quart, C-839 .... 1.00
Drey Mason, Beaded Neck Seal, Quart, C-840 .... .75
Drey Mason, 1/2 Gallon, C-839 .... 1.00
Drey Pat'd.1920 Improved Everseal, Pint, C-834 .... 5.00
Drey Pat'd.1920 Improved Everseal, Quart, C-834 .... 2.00
Drey Perfect Mason, Aqua, Quart, C-842 .... 18.00
Drey Perfect Mason, Round, Pint, C-842 .... 1.00
Drey Perfect Mason, 1/2 Gallon, C-842 .... 1.00
Drey Perfect Mason, 1/2 Pint, C-842 .... 3.00 To 6.00
Drey Square Mason, Carpenter's Square, Quart, C-847 .... 3.00
Drey Square Mason, Pint, C-848 .... 3.00
Drey Square Mason, 1/2 Gallon, C-848 .... 2.00
Eagle, Pint, C-871 .... 195.00
East India Pickles, 1894 On Base, Light Green, Quart, C-876 .... 8.00
Easy Vacuum Jar, Trademark, Aqua, 1/2 Gallon, C-878 .... 30.00
Eclipse, The, Ground Lip, Aqua, 1/2 Gallon, C-885 .... 90.00
Economy Sealer, Ghosted Lettering, Aqua, Quart, C-904 .... 15.00
Economy Trademark, Lid & Clip, Clear, Pint, C-894 .... 3.00

Fruit Jar, Electric, Aqua, Pint

Economy Trademark, Lid & Clip, Clear, 1/2 Gallon, C-894	3.00
Economy Trademark, Lid & Clip, Underlined, Quart, C-895	2.50
Economy, Pat'd Sept 15th 1885, Aqua, C-906	17.00
Economy, Underlined, Closed End, Quart, C-887	3.00
Eddy & Eddy Pure Food Products, Glass Stopper, 1/2 Pint, C-909	20.00
EGCO, Imperial, Aqua, Quart, C-962	20.00
EGCO, Imperial, Midget, C-962	27.50
EGCO, Imperial, Zinc Ring, Aqua, 6 In.	12.50
Electric Trademark, In Circle, Aqua, Pint, C-917	7.00
Electric, Aqua, Pint	*Illus* 145.00
Electric, Fruit Jar, Globe, Aqua, Original Clamp, Pint, C-922	125.00
Electric, Fruit Jar, Globe, Aqua, 1/2 Gallon, C-922	65.00 To 70.00
Electric, Fruit Jar, World Globe, Aqua, Quart, C-922	50.00 To 65.00
Electric, In Circle, Aqua, Pint, C-915	10.00
Empire, Aqua, 1/2 Gallon, C-924	425.00
Empire, In Cross, Old Style Seal, 1/2 Pint, C-925	10.00
Empire, The, Pat. Feb 13 1866, Aqua, 1/2 Gallon, C-927	65.00
Empire, Within Cross, Quart, C-925	10.00
Eureka 1, Pat'd.Dec.27, 1864, Aqua, Quart, C-948	65.00
Eureka 3, Pat'd.Dec.27th, 1864, 1/2 Gallon, C-948	60.00
Eureka 4, Pat.Dec.27th, 1864, Aqua, Quart, C-948	37.50 To 40.00
Eureka 5, Dec.27th, 1864, Repro Lid, Quart, C-948	60.00
Everlasting, Aqua, Pint, C-953	20.00
Everlasting, Aqua, Quart, C-953	20.00
Excelsior Improved, Aqua, Quart, C-959	40.00
Excelsior, Aqua, 1/2 Gallon, C-958	50.00
Exwaco, On Base, Repro, Lid & Band, Amber, Pint, C-965	27.00
Exwaco, On Base, Repro, Lid & Band, Green, Pint, C-965	25.00
F A & Co., Pontil, Aqua, Pint, C-968	175.00
F A & Co., Pontil, Aqua, Quart, C-968	100.00 To 150.00
F. & J.Bodine, Philadelphia, Aqua, 1/2 Quart, C-474	100.00
F. & J.McKee, Pittsburgh, Pa., Pontil, 1 1/2 Quart, C-2160	450.00
F. & S., Aqua, Quart, C-1043	14.00
F.C.G. Co., Amber, 1/2 Gallon	120.00
F.C.G. Co., Deep Apple, Wax Sealer, 1/2 Gallon	80.00
F.C.G. Co., On Base, Lime Green, 1/2 Gallon, C-990	40.00
F.C.G. Co., On Base, Wax Sealer, Aqua, Quart, C-988	18.00
F.C.G. Co., On Base, Wax Sealer, Dark Amber, 1/2 Gallon, C-990	120.00
F.C.G. Co., Wax Sealer, Cobalt Blue, 1/2 Gallon	3500.00
F.G.F.C.G. Co., On Base, Wax Sealer, Aqua, Quart, C-992	15.00
F.H.G.W., Wax Sealer, Aqua, Quart, C-1000	7.50
F.H.G.W.No.4, On Base, Aqua, 1/2 Gallon	15.00
Federal, Aqua, 1/2 Gallon, C-996	100.00
Federal, Flag, Light Green, Quart, C-996	140.00
Flaccus Bros., Amber, Pint	350.00

Flaccus Bros., Green, Pint	475.00
Flaccus Bros., Mustard Fruit Jar, Repro Lid & Band, Pint, C-1011	90.00
Flaccus Bros., Table Delicacies, Embossed, SCA, 1/2 Pint, C-1010	40.00
Flaccus Bros.Steershead, C-1014	50.00
Flaccus Bros.Steershead, Glass Screw Lid	32.00 To 50.00
Flaccus Bros.Steershead, Pint, C-1013	40.00
Flaccus Bros.Steershead, Repro Plastic Lid, Amber, Pint, C-1014	165.00
Flaccus Bros.Steershead, Yellow, Pint	280.00
Flaccus Bros.Table Delicacies, 1/2 Pint, C-1008	25.00
Flaccus Type, Amber, Pint, C-3087	12.00
FRUIT JAR, FOSTER, see Fruit Jar, Sealfast, Foster	
Franklin Dexter, Aqua, Quart, C-1034	20.00 To 35.00
Franklin, Aqua, 1/2 Gallon, C-1033	28.00
Fruit Keeper, GCCO, Original Clamp, Aqua, Quart, C-1042	48.00
Fruit Keeper, GCCO, Original Metal, Aqua, Pint, C-1042	48.00
G J Co., Aqua, Pint, C-1109	35.00
G J Co., Aqua, Quart, C-1109	22.00
G J Co., Aqua, 1/2 Gallon, C-1109	25.00
Gem, Aqua, Midget, C-1053	29.00
Gem, Cross, Midget, C-1064	24.00
Gem, The, Aqua, Quart, C-1066	5.00 To 10.00
Gem, The, CFJ Monogram, Aqua, Quart, C-1078	6.50
Gem, The, Gallon	425.00
Gem, The, On 2 Lines, H.G.W.Monogram On Reverse, Aqua, 1/2 Gallon	17.00
Genuine Boyds Mason, Aqua, Quart, C-496	4.00
Genuine Boyds Mason, Green, Quart, C-496	3.00
Genuine Boyds Mason, Light Green, 1/2 Gallon, C-497	4.00
Genuine Mason, Aqua, Pint, C-1103	6.00
Geo.D.Brown & Co., Quart, C-525	25.00 To 28.00
Gilberds Improved, Aqua, Quart, C-1108	90.00
Gilberds Improved, Star, Aqua, Pint, C-1108	350.00
Gilberds Jar, Star, Aqua, 1/2 Gallon, C-1107	190.00
Gilberds Jar, Star, Aqua, Quart, C-407	20.00
FRUIT JAR, GILCHRIST, see Fruit Jar, G J Co.	
Glassboro Improved 2, Aqua, Quart, C-1117	12.00
Glassboro Improved, Quart, C-1115	22.00
Glenshaw G Mason, Pint, C-1122	4.00
Glenshaw G Mason, Zinc Lid, Quart, C-1122	4.00
Globe, Amber, Pint, C-1123	72.00 To 75.00
Globe, Amber, Quart, C-1123	40.00
Globe, Amber, 1/2 Gallon, C-1123	20.00 To 65.00
Globe, Aqua, Pint, C-1123	9.00 To 18.00
Globe, Aqua, Quart, C-1123	15.00
Globe, Aqua, 1/2 Gallon, C-1123	14.00 To 18.00
Globe, Dark Amber, 1/2 Gallon, C-1123	49.00
Globe, Light Amber, 1/2 Gallon, C-1123	55.00
Globe, Orange Amber, 1/2 Gallon, C-1123	65.00
Globe, Pint, C-1123	80.00
Globe, Red, Quart, C-1123	67.00
Globe, Small Lettering, Honey Amber, Pint	80.00
Globe, Widemouth, Aqua, Quart, C-1124	20.00
Globe, Widemouth, No Closure, Aqua, Quart, C-1124	17.00
Glocker, Aqua, Quart, C-1126	10.00
Golden State Mason, A Has No Cross, Pint	5.00
Golden State Masons, SCA, Pint, C-1132	2.50 To 10.00
Golden State Trade, Pat.Dec.20th, 1910, SCA, Pint, C-1133	12.00
Golden State Trade, Pat.Dec.20th, 1910, 1/2 Gallon, C-1133	12.00
Golden State, Amethyst, Pint, C-1133	12.00
Golden State, SCA, Quart, C-1133	5.00
Good House Keepers, Glass Lid, Screw Band, Quart, C-1144	2.00
Gray & Hemingray, Original Lid, Aqua, 1/2 Gallon	115.00
Greek Key Design, Glass Lid, Wire & Tin Closure, Aqua, 2 Gallon	20.00
Green Mountain, C.A.Co., Aqua, Quart, C-1151	15.00

Griffen's Patent, Iron Clamp & Glass Top, Quart, C-1155 .... 125.00
H Over A, On Base, Safety Valve Closure, Label, Quart 8.00
H.K.Mulford & Co. Chemists Philadelphia, Amber, 22 Oz., C-2215 .... 16.00
H.W.Pettit, Salem, N.J., Aqua, Quart, C-2363 .... 10.00
H.W.Pettit, Westville, Aqua, 1/2 Pint, C-2362 .... 22.00
H.W.Pettit, Westville, N.J., Base, Aqua, Quart, C-2362 .... 6.00 To 15.00
Hahne & Co., Newark, N.J., Aqua, Quart, C-1163 .... 35.00
Haines Combination, Aqua, Quart, C-1168 .... 17.00
Haines, March 1, 1870, Aqua, 7 In. ....*Illus* 80.00
Hamilton No.3 Glassworks, Aqua, 1/2 Gallon, C-1196 .... 185.00 To 195.00
Hamilton, Clear, Quart, C-1188 .... 60.00
Handy Jar, Original Dated Closure, Handle, Cork, Quart, C-1205 .... 35.00
Hansee's Palace Home, Pint, C-1206 .... 65.00
Hansee's Palace Home, Quart, C-1206 .... 40.00
Hartell's, Aqua, Quart, C-1211 .... 55.00
Hartell's, Black, Quart, C-1211 .... 1350.00
Hartell's, Light Green, Pint, C-1211 .... 150.00
Hartell's, Patented Oct.19, 1858, Deep Amethyst, 7 In., C-1211 .... 170.00
Harvest Mason, Quart, C-1215 .... 4.00
Haserot, The, Company, Cleveland, Mason Patent, Aqua, Quart, C-1216 .... 9.00
Hazel HA Preserve Jar, Pint, C-1231 .... 4.00
Helme's Railroad Mills, Amber, Snuff, C-1235 .... 14.00
     FRUIT JAR, HERO CROSS, see Fruit Jar, Mason's Cross
Hero, Lettered Cross, Widemouth, Wire Bail, Quart, C-1240 .... 25.00
Heroine, The, 3-Piece Glass & Tin Closure, Aqua, Quart, C-1248 .... 35.00
Holman's Baking Powder, Buffalo, N.Y., Greenish Aqua, Pint 150.00
Home Pak Mason, Quart, C-1262 .... 3.00
Honest Mason Jar Pat.1858, Amethyst Tint, Quart, C-1264 .... 10.00
Honest Mason Pat.1858, Clear, Pint, C-1264 .... 14.00
Hormel Good Food, Pint, C-1270 .... 1.00
Howe Jar, The, Scranton, Pa., Aqua, Quart, C-1274 .... 37.00
I.G.Co., On Base, Midget, Aqua, C-1286 .... 55.00
Ideal, The, 1/2 Gallon, C-1280 .... 15.00
Imperial Patented April 20th, 1886, On Lid, Aqua, Quart, C-1293 .... 115.00
Imperial Trademark, Arm, Mace, Aqua, Pint, C-1291 .... 800.00
Imperial Trademark, Arm, Mace, Aqua, Quart, C-1291 .... 175.00
Imperial, Embossed Delicious Crushed Fruits, 1/2 Gallon 55.00
Improved Gem, Canadian, Quart, C-1301 .... 1.00
Improved Jam, L.G.Co., Aqua, Pint, C-1302 .... 80.00
Improved Jewel, Made In Canada, Quart, C-1332 .... 1.50
Independent, Pat Oct 24 1882, Midget, C-1310 .... 29.00
Iron Pontil, Cork Seat, Deep Aqua, Quart, 9 1/4 In. 88.00

Fruit Jar, Haines, March 1,
1870, Aqua, 7 In.

J.& B., Pat'd.June 14th, 1898, Aqua, Pint, C-1321 .... 42.00 To 65.00
J.& B., Pat'd.June 14th, 1898, Quart, C-1321 .... 35.00
J.D.Willoughby, 2 3/8, Pat.Jan.4, 1859, 1/2 Gallon, C-3012 .... 40.00
J.J.Squire, Patd Octr 18th 1864, Aqua, Quart, C-2693 .... 500.00
J.P.Smith Son & Co. Pittsburgh, Wax Seal, Aqua, 7 3/4 In., C-2670 .... 25.00
Jar Salt Detroit Salt Co., Mason's Pat., Aqua, Quart, C-1323 .... 25.00
Jeanette J, In Square, Mason Home Packer, Quart, C-1324 .... 5.00
Jos.Middleby Jr., Inc., 1/2 Gallon, C-2175 .... 8.00
Joseph Campbell, JC Mono., Aqua, Quart 40.00
Joshua Wright, Aqua, 1/2 Gallon, C-3036 .... 450.00
Jumbo Peanut Butter, Good Enuf For Me On Base, Pint, C-1347 .... 3.00
K.Y.G.W., On Base, Wax Sealer, Aqua, 1/2 Gallon, C-1446 .... 15.00
Keene, Freeblown, Open Pontil 300.00
Kerr Economy Trademark, Chicago, Pale Green, Pint, C-1364 .... 7.50
Kerr Economy Trademark, Green, Pint, C-1366 .... 7.50
Kerr Mason, 65th Anniversary, Amber, Quart, C-1387 .... 10.00
Kerr Self Sealing Mason, Embossed Insert, Amber, Quart 10.00
Kerr Self Sealing Mason, Trademark, 1/2 Pint, C-1385 .... 3.00
Kerr Self Sealing Mason, 1615 Base, Quart, C-1377 .... 1.00
Kerr Self Sealing, Mason, 1/2 Pint, C-1379 .... 2.00
Kerr, Bicentennial, Bell Shape, Cobalt Blue, Quart, C-1389 .... 25.00
Kerr, Bicentennial, Bell Shape, Red, Quart, C-1389 .... 25.00
Kerr, Bicentennial, Bell Shape, White, Quart, C-1389 .... 25.00
Kerr, 65th Anniversary, Blue Streaked, Quart, C-1387 .... 12.50
Keystone, Circled Over Mason, Aqua 6.00
Keystone, Mason's Patent Nov.30th, 1858, Aqua, 1/2 Gallon, C-1961 .... 6.00
Keystone, Trademark Registered, Pint, C-1392 .... 10.00
Keystone, Trademark Registered, Quart, C-1392 .... 6.00
King, King's Head, Aqua, Quart, C-1416 .... 6.50
King, On Banner Below Crown, Quart, C-1414 .... 12.00
Kinsella 1874 True Mason, Quart, C-1421 .... 4.00
Kline, Applied Collar, Folded Rim, Iron Pontil, Aqua, 9 1/2 In. 40.00
Kline's Patent Oct.27 '63, On Stopper, 1/2 Gallon, C-1422 .... 100.00
Knowlton Vacuum, Star, Aqua, Pint .... *Illus* 25.00
Knowlton Vacuum, Star, Aqua, Quart, C-1432 .... 10.00 To 20.00
Knox Genuine Mason, Pint, C-1434 .... 3.50
Knox K Mason, Pint, C-1435 .... 3.00
Knox K Mason, Quart, C-1435 .... 2.00
Knox K Mason, Zinc Lid, 1/2 Pint, C-1435 .... 5.00
Knox Mason, Closure Churn, Tulsa, Handle, 1/2 Gallon, C-1435 .... 18.00
Koenig 5 Cent, Quart, C-1439 .... 5.00
L & S, On Base, Quart, C-1563 .... 2.00

Fruit Jar, Knowlton Vacuum, Star, Aqua, Pint

L & W, Dictator, Aqua, Quart 15.00
L & W, Embossed, 1/2 Gallon, C-1523 .... 35.00
L & W, Pet, C-1524 .... 40.00
L & W's X L, Ghosted Except W, Wax Sealer, Aqua, Quart, C-1532 .... 17.00
L & W's X L, Swirled Glass, Aqua, Quart, C-1531 .... 75.00
L G Co., Wax Sealer, Original Tin Lid, Aqua, 1/2 Gallon, C-1482 .... 15.00
L G Co., Yellow Green, 1/2 Gallon, C-1482 .... 55.00 To 60.00
L.& W., Kline Stopper, Large Bubbles, Aqua, Quart, C-1528 .... 65.00
Lafayette, Aqua, Quart, C-1452 .... 75.00 To 85.00
Lafayette, Clear, Pint, C-1450 .... 300.00
Lafayette, In Script, Aqua, 1/2 Gallon, C-1452 .... 95.00
Lamb Mason, Round, Quart, C-1455 .... 2.00
Lamb Mason, Round, 1/2 Gallon, C-1455 .... 3.00
Lamb Mason, Square, Quart 3.00
Leader, Amber, Quart ....*Color* 145.00
Leader, The, Amber, Pint, C-1466 .... 275.00
Leader, The, Amber, 1/2 Gallon, C-1465 .... 165.00
Leader, The, On 1 Line, Amber, Pint, C-1465 .... 300.00
Leader, The, On 2 Lines, Repro Wire, Amber, Quart, C-1466 .... 90.00
Leader, The, On 2 Lines, Repro Wire, Aqua, Quart, C-1466 .... 40.00
Legrand Ideal Vacuum Jar, Quart, C-1972 .... 95.00 To 105.00
Leotric, Aqua, Pint, C-1473 .... 9.00
Lightning Trademark Putnam, On Base, Amber, 1/2 Pint 600.00
Lightning Trademark, Amber, Quart, C-1498 .... 25.00 To 39.50
Lightning Trademark, Amber, 1/2 Gallon, C-1491 .... 30.00
Lightning Trademark, Amber, 1/2 Gallon, C-1498 .... 35.00 To 39.00
Lightning Trademark, Aqua, Pint, C-1496 .... 5.00
Lightning Trademark, Aqua, Quart, C-1496 .... 5.00
Lightning Trademark, Closure, Citron, Quart, C-1499 .... 55.00
Lightning Trademark, Closure, Yellow Green, Quart, C-1499 .... 45.00
Lightning Trademark, Closure, Yellow, 1/2 Gallon, C-1499 .... 70.00
Lightning Trademark, Dark Amber, Quart, C-1499 .... 30.00
Lightning Trademark, Light Amber, Quart, C-1499 .... 25.00
Lightning Trademark, Light Green, Quart, C-1499 .... 20.00
Lightning Trademark, Medium Dark Amber, 1/2 Gallon, C-1489 .... 45.00
Lightning Trademark, Medium Golden Amber, 1/2 Gallon, C-1489 .... 53.00
Lightning Trademark, Pint, C-1496 .... 5.00
Lightning Trademark, Reg.Patent Office, Aqua, Quart, C-1502 .... 4.00
Lockport, Mason, Aqua, Pint, C-1512 .... 4.00
Lockport, Mason, Aqua, Quart, C-1512 .... 5.00
Longlife, Mason, Widemouth, Pint, C-1515 .... 1.00
Ludlow's Patent June 28th, 1859, Aqua, Quart, C-1547 .... 125.00
Ludlow's Patent June 28th, 1859, 1/2 Gallon, C-1547 .... 145.00
Lustre, R.E.Tongue & Bros.Phila., Aqua, Quart, C-1554 .... 4.00
Lynchburg Standard Mason, Aqua, Quart, C-1594 .... 18.00
M.G.Co., A On Base, Wax Sealer, Green, Quart 50.00
M.Hose & Lyon, Dayton, 3-Lipped, Wax Sealer, 1/2 Gallon 25.00
Macomb Pottery Co., Pat.Jan.24, 1899, Stoneware, Quart, C-1602 .... 8.00
Magic Star, Dudley Clamp, Aqua, C-1606 .... 95.00
Magic TM Mason, Pint, C-1611 .... .25
Magic, The, Star, Original Clamp, Aqua, 1/2 Gallon, C-1606 .... 110.00
Maine Condensed Milk Company, 1/2 Pint, C-1614 .... 8.00
Maine-Morro Castle, Pictured, C.1898, SCA, Pint, C-3086 .... 120.00
Marion Jar, The, Mason's Pat., Lettering, Aqua, 1/2 Gal., C-1625 .... 10.00
Marion Jar, The, Mason's Pat.Nov.30th, 1858, Aqua, Pint, C-1625 .... 12.00
Marion Jar, The, Mason's Pat.Nov.30th, 1858, Aqua, Quart, C-1625 .... 10.00
Mason Of 1858, Trademark, Aqua, 1/2 Gallon, C-1748 .... 45.00
Mason Of 1872, Trademark, Aqua, 1/2 Gallon, C-1751 .... 75.00
Mason, H Over Anchor, Pint, C-83 .... 1.00
Mason, H Over Anchor, Quart, C-83 .... 1.00
Mason, In Straight Line, 1/2 Gallon, C-1642 .... 4.00
Mason, Loop Underline, Aqua, Quart, C-1636 .... 5.00
Mason, Loop Underline, Light Vaseline, Pint, C-1636 .... 6.50

Mason, Over Shepherd's Crook, Aqua, 1/2 Gallon, C-1633	5.00
Mason, Rounded Shepherd's Crook, Aqua, 1/2 Gallon, C-1637	5.00
Mason, Shepherd's Crook Underline, Aqua, Pint, C-1633	4.00
Mason, Shepherd's Crook Underline, Aqua, Quart, C-1632	5.00
Mason, Star, 2-Piece Lid, Pint, C-1746	1.00
Mason, Straight Line, Amber, Pint, C-1641	35.00 To 60.00
Mason, The, Within Initial Stroke Of M, Aqua, 1/2 Gal., C-1651	4.00
Mason's C.F.J., Midget	9.00
Mason's C.F.J., Pat.Nov.30th, 1858, Aqua, 1/2 Gallon, C-1920	4.00
Mason's C.F.J.Co., Improved, Aqua, Quart, C-1722	5.00
Mason's C.F.J.Co., Pat.Nov.30th, 1858, Green, Quart, C-1920	20.00
Mason's C.F.J.Co., Patent Nov.30th, 1858, Aqua, C-1920	10.00
Mason's C.F.J.Co.Improved, 2 Piece Lid, Amber, 1/2 Gallon	128.00
Mason's Cross, Improved, Light Aqua, Pint, C-1727	4.00
Mason's Cross, Patent Nov.30th, 1858, Amber, 1/2 Gal., C-1939	75.00
Mason's Cross, Patent Nov.30th, 1858, Aqua, Quart, C-1939	3.00
Mason's Cross, Patent 1858, Original Lid, Olive Green, Quart	65.00
Mason's I.G.Co., Patent Nov.30th, 1858, Quart, C-1955	12.00
Mason's Improved, Aqua, Quart, C-1702	4.00
Mason's Improved, Aqua, 1/2 Gallon, C-1711	3.00
Mason's Improved, Aqua, 1/2 Gallon, C-1721	3.00
Mason's Improved, Aqua, 1/2 Gallon, C-1725	3.00
Mason's Improved, Aqua, 1/2 Gallon, C-1726	3.00
Mason's Improved, Ghosted Disk Immerser, Amber, 1/2 Gallon	105.00
Mason's Improved, Mabel Insert, Bottom Irregular, Amber, 9 In.	95.00
Mason's J Patent Nov.30th, 1858, Aqua, 1/2 Gallon, C-2002	20.00
Mason's Jar Of 1872, Aqua, Quart, C-1750	35.00
Mason's Jar Of 1872, Aqua, 1/2 Gallon, C-1749	44.00
Mason's K.B.G.Co., Patent Nov.30th, 1858, Aqua, Quart, C-1958	12.00
Mason's L.G.Co., Patent Nov.30th, 1858, Aqua, Quart, C-1970	10.00
Mason's M.F.J.Co.Patent Nov.30th, 1858, Aqua, 1/2 Gal., C-1971	135.00
Mason's N Patent Nov.30th, 1858, Aqua, Pint, C-2007	10.00
Mason's N Patent Nov.30th, 1858, Aqua, Quart, C-2008	9.00
Mason's N Patent Nov.30th, 1858, Aqua, 1/2 Gallon, C-2007	10.00
Mason's N Patent 1858, Aqua, Pint, C-2008	14.00
Mason's Patent Nov.30th, 1858, Amethyst, 1/2 Gallon *Color*	
Mason's Patent Nov.30th, 1858, Apple Green, Quart, C-1778	18.00
Mason's Patent Nov.30th, 1858, Aqua, Pint *Illus*	4.00
Mason's Patent Nov.30th, 1858, Aqua, Pint, C-1787	3.00
Mason's Patent Nov.30th, 1858, Aqua, Quart, C-1787	3.00
Mason's Patent Nov.30th, 1858, Aqua, Quart, C-1927	3.00
Mason's Patent Nov.30th, 1858, Aqua, 1/2 Gallon, C-1	6.00 To 8.00
Mason's Patent Nov.30th, 1858, Aqua, 1/2 Gallon, C-1927	2.00

Fruit Jar, Mason's Patent Nov.30th,
1858, Aqua, Pint

Mason's Patent Nov.30th, 1858, Cross Rev., Aqua, Midget, C-1941 .... 15.00
Mason's Patent Nov.30th, 1858, Moore Bro's.Glass, Aqua, C-1889 .... 12.00
Mason's Patent Nov.30th, 1858, Port Base, Aqua, At., C-1894 .... 3.50
Mason's Patent Nov.30th, 1858, Port, Aqua, 1/2 Gallon, C-1894 .... 5.00
Mason's Patent Nov.30th, 1858, SCA, Quart, C-1778 .... 1.00
Mason's Patent Nov.30th, 1858, U.G.Co., Aqua, 1/2 Gallon, C-1866 .... 12.00
Mason's Patent Nov.30th, 1858, U.G.Co., Reverse, Aqua, 1/2 Gallon 15.00
Mason's Patent Nov.30th, 1858, W.C.D., Aqua, Quart, C-1900 .... 6.00
Mason's Patent Nov.30th, 1858, W.C.D., Aqua, 1/2 Gallon, C-1900 .... 6.00
Mason's Patent November 30th, 1858, Zinc Cap, Aqua, 5 3/4 In. 7.50
Mason's Patent 1858, H.C. & T. On Base, No.5, Aqua, Quart 16.00
Mason's Patent 1858, L. & W. On Base, Aqua, Quart, C-1886 .... 6.00
Mason's Patent 1858, Port In Script, Aqua, Quart, C-1864 .... 4.00
Mason's Patent 1858, Port On Reverse, Aqua, 1/2 Gal., C-1864 .... 4.00
Mason's Patent 1858, Port Printed At Base, Quart, C-1893 .... 25.00
Mason's Patent 1858, Reverse Tudor Rose, Aqua, Quart, C-1875 .... 22.00
Mason's Patent 1858, Reverse Tudor Rose, 1/2 Gallon, C-1875 .... 20.00
Mason's Patent 1858, 1/2 Gallon, C-1776 .... 2.00
Mason's Patent, Aqua, Pint, C-1756 .... 3.00
Mason's Patent, Aqua, 1/2 Gallon, C-1756 .... 2.00
Mason's Patent, 1/2 Gallon, C-1755 .... 1.00
Mason's S Patent Nov.30th, 1858, Cross, Aqua, Quart, C-1949 .... 12.00
Mason's S Patent 1858, Aqua, Quart, C-1770 .... 12.00
Mason's S Patent 1858, Quart, C-1770 .... 6.00
Mason's S.G.Co., Patent Nov.30th, 1858, Aqua, Quart, C-1974 .... 6.00
Mason's Union, Shield, Aqua, Quart, C-2133 .... 90.00
Mason's Union, Shield, Unlined Lid, Aqua, 1/2 Gallon, C-2133 .... 125.00
Mason's 1858, Monogram G.C.Co., Amber, Pint 245.00
Mason's 1858, N.C.L.Co.On Reverse, Quart, C-1861 .... 7.00
Mason's 2 Patent 1858, Aqua, 1/2 Gallon, C-2032 .... 16.00
Mason's 3 Patent Nov.30th, 1858, Clear To Gray, Quart, C-2039 .... 8.00
Mason's 6 Patent Nov.30th, 1858, Aqua, Quart, C-2053 .... 8.00
Mason's, Black Glass, Quart 600.00
Mason's, C.F.J., Improved, Clyde, N.Y., Aqua, Midget, C-1921 .... 15.00
Mason's, C.F.J., Patent Nov.30th, 1858, Aqua, Midget, C-1920 .... 12.50
Mason's, C.F.J., Patent Nov.30th, 1858, Olive Green, Quart, C-1920 .... 50.00
Mason's, C.F.J.Co., Improved, Aqua, Quart, C-1711 .... 3.00
Mason's, C.F.J.Co., Patent Nov.30th, 1858, Midget, C-1920 .... 9.00
Mason's, Keystone, Circle, Pat.Nov.30th, 1858, Aqua, Quart, C-1964 .... 6.00
Mason's, Keystone, Patent Nov.30th, 1858, Aqua, Quart, C-1965 .... 6.00
McDonald Perfect Seal, Bead Neck Lightning, Blue, Qt., C-2148 .... 5.00
McDonald Perfect Seal, In Circle, Blue, Quart, C-2147 .... 5.00
McMechen's Always The Best Of Old Virginia, White, Pint, C-2161 .... 80.00 To 125.00
Michigan Mason, Aqua, Pint, C-2172 .... 25.00
Millville Atmospheric Fruit Jar, Pint, C-2181 .... 40.00
Millville Atmospheric Fruit Jar, Repro Clamp, Quart, C-2181 .... 16.00
Millville Atmospheric Jar, Squared Shoulder, Aqua, Quart, C-2183 .... 75.00
Millville Atmospheric, Aqua, Quart, C-2181 .... 20.00 To 25.00
Millville Atmospheric, Aqua, 1/2 Gallon, C-2181 .... 20.00
Millville Improved, Complete With Lid, Aqua, Quart 50.00
Millville WTC, Closure, Quart, C-2187 .... 48.00
Millville, Amber, Quart 2500.00
Mission Trade Mark Mason, Aqua, Pint, C-2190 .... 11.00
Mission Trade Mark Mason, Bell, Aqua, Pint 8.00
Mission Trade Mark Mason, Pint, C-2190 .... 10.00
Model Mason, Quart, C-2196 .... 12.00
Mom's Mason Jar, Pint, C-2198 .... 1.00
Mom's Mason Jar, Quart, C-2198 .... 1.00 To 1.25
Monarch Finer Foods, Circle With Lion's Head, Quart, C-2200 .... 3.00
Moore's, Patent Dec.3rd, 1861, Aqua, C-2204 .... 50.00 To 80.00
Mother's Jar, Tin Lid, Aqua, Quart, C-2211 .... 25.00
Mrs.G.E.Haller Pat'd.Feb.25, '73, Stopper, Aqua, 1/2 Gallon, C-1178 .... 110.00
Mrs.G.E.Haller, Clear Stopper, Aqua, 1/2 Gallon, C-1179 .... 105.00

Mudge's Canner, 4 Barrel 225.00
Myer's Test Jar, Aqua, Quart, C-2218 .... 90.00
N E Plus Ultra Airtight, Bodine & Bros., Aqua, C-475 .... 650.00
Nelson Morris & Co., Chicago, Ill., Base, 1/2 Pint 5.00
New Paragon 5, Repro Band, Aqua, Quart, C-2291 .... 95.00
O.C.Monogram, Aqua, 8 1/2 In., 2 1/2 In.Diam., Pint, C-2256 .... 75.00
Ohio Quality Mason, H & I Repositioned & Peened Out, Quart 14.00
Ohio Quality Mason, 1/2 Gallon, C-2263 .... 10.00
Old Judge Coffee, Quilted, Owl On Branch, Quart, C-2271 .... 2.25
Old Style Mustard, Ball, Pint, C-2272 .... 2.50
One Of The Best Foods, On Base, Quart 1.50
Open Pontil, Blue, 8 In. ....Color 250.00
Opler Bros., Inc., Cocoa & Chocolate, New York, Quart, C-2274 .... 4.00
Opler Brothers, Inc., Cocoa & Chocolate, Quart, C-2273 .... 5.00
Osotite, Quart, C-2279 .... 65.00
Owl, Milk Glass, C-3085 .... 50.00
P.Lorillard Co., Amber, Pint, C-1543 .... 15.00
P.Lorillard Co., On Base, Closure, Amber, Quart, C-1542 .... 7.00
Pacific Mason, Clear, Quart, C-2283 .... 15.00
FRUIT JAR, PALACE HOME, see Fruit Jar, Hansee's
Pareil, Aqua, Quart 200.00
Patent June 9, 1863, Cin.O., Aqua, 1/2 Gallon 115.00
Patented Oct.19, 1858, On Lid, Aqua, 1/2 Gallon 50.00
Pearl, The, Aqua, 1/2 Gallon, C-2318 .... 28.00
Pearl, The, Dated Base, Aqua, Quart, C-2318 .... 30.00
Penn, The, Quart, C-2326 .... 95.00
Peoria, Brown Glazed Wax Sealer, Quart, C-2329 .... 9.00
Peoria, Brown Glazed Wax Sealer, 1/2 Gallon, C-2329 .... 10.00
Perfect Seal, Pint, C-2333 .... 5.00
Perfect Seal, Quart, C-2333 .... 3.00
Perfect Seal, Square With Vines, Quart, C-2349 .... 2.00
Perfection, Amber, Pint, C-2330 .... 1350.00
Perfection, Thrine Band & Bail, Quart, C-2330 .... 25.00
Perfection, 1/2 Gallon, C-2330 .... 27.00
Pet, Aqua, 1/2 Gallon, C-2359 .... 55.00 To 60.00
Pet, L & W Ghosted, Original Wire, Aqua, 1/2 Gallon, C-1527 .... 65.00
Petal, Iron Pontil, Olive Emerald Green, 1/2 Gallon 85.00
Petal, Pontil 150.00
Petal, Sapphire Blue, Quart 995.00
Petal, 10, Aqua, Quart 90.00
Petal, 12, Applied Lip, Aqua, 9 1/4 In. 45.00
Pine De Luxe Jar, Quart, C-2366 .... 3.00 To 5.00
Pine De Luxe, Clear, 1/2 Gallon, C-2366 .... 5.00
Pine P Mason, Clear, Pint, C-2367 .... 3.00
Pine P Mason, Clear, Quart, C-2367 .... 2.00
Pint Standard, Wax Sealer, Original Lid, Aqua, C-2368 .... 75.00
Porcelain Lined, Aqua, Quart, C-2374 .... 18.00
Porcelain Lined, Midget, C-2374 .... 49.00
Port Q, On Base, Wax Sealer, Aqua, Quart, C-2379 .... 15.00
FRUIT JAR, POTTER & BODINE, see also Fruit Jar, Airtight
Potter & Bodine Airtight, Barrel, Pontil, Quart, C-2387 .... 525.00
Potter & Bodine, Barrel, Pontil, Aqua, 1/2 Quart, C-2387 .... 750.00
Potter & Bodine, Barrel, Pontil, Aqua, Quart, C-2388 .... 495.00
Potter & Bodine, Pat.April 13th, 1858, Aqua, 1/2 Gallon, C-2387 ...... 350.00
Potter & Bodine, Philadelphia, Aqua, 1/2 Gallon, C-2381 .... 100.00
Premium, Coffeyville, Kansas, Clamp & Lid, Clear, Quart, C-2395 .... 17.50
Presto Glass Top, Glass Lid, Wire Bail, 1/2 Pint, C-2402 .... 5.00
Presto Glass Top, Widemouth, Glass Lid, 1/2 Gallon, C-2414 .... 2.50
Presto Supreme Mason, Correct Closure, Quart, C-2407 .... 1.25
Presto Supreme, Duraglas, Pint, C-2412 .... .50
Protector, Arched, 1/2 Gallon, C-2423 .... 30.00
Protector, Embossed Panel Recessed, Aqua, Quart, C-2421 .... 17.00
Protector, Round, Aqua, Quart, C-2420 .... 25.00

Fruit Jar, Root Mason,

Aqua, Pint, C-2510

Protector, 6 Panel, Thrine Repro.Closure, Aqua, Quart, C-2421 .... 50.00
Purity, Oats, Paneled, Original Embossed Lid, Widemouth, Quart 20.00
Queen, The, Aqua, Quart, C-2433 .... 9.00 To 18.00
Quick Seal Pat'd.July 14, 1908, Aqua, Quart, C-2454 .... 3.50
Quick Seal, Aqua, Pint, C-2452 .... 4.00
Quick Seal, Aqua, Quart, C-2452 .... 4.00
Quick Seal, Pat'd.July 14, 1908 On Reverse, Pint, C-2454 .... 2.00
Quick Seal, Quart, C-2452 .... 4.00
Quong Hop Sing & Co., Chinese Characters, Pint, C-2460 .... 5.00
    FRUIT JAR, RAILROAD, see Fruit Jar, Helme's
Rath's Black Hawk Food Products, Quart, C-2468 .... 2.00
Red Key Mason, Aqua, Quart, C-2474 .... 6.00
Red Key Mason, Aqua, 1/2 Gallon, C-2474 .... 5.00
Red Key Mason, Patent Nov.30th, 1858, Aqua, Quart, C-2477 .... 6.00
Reeds Patties, 1/2 Gallon, C-2484 .... 6.00
Reid, Murdoch & Co., Chicago, Embossed, Quart, C-2488 .... 10.00
Reliable Home Canning Mason, Correct Insert, Quart, C-2489 .... 4.00
Reliable Home Canning Mason, Pint, C-2489 .... 1.50
Reservoir Jar Of 1876, 1 Ounce, C-2497 .... 149.00 To 165.00
Robert Arthur's 1855, Yellow Ware, Sealer, Quart, C-98 .... 75.00
Robinson, On Base & Clamp, Quart, C-2507 .... 5.50
Root Mason, Aqua, Pint, C-2510 .... Illus 5.00
Root Mason, Aqua, Quart, C-2510 .... 1.00 To 3.00
Root Mason, Aqua, 1/2 Gallon, C-2510 .... 2.00 To 4.00
Rose, Crown Inset, Lip Clip, Aqua, 1/2 Gallon, C-2511 .... 30.00
Royal Crown, 1/2 Gallon, C-2516 .... 6.00
Royal Of 1876, Aqua, 1/2 Gallon, C-2515 .... 185.00
Royal Of 1876, Original Closure, Aqua, 1/2 Gallon, C-2515 .... 195.00
Royal Trademark, Amber, Quart, C-2517 .... 50.00
Royal, On Neck, Trademark, Janney & Monzani, Pint 20.00
Royal, Whittled, Original Closure, Aqua, 1/2 Gallon, C-2514 .... 165.00
S.McKee & Co., On Base, Aqua, 1/2 Gallon, C-2155 .... 7.00
S.McKee & Co., Wax Sealer, Aqua, Quart, C-2155 .... 15.00
Safety Seal, Made In Canada, Quart, C-2536 .... 5.00
Safety Valve, Greek Key, Pat'd 1895, Aqua, 1/2 Gallon, C-2538 .... 30.00
Safety Valve, On Base, Label, Quart, C-2538 .... 10.00 To 16.00
Safety Valve, On Base, Light Aqua, Quart, C-2538 .... 5.00
Safety Valve, Patent 1895, Metal Clamp, Clear, 1/2 Pint, C-2538 .... 20.00
Safety Valve, Pint, C-2538 .... 8.00
Safety Widemouth Mason, Salem Glass Works, Aqua, Pint, C-2549 .... 12.50
Safety, Amber, 1/2 Gallon, C-2535 .... 130.00 To 165.00
Safety, Embossed, Original Bail & Lid, Amber, Pint, C-2535 .... 155.00
Samco Genuine Mason, Samco In Circle, Quart, C-2545 .... 2.00
Samco Super Mason, Quart, C-2548 .... 1.50 To 2.00

Sanford's, Quart, C-2551	10.00
Saratoga, N.Y., Widemouth, Embossed, Olive Green, Quart	400.00
Schram Automatic Sealer B, Pint, C-2568	9.00
Schram Automatic Sealer B, Quart, C-2568	5.00
Schram Automatic Sealer, Script, Closure, 1/2 Gallon, C-2566	6.50
Schram Automatic Sealer, Tin Lid, Clamp, Pint, C-2569	5.00
Schram, Flag, 1/2 Gallon, C-2572	7.00
Sealfast, Foster, Foster On Base, Pint	3.00
Sealfast, Foster, Quart, C-2580	1.00
Sealfast, Foster, 1/2 Pint, C-2581	6.00
Security Seal, F G Co, Pint, C-2608	5.00
Security Seal, F G Co, Quart, C-2608	1.50
Silver Moon Coffee, Olive Finne Co, Quart, C-2631	3.00
Simplex, Contents & Label, 1/2 Pint, C-2632	10.00
Simplex, Pint, C-2632	5.00
Simplex, 1/2 Pint, C-2633	5.00
SKO Queen Trademark, Pint, C-2444	4.00
SKO Queen Trademark, Widemouth, Quart, C-2445	2.50
Smalley Kivlan & Onthank, Boston, Label, Quart, C-2663	10.00
Smalley Nu-Seal, Clear, Quart, C-2657	6.50
Smalley Nu-Seal, In Diamond, Quart, C-2659	8.00
Smalley Self Sealer, Widemouth, Quart, C-2667	4.00
Smalley's Royal Trade Mark Nu-Seal, Quart, C-2661	8.50
Snowflake, Greenish Aqua, Midget	200.00
Solidex, Deep Green, 1/2 Gallon, C-2678	25.00
Southern Double Seal Mason, Quart, C-2680	12.00
Spratt's, Patent July 18, 1854, Aqua, Quart, C-2690	210.00 To 325.00
Square G Mason, Pint, C-2691	2.00 To 5.00
Square G Mason, Quart C-2691	4.00 To 5.00
St.Louis Syrup & Preserving, Aqua, Pint, C-2742	28.00
Standard, Aqua, Quart, C-2701	8.00
Standard, Blue, Quart, C-2701	75.00
Standard, Looped Underline, Wax Sealer, Quart, C-2709	18.00
Standard, Shepherd's Crook, Aqua, 1/2 Gallon, C-2711	15.00
Star & Crescent, Self Sealing, Paper Label, C-2772	250.00
Star Glass Co., Wax Sealer, Aqua, Quart, C-2729	35.00 To 40.00
Star, With Picture, Canadian Jar, Aqua, 1/2 Gallon, C-2718	85.00
Star, With Picture, The American Haller Jar, Aqua, Quart, C-2721	65.00
Stark, Original Closure, Quart, C-2730	65.00
Stark, Patented 1923, Quart	65.00
Stark, Patented, K Within Star, Quart, C-2730	70.00
FRUIT JAR, STEER'SHEAD, see Fruit Jar, Flaccus	
Sterling Mason, Quart, C-2735	2.00
Steven's Tin Top, Lewis & Neblett, Repro Lid, C-2741	145.00
Stone Mason, The, Brown & White Stoneware, 1/2 Gallon, C-2754	15.00
Strittmatter's Pure Honey, Blue, Pint, C-2757	42.00
Sun Trade Mark, Glass Cap, Closure, Aqua, Quart, C-2761	50.00
Sun Trade Mark, Original Closure, Pint, C-2761	50.00
Sun Trade Mark, Within Circle, Light Green, Pint, C-2761	60.00
Sun Trade Mark, Within Circle, Light Green, Quart, C-2761	55.00
Sure Seal, Script, Aqua, Pint, C-2772	4.50
Sure Seal, Script, Aqua, Quart, C-2773	3.50
Sutcliffe, No Lid, C-2774	25.00
Swayzee's Improved Mason, Aqua, Pint, C-2780	4.50
Swayzee's Improved Mason, Aqua, Quart, C-2780	2.00 To 4.00
Swayzee's Improved Mason, Aqua, 1/2 Gallon, C-2780	3.75
Swayzee's Improved Mason, Fleur-De-Lis, Aqua, 1/2 Gallon, C-2780	4.00
Sydney, Trade Mark Dingo F.J., Green Aqua, Quart, C-2785	160.00
T.W.Beach Fruit Growers, Light Apple Green, Quart	20.00
Telephone, The, Whitney Glass Works, Aqua, Quart, C-2790	9.00
Telephone, The, Widemouth, Aqua, Quart, C-2792	8.00
Telephone, The, Widemouth, Trademark Reg., Aqua, Pint, C-2792	5.00
Texas Mason, Pint, C-2796	10.00

Fruit Jar, Van Vliet, 1881,
Aqua, Pint, C-2878

Texas Mason, Quart, C-2796	8.00 To 13.00
Three Rivers, Barrel Shape, Zinc Lid, Clear, Pint, C-2800	2.00
Thrift, Buck Glass Co., Baltimore, Clear, Pint, C-2802	12.00
Thrift, Thrift Jar Co., Baltimore, Embossed, Quart, C-2802	12.50
Tight Seal, In Circle, Date On Reverse, Aqua, Pint, C-2806	3.00
Tight Seal, Pat'd.July 14, 1908, Aqua, 1/2 Gallon, C-2806	5.00
Tight Seal, Pat'd, July 14, 1908, Aqua, Pint, C-2806	2.75
Tillyer, Aqua, Quart, C-2810	65.00 To 95.00
Trade Mark Climax Registered, Date On Reverse, Aqua, Pint, C-613	5.00
Tropical Canners, TF In Diamond, 1/2 Gallon	3.50
Trues Imperial Brand, Pint, C-2828	8.00
Trues Imperial Brand, Portland, Me., 1/2 Gallon, C-2828	8.50
Turnmold, Unmarked, Wax Sealer, Amber	87.50
Union No.1, Wax Sealer, Aqua, C-2838	50.00
Vacuum Seal, Original Clamp, Quart, C-2866	4.00
Valve Jar Co., Phil., March 10, 1868, Aqua, 1/2 Gallon, C-2875	175.00
Valve Jar Co., Philadelphia, Aqua, 1/2 Pint, C-2873	145.00
Valve Jar, Original Coil, 1/2 Gallon	170.00
Valve Jar, Philadelphia, Quart, C-2873	153.00
Van Vliet, 1881, Aqua, Pint, C-2878	*Illus* 475.00
Veteran, Bail, Clear, Quart	10.00
Veteran, Bust In Circle, Pint, C-2884	15.00
Veteran, Bust In Circle, Quart, C-2884	18.00
Victor, The, M In Diamond, Pat.1899, Paper Label, Quart, C-2886	50.00
Victor, The, M In Diamond, Pat. 1899, Repro Clamp, Aqua, Pint, C-2886	35.00
Victor, The, Pat.1900, Aqua, 1/2 Gallon, C-2887	19.00
Victor, The, Pat'd.Feb.20th, 1900, 1/2 Gallon, C-2887	19.00
Victor, The, Patented 1899, Aqua, Quart, C-2886	20.00
Victory Home-Pak Mason, Quart, C-2904	1.50
Victory 1, Circle Of Dates, Aqua, Quart, C-2893	35.00
Victory 2, Circle Of Dates, Aqua, 1/2 Gallon	35.00
Vliet, 1881, Aqua, Quart, C-2978	275.00
W & Co., Wax Sealer, Base Embossed, Aqua, Quart, C-1540	11.00
W.& J.Flett Liverpool, Green, Quart, C-1018	35.00
W.McCully & Co., Standard, Light Blue, 1/2 Gallon	20.00
W.W.Lyman 4, Patent 1862 & 1864, Aqua, 1/2 Gallon	25.00
W.W.Lyman 5, Pat'd. Feb.9th, 1864, Aqua, C-1572	25.00
W.W.Lyman 18, Patent 1864, Original Lid, Aqua, 1/2 Gallon, C-1589	65.00
W.W.Lyman 27, Original Tin Press On Lid, Aqua, Quart	75.00
W.W.Lyman 27, Pat'd.Feb.9th, 1864, Aqua, Quart	22.00
W.W.Lyman, Circle Dates, 1864 & 1867, 2 Stars, Aqua, Quart, C-1579	75.00
Wan-Eta Cocoa, Boston, Amber, Pint, C-2909	12.00
Wan-Eta Cocoa, Boston, Amber, Quart, C-2909	5.00 To 7.00
Wax Corker, Heavy Glass, Pale Green, Imperial Size, Quart	12.00

Wax Sealer, Amber .... 85.00 To 100.00
Wax Sealer, Applied Handle, Tin Lid, White Salt Glaze, Gallon 45.00
Wax Sealer, Bell-Shaped, Iron Pontil, Aqua, Quart 235.00
Wax Sealer, Orange Amber, Quart 85.00
Wax Sealer, Turnmold, Amber, Quart 60.00
Wax Sealer, Turnmold, Amber, 1/2 Gallon 103.00
Wears Jar, The, Glass Lid, Side Clamps, Pint, C-2920 .... 7.50
Wears, Name In Circle, Aqua, Quart, C-2916 .... 9.00
Weideman Boy Brand, Cleveland, Quart, C-2931 .... 5.00
Weir, The, Pat.March 1, 1892, Brown, White Stoneware .... 15.00 To 18.00
Wesk, 6 D, Correct Glass Closure, Pint, C-2926 .... 4.00
Western Pride, Pat.June 22, 1875, Aqua, Quart, C-2945 .... 110.00
Western Pride, Pat.June 22, 1875, Aqua, 2 Gallon, C-2945 .... 85.00
White Crown Mason, Aqua, 1/2 Gallon, C-2961 .... 6.00
White Crown Mason, Quart, C-2961 .... 5.00 To 8.00
Whitney Mason Pat'd.1858, Aqua, Pint, C-2970 .... 8.00
Whitney Mason, Patented 1858, Aqua, Quart, C-2970 .... 8.00
Whittled, Iron Pontil, Applied Lip, Aqua, 7 3/4 In. 65.00
Whittled, 3 Part, Attributed To Zettle, Aqua, 7 3/8 In. 50.00
Windsor Cocoanut, On Base, Aqua, Pint 3.00
Winslow, Aqua 40.00
Wm.Culley & Co., Blue, 1/2 Gallon 20.00
Wm.Frank & Sons, Pitts., On Base, Aqua, Quart, C-1031 .... 10.00
Wm.Frank & Sons, Pitts., On Base, Aqua, 1/2 Gallon, C-1031 .... 20.00
Wm.L.Haller, Carlisle, Pa., Ladies Favorite, Quart, C-1182 .... 1600.00
Wm.L.Haller, Carlisle, Pa., Pint, C-1179 .... 400.00
Woodbury Improved, WGW Monogram, Aqua, 1/2 Gallon, C-3028 .... 28.00
Woodbury Improved, WGW, Aqua, Pint, C-3029 .... 36.00
Woodbury WGW, Aqua, Quart, C-3028 .... 25.00
Woodbury, Woodbury, New Jersey, Aqua, Quart, C-3027 .... 25.00
X Ray 200.00
Yeoman's Fruit Bottle, Aqua, Quart, C-3079 .... 25.00
Yeoman's, Aqua, 1/2 Quart, C-3039 .... 50.00

GALLIANO, Guard, 10th, Figural 8.00

Garnier bottles were first made in 1899 to hold Garnier Liqueurs. The firm was founded in 1859 in France. Figurals have been made through the twentieth century, except for the years of prohibition and World War II.

GARNIER, Acorn, 1910 .... 33.00
Aladdin's Lamp, 1963 .... 43.00
Alfa Romeo, 1913 .... 16.00
Alfa Romeo, 1924 .... 16.00
Angel Wing 5.00
Antique Coach, 1970 .... 20.00
Apollo, 1969 .... 16.00
Aztec, 1965 .... 11.00
Baby Foot, 1963 .... 15.00
Bacchus, 1967 .... 14.00
Bahamas Policeman, 1970 .... 24.00
Bedroom Candlestick, 1967 .... 19.00
Bellows, 1969 .... 17.00
Bluebird, 1970 .... 15.00
Bouquet, 1966 .... 20.00
Burmese Man, 1965 .... 19.00
Candlestick No.134, 1955 .... 38.00
Cannon, 1964 .... 53.00
Cardinal, 1969 .... 12.00
Cat No.52, 1930 .... 75.00
Cat, Gray, 1962 .... 20.00
Chalet, 1955 .... 45.00
Chimney, 1956 .... 58.00

Chinese Man, 1970	20.00
Chinese Woman, 1970	20.00
Christmas Tree, 1956 *Illus*	50.00
Citroen, 1922	17.00
Clock, 1958	23.00
Clown No.20, 1910	42.00
Clown With Tuba, 1955	18.00
Clown's Head, 1931	75.00
Coffee Mill, 1966	27.00
Coffeepot, 1961	33.00
Country Jug, 1937	31.00
Diamond Bottle, 1969	13.00
Duck, No.21, 1910	13.00 To 20.00
Duckling, 1956	38.00
Duo Firefly, 1959	15.00
Egg, 1956	73.00
Eiffel Tower, 1950	21.00
Elephant No.66, 1932	75.00 To 125.00
Elephant No.183, 1961	22.00
Empire Vase, 1962	13.00
Fiat Nuevo, 1913, 1969	16.00
Ford, 1913, 1969	15.00
Fountain, 1964	27.00
Giraffe, 1961	17.00
Goddess, 1963	43.00
Goldfinch, 1970	13.00
Goose, 1955	17.00
Greyhound, 1930	75.00
Harlequin No.166, 1958	35.00
Horse Pistol, 1964	19.00
Hula Hoop, 1959	28.00
Hunting Vase, 1964	28.00
Inca, 1969	16.00
Indian, 1958	17.00
Jockey, 1961	19.00
Jug, 5-Handled, 1959	21.00
LaDonna, 1963	35.00
Lafayette, 1949	19.00
Laurel Crown, 1963	21.00
Locomotive, 1969	14.00

Garnier, Christmas Tree, 1956

Log, Round, 1958	23.00
Loon, 1970	14.00
Maharajah, 1958	73.00
Marquis, 1931	73.00
Marseillaise, 1970	19.00
MG, 1933, 1970	17.00
Milord Drunkard, 1956	22.00
Mockingbird, 1970	13.00
Montmartre Jug, 1960	15.00
Napoleon, 1969	25.00
Oasis, 1959	20.00
Packard, 1930, 1970	17.00
Painting, 1961	25.00
Paris Taxi, 1960	26.00
Parrot, 1910	24.00
Partridge No.177, 1961	39.00
Partridge No.254, 1969	14.00
Pegasus, 1958	55.00
Penguin, 1930	75.00
Pheasant, 1969	24.00
Pony, 1961	17.00
Poodle, Black, 1954	14.00
Poodle, White, 1954	12.00
Rainbow, 1952	29.00
Renault, 1911, 1969	17.00
Roadrunner, 1969	13.00
Robin, 1970	13.00
Rolls-Royce, 1908, 1970	17.00
Rooster, Black, 1952	14.00
Rooster, Maroon, 1952	20.00
Rouen Vase, 1962	24.00
Scarecrow, 1960	22.00
Sheriff, 1958	19.00
Snail, 1959	39.00
Soccer Shoe, 1962	35.00
SS Queen Mary, 1970	22.00
St.Tropez Jug, 1961	15.00
Stanley Steamer, 1907, 1970	20.00
Tam Tam, 1976	50.00
Tea Pot, No.180, 1961	18.00
Trio, 1955	15.00
Trout, 1967	14.00
Violin, 1966	19.00
Water Pitcher, 1965	15.00
Watering Can, 1958	15.00
Woman With Jug, 1930	50.00
Young Deer, 1964	28.00

Gin was first made in the 1600s and gin bottles have been made ever since. Gin has always been an inexpensive drink. That is why so many of these bottles were made. Many were of a type called case bottles today.

GIN, African, W.Hoytema & Co.	19.50
African, Yellow Green	14.00
Avan Hoboken & Co., Rotterdam, A.H.In Seal On Shoulder, Olive Green	22.50
Avan Hoboken & Co., Rotterdam, A.H.In Seal, Amber	25.00
Avan Hoboken & Co., Rotterdam, Olive Amber, Embossed, Square, 11 3/8 In.	80.00
GIN, BININGER, see Bininger	
Blankenheym & Nolet, Olive Green, Pint	15.00
Blankenheym & Nolet, Olive Green, Quart	15.00
Blankenheym & Nolet, Tapered, Amber, 9 1/2 In.	15.00
Blown, Black Glass, Flared Lip	12.00
Booth & Sedgwick Cordial, London, Iron Pontil, Square, Green, 9 In.	75.00

Booth & Sedgwick, London Cordial Gin, Amber, 8 1/2 In.	75.00
Booth & Sedgwick, London Cordial, Square, Green, IP, Quart	55.00
Burnett's & Gordon's, Aqua	2.00
Burroughs, Paper Label	*Color*
C.G.& Co., Open Pontil, Sea Washed, Applied Seal	175.00
Case, A.Miller & Co., Dark Olive	22.50
Case, A.Miller BZ & Co., Green Amber, 9 In.	28.00
Case, African, Black	15.00
Case, African, Light & Dark Green	22.50
Case, Applied Seal, Vandenberg Mushroom Top	25.00
Case, Avan Hoboken, Sealed, Olive Green, 12 In.	75.00
Case, Black Glass	12.00
Case, Blankenheym & Nolet, Olive Green	15.00
Case, Blankenheym & Nolet, Partial Label, Green, 9 In.	35.00
Case, Blown, Olive Green, 8 1/2 In.	30.00
Case, Blown, Open Pontil, Deep Olive Amber	45.00
Case, Colonial, Bubbly	49.50
Case, Colonial, Open Pontil	49.50
Case, Daniel Visser & Zonen	10.00
Case, Dutch Porter, Water Wash, Open Pontil	49.50
Case, E.Kiderlin, Black	20.00
Case, E.Kiderlin, Label, 12 In.	50.00
Case, E.Kiderlin, Rotterdam, Green, 8 In.	28.00
Case, Flower Design Base, Green	6.00
Case, Forward, Dark Olive	30.00
Case, G.W.Herwig, Black	30.00
Case, Graphite Pontil, Flat Lip	35.00
Case, Hartwig Kantorowicz, Germany, Milk Glass	50.00
Case, Henry H.Shufeldt & Co., Rye, Malt, & Gin, Amber	25.00
Case, J.J.W.Peters, Embossed Dog, Bird In Mouth, Olive Green	35.00
Case, J.J.W.Peters, Embossed Dog, Light & Dark Green, Ribbed Sides	45.00
Case, John De Kuyper & Son, Rotterdam, Olive	15.00
Case, Louis Meeus, Anvers	18.00
Case, P.Loopuyt & Co., Distillers	18.00 To 25.00
Case, Tubular Pontil, 2 1/4 Gallon	750.00
Case, V.Hoytema & Co., Black	15.00
Case, V.Hoytema & Co., Embossed, Olive Green, Quart	12.00
Case, V.Hoytema & Co., Olive Amber & Green	22.50
Case, V.Marken & Co., Black	15.00
Case, V.Marken & Co., Olive Amber & Green	22.50
Case, V.Meerten & Co., Black	20.00
Case, Vandenberg & Co., Bell, Ring Top, Olive	45.00
Case, Vandenberg & Co., Sealed, Light Olive, Quart	40.00
Case, Vanderveer's Medicated, Schiedam Schnapps, Dark Olive Green, 9 In.	75.00
Case, Vert Wood Pattern Mold, 11 In.	25.00
Case, 18th Century, Emerald	69.50
Case, 18th Century, Olive Green	49.50
Classic Busts, Highest Medal, Vienna, 1873, Teal Green	60.00
Cloverdale Spring Co., Newville, Penn., Bail & Stopper, Green, 10 In.	5.00
Cosmopoliet, Honey Yellow	80.00
DeKuyper's, Embossed, Odd Coffin Shape, Green, Large	6.00
Dog & Bird, Vertical Marks, Olive Green, 8 In.	50.00
Dr.Bouvier's Buchu, Clear, 1/2 Pint	5.00
Herman Jansen, Aschiedam, Holland, On Seal, Olive Green	20.00
Imperial, Cobalt Blue, Quart	250.00
J.J.W.Peters, Hamburg, Trademark, Dog With Bird In Mouth, Amber	25.00
J.J.W.Peters, Hamburg, Trademark, Dog With Bird In Mouth, Deep Red	45.00
London Charles Cordial, Emerald Green, 9 In.	35.00
London Charles Cordial, Olive Green, 2 1/4 X 2 1/4 X 7 3/4 In.	75.00
London Jockey Clubhouse, Embossed Horse & Jockey, IP, Light Citron	325.00
R.E.Messenger & Co., London, Olive Green, 2 1/4 X 2 1/4 X 8 In.	65.00
Rooster Riding Bike On Front, Oval, Amber	75.00
Simon, Rynbende & Zonein Schiedam, Tapered, Amber, 11 In.	15.00

Ginger Beer, Niagara Bottling
Co., Pottery, 7 In.

Ginger Beer, M.Nortz & Sons,
Lowville, N.Y., 7 In.

Ginger Beer, Titus Greenwood,
Pottery, 8 In.

T.J.Dunbar & Co., Green, Pint	18.00
V.Marken & Co., Olive Green	10.00
V.Marken & Co., Tapered, Amber, 9 1/2 In.	15.00
Van Bergh & Co.Seal, Blown, Yellow Green	75.00
Vandenberg & Co., Embossed, Around Bell In Seal, Olive Green	35.00
GINGER BEER, Ginger Beer Co., Syracuse, 20 In.High, 13 Pounds	225.00
Hill's Reliable, Dumbfries, Inside Screw	8.00
M.Nortz & Sons, Lowville, N.Y., 7 In. ....*Illus*	8.00
Niagara Bottling Co., Pottery, 7 In. ....*Illus*	7.00
Pottery, Tan & White	5.00
Titus Greenwood, Pottery, 8 In. ....*Illus*	8.00
GLOBULAR, Blown, Applied Lip, Light Green, 7 5/8 In.	65.00
Blown, Aqua, 10 3/4 In.	65.00
Blown, Light Green, 8 In.	35.00
Blown, Light Olive Amber, 9 X 7 3/4 In.	150.00
Blown, Light Olive, 15 In.	50.00
Blown, 20 Swirled Ribs, Flared Lip, Golden Amber, 7 1/2 In.	50.00
Blown, 20 Vertical Ribs, Light Blue, 6 5/8 In.	25.00
Kent, 20 Swirled Ribs, Applied Lip, Aqua, 5 3/8 In.	115.00
New England, Olive Green, 3 1/4 In.	60.00
Olive Amber, 3 1/2 In.	70.00
Sapphire Blue, 2 In.	260.00
Zanesville, Blown, 24 Swirled Ribs, Amber, 7 3/4 In.	300.00
30 Vertical Ribs, Folded-Over Lip, Aqua, 5 3/4 In.	15.00

*Glue bottles are often included with information about ink bottles. The
numbers in the form C-0 refer to the book "Ink Bottles and Inkwells" by
William E. Covill, Jr.*

GLUE, Carter's Mucilage, Clear	15.00
Spaulding's	10.00
GRENADIER, American Saddle Bred, 1978	22.00 To 28.00
American Thoroughbred, 1978	22.00 To 28.00
Appaloosa, 1978	22.00 To 38.00
Arabian, 1978	22.00 To 35.00
Coit Fireman Statue, 1974	40.00

Comte De Rochambeau, 1978 .... 28.00
Father's Gift, 1979 .... 35.00 To 40.00
Fire Chief, 1973 .... 30.00 To 40.00
Fireman Statue, 1974 .... 68.00
Ford T-Bird No.15, 1979 .... 46.00 To 50.00
Fray Junipero Serra, 1974 .... 20.00 To 25.00
Frosty The Snowman, 1978 .... 29.00 To 35.00
Gen.Billy Mitchell, 1975 .... 24.00
Joan Of Arc, 1972 .... 75.00 To 95.00
    GRENADIER, MINIATURE, see Miniature, Grenadier
Mission San Carlos, 1977 .... 22.00
Mission San Francisco De Asis, 1978 ....*Illus* 30.00
Mission San Gabriel, 1978 .... 22.00
Mission Santa Clara .... 22.00 To 24.95
Molly Pitcher, Bicentennial, 1976 .... 15.00
Moose Lodge, 1970 .... 18.00 To 20.00
Mr.Spock, 1979 .... 38.00 To 49.95
Nancy Holt, Bicentennial, 1976 .... 15.00
Pancho Villa & Carranza, 1977 .... 20.00
Pancho Villa & Maytorena, 1977 .... 20.00
Pancho Villa & Obregon, 1977 .... 20.00
Pancho Villa & Zapata, 1977 .... 20.00
Pancho Villa At Palacio, 1977 .... 20.00
Pancho Villa Into Battle, 1977 .... 20.00
Pontiac Trans-Am, 1979 .... 44.00 To 50.00
San Fernando Electric Co., 1977 .... 55.00 To 80.00
Santa Claus, Green Sack, 1978 .... 26.00
Shrine Jester, 1977 .... 47.00 To 60.00
Soldier, Baron General Von Steuben, 1978 .... 27.00 To 28.00
Soldier, Baron Johann DeKalb, 1978 .... 28.00 To 33.00
Soldier, Baylor's 3rd, 1969 .... 25.00 To 28.00
Soldier, Bicentennial, Set Of 12 .... 469.00
Soldier, Brunswick Dragoon, Bicentennial, 1976 .... 15.00
Soldier, Capt.Confederate, 1970 .... 18.00 To 21.00
Soldier, Capt.Union Army, 1970 .... 18.00
Soldier, Continental Marines, 1969 .... 47.00 To 60.00
Soldier, Corporal Grenadier, 1970 .... 20.00 To 22.00
Soldier, Count Pulaski, 1978 .... 28.00 To 42.00
Soldier, Dragoon 17th Regiment, 1970 .... 17.00 To 20.00
Soldier, Eugene, 1969 .... 21.00 To 25.00
Soldier, Field Marshal Rochambeau, 1978 .... 28.00
Soldier, Gen.George Washington, 1973 .... 30.00
Soldier, Gen.Ulysses S.Grant, 1975 .... 25.00
Soldier, General Custer 21.00
Soldier, General Douglas MacArthur, 1975 .... 17.00 To 23.00
Soldier, General Lafayette, 1978 .... 27.00
Soldier, Hesse-Cassel, Bicentennial, 1976 .... 15.00
Soldier, Jeb Stuart, 1970 .... 18.00 To 20.00
Soldier, John Paul Jones, 1976 ....*Illus* 25.00
Soldier, King's African Rifle Corps, 1971 .... 18.00
Soldier, King's African, Quart, 1970 .... 35.00
Soldier, Kosciuszko 29.00
Soldier, Lannes, 1970 .... 18.00 To 30.00
Soldier, Lassal, 1969 .... 40.00 To 45.00
Soldier, LCMC Foot Guard, 1972 .... 22.00
Soldier, Minute Man, Bicentennial, 1976 .... 15.00
Soldier, Murat, 1970 .... 20.00 To 24.00
Soldier, Napoleon, 1969 .... 51.00 To 70.00
Soldier, Ney, 1969 .... 25.00
Soldier, Officer Scots Fusileer, 1971 .... 21.00
Soldier, Officer 3rd Guard, 1971 .... 18.00 To 20.00
Soldier, Queen's Rangers, Bicentennial, 1976 .... 15.00

Grenadier, Mission San Francisco De Asis, 1978   Grenadier, Soldier, John Paul Jones, 1976

Soldier, Rhode Island, Bicentennial, 1976	15.00
Soldier, Robert E.Lee, 1/2 Gallon	120.00
Soldier, Sgt.Maj.Coldstream, 1971	20.00
Soldier, Stonewall Jackson, 1976	35.00 To 40.00
Soldier, Teddy Roosevelt, 1977	26.00 To 30.00
Soldier, Texas Ranger, 1977	27.00
Soldier, Thaddeus Kosciuszko, 1978	23.00
Soldier, Valley Forge, Bicentennial, 1976	15.00
Soldier, Washington's Guard, Bicentennial, 1976	15.00
Soldier, 1st Georgia Regiment, Bicentennial, 1976	15.00
Soldier, 1st Pennsylvania, 1970	43.00 To 50.00
Soldier, 1st U.S.Regulars, Bicentennial, 1976	15.00
Soldier, 18th Continental, 1970	21.00
Soldier, 2nd Maryland, 1969	38.00 To 50.00
Soldier, 3rd New York, 1969	19.00 To 22.00
Soldier, 38th Regiment On Foot, Bicentennial, 1976	15.00
Tennessee Walking Horse, 1978	23.00

     HAIR PRODUCTS, see Cosmetic; Medicine
     HAND LOTION, see Cosmetic; Medicine

HOFFMAN, Alaska Pipeline, 1975	27.00
Androcles & Lion, 1978	27.00
Baby Egret, 1979	18.00 To 21.00
Bear & Cub, 1978	35.00 To 48.00
Betsy Ross, 1974	52.00
Big Red Machine, 1973	25.00
Big, Big Trouble On The Trail, 1978	300.00 To 350.00
Blue Jay, Pair	50.00
Bobcat & Pheasant, 1978	48.00
Buffalo Hunter, 1978	33.00
Buffalo Man, 1976	26.00
Calf Roping, 1978	33.00
Canada Goose Decoy, 1977	17.00
Caroliers, 1979	45.00 To 50.00
Clown, 1978	29.00 To 32.00
Concord Soldier, 1973	27.00
Coon Dog, 1979	50.00 To 60.00
Cowboy, 1978	31.00
Dallas Cheerleader, Topless	150.00 To 200.00
Dallas Cheerleader, 1980	27.00 To 29.00
Doe & Fawn, 1975	49.00 To 51.00
Dogs Playing Pool, 1979	38.00

Hoffman, Mark Donohue's No.66, Sunoco McLaren

Hoffman, Mr.Doctor, 1974

Donahue Commemorative, 1972	25.00
Dove, Closed Wing, 1979	28.00
Dove, Open Wing, 1979	28.00
Doves, Pair, 1979	48.00
Eagle & Fox, 1978	45.00 To 60.00
Eagle, Bicentennial, 1976	75.00 To 79.00
Eagle, Open Wing, 1979	22.00 To 23.00
Falcon & Rabbit, 1978	46.00
Flathead Squaw, 1976	29.00
Fox & Grapes, 1978	24.00
Foyter, No.2, 1973	79.00
Geese, Pair, 1980	18.00
German Shepherd, 1980	35.00
Golden Eagles, U.S.M., 1981	*Color* 35.00
Goose With Golden Egg, 1978	25.00
Half-Breed Trader, 1978	32.00
Hare & Tortoise, 1978	22.00
Jaguar, 1978	47.00
Johncock Commemorative, 1973	24.00
Johncock No.20, 1974	30.00
Kangaroo, 1978	40.00
Kentucky Flintlock, 1975	27.00
Lady Godiva, 1974	25.00 To 40.00
Last Of The 5000, 1975	27.00 To 30.00
Lion & Dall Sheep, Set, 1977	145.00 To 180.00
Lion, 1979	44.00 To 46.00
Louisiana State University Tiger, 1978	50.00
Lovebirds, 1979	18.00 To 20.00
Mallards, Open Wing, 1980	30.00 To 35.00
Mark Donohue's No.66, Sunoco McLaren	*Illus* 25.00
Merganser, 1978	43.00
HOFFMAN, MINIATURE, see Miniature, Hoffman	
Mississippi Bulldogs, 1977	*Color* 58.00
Mississippi Rebels, 1977	*Color* 58.00
Mr.Baker, 1978	38.00
Mr.Barber, 1980	20.00 To 46.00
Mr.Bartender, 1975	32.00
Mr.Blacksmith, 1976	32.00
Mr.Butcher, 1979	35.00
Mr.Carpenter, 1979	35.00 To 36.00
Mr.Charmer, 1974	31.00
Mr.Cobbler, 1973	29.00
Mr.Dancer, 1974	30.00
Mr.Dentist, 1980	25.00 To 46.00
Mr.Doctor, 1974	*Illus* 30.00
Mr.Electrician, 1978	35.00 To 36.00
Mr.Farmer, 1980	20.00 To 45.00

Mr.Fiddler, 1974 .... 30.00 To 60.00
Mr.Fireman, 1976 .... 32.00
Mr.Guitarist, 1975 .... 29.00 To 29.50
Mr.Harpist, 1974 .... 25.00 To 29.50
Mr.Lucky Retired, 1978 .... 44.00
Mr.Lucky, White & Gold, 100th Anniversary 200.00
Mr.Lucky, 1973 .... 50.00 To 75.00
Mr.Mailman, 1976 .... 29.00
Mr.Mechanic, 1979 .... 34.00
Mr.Photographer, 1980 .... 20.00 To 47.00
Mr.Plumber, 1978 .... 35.00
Mr.Policeman, 1975 .... 28.00
Mr.Railroad Engineer, 1980 .... 20.00 To 45.00
Mr.Sandman, 1974 .... 30.00
Mr.Saxophonist, 1975 .... 29.50 To 30.00
Mr.Schoolteacher, 1976 .... 32.00
Mr.Stockbroker, 1976 .... 30.00
Mr.Tailor, 1979 .... 30.00 To 35.00
Mr.Tourist, 1980 .... 20.00 To 45.00
Mrs.Lucky, 1974 .... 29.00
Musk Ox, Pair, 1979 .... 65.00 To 84.00
Nevada Wolf Pack, 1979 .... 39.00
Northern Cree, 1978 .... 34.00
Organ Player, 1979 .... 45.00 To 50.00
Owl & Chipmunk, 1978 .... 63.00
Panda, 1976 .... 48.00 To 53.00
Penguins, 1979 .... 41.00
Pointer, 1979 .... 60.00
Prospector, 1976 .... 28.00
Pup Seals, 1979 .... 18.00 To 20.00
Russell & Goat, Pair, 1978 .... 59.00
Russell Bust, 1978 .... 32.00
Rutherford No.3, 1974 .... 43.00
Saddle Bronc Rider, 1978 .... 36.00
Saddle, 1978 .... 41.00
Scout, 1978 .... 34.00
Setter, 1979 .... 59.00
Shepherd's Boy, 1978 .... 22.00
Sow Grizzly & Cub Fishing, 1981 ....*Color* 99.00
Springer Spaniel, 1979 .... 50.00 To 60.00
Stage Robber, 1978 .... 29.00 To 30.00
Stagecoach Driver, 1976 .... 27.00
Steer Wrestling, 1978 .... 36.00
Stranger, This Is My Land, 1979 ....*Illus* 500.00

Hoffman, Stranger, This Is My Land, 1979

Swans, Pair, 1/2 Pint, 1980	38.00
Tower Flintlock, 1975	29.00
Trapper, 1976	26.00
Turkeys, 1980	39.00
Widgeon, 1978	38.00
Wolf & Raccoon, 1978	39.00 To 60.00
Wood Duck, 1978	36.00
Wood Ducks, 1981	*Color* 350.00
HOLLY CITY, see Millville Art Glass	
HOUSEHOLD, C.C.Parsons Ammonia, Aqua, 10 In.	*Color* 4.00
Osborn's Liquid Polish, Amber, Open Pontil, Round	325.00
Osborn's Liquid Polish, Honey Green Amber	225.00
HOUSEHOLD, SHOE POLISH, see Shoe Polish	
I.W.HARPER, Flags Of Nations, 1966	8.00
Gold Medal, Whiskey, Pottery, Blue, 9 In.	20.00
Grand Prize, 1960	10.00
Harper Man, Blue, 1968	10.00
Harper Man, Gray, 1968	10.00
Southern Gentlemen, Wheel Cut, Pint, No Stopper	35.00

Ink bottles were first used in the United States in 1819. Early ink bottles were of ceramic and were often imported. Inks can be identified by their shape. They were made to be hard to tip over. The numbers used in entries in the form C-0 or McK G I-0 refer to the books "Ink Bottles and Inkwells" by William E. Covill, Jr., and "American Bottles and Flasks" by Helen McKearin and Kenneth M. Wilson.

INK, A.D.R., Albany, Igloo, Aqua, 2 X 2 In.	45.00
Alling's Pat'd.Apr.25, 1871, C-704	85.00
AM Bertinguiot, Open Pontil, Deep Cobalt Blue, C-576	475.00
Antes, Patent 1890, Top	12.00
Arnold, Pottery, 6 In.	7.50
B.G.S., On Base, Umbrella, Pontil	129.00
B.P.Co., Cobalt, 3 In.	*Illus* 8.00
Babbettonian Black, N.Y., 16-Sided Umbrella, Olive Amber, Open Pontil	185.00
Ball, Fountain, Metal Frame, 3 3/4 X 4 3/4 In., C-1308	80.00
Ball, Patented, Milk Glass Ball On Leaf Frame, No Font, 4 1/4 In.	35.00
Banana Shape, Aqua	30.00
Barrel, A.Dinka Co., Aqua, C-660	52.00
Barrel, BIMAL, Oval Label Panel, Aqua, C-658	20.00
Barrel, BIMAL, Pat.March, 1870, Clear, C-672	65.00
Barrel, Pat.March 1st, 1870, BIMAL, Clear, 2 In., C-671	50.00
Barrel, Pontil, Clear, 2 X 2 1/4 In., C-668	95.00
Bertinguiot, Domed, Label, Deep Olive Amber, 2 X 2 1/2 In.	110.00
Bertinguiot, Domed, Light Olive Amber, 2 X 2 1/2 In.	140.00
Bertinguiot, Domed, Open Pontil, Cobalt Blue	525.00
Bertinguiot, Domed, Open Pontil, Dark Amber, C-576	175.00
Bertinguiot, Domed, Open Pontil, Light Olive Green	185.00
Bird, Embossed, BIMAL, Aqua, C-638	39.00
Blacking Oval, Open Pontil, Crude, Green, 4 3/4 In.	45.00
Blackstone's, U.S.A., BIMAL, 2 3/8 In., C-41	10.00
Blake, N.Y., Umbrella, Aqua, 2 7/8 X 2 3/4 In.	120.00
Blown, Applied Rigaree Rim, Light Blue Opaque, 24 Ribs, 2 In.	65.00
Blown, Bulbous, Dark Olive Amber, 1 1/4 X 2 In., C-1023	160.00
Blown, Bulbous, Pontil, Light Olive Amber, 2 X 2 3/4 In., C-1030	200.00
Blown, Conical Shaped, Double Font, Handled, 4 3/4 X 3 In., C-1098	160.00
Blown, Covered, Aqua, 4 1/2 X 4 1/8 In., C-1062	55.00
Blown, Covered, Pedestal Base, Greenish Aqua, 5 5/8 In., C-1047	300.00
Blown, Funnel Type, Pedestal Base, Deep Golden Amber, 2 7/8 In.	225.00
Blown, Horizontally Ribbed, Applied Handle, Greenish Aqua, 2 1/8 In.	180.00
Blown, Hourglass Shaped, Aqua, 3 X 2 1/4 In.	110.00
Blown, Pale Green, 2 1/4 X 2 3/4 In.	60.00

Ink, B.P.Co., Cobalt, 3 In.

Blown, Pale Green, 3 5/8 X 3 In., C-1044 .... 65.00
Blown, Paperweight, Stopper, Green Aqua, 5 X 4 In. 160.00
Blown, Pontil, Dark Olive Amber, 2 X 2 1/8 In., C-1022 .... 180.00
Blown, Pontil, Olive Amber, 2 1/8 X 2 3/8 In., C-1024 .... 290.00
Blown, Round, Deep Olive Amber, 2 3/4 X 3 1/2 In., C-1034 .... 175.00
Blown, Round, Horizontal Ribs, Applied Handle, Greenish Aqua, 2 1/8 In. 210.00
Blown, Round, Pontil, Citron, 2 1/2 X 2 7/8 In., C-1041 .... 110.00
Blown, Round, Pontil, Deep Olive Amber, 1 1/2 X 2 1/2 In., C-1033 .... 160.00
Blown, Round, Red, 2 1/8 X 2 3/8 In. 120.00
Blown, Round, Swagging, Pontil, Deep Aqua, 1 1/2 X 2 1/2 In., C-1094 .... 250.00
Blown, Square, Dark Amber, 2 1/4 X 2 In., C-1080 .... 220.00
Blown, Turtle, Double Neck, 2 1/8 In., C-1095 .... 875.00
Blown, 3 Mold, Aqua With Moonstone Effect, 2 X 2 5/8 In. 150.00
Blown, 3 Mold, Boston & Sandwich, 1 3/4 X 2 In., C-1212 .... 450.00
Blown, 3 Mold, Boston & Sandwich, 2 X 2 In., C-1202 .... 425.00
Blown, 3 Mold, Boston & Sandwich, 2 1/8 X 2 1/8 In., C-1214 .... 325.00
Blown, 3 Mold, Bright Green, 2 X 2 1/4 In., C-1178 .... 300.00
Blown, 3 Mold, Bulbous, Dark Olive Amber, 1 1/2 X 2 In., C-1204 .... 1750.00
Blown, 3 Mold, Clear, 1 7/8 X 2 1/8 In., C-1206 .... 425.00
Blown, 3 Mold, Clear, 2 X 2 In., C-1207 .... 450.00
Blown, 3 Mold, Clear, 2 1/8 X 2 In., C-1203 .... 500.00
Blown, 3 Mold, Clear, 2 5/8 X 2 In., C-1216 .... 575.00
Blown, 3 Mold, Conical, Clear, 2 1/8 X 2 1/8 In., C-1205 .... 475.00
Blown, 3 Mold, Corset, 2 X 2 In., C-1213 .... *Illus* 1600.00
Blown, 3 Mold, Deep Amber, 1 5/8 X 2 3/8 In. 80.00
Blown, 3 Mold, Deep Cobalt Blue, 1 7/8 X 2 In., C-1186 .... 2100.00
Blown, 3 Mold, Deep Emerald Green, 2 X 2 5/8 In., C-1200 .... 160.00
Blown, 3 Mold, Deep Golden Amber, 1 1/2 X 2 1/4 In. .... 80.00 To 95.00
Blown, 3 Mold, Deep Golden Amber, 1 5/8 X 2 3/8 In., C-1182 .... 75.00
Blown, 3 Mold, Deep Olive Amber, 1 1/2 X 2 1/4 In., C-1182 .... 40.00 To 100.00

Ink, Blown, 3 Mold, Corset, 2 X 2 In., C-1213

Blown, 3 Mold, Deep Olive Amber, 1 3/4 X 2 5/8 In., C-1196 .... 45.00 To 100.00
Blown, 3 Mold, Deep Olive Amber, 1 5/8 X 2 1/4 In., C-1182 .... 70.00
Blown, 3 Mold, Deep Olive Green, 1 1/2 X 2 1/4 In., C-1221 .... 250.00
Blown, 3 Mold, Deep Olive Green, 2 1/4 X 3 In., C-1174 ....*Illus* 950.00
Blown, 3 Mold, Deep Yellow Olive, 1 1/2 X 2 1/4 In., C-1194 .... 80.00
Blown, 3 Mold, Dense Amethyst, 2 1/2 X 2 5/8 In., C-1210 ....*Illus* 700.00
Blown, 3 Mold, Dense Olive Amber, 1 1/2 X 2 1/4 In., C-1182 .... 25.00
Blown, 3 Mold, Light Olive Amber, 1 1/2 X 2 1/4 In., C-1181 .... 30.00
Blown, 3 Mold, Light Yellow Green, 2 X 2 In., C-1185 ....*Illus* 625.00
Blown, 3 Mold, Light Yellow Olive, 1 3/4 X 2 1/8 In., C-1215 .... 325.00
Blown, 3 Mold, Olive Amber, 2 X 2 In. ....*Illus* 775.00
Blown, 3 Mold, Olive Amber, 2 X 2 1/4 In., C-1175 .... 50.00
Blown, 3 Mold, Olive Green, 1 3/4 X 1 7/8 In., C-1184 .... 70.00
Blown, 3 Mold, Olive Green, 9 3/4 In. 20.00
Blown, 3 Mold, Open Pontil, Olive Amber, C-1221 .... 100.00
Blown, 3 Mold, Pale Electric Blue, 2 X 2 In., C-1218 .... 550.00

Ink, Blown, 3 Mold, Deep Olive Green,
2 1/4 X 3 In., C-1174

Ink, Blown, 3 Mold, Dense Amethyst,
2 1/2 X 2 5/8 In., C-1210

Ink, Blown, 3 Mold, Light Yellow Green,
2 X 2 In., C-1185

Ink, Blown, 3 Mold, Olive Amber,
2 X 2 In.

Blown, 3 Mold, Vertically Ribbed, Emerald Green, 1 3/4 X 2 In. 150.00
Blown, 3 Mold, Vertically Ribbed, Fiery Opalescent, 1 7/8 X 2 In. 150.00
Blown, 3 Mold, Vertically Ribbed, Milk Glass, 1 3/4 X 1 7/8 In. 90.00
Blown, 3 Mold, Vertically Ribbed, Violet Blue, 1 5/8 X 2 In., C-1173 .... 150.00
Blown, 3 Mold, Violet, 1 7/8 X 1 7/8 In., C-1172 ....*Illus* 300.00
Blown, 3 Mold, Yellow Green, 1 7/8 X 2 1/4 In., C-1179 .... 200.00
Blown, 3 Mold, Yellow Olive, 1 7/8 X 2 5/8 In., C-1198 .... 120.00
Boat, Patented, Milk Glass, Painted Decoration, Metal Cap, 5 1/2 In. 250.00
Boat, Patented, Pewter Cap, Clear, 2 1/4 X 5 1/2 In., C-1421 .... 75.00
Boot, Amber 35.00

Ink, Blown, 3 Mold, Violet,
1 7/8 X 1 7/8 In., C-1172

Ink, Booth's, Round, IP, Deep Aqua,
9 3/4 X 3 5/8 In.

Booth's, Round, IP, Deep Aqua, 9 3/4 X 3 5/8 In. .... *Illus* 100.00
Boss Patent, 6 Sided, Umbrella, Aqua, 2 5/8 X 2 1/2 In. 150.00
Boston Ink, Round, Aqua, 2 1/4 X 2 In. 80.00
Bourne Pottery, Embossed, Quart 5.00
Brass Demon Head 60.00
Brickett & Thayer, Labeled, Round, Deep Olive Amber, 4 3/8 X 1 5/8 In. 30.00
Bristol's Recorder, Amber, ABM, C-394 .... 12.00 To 18.00
Building, BIMAL, Greenish Aqua, 4 X 3 1/4 In., C-694 .... 50.00
Building, BIMAL, 1776, 1876, Clear, 3 3/8 X 3 3/4 In., C-695 .... 50.00
Bulldog Bust, Light Amber 48.00
Bulldog Head, Light Amber, 4 In. 55.00
Bulldog, Head & Bust Type, Topaz, 4 In. 60.00
Burham's & Co., Burlington, Iowa, Umbrella, Aqua, 2 1/4 In. 390.00
Burham's & Co., Umbrella, Aqua, 2 1/4 X 2 In. 390.00
Butler's, Cincinnati, Olive Yellow, 2 3/4 X 2 In., C-519 ....*Illus* 1350.00
Butler's, Cincinnati, 12-Sided, Aqua, 2 3/4 X 2 1/4 In. 85.00
Butler's, Cincinnati, 12-Sided, Olive Yellow, 2 3/4 In., C-519 .... 1350.00
Butler's, Cincinnati, 12-Sided, Open Pontil, Aqua, 2 7/8 In. 225.00
C.G.Geer, Labeled, Umbrella, Aqua, 2 1/2 X 2 3/8 In., C-125 .... 25.00
Cabin, BIMAL, 2 1/2 X 2 1/2 In., C-680 .... 175.00
Cabin, BIMAL, 2 1/4 X 1 5/8 In., C-679 .... 250.00
Cabin, Pontil, 3 1/8 X 2 3/8 In., C-675 .... 100.00
Cabin, 3 1/8 X 2 1/2 In., C-677 ....*Illus* 350.00

Ink, Butler's, Cincinnati, Olive
Yellow, 2 3/4 X 2 In., C-519

Ink, Cabin, 3 1/8 X 2 1/2 In., C-677

Carter's Black Letter Ink, Cone, Full Label, Clear 9.50
Carter's Black Letter, Cone, Full Label, Clear 12.50
Carter's Cathedral, Cobalt Blue, 1/2 Pint 95.00
Carter's Ink Co., Pottery, Handled Jug, Cream & Brown Glazes, Gallon 45.00
Carter's Spanish Mixture, IP, Green 150.00
Carter's Spanish Mixture, Iron Pontil, Olive Green 140.00
Carter's 1897, Cone, Olive Green, C-47 .... 20.00
Carter's, BIMAL, Amber, 7 5/8 In., C-814 .... 10.00
Carter's, Cathedral, ABM, Cobalt Blue, Quart .... 28.00 To 49.00
Carter's, Cathedral, Cap, Cobalt Blue, 9 3/4 In. 65.00
Carter's, Clear, 2 1/2 In. .... *Illus* 6.00
Carter's, Cloverleaf Panels, Stopper, 6-Sided, Label 87.50
Carter's, Cobalt Blue, 3 X 3 1/4 In., C-555 .... 55.00
Carter's, Cone, Emerald Green .... 12.00 To 12.50
Carter's, Labels, Cap, Quart, C-820 .... 65.00
Carter's, Master, Honey Amber, 1/2 Pint, C-812 .... 9.50
Carter's, Pottery, Handled Jug, Cream & Brown Glazes, Gallon 55.00
Carter's, Turtle, Doors & Windows, Aqua, 1 5/8 In., C-614 .... 75.00
Carter's, Turtle, Doors & Windows, Aqua, 1 7/8 X 2 1/4 In. 140.00
Carter's, Umbrella, Green 20.00
Carter's, Widemouth, 2 3/4 In. 2.00
Carter's, 1897, Bright Green 20.00
Carter's, 6 Panel, 5 Embossed Cloverleaves, Cobalt Blue, 2 3/4 In. 100.00
Cathedral, Carter's, Labels & Stopper, Quart, C-819 .... 50.00
Caw's Ink & Pen Co. 8.00
Caw's Ink, N.Y., Small 5.00
Chadwick's Black, Labeled, Olive Green, 4 7/8 X 1 3/4 In. 50.00
Chas.M.Higgins Co., N.Y., Round, Master, Aqua, 5 3/4 In. 5.00
Christey, Buffalo, N.Y., Cone, Aqua, 2 1/8 X 2 1/2 In. 20.00
Christey, Patent, Cone, Wire Pen Rack, Aqua, 2 1/8 In. 40.00
Clark's Ink Co., Pouring Spout, Master, Aqua, Small 15.00
Columbian Exhibition Building, Pressed Glass, 3 1/2 In., C-1513 ...... 160.00
Cone, BIMAL, Blue-Green, 2 7/8 In., C-45 .... 10.00
Cone, BIMAL, Dark Amber, 2 7/8 In., C-45 .... 7.50
Cone, BIMAL, Light Amber, 2 7/8 In., C-45 .... 6.00
Cone, BIMAL, Light Blue, 2 1/2 In., C-47 .... 25.00
Cone, BIMAL, Olive Green, 2 7/16 In., C-97 .... 15.00
Cone, BIMAL, Teal Blue, C-97 .... 20.00
Cone, Brown Stoneware 10.00
Cone, Deep Sapphire Blue, 2 1/2 X 2 3/8 In. 70.00
Cone, Golden Amber, 2 1/4 X 2 3/8 In. 65.00
Cone, Green 12.00
Cone, Light Green, Pontil, C-113 .... 20.00
Cone, Medium Green, 2 5/8 X 2 1/4 In., C-22 .... 80.00
Cone, Olive Amber, 2 1/4 X 2 1/4 In., C-18 .... 75.00
Cone, Pontil, Aqua, 2 1/2 X 4 1/8 In., C-13 .... 80.00
Cone, Pontil, Bright Medium Green, 2 3/4 X 2 1/4 In., C-21 .... 45.00
Cone, Pottery, Red Brown 8.00
Cone, Puce, 2 1/4 X 2 3/8 In. 80.00
Cone, Sapphire Blue, 2 1/2 X 2 1/4 In. 175.00
Cone, Stoddard Type, Open Pontil, Olive Amber 85.00
Cone, Stoddard, N.H., Open Pontil, Olive Amber, C-15 .... 65.00
Cone, Swag Decorated, Sapphire Blue, 4 X 3 In., C-28 .... *Illus* 725.00
Continental Jet Black, Label, 90 Percent, Aqua 12.50
Continental Philadelphia, For School Desk, BIMAL, Aqua, C-722 ...... 25.00
Cooke's Carmine, Cone, Aqua, 2 X 1 3/4 In., C-9 .... *Illus* 100.00
Cylinder, Horizontal Ribs, Pale Yellow Green, 2 5/8 In. 90.00
Darling, Octagonal, Patent, 1 1/2 X 2 3/8 In. 15.00
Davids & Black, Labeled, Deep Olive Amber, Double Mouth, 6 1/2 In. 50.00
Davids & Black, New York, Master, Emerald Green, 8 In. 155.00
Davids & Black, Round, Spout, Iron Pontil, Light Green, C-752 .... 80.00
Davids Black Ink, Open Pontil, Aqua, 5 1/2 In. .... *Color* 80.00
Davids, New York, Pottery, Master, Pint 30.00

Davids, New York, Round, Pale Yellow Green, 5 1/4 X 1 1/3 In. 35.00
Davids, New York, Round, Spout, Bright Green, 8 3/4 X 3 3/4 In., C-752 .... 240.00
Davis & Miller, Umbrella, Vertically Ribbed, Aqua, 2 1/2 X 2 1/8 In. 150.00
De Halsey, Patente, Domed, Dark Olive Amber, 3 X 3 3/8 In., C-578 .... 150.00
De Halsey, Patente, Olive Amber, 2 3/4 X 3 1/4 In., C-577 .... *Illus* 130.00
Denby All British, Contents, Cork, Wax, Triangular, Aqua, C-709 .... 25.00
Denby Pottery, P & J Arnold, London, 6 In. .... *Illus* 6.00
Desk, Heavy Glass, Pen Rest, Brass Hinged Top, Mame, Saratoga, 1893 .... 29.50

Ink, Carter's, Clear, 2 1/2 In.

Ink, Cone, Swag Decorated, Sapphire
Blue, 4 X 3 In., C-28

Ink, Cooke's Carmine, Cone,
Aqua, 2 X 1 3/4 In., C-9

Ink, De Halsey, Patente, Olive Amber,
2 3/4 X 3 1/4 In., C-577

Ink, Denby Pottery, P & J Arnold, London, 6 In.

Dessauer's Jet Black, Turtle, Aqua, 1 7/8 X 2 1/8 In., C-618 .... 15.00
Diamond Ink Co., Milwaukee, BIMAL, 2 7/16 In., C-740 .... 15.00
Dog's Head, Milk Glass, Square Metal Stand, 4 1/2 X 4 1/2 In. 160.00
Dome, BIMAL, Deep Golden Amber, 1 7/8 X 1 7/8 In., C-647 .... 100.00
Dome, Clear, Blue & White Swirls, Pewter Cover, 2 1/2 X 3 In., C-1382 .... 600.00
Dome, Electric Blue, Metal Cap, 1 7/8 X 2 3/4 In., C-1472 .... 85.00
Dome, Round, Olive Amber, 2 X 2 1/2 In., C-573 .... 120.00
Dome, 9-Sided, Stone, Brass Cap, 1 7/8 X 3 In. 120.00
Drape Pattern, Cone, Bright Green, 2 1/2 X 2 1/4 In. 60.00
Draper's Patent, Overlay, Green Cut To Clear, Gilt, 2 7/8 In., C-1416 .... 275.00
Draper's Patent, 12-Sided, Clear, Pewter Cap, 2 7/8 X 4 In., C-1414 .... 65.00
Draper's Patent, 12-Sided, Violet, Pewter Cap, 2 7/8 X 4 In. 290.00
E.Waters, Troy, N.Y., Aqua, 5 1/2 X 3 1/2 In., C-773 .... 150.00
E.Waters, Troy, N.Y., Aqua, 6 3/4 X 4 3/8 In., C-774 ....*Illus* 250.00
E.Waters, Troy, N.Y., Open Pontil, Light Green, C-208 .... 275.00
E.Waters, Troy, N.Y., Pontil, C-773 .... 110.00
E.Waters, Troy, N.Y., Round, Aqua, 2 1/4 X 1 1/2 In., C-207 .... 90.00
E.Waters, Troy, N.Y., Round, Aqua, 8 1/2 X 5 3/8 In. 150.00
Encre De La Grande Vertu Bordeaux, Citron, 2 1/8 X 2 1/2 In. 40.00
English, Debossed Scott, Salt Glazed, Miniature 15.00
Estes, N.Y., Octagonal, Aqua, 6 3/4 X 2 3/4 In., C-756 .... 140.00
Estes, N.Y., Octagonal, Light Golden Amber, 5 1/2 X 2 In. ....*Illus* 425.00
Excelsior Pattern, Molded, Clear, 2 5/8 X 3 1/2 In., C-1389 .... 70.00
F.Kidder Improved Indelible, Aqua, Flared Lip, Square 55.00
Farley's, Label, Pour Spout, IP, Deep Olive Amber, 7 3/8 In., C-757 .... 110.00
Farley's, Octagonal, Olive Amber, 1 3/4 X 1 7/8 In., C-526 ....*Illus* 225.00
Felix The Cat 40.00
Fellows & Co., Chemists, St.John, N.B., Dark Cobalt Blue 20.00
Felt Stationer's Hall, N.Y., Pottery, 4 1/2 In. ....*Color* 80.00
Fountain, Clear, Black Painted Cast Iron & Gold Decoration, 3 1/2 In. 30.00
Fountain, Floral, Emerald Green, 2 1/2 X 2 3/4 In. ....*Illus* 300.00
Fountain, Patented, Vaseline, 3 1/8 X 4 3/4 In., C-1316 .... 150.00
Fountain, Pontil, Cut, Hexagonal, 2 3/8 X 2 1/2 In., C-1243 .... 20.00
Fountain, Pontil, Quill Holder, Hexagonal, 2 3/4 X 2 3/4 In., C-1244 .... 10.00
Fountain, 12-Panel Dome, BIMAL, Cap & Box, 2 9/16 In., C-1297 .... 30.00
Fred Allings, Rochester, Clear 16.00
Funnel, Hole, Rubber Stopper In Base, BIMAL, C-1360 .... 12.00
G. & R.'s Carmine, Round, Aqua, 2 7/8 X 1 3/8 In. 100.00
G.A.Miller, Quincy, Ill., 12-Sided, Embossed, Pale Citron 100.00
G.E.Hatch, Milk Glass, Painted Pear, Leaves, 2 1/2 In., C-1426 .... 300.00
G.E.Hatch, Round, Embossed Pear Decoration, 2 1/2 X 3 7/8 In. 90.00
G.M.W. & A.A.S., Pen Ledge, BIMAL, Aqua, 1 3/8 In., C-635 .... 20.00
Garret & Co., Penn Mfg. Works, Stopper, Milk Glass, C-563 .... 60.00 To 100.00
Gaylord's Superior Record, Light Olive Amber, 6 In. ....*Illus* 250.00
Glazed Stoneware, White, Master, 10 In. 12.00
Gross & Robinson, IP, Deep Aqua, 9 1/8 X 4 3/4 In. ....*Illus* 575.00
Gross & Robinson's, Aqua, 4 1/4 X 2 1/8 In. 150.00
Gross & Robinson's, Round, Iron Pontil, Aqua, 5 7/8 X 3 1/4 In. 80.00
H.G.Hotchkiss, Pouring Lip, Master, Cobalt Blue, 9 3/4 In., C-860 .... 35.00
Haley Ink Co., New York, Round, Clear 14.00
Halsey's Patente, Open Pontil, Olive Green, 3 X 3 1/4 In. 350.00
Harrison, Tippecanoe, Cabin, 3 7/8 X 3 X 1 3/4 In., C-676 ....*Illus* 2900.00
Harrison's Columbian, Aqua, 11 3/8 X 6 1/4 In., C-762 .... 375.00
Harrison's Columbian, Aqua, 3 3/4 X 2 1/8 In., C-536 .... 40.00
Harrison's Columbian, Aqua, 3 7/8 X 2 In., C-537 .... 75.00
Harrison's Columbian, Cobalt Blue, 2 1/8 X 2 1/8 In., C-194 .... 225.00
Harrison's Columbian, Cobalt Blue, 4 1/8 X 1 7/8 In., C-195 .... 350.00
Harrison's Columbian, Deep Sapphire Blue, 10 1/2 X 6 1/8 In. 8000.00
Harrison's Columbian, Deep Sapphire Blue, 5 7/8 X 2 3/4 In., C-764 .... 325.00
Harrison's Columbian, Flared Applied Mouth, 8 1/2 In. 600.00
Harrison's Columbian, Labeled, Cobalt Blue, 5 3/4 X 2 3/4 In. 120.00
Harrison's Columbian, Light Blue Green, 8 1/2 X 5 In. ....*Illus* 600.00
Harrison's Columbian, Octagonal, Aqua, 2 X 2 1/8 In., C-531 .... 35.00

Ink, E.Waters, Troy, N.Y., Aqua,
6 3/4 X 4 3/8 In., C-774

Ink, Estes, N.Y., Octagonal,
Light Golden Amber,
5 1/2 X 2 In.

Ink, Farley's, Octagonal, Olive Amber,
1 3/4 X 1 7/8 In., C-526

Ink, Fountain, Floral, Emerald
Green, 2 1/2 X 2 3/4 In.

Ink, Gaylord's Superior Record,
Light Olive Amber, 6 In.

Ink, Gross & Robinson,
IP, Deep Aqua,
9 1/8 X 4 3/4 In.

Ink, Harrison, Tippecanoe, Cabin,
3 7/8 X 3 X 1 3/4 In., C-676

Ink, Harrison's Columbian,
Light Blue Green,
8 1/2 X 5 In.

Harrison's Columbian, Octagonal, Aqua, 2 1/2 X 1 1/4 In., C-534 .... 65.00
Harrison's Columbian, Octagonal, Turtle, Aqua, 1 5/8 In., C-623 .... 190.00
Harrison's Columbian, Partial Label, Aqua, 2 7/8 X 1 1/2 In., C-535 .... 65.00
Harrison's Columbian, Pontil, Aqua, 1 7/8 X 1 5/8 In., C-530 .... 95.00
Harrison's Columbian, Pontil, Cobalt Blue, 5 3/4 In., C-764 .... 600.00
Harrison's Columbian, Pontil, Sapphire Blue, 5 3/4 In., C-764 .... 415.00
Harrison's Columbian, Reversed N, Pontil, Aqua, C-537 .... 100.00
Harrison's Columbian, Round, Cobalt Blue, 3 3/8 In., C-765 .... 675.00
Harrison's Columbian, Sapphire Blue, Applied Mouth, Iron Pontil, 7 In. 200.00
Harrison's Columbian, Sapphire Blue, 10 1/2 X 6 1/8 In. ....*Illus* 8000.00
Harrison's Columbian, Turtle, Aqua, 1 7/8 X 2 1/4 In., C-624 .... 330.00
Harrison's Columbian, 12-Sided, Aqua, 5 7/8 X 3 1/4 In., C-760 .... 175.00
Harrison's Columbian, 12-Sided, 7 1/8 X 4 In., C-1661 .... 100.00 To 150.00
Harrison's Indelible Preparation, Octagonal, Clear 55.00
Harrison's Indelible, Clear, 2 3/8 X 1 1/2 In., C-533 .... 95.00
Harrison's, Cylindrical Pontil, Cobalt Blue, 2 1/16 In., C-194 .... 275.00
Head, Benjamin Franklin, Aqua, 2 3/4 X 4 1/8 In., C-1291 .... 90.00
Head, Benjamin Franklin, Fountain, 2 3/4 X 4 1/2 In., C-1290 .... 90.00
Heath's Indelible, 12-Sided, Aqua, 5 7/8 X 3 3/4 In. 200.00
Hexagonal, Sapphire Blue, 2 5/8 X 1 3/4 In., C-540 .... 80.00
Higgs, 12-Sided, Umbrella, Deep Aqua, 2 3/4 X 2 3/8 In. 60.00
Hogan & Thompson, Pale Yellow Green, 2 5/8 X 2 5/8 In. ....*Illus* 160.00
Hogan & Thompson, Red Ink, Conical, Aqua, 2 X 2 1/2 In. 30.00
Hohenthal Brothers & Co., Indelible Writing Ink, Green, 7 1/4 In. 600.00
Hohenthal Brothers & Co., Indelible, Embossed, OP, Olive Amber, C-766 .... 450.00
Hohenthal Brothers & Co., N.Y., OP, Deep Olive Amber, 9 In., C-766 .... 500.00
Hohenthal Brothers, Round, Olive Amber, Spout, IP, 7 1/8 In., C-766 .... 200.00
Horse & Rider, Round, Deep Golden Amber, 1 3/8 In., C-1039 ....*Illus* 1700.00
Hotchkiss & Sons, Pour Spout, Marked, Cobalt Blue 10.00
House, BIMAL, Aqua, 2 5/8 In., C-684 .... 165.00
House, Medium Green, 2 5/8 X 1 3/4 In., C-693 .... 30.00
House, Rectangle, Aqua, 2 5/8 X 2 3/8 In., C-678 ....*Illus* 100.00
House, Square, Aqua, 2 3/4 X 2 In., C-688 .... 100.00
House, Square, NE, Aqua, 2 1/2 X 2 In., C-689 ....*Illus* 130.00
Houston Ink Co., Houston, Texas, Full Label & Contents, Cobalt Blue 50.00
Hover, Open Pontil, Royal Blue, 5 In. ....*Illus* 550.00
Hover, Phila., Round, Light Yellow Green, 6 X 2 1/8 In., C-767 .... 100.00
Hover, Phila., Round, Yellow Green, Spout, Iron Pontil, 9 1/4 In. 70.00
Hover, Phila., Umbrella, Blue Green, 2 3/8 X 2 1/4 In., C-118 .... 265.00
Hover, Phila., 12-Sided, Umbrella, Light Yellow Green, 1 7/8 In., C-119 .... 170.00
J & I E M, BIMAL, Aqua, C-627 .... 15.00
J & I E M, Dated October 31, 1865, Turtle 15.00
J & I E M, Full Label On Front, Aqua, Embossed, C-626 .... 25.00
J & I E M, Turtle, Amber, 1 5/8 X 2 1/4 In., C-627 .... 65.00 To 95.00
J & I E M, Turtle, Citron, 1 5/8 X 2 1/4 In., C-628 .... 145.00
J & I E M, Turtle, Cobalt Blue, 1 3/4 X 2 1/4 In. 390.00
J & I E M, Turtle, Cornflower Blue, 1 5/8 X 2 1/4 In. 120.00
J & I E M, Turtle, Light Golden Amber, 1 5/8 X 2 1/4 In. .... 80.00 To 120.00
J & I E M, Turtle, Light Yellow Green, 1 5/8 X 2 1/4 In. 45.00
J Kidder Improved Indelible, 2 1/2 X 1 1/2 In., C-481 .... 40.00
J.& I.E.Moore, Pottery Handled, Label, Cream & Brown Glaze, Gallon 30.00
J.B.Fondersmiths, Aqua, 3 X 1 7/8 In., C-572 .... 120.00
J.J.Butler, Cin., Pontil, Aqua, C-478 .... 85.00
J.J.Butler, Ohio, BIMAL, C-613 .... 60.00
J.Kidder Improved Indelible, Pontil, 2 1/6 In., C-481 .... 100.00
J.Kidder, Square, Aqua, 2 1/2 X 1 1/2 In. 40.00
J.M. & S., Dome, BIMAL, Aqua, 1 7/8 In., C-633 .... 20.00
J.S.Dunham, St.Louis, 12-Sided, Pontil, Aqua, C-525 .... 100.00 To 175.00
J.S.Dunham, Umbrella, Deep Aqua, 2 3/4 X 2 3/8 In., C-116 ...... 90.00 To 140.00
J.S.Mooris & Co., 12-Sided, Aqua, 2 1/8 X 1 3/4 In. 75.00
J.W.Pennell, Hexagonal, BIMAL, Aqua, C-560 .... 25.00
J.W.Seaton, Umbrella, 10-Sided, Light Yellow Green, 2 1/4 X 2 In. 240.00
Jackson's, Pottery, Labeled, Brown Glaze, 8 1/2 X 3 3/4 In., C-1016 .... 35.00

Ink, Harrison's Columbian, Sapphire
Blue, 10 1/2 X 6 1/8 In.

Ink, Hogan & Thompson, Pale Yellow
Green, 2 5/8 X 2 5/8 In.

Ink, Horse & Rider, Round, Deep
Golden Amber, 1 3/8 In., C-1039

Ink, House, Rectangle, Aqua,
2 5/8 X 2 3/8 In., C-678

Ink, House, Square, NE, Aqua,
2 1/2 X 2 In., C-689

Ink, Hover, Open Pontil,
Royal Blue, 5 In.

Jacob's Brown, Hamilton, C., 12-Sided, Greenish Aqua, 2 1/2 X 2 In. 130.00
James S.Mason & Co., Umbrella, Aqua, 2 3/8 X 2 1/4 In. 80.00
JBC Embossed, BIMAL, Aqua, 2 7/16 In., C-741 .... 8.50
Johnson, Knoxville, Pa., Pat.Jan.22, 1889, 2 1/8 In., C-135 .... 27.50
Johnson's Writing, Labeled, Deep Olive Amber, 6 1/8 In., C-768 .... 25.00
Jones' Empire, N.Y., 12-Sided, Label, Deep Yellow Olive, C-769 .... 500.00
Josiah Jonson, Japan Writing Fluid, C-1242 .... 150.00
Jug, U.S.Treasury Inks & Mucilage, Wood Stopper, 3 Gallon 135.00
Keene, Blown, 3 Mold, Olive Amber, 1 1/2 X 2 1/4 In., C-1221 .... 80.00
Keene, Cone, Olive Green 85.00
Keller, Detroit, Embossed Shoulder, Aqua 8.00
Kent's, Round, Labeled, Olive Green, 4 7/8 X 1 5/8 In., C-197 .... 90.00
Kimball's Superior Black, Cylinder, Open Pontil, Deep Aqua 365.00
Kimball's Superior, Round, Ice Blue, 4 1/4 X 1 5/8 In. 170.00
Kirtland's Ink, W. & H., Dome, BIMAL, Aqua 170.00
Kirtland's, Poland, Ohio, Round, Aqua, 2 3/8 X 2 In. ....*Illus* 230.00
L.H.Thomas, Cone 9.00
L.S.Learned, Cambridgeport, Mass., Label, Aqua, 1 3/4 X 2 In., C-625 .... 20.00
Laughlin's & Bushfield, Octagonal, Deep Aqua, 2 3/4 X 1 3/4 In. 150.00
Lochman's Locomotive, Aqua, 2 X 2 1/8 In., C-715 .... 575.00
Locomotive, English, Greenish Aqua, 2 3/8 X 2 5/8 In. 450.00
Lowell Record, 16-Sided, Umbrella, Labeled, Deep Olive Amber, 2 In. 225.00
Mass.Glass Co., Umbrella, Greenish Aqua 75.00
Mayhew College, Turtle, Aqua, 1 3/4 X 2 1/4 In. 40.00
Maynard & Noyes, Round, Label, Olive Green, 4 1/2 X 1 5/8 In. 40.00
McK G II-016, Blown, 3 Mold, Drum Top, Dark Amber, 2 1/4 In. 55.00
McK G II-018, Blown, 3 Mold, 1 5/8 X 1 7/8 In. 150.00
McK G II-018c, Geometric, Olive Green, 1/2 Size 275.00
McK G II-018e, Coventry, Conn., Olive Amber, 2 3/4 X 1 13/16 In. 135.00
McK G III-019, Keene, Dark Olive Green, 1 1/2 In. 95.00
McK G III-019, Keene, Light Cinnamon Amber, 1 1/2 In. 165.00
McK G III-030, 3 Mold, Sandwich, Miniature 175.00
McK G VII-004, Booz's Cabin, Straight Roof, Amber 300.00
Monks & Arches, 6 Panel 80.00
Mr. & Mrs.Carters, Pat.Jan.6, 1914, Germany, C-1619 ....*Color* 100.00
Muspratt's, Dome, Label, Aqua, 2 X 1 7/8 In., C-634 .... 30.00
N.Wood, Portland, Maine, Interior Etching, Amber, 7 1/4 In. 415.00
Ne Plus Ultra, House, Aqua, 2 5/8 X 2 1/8 In. .... 100.00 To 210.00
Octagonal, Cut, Clear, C-1407 .... 45.00
Octagonal, Sheared Top, Emerald Green 15.00
P & J Arnold, Cone, Aqua, C-35 .... 11.00
P & J Arnold, Pottery, 16 Ounce 8.00
Pacific, Umbrella, Label, Deep Aqua, Yellow Mouth Streak, 2 7/8 In. 35.00
Palmer's Superior Blue, Label, Olive Green, 4 7/8 X 1 7/8 In., C-202 .... 30.00
Panok, Clear 15.00
Paperweight, Lion's Head Cover, Clear & Frosted, 4 3/8 X 2 7/8 In. 85.00
Patd., Pen Ledge, BIMAL, 2 3/4 In., C-1445 .... 35.00
Patent, 12-Sided, Cobalt Blue, 2 3/4 X 4 In., C-1415 ....*Illus* 230.00
Patented, Head & Font In Cast Iron Frame, Milk Glass, 6 1/2 In., C-1417 .... 175.00
Patterson's Excelsior, Aqua, 2 1/2 X 1 5/8 In. 110.00
Paul's Safety Bottle & Ink Co., New York, BIMAL, Label, Aqua, C-879 .... 18.00
Pen Ledges, BIMAL, Green, 2 In., C-514 .... 15.00
Penn.Mfg.Works, Garret & Co., Philada., Milk Glass, C-563 .... 75.00 To 120.00
Phrenology, C.1820, Signed 400.00
Pitkin Type, Double Opening, Swirled To Right, Olive Amber, 1 5/8 In. 235.00
Pitkin Type, Melon, Olive Amber, 2 X 2 3/4 In., C-1129 ....*Illus* 450.00
Pitkin Type, Olive Amber, C-1151 .... 240.00
Pitkin Type, Olive Amber, 1 3/4 In., C-1117 ....*Illus* 475.00
Pitkin Type, Olive Amber, 1 3/8 X 2 3/4 In., C-1158 ....*Illus* 260.00
Pitkin Type, Ribbed & Swirled To Left, Olive Amber .... 55.00 To 220.00
Pitkin Type, Ribbed & Swirled To Left, Olive Amber, 2 1/4 In., C-1141 .... 60.00
Pitkin Type, Ribs Swirled To Left, Deep Olive Green, 1 1/2 In., C-1123 .... 170.00
Pitkin Type, Ringed, Dark Olive Green, 1 1/2 X 2 1/2 In., C-1169 .... 180.00

Pitkin Type, Round, Swirled To Right, Deep Olive Green, 2 X 2 1/2 In. 50.00
Pitkin Type, Square, Honey Amber, C-1121 .... 445.00
Pitkin Type, Square, Olive Green, 1 1/2 In., C-1119 .... 350.00
Pitkin Type, Square, Swirled To Right, Olive Amber, 1 3/4 In., C-1117 .... 475.00
Pitkin Type, Swirled To Left, Deep Forest Green, 1 5/8 In., C-1140 .... 140.00
Pitkin Type, Swirled To Left, Deep Olive Amber, 1 1/2 In., C-1138 .... 190.00
Pitkin Type, Swirled To Left, Deep Olive Amber, 1 5/8 In., C-1136 .... 140.00
Pitkin Type, Swirled To Left, Light Olive Amber, 1 7/8 In., C-1144 .... 160.00
Pitkin Type, Swirled To Left, Olive Amber, 2 3/8 In., C-1149 .... 175.00
Pitkin Type, Swirled To Left, Olive Green, 1 1/2 X 2 1/2 In., C-743 .... 55.00
Pitkin Type, Swirled To Left, Olive Green, 1 1/2 X 2 5/8 In., C-1147 .... 110.00
Pitkin Type, Swirled To Left, Olive Green, 2 1/4 X 2 5/8 In., C-1146 .... 35.00

Ink, Kirtland's, Poland, Ohio,
Round, Aqua, 2 3/8 X 2 In.

Ink, Patent, 12-Sided, Cobalt
Blue, 2 3/4 X 4 In., C-1415

Ink, Pitkin Type, Melon, Olive Amber,
2 X 2 3/4 In., C-1129

Ink, Pitkin Type, Olive Amber, 1 3/4 In., C-1117

Ink, Pitkin Type, Olive Amber,
1 3/8 X 2 3/4 In., C-1158

Pitkin Type, Swirled To Right, Deep Forest Green, 2 3/8 In., C-1157 .... 130.00
Pitkin Type, Swirled To Right, Deep Olive Amber, 1 1/2 In., C-1122 .... 80.00
Pitkin Type, Swirled To Right, Deep Olive Amber, 1 3/4 In., C-1153 .... 80.00
Pitkin Type, Swirled To Right, Deep Olive Amber, 1 5/8 In., C-1150 .... 50.00
Pitkin Type, Swirled To Right, Olive Amber, 1 5/8 X 2 1/4 In., C-1151 .... 140.00
Pitkin Type, Swirled To Right, Olive Amber, 2 3/8 X 2 7/8 In., C-1160 .... 200.00
Pitkin Type, Swirled To Right, Oliver Amber, 1 3/8 In., C-1158 .... 260.00
Pitkin Type, Vertically Ribbed, Deep Olive Green, 1 3/4 In., C-1133 .... 280.00
Pitkin Type, Vertically Ribbed, Light Olive Amber, 1 1/2 In., C-1126 .... 250.00
Pitkin Type, Vertically Ribbed, Olive Amber, 1 3/4 In., C-1131 .... 425.00
Pitkin Type, Vertically Ribbed, Olive Amber, 1 3/4 X 2 1/2 In., C-1127 .... 325.00
Pitkin Type, Vertically Ribbed, Olive Green, 2 X 2 3/4 In., C-1128 .... 425.00
Pitkin Type, 5 Rings, Dark Olive Green, 1 5/8 In., C-1167 .... 275.00
Porcelain, Floral Decorated, 4 Sides, 2 X 2 X 3 In. 45.00
Pottery, Cone, Light Tan Satin Glaze, 3 In. 5.00
Pottery, Lion's Head, Rockingham Glaze, 2 X 2 7/8 In., C-1589 .... 90.00
Pottery, Reclining Boy, Rockingham Glaze, 3 5/8 X 5 1/4 In., C-1597 .... 50.00
Pottery, Reclining Girl, Rockingham Glaze, 3 5/8 X 4 3/4 In., C-1598 .... 90.00
Pottery, Ugly Woman, Rockingham Glaze, 2 X 3 In. 25.00
Pour Spout, Double-Collared Mouth, Master, Deep Golden Amber, 9 3/4 In. 50.00
Pour Spout, Wicker Covering With Handle, Master, Green, 3 1/4 X 10 In. 50.00
Pour Spout, 18-Sided, Deep Purple Cobalt, 3 X 6 1/4 In. 35.00
Pouring Lip, Round, 32 Ounce, ABM, Master, Light Cobalt Blue, 9 In. 10.00
Premium, Dome, Labeled, Aqua, 2 In., C-615 .... 25.00
Pridge's Inks, Pour Spout, Debossed, London, White Glaze 8.00
Pyramid, Octagonal, Amber, 2 1/2 In. 40.00
Pyramid, Octagonal, Deep Greenish Aqua, 2 3/8 In. 15.00
Pyramid, Octagonal, Olive Amber, 2 1/4 In. 40.00
R.B.Snow, St.Louis, Umbrella, Aqua, 2 1/2 X 2 1/2 In. 60.00
R.B.Snow, St.Louis, 12-Sided, Umbrella, Aqua, 1 7/8 X 1 7/8 In. 60.00
R.F., Round, Dark Amethyst, 2 1/8 X 2 1/2 In., C-203 .... 120.00 To 250.00
Rectangle, Roofed, BIMAL, Aqua, 2 3/8 X 2 In., C-505 .... 15.00
Red & White Swirl Stripes, 2 1/4 X 3 1/4 In. ....*Illus* 1050.00
Red Ink, Hogan & Thompson, Philadelphia, Conical, Green, 2 5/8 In. 160.00
Revolving, Cast Iron Wheelbarrow Frame, Milk Glass, 3 In., C-1455 .... 300.00
Revolving, Double, Milk Glass & Cobalt Blue, 3 1/2 X 5 In., C-1459 .... 115.00
Revolving, Milk Glass, Cast Iron Frame, 4 X 4 1/2 In., C-1456 .... 65.00
Ringed, Forest Green, C-1169 .... 195.00
Robert Keller Inks & Mucilage, Pour Spout, Aqua 10.00
Robert Whitfield's, Dome, Pottery, Tan & Brown Glazes, 1 5/8 In. 75.00
Rolled Lip, Open Pontil, Aqua .... 17.00 To 40.00
Ross's Excelsior, 12-Sided, Labeled, Aqua, 5 X 2 1/2 In. 50.00
Round, Cobalt Blue, 2 X 2 1/4 In., C-1029 ....*Illus* 470.00

Ink, Round, Cobalt Blue, 2 X 2 1/4 In., C-1029

Ink, Red & White Swirl Stripes, 2 1/4 X 3 1/4 In.

Ink, Simmond's, 12-Sided, Deep
Aqua, 8 X 4 1/2 In.

Ink, Smith's Perpetual Calendar,
Aqua, 3 1/4 X 2 1/4 In.

Round, Fluted, Blue Milk Glass, Brass Cap, 1 3/4 X 2 1/2 In. 130.00
Round, Pattern Mold, Vertically Ribbed, Golden Amber, 1 7/8 In., C-1335 .... 375.00
Round, Pontil, Cobalt Blue, 2 X 2 In., C-219 .... 40.00
Round, Purple, Applied Milk Glass Mouth & Base Rigaree, 2 In., C-1068 .... 130.00
Round, 17 Vertical Ribs, Cobalt Blue, 2 3/4 X 2 1/2 In., C-222 .... 285.00
S.Fine Blk., Cylindrical, Pontil, Green, 3 1/8 In., C-192 .... 50.00
S.Fine Blk., Round, Golden Amber, 3 1/8 X 1 1/2 In. 90.00
S.Fine Blk., Round, Light Blue Green, 3 1/8 X 1 1/2 In., C-192 .... 60.00
S.Fine Blk., Round, Yellow Green, 3 X 1 1/2 In., C-193 .... 185.00
S.I.Comp., Barrel, Original Stopper, Milk Glass, 2 1/2 In., C-666 .... 275.00
S.I.Comp., House, Full Label, Aqua, 2 5/8 X 2 In., C-682 .... 210.00
S.I.Comp., House, Milk Glass, 2 3/4 X 2 In., C-683 .... 300.00 To 400.00
S.O.Dunbar, Octagonal, Aqua, 2 1/2 X 1 3/8 In. 50.00
S.O.Dunbar, Pontil, Aqua, Pint, C-755 .... 45.00
S.O.Dunbar, Round, Aqua, Pour Spout, 8 1/2 X 3 7/8 In., C-754 .... 50.00
S.O.Dunbar, Taunton, Cylinder 30.00
S.O.Dunbar, Taunton, Umbrella, 2 1/2 X 2 1/4 In., C-115 .... 70.00 To 95.00
S.O.Dunbar, 12-Sided, Aqua, 2 1/4 X 2 In., C-520 .... 85.00
S.O.Dunbar, 12-Sided, Light Yellow Green, 2 1/4 X 2 In. 175.00
S.S.Stafford, Cobalt, 16 Ounces 15.00
S.S.Stafford's Master Ink, Cobalt Blue 25.00
S.S.Stafford's, Cobalt Blue, 6 In. 12.50
Sanford, Patent Applied For, BIMAL, Aqua, 2 In., C-719 .... 15.00
Sanford's Inks & Library Paste, Pint 8.00
Sanford's Inks & Library Paste, Quart 8.00
Sanford's, Square, 4-Sided, ABM, 3 In. 3.00
Sanford's, 6 Ounce, 4 1/4 X 2 1/2 In. 20.00
Saratoga Type, Cone, Blown, Deep Green, White Flecks, 4 5/8 In., C-17 .... 320.00
Shipman's, Turtle, Aqua, 1 5/8 X 2 1/4 In. 20.00
Shipman's, Utica N.Y., Pour Lip, Stoneware, 7 In. 39.00
Shipman's, Utica, N.Y., Turtle, 1 5/8 X 2 1/4 In. 35.00
Shoe, Aqua, 1 7/8 X 4 1/4 In., C-725 .... 25.00
Shoe, Clear, C-726 .... 25.00
Shoe, Clear, 2 1/2 X 4 1/4 In. 20.00
Shoe, Clear, 3 5/16 X 4 In., C-726 .... 25.00
Simmond's, 12-Sided, Deep Aqua, 8 X 4 1/2 In. .... *Illus* 310.00
Simon Clarke's, Round, Applied Base, Bright Green, 3 X 3 3/4 In. 180.00
Smith's Perpetual Calendar, Aqua, 3 1/4 X 2 1/4 In. .... *Illus* 150.00
Snail, Fountain, 1 3/4 X 3 1/2 In., C-1292 .... 100.00
Snow & Quirk, St.Louis, 12-Sided, Aqua, 3 X 2 1/8 In. 120.00
Square, ABM, Cobalt, Small 5.00
Square, Blown, Milk Glass, Painted Floral Design, 2 1/8 In., C-1074 .... 100.00
Square, Chinese Writing, BIMAL, Aqua, C-475 .... 8.00

Ink, Square, Forest Green, 1 1/2 X 2 1/8 In., C-1103

Square, Forest Green, 1 1/2 X 2 1/8 In., C-1103	*Illus*	90.00
Square, Swirl Ribbed, Milk Glass, Brass Cover, 2 3/4 X 2 In.		30.00
Square, Vertically Ribbed, Yellow Olive, Red Streaks, 1 1/2 In., C-1116		250.00
Stafford's Ink, Pouring Lip, Label, BIMAL, Aqua, C-897		20.00
Stafford's Ink, Teal Green, C-897		25.00
Stafford's, Sapphire Blue, Pint		25.00
Standard, Stoneware, Debossed, Handled, Cream Glaze, Pour Spout, Gallon		30.00
Stoddard, Cylinder, Open Pontil, Olive Amber, 2 1/2 In.		45.00
Stoddard, Embossed Indelible Writing Ink, Olive Amber, Master		300.00
Stoddard, Spout, Open Pontil, Olive, Quart, 9 3/4 In.		29.50
Stoddard, Umbrella, Open Pontil, Yellowish Olive		110.00
Stoddard, Umbrella, 8-Sided, Open Pontil	105.00 To	110.00
Stoddard, 8-Sided, Open Pontil, Olive Green		80.00
Stout, Dyer & Wicks, New York, Bulbous Base, Aqua, 7 7/8 In.		80.00
Swan, Pottery, Rockingham Glaze, 4 1/8 X 3 3/4 In.		90.00
T & M, Pontil, Aqua, 1 7/8 X 1 3/8 X 2 1/2 In.		20.00
Teakettle, Barrel, Amethyst, Brass Cap, 2 1/8 X 2 In.		300.00
Teakettle, Barrel, Cobalt Blue, 2 1/4 X 2 In., C-1286	*Illus*	375.00
Teakettle, Barrel, Medium Blue, 2 1/8 X 2 In., C-1285		300.00
Teakettle, Ben Franklin, BIMAL, Aqua, C-1291		115.00
Teakettle, BIMAL, Amethyst, C-1231		260.00
Teakettle, BIMAL, Amethyst, C-1261		255.00
Teakettle, BIMAL, Aqua, C-1255		78.00

Ink, Teakettle, Barrel, Cobalt Blue, 2 1/4 X 2 In., C-1286

Teakettle, Brass Cap, Cut, Clear, C-1268 .... 100.00
Teakettle, Clear, Blue & Gold Painted Design, Miniature, 1 1/8 In. 190.00
Teakettle, Clear, Copper Cap, 3 3/4 X 2 5/8 In., C-1274 .... 50.00
Teakettle, Clear, Gold Leaf Decoration, C-1248 .... 265.00
Teakettle, Cobalt Blue, Brass Cap, 1 7/8 X 2 3/8 In., C-1232 .... 175.00
Teakettle, Cobalt Blue, Brass Cap, 2 X 2 3/8 In., C-1255 .... 170.00
Teakettle, Corseted, Amethyst, 2 1/8 X 2 1/8 In. 450.00
Teakettle, Corseted, Fiery Opalescent, Gold, Blue Design, 2 1/8 In. 200.00
Teakettle, Deep Ice Blue, Brass Cap, 2 X 2 3/9 In., C-1257 .... 175.00
Teakettle, Deep Sapphire Blue, Cap Missing, 2 In., C-1254 .... 160.00
Teakettle, Deep Sapphire Blue, Copper Cap, 2 1/4 X 2 1/4 In. 400.00
Teakettle, Double Font, Tooled Mouth, 11-Sided, Cobalt Blue, 4 In. 700.00
Teakettle, Double Font, 6 1/4 X 2 3/4 In., C-1276 .... 270.00
Teakettle, Fiery Blue Opalescent, Brass Cap, 2 X 1 7/8 In. 375.00
Teakettle, Fiery Opalescent, Multicolor Floral, Brass Cap, 2 3/8 In. 175.00
Teakettle, Floral Decorated, Fiery Opalescent, 2 3/8 In., C-1227 .... 325.00
Teakettle, Floral, Fiery Opalescent, Brass Cap, 2 3/8 In., C-1239 .... 210.00
Teakettle, Greenish Aqua, 1 5/8 X 1 7/8 In., C-1251 .... 45.00
Teakettle, Ice Blue, 1 1/2 X 1 3/4 In., C-1250 .... 65.00
Teakettle, Octagonal, Amethyst, Brass Cap, 2 1/8 X 2 1/4 In., C-1257 .... 230.00
Teakettle, Octagonal, Amethyst, 2 In., C-1268 .... 110.00
Teakettle, Octagonal, Amethyst, 2 1/8 X 2 3/8 In., C-1263 .... 180.00
Teakettle, Octagonal, Cobalt Blue, Copper Cap, 2 1/8 X 2 3/8 In. 190.00
Teakettle, Octagonal, Copper Cap, 2 5/8 X 2 3/4 In., C-1271 .... 50.00
Teakettle, Octagonal, Electric Blue, Brass Cap, 2 X 2 1/8 In. 230.00
Teakettle, Octagonal, Vaseline, 2 1/8 X 2 3/8 In. 350.00
Teakettle, Octagonal, White Porcelain, 2 1/4 X 2 3/8 In., C-1265 .... 60.00
Teakettle, Octagonal, 3 3/8 X 2 5/8 In., C-1273 .... 50.00
Teakettle, Polished Pontil, 1 1/4 X 1 3/16 In., C-1248 .... 150.00
Teakettle, Porcelain, Octagon, White, Blue Designs, 2 1/4 In. 120.00
Teakettle, Pottery, Blue Glaze, Religious Scene, Brass Cap, 2 5/8 In. 400.00
Teakettle, Pottery, Hexagonal, Red, White Glaze, 2 1/8 In. .... 50.00 To 80.00
Teakettle, Pottery, Vertically Ribbed, White Glaze, 3 X 2 3/4 In. 120.00
Teakettle, Sapphire Blue, 1 1/2 X 1 1/8 In., C-1247 .... *Illus* 450.00
Teakettle, Square, Amethyst, Cap Missing, 1 7/8 X 2 In., C-1231 .... 175.00
Teakettle, Square, Aqua, Deep Amber Body Swirls, Brass Cap, 1 5/8 In. 250.00
Teakettle, Square, Sapphire Blue, 1 3/4 X 1 1/2 In., C-1229 .... 150.00
Teakettle, Stoneware, Compliments Of Letort Hotel, Carlisle, Pa. 250.00
Teakettle, Turtle, 1 7/8 X 3 7/8 In., C-1288 .... 50.00
Teakettle, Yellow Amber, Painted Gold Design, Brass Cap, 1 7/8 In. 350.00
Teakettle, Yellow Green, Painted Gold Design, 2 X 2 3/8 In., C-1259 .... 240.00
Teakettle, 5-Lobed, Floral Design, Fiery Opalescent, 2 In., C-1233 .... 225.00

Ink, Teakettle, Sapphire Blue, 1 1/2 X 1 1/8 In., C-1247

Ink, Teakettle, 11-Sided, Double Font,
Cobalt Blue, 4 In.

Ink, Turtle, Double Neck, Olive Amber,
2 1/8 In., C-1095

Teakettle, 6-Lobed, Opaque Light Blue, Brass Cap, 2 3/4 In., C-1237	500.00
Teakettle, 10-Sided, Floral Design, Fiery Opalescent, 3 In., C-1277	210.00
Teakettle, 10-Sided, Floral, Fiery Opalescent, 2 5/8 X 2 7/8 In., C-1278	220.00
Teakettle, 11-Sided, Double Font, Cobalt Blue, 4 In. .... *Illus*	700.00
Teakettle, 11-Sided, Emerald Green, 2 1/4 X 3 In., C-1280	200.00
Teakettle, 11-Sided, S.Mordan & Co., London, Amethyst, C-1280	245.00
Thaddeus David's & Co., Label & Contents, Spout, Cobalt Blue, 1/2 Pint	14.50
Thaddeus David's & Co., Stoneware Jug, Yellow & Cream Glazes, Gallon	60.00
Thaddeus David's, Labeled, Deep Golden Amber, 5 5/8 X 1 7/8 In., C-751	55.00
Thaddeus David's, Round, Labeled, Olive Amber, 5 1/8 X 1 3/4 In., C-750	40.00
Thaddeus David's, Umbrella, Labeled, Greenish Aqua, 2 5/8 X 2 1/2 In.	35.00
Thomas & Co., ABM, Aqua, 2 1/4 In., C-455	12.00
Thomas Hollis, Round, Labeled, Light Green, 4 7/8 In.	25.00
Tippecanoe, Hard Cider, Barrel, 1 7/8 X 2 1/4 In., C-667 .... 100.00 To	275.00
Toilet With Tank, 2 Pen Grooves, Fortschritt, Embossed, 5 X 1 1/2 In.	75.00
Traveling, Carved Initials, J.P.H., Wood Encased	24.50
Traveling, Hinged Brass Bottle, Johann Hoff, Leather Closure, 3 In.	42.00
Traveling, Wood Encased, Civil War Period, Cylindrical	29.50
Tree Trunk Base, Clear, 2 X 3 1/8 In.	25.00
Turtle, Blue-Green, 1 5/8 X 2 1/4 In.	75.00
Turtle, Cardinal Embossed On Dome	25.00
Turtle, Cardinal, Ice Blue, 1 1/2 X 2 1/4 In.	50.00
Turtle, Cast Metal, Silver Gray, 1 1/2 X 2 1/4 In., C-643	70.00
Turtle, Citron, 1 3/4 X 2 1/8 In., C-636	120.00
Turtle, Continental Black, Partial Label, Deep Bluish Aqua	12.50
Turtle, Double Neck, Olive Amber, 2 1/8 In., C-1095 .... *Illus*	875.00
Turtle, Fountain, Deep Amethyst, 1 1/2 X 4 1/2 In., Brass Cap, C-1287	275.00
Turtle, Golden Amber, 1 1/2 X 2 1/8 In.	45.00
Turtle, Pale Blue-Green, 1 5/8 X 2 1/8 In.	35.00
Umbrella, Amethyst, 2 1/2 X 2 1/4 In. .... *Illus*	200.00
Umbrella, Aqua, Silver Cap, C-175	15.00
Umbrella, BIMAL, Yellow, C-179	55.00
Umbrella, Electric Blue, 2 5/8 X 2 5/8 In.	100.00
Umbrella, Embossed R, Yellow Olive, 2 1/4 X 2 1/8 In., C-122	175.00
Umbrella, Emerald, 2 3/8 In., C-127	47.00
Umbrella, Golden Amber, 2 1/2 X 2 1/2 In. .... 45.00 To	85.00
Umbrella, Light Blue, C-169	25.00
Umbrella, Medium Green, 2 5/8 X 2 1/2 In. .... 35.00 To	55.00
Umbrella, Octagonal, Sapphire Blue, 2 1/4 X 2 1/8 In. .... *Illus*	370.00
Umbrella, Olive Amber, 2 3/8 X 2 1/4 In. .... 65.00 To	75.00
Umbrella, Open Pontil, Aqua, C-136	45.00
Umbrella, Open Pontil, Black Olive Green, C-141	180.00

Ink, Umbrella, Amethyst,
2 1/2 X 2 1/4 In.

Ink, Umbrella, Octagonal, Sapphire
Blue, 2 1/4 X 2 1/8 In.

Umbrella, Open Pontil, Reddish Amber, C-135 .... 200.00
Umbrella, Open Pontil, Rolled Lip, Dark Golden Amber, C-129 .... 125.00
Umbrella, Open Pontil, Rolled Lip, Dark Yellow Green, C-129 .... 65.00
Umbrella, Open Pontil, Rolled Lip, 12-Sided, Aqua 40.00
Umbrella, Partial Label, Olive Amber, 2 1/2 X 2 3/8 In. 35.00
Umbrella, Pontil, Aqua, C-150 .... 28.00
Umbrella, Pontil, Aqua, 2 1/4 In., C-141 .... 20.00
Umbrella, Pontil, Dark Amber, 2 1/2 In., C-129 .... 66.00
Umbrella, Pontil, Green, 2 1/4 X 2 1/4 In. .... 25.00 To 40.00
Umbrella, Pontil, Olive Green, C-143 .... 125.00
Umbrella, Puce, 2 5/8 X 2 1/2 In., C-129 .... 225.00
Umbrella, Red Amber, 2 1/2 X 2 1/4 In., C-134 .... 100.00
Umbrella, Rolled Lip, Cobalt Blue, 2 1/2 X 2 1/2 In., C-180 .... 150.00
Umbrella, Sapphire Blue, 2 1/4 X 2 1/4 In. 150.00
Umbrella, Wine, 2 1/4 X 2 1/4 In. 170.00
Umbrella, Yellow Olive, 2 1/2 X 2 1/2 In., C-143 .... 75.00
Umbrella, Yellow Olive, 2 3/4 X 2 3/8 In., C-173 .... 30.00
Umbrella, 8-Sided, Rolled Lip, 2 1/2 In. .... 8.00 To 15.00
Umbrella, 10-Sided, Light Blue, 1 7/8 X 2 1/4 In. 48.00
Umbrella, 12-Sided, Golden Amber, 1 3/4 X 1 7/8 In. 35.00
Umbrella, 12-Sided, Green Aqua, 1 3/4 X 1 7/8 In. 48.00
Umbrella, 12-Sided, Pontil, Aqua, 2 In., C-149 .... 35.00
Umbrella, 12-Sided, Pontil, Emerald, 2 In., C-149 .... 10.00
Umbrella, 16-Sided, Deep Olive Amber, 2 1/8 X 2 1/8 In., C-153 .... 140.00
Underwood, ABM, Master, Cobalt Blue 22.00
Underwood, 2 Pen Slots, Round 16.00
Underwood's Inks, BIMAL, Aqua, 2 5/8 In., C-562 .... 16.00
Union Ink Co., Springfield, Mass., BIMAL, Aqua, C-600 .... 20.00
Upton's Refined Liquid Glue, 12-Sided, Aqua, 3 In., C-1753 .... 20.00
Use Dovell's Inks & Fluids, Aqua, 3 1/4 In. 40.00
W.E.Bonney, Barrel, Pour Spout, Aqua, 6 X 3 1/4 In. 65.00
W.E.Bonney, Umbrella, Labeled, Aqua, 2 1/2 X 2 1/2 In. 30.00
W.F.Bonney, Barrel, Open Pontil, C-653 .... 75.00
W.G.Nixey, 12 Soho Square, London, Embossed, White Glazed 8.00
Ward's, Whittled, Mini Master, Green 160.00
Warren's Congress, IP, Olive Green, 7 1/4 X 2 5/8 In. .... *Illus* 650.00
Warren's Congress, Octagonal, Aqua, Pour Spout, 9 X 3 1/4 In. 120.00
Warren's Congress, Octagonal, Aqua, 2 3/4 X 1 5/8 In. 100.00
Warren's Congress, Octagonal, Deep Aqua, 4 3/8 X 1 7/8 In. 80.00
Water's, Troy, N.Y., Umbrella, Aqua, 2 3/4 X 2 In., C-171 .... 60.00

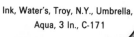

Ink, Warren's Congress, IP, Olive
Green, 7 1/4 X 2 5/8 In.

(See Page 143)

Ink, Water's, Troy, N.Y., Umbrella,
Aqua, 3 In., C-171

Ink, Wood's Black, Portland, Amber,
2 1/2 X 2 1/4 In., C-12

Water's, Troy, N.Y., Umbrella, Aqua, 3 In., C-171 ....*Illus* 190.00
Weiner Ink, BIMAL, Aqua, C-713 .... 15.00
Western Ink Co., Bloomington, Ill., Schoolhouse Type 18.00
William A.Davis Co., Labels, BIMAL, Aqua, C-843 .... 25.00
William's Ink Pot, Beehive, Glazed Crockery, Screw-On Lid 75.00
William's Ink Pot, Pottery, Beehive-Shaped, Black Glaze, 4 1/4 In. 80.00
William's Ink Pot, Pottery, Beehive-Shaped, White Glaze, 4 1/4 In. 60.00
Winslow's Indelible, Labeled, Round, Olive Amber, 5 X 1 7/8 In. 65.00
Wood Case, Clear Ink, 4 1/2 In. ....*Color* 10.00
Wood's Black, Portland, Amber, 2 1/2 X 2 1/4 In., C-12 ....*Illus* 450.00
Wood's Black, Portland, Cone, Aqua, 2 3/8 X 2 1/4 In., C-12 .... 90.00

Ink, 6 Ring, 2 Quill Holes, Olive Amber, 1 3/4 X 2 3/4 In.

Ink, 12-Sided, IP, Deep Olive
Green, 12 X 6 In., C-781

Ink, Zieber & Co., 12-Sided, Deep
Green, 7 1/4 X 4 In., C-775

Jack Daniel, Decanter

Zieber & Co., Excelsior, 12-Sided, Deep Yellow Green, IP, 5 7/8 In. 600.00
Zieber & Co., 12-Sided, Deep Green, 7 1/4 X 4 In., C-775 ....*Illus* 1300.00
Zierlein's Ink, St.Louis, 12-Sided, Deep Aqua, 2 5/8 X 2 1/4 In. 110.00
6 Ring, 2 Quill Holes, Olive Amber, 1 3/4 X 2 3/4 In. ....*Illus* 675.00
12-Sided, Bright Green, 1 5/8 X 1 5/8 In. 65.00
12-Sided, Bright Green, 2 7/8 X 2 In. 50.00
12-Sided, Deep Purple, 2 1/4 X 4 1/2 In. 125.00
12-Sided, IP, Deep Olive Green, 12 X 6 In., C-781 ....*Illus* 1000.00
12-Sided, Pontil, Aqua, 2 9/16 X 2 In., C-549 .... 25.00
12-Sided, Pontil, Olive Amber, 1 7/8 X 2 1/8 In., C-548 .... 100.00
36 Vertical Ribs, Swirled To Left, Pontil, Dark Green, 1 1/2 In. 75.00

IRISH MIST, Decanter, Wade 9.00
 Guard 25.00

JACK DANIEL, Decanter ....*Illus* 60.00
 Jug ....*Illus* 40.00
 Lem Motlow's, Paper Label ....*Illus* 20.00
 Old No.7, Gallon 20.00

Jack Daniel, Jug   Jack Daniel, Lem Motlow's, Paper Label

JAR, Armour's Meat Sauce, Handled 22.00
Canadian, Ring & Glass Lid, Amber, 1 Quart 200.00
Cudahey Packing Co., Meat Sauce, Handled 22.00
F. & J.McKee, Pittsburgh, Pa., Open Pontil 365.00
Loydsville, Ohio, Pottery .... *Illus* 120.00

JON-SOL, Baby Robin .... *Illus* 10.00
Blue Jay .... *Illus* 11.00
Red-Eyed Vireo 6.00
Redheaded Woodpecker .... *Illus* 10.00

JUG, Chas.S.Gove Co.Liquor Merchants, Brown & Tan Stoneware, 1/4 Pint 17.00
Chestnut Grove, Whiskey C.W., Round Medallion, Amber, 9 In. 85.00
Collignon Bros., Troy, Ind., Cobalt Letters, Brown & Cream, 2 Gallon 46.00
Compliments I.W.Harper, Nelson Co., Kentucky, Miniature, Cream 35.00
Compliments Of Langert Wine Co., Brown Top, Creme Bottom, 1/2 Pint 80.00
Detrick Distilling Co., If You Try Me Once 21.00
Detrick Distilling, As I Go Up Hill Of Prosperity, Blue Print 30.00
E.Bloch, Cleveland, Ohio, Blue Star Monogram, Whiskey, Brown & Tan, Quart 46.00
Flora Temple, Flattened Handle, Red Amber, Quart 240.00
Gilbert Riding's New Inn & Central Hotel, Wicker Holder, Pint 25.00
Golden Cream Whiskey, Script Within Border, Cream, Miniature 34.00
J.S.Bloch, Monroe, La., Brown & Cream, 1/2 Gallon 29.00
Jones Bros.Blue Grass Belle, Vinegar, Louisville, Miniature, Cream 24.00
K.T.& K.China, Pennsylvania Club Pure Rye Whiskey, Quart 95.00
Louis Zapp & Co., Louisville, Incised Script, Chocolate Brown, Gallon 46.00
       JUG, MINIATURE, see also Miniature, Jug
M.Salzman Co., Purity Above All, Brown & Cream, 1/2 Gallon 25.00
Meiers Sherry, Pink, 1 Handle 3.00
Old Continental Whiskey, Within Acorn Outline, Cream, Miniature 24.00
Overland Liquor Co., Butte, Montana, 1 Gallon 90.00
Rheinstrom Bros., N.Y.& Cincinnati, Silvered Over Amber, Handled 65.00
Rothschild & Co., State & Van Buren Sts., Cream & Brown, 1/2 Gallon 17.50
Salzman & Siegelman, Brooklyn, N.Y., Port 30.00
Simmons & Hammond, Portland, Maine, Root Beer Syrup 35.00
Souvenir, Excelsior Springs, Missouri, Pint 20.00
W.A.Baird & Co., Handled, Tan & Brown, Quart 30.00
Whiskey, Casper Co., Wire Bail, Handle, Gray, Blue Lettering, Gallon 69.00
Whiskey, Griffith & Hyatt Co., Handle On Right Side, Amber 265.00
Whiskey, Mike & Jim's Pure Rye, China 125.00
White Lily, Pure Rye, China, Maroon Letters, Flowers, Animal Head, White 58.00
White Rose Rye Whiskey, St.Paul, Handled, Embossed, Pint 125.00

KENTUCKY GENTLEMAN, Confederate Soldier, 1969 .... 12.00
Frontiersman, 1969 .... 15.00
Gentleman With Cane, 1969 .... 15.00
Pink Lady, 1969 .... 27.00
Revolutionary Soldier, 1969 .... 12.00
Union Soldier, 1969 .... 12.00

KENTUCKY TAVERN, Captain's Quart, Gold, 1968 .... 10.00
Country Scene 9.00
Decanter, 1952 .... 20.00
Dresser, 1978 .... 40.00
Treasure Island .... 5.00 To 9.00

KONTINENTAL CLASSICS, Car, Corvette, 1 3/4 Liter 74.95
Corvette, 1963 .... 28.00
Dock Worker, 1978 .... 34.00
Editor, 1976 .... 35.00
Gandy Dancer, 1976 .... 33.00
Gunsmith, 1977 .... 37.00
Homesteader, 1978 .... 35.00

Jar, Loydsville, Ohio, Pottery

Jon-Sol, Blue Jay, Baby Robin, Redheaded Woodpecker

Kontinental Classics, Statue
Of Liberty, 1976

Kontinental Classics, Stephen
Foster, 1975

Innkeeper, 1978	35.00
Land Surveyor, 1978	36.00
Lumberjack, 1978	30.00 To 34.00
Medicine Man, 1977	33.00
Pioneer Dentist, 1978	38.00
Prospector & Burro, 1977	39.00
Saddlemaker, 1977	30.00 To 38.00
Santa Claus, 1973	20.00
Schoolmarm, 1977	35.00
Statue Of Liberty, 1976	*Illus* 30.00
Stephen Foster With Striped Pants, 1976	100.00
Stephen Foster, 1975	*Illus* 30.00
Village Pharmacist, 1977	30.00 To 35.00
KORD, Coach	38.00
Country Scene	39.00
Dancing Scene	39.00
Dolphin	12.00
Horsehead	14.00
Milk Glass	9.00
Sleigh	38.00
KUMMEL BEAR, see Figural	

Lacey, Bank Exchange, 1976

W.A. LACEY, see also Cyrus Noble

LACEY, Bank Exchange, 1976 ....*Illus*	16.00
Continental Navy, 1975	8.00
Faro Bank, 1975	12.00
Harold's Club, 1970	20.00
Tennis Players, Pair, 1976	32.00
Tonopah Saloon, 1975	12.00
Tun Tavern, 1975	8.00
Willets Frontier Days, 1976	115.00
LADY'S LEG, Fleischman Co., Congress Hall, Maryland, Rye, Amber	30.00
M.Shaughnessy Co., St.Louis, Amber	25.00
Yellow Green, Quart	20.00
LAIRD'S, Heritage Vase	14.00
Jug, 1 Handle, New	9.00
Jug, 1 Handle, Old	12.00
Jug, 2 Handle	40.00
LARSEN, Viking Ship, China	32.00
Viking Ship, Glass	17.00
LAST CHANCE, Banker	15.00
Wyoming Stock Growers	92.00
LEWIS & CLARK, Charbonneau, 1972	59.00
Clark, 1971	96.00
Curlee, Indian Scout, 1974	53.00
General Custer, 1974	59.00
Indian Peace Pipe, 1978	38.00
Lewis, 1971	102.00
Major Reno, 1975	50.00
Montana	49.00
Montana, 1976	49.00
Pioneer Family, Pair, 1978	118.00
Prowling Panther	47.00
Sacajawea, 1972	121.00
Sheepherder	40.00
Sitting Bull, 1976 .... 110.00 To	126.00
Trader	55.00
Troll, Cousin, 1979	30.00
Troll, Daughter, 1978	32.00
Troll, Father, 1979	30.00
Troll, Grandfather, 1978	31.00

Troll, Grandmother, 1979 .... 32.00
Troll, Mother, 1978 .... 30.00
Trooper, 1975 .... 52.00

LIONSTONE, Annie Christmas, 1969 .... 19.00 To 150.00
Annie Oakley .... 22.00 To 40.00
Backpacker, 1980 .... 33.00 To 42.00
Bar Scene No.2, With Nude, 1970 .... 171.00
Bar Scene, Nude Painting, Set Of 4, 1970 .... 500.00
Bar Scene, Set Of 4, Framed 600.00
Barber, 1976 .... 40.00 To 45.00
Bartender, 1969 .... 20.00 To 120.00
Baseball Players, 1974 .... 30.00
Basket Weaver, 1974 .... 33.00
Basketball Players, 1974 .... 24.00
Belly Robber, 1969 .... 14.00 To 60.00
Betsy Ross, 1976 ....Illus   28.00
Blacksmith, 1973 .... 20.00 To 60.00
Blue Jay, 1971 .... 24.00 To 26.00
Bluebird, Eastern, 1972 .... 26.00
Bluebird, Western, 1972 .... 19.00 To 30.00
Boxers, 1974 .... 24.00
Buccaneer, 1973 .... 25.00 To 32.00
Buffalo Hunter, 1973 .... 33.00 To 50.00
Calamity Jane .... 25.00 To 28.00
Camp Cook .... 26.00 To 50.00
Camp Follower, 1969 .... 18.00 To 40.00
Canada Goose, 1980 .... 80.00 To 90.00
Cannonade, 1976 .... 43.00
Canvasback, 1980 .... 75.00 To 80.00
Capistrano Swallow, 1972 .... 28.00
Cardinal, 1972 .... 32.00 To 45.00
Casual Indian .... 11.00 To 25.00
Cavalry Scout, 1969 .... 10.00 To 30.00
Cherry Valley, Gold, 1971 .... 25.00
Cherry Valley, Silver, 1971 .... 34.00
Chinese Laundryman, 1969 .... 16.00 To 40.00
Circuit-Riding Judge, 1969 .... 14.00 To 35.00
Circus Series, 1973 .... 39.00
Clown, No.I, Monkey Business, 1978 .... 32.00 To 41.00
Clown, No.3, Pie In Face, 1979 .... 32.00 To 40.00

Lionstone, Betsy Ross, 1976

Clown, No.3, Say It With Music, 1978 .... 32.00 To 39.00
Clown, No.4, Salty Tails, 1978 .... 32.00 To 40.00
Clown, No.5, Lampy, 1979 .... 32.00 To 40.00
Clown, No, 2, Sad Sam, 1978 .... 34.00
Country Doctor, 1969 .... 15.00 To 40.00
Cowboy, 1969 .... 12.00 To 25.00
Cowgirl, 1973 .... 30.00
Custer's Last Stand, 1979 .... 250.00 To 300.00
Dancehall Girl, 1973 .... 69.00
Delta Queen 50.00
Dogs Playing Pool 36.00
Doves Of Peace, 1977 .... 45.00
Egg Merchant, 1974 .... Illus   38.00
European Workers, 1974 .... 27.00
Falcon, 1973 .... 20.00 To 25.00
Fireman, No.l, Yellow Hat, 1972 .... 100.00 To 115.00
Fireman, No.2, With Child, 1974 .... 100.00 To 106.00
Fireman, No.3, Down Pole, 1975 .... 56.00 To 65.00
Fireman, No.4, Emblem, 1978 .... 42.00
Fireman, No.5, 60th Anniversary, 1979 .... 33.00 To 43.00
Fireman, No.6, Fire Hydrant, 1981 .... 54.00
Fireman, No.7, Red Hat, 1972 .... 100.00 To 112.00
Fisherman, 1980 .... 33.00 To 42.00
Football Players, 1974 .... 18.00
Frontiersman, 1969 .... 15.00 To 60.00
Gambler, 1969 .... 12.00 To 30.00
George Washington, 1976 .... Illus   25.00
God Of War, 1978 .... 38.00
Goddess Of Love, 1978 .... 38.00
Gold Panner .... 45.00 To 160.00
Goldfinch, 1972 .... 23.00
Golfer, 1974 .... 22.00
Highway Robber, 1969 .... 10.00 To 12.00
Hockey Players, 1974 .... 18.00 To 24.00
Hunter, 1980 .... 40.00 To 48.00
Indian Bust, No.l, 1980 .... 54.00
Indian Bust, No.2, 1980 .... 54.00
Indian Squaw, 1973 .... 20.00 To 27.00
Indian Weaver, 1976 .... 15.00 To 45.00
Japanese Workers 37.00
Jesse James, 1969 .... 14.00 To 35.00
Johnnie Lightning, No.1, 1972 .... 53.00
Johnnie Lightning, No.2, 1973 .... 51.00
Judge Roy Bean, 1973 .... 28.00
Koala, 1977 .... 17.00
Lion & Cub, 1977 .... 25.00 To 32.00
Lonely Luke, 1974 .... 35.00 To 70.00
Lucky Buck, 1974 .... 25.00 To 32.00
Madame, 1969 .... 45.00 To 60.00
Mailman, 1974 .... 15.00 To 21.00
Meadowlark, 1969 .... 21.00 To 35.00
Mecklenburg, 1975 .... 20.00 To 28.00
        LIONSTONE, MINIATURE, see Miniature, Lionstone
Molly Brown, 1973 .... 20.00 To 28.00
Molly Pitcher, 1975 .... 19.00 To 30.00
Mountain Man, 1969 .... 16.00 To 60.00
North American Wood Duck, 1980 .... 65.00 To 80.00
Northern Mallard, 1980 .... 65.00 To 80.00
Northern Pintail, 1980 .... 65.00 To 73.00
Olsonite Eagle, No.6 .... 40.00
Owls, 1973 .... 35.00
Paul Revere, 1976 .... Illus   26.00
Pheasant, 1977 .... 39.00 To 65.00

Lionstone, Egg Merchant, 1974

Lionstone, George Washington, 1976

Lionstone, Paul Revere, 1976

Photographer, 1976	30.00 To 45.00
Police Association Convention, 1980	20.00 To 33.00
Policeman	42.00
Prima Donna Club Set, 1978	230.00
Professor, 1973	60.00
Proud Indian, 1969	18.00 To 30.00
Quail, 1969	14.00
Railroad Engineer, 1969	14.00 To 35.00
Rainmaker, 1976	15.00 To 33.00
Renegade Trader, 1969	22.00 To 35.00
Riverboat Captain, 1969	10.00 To 35.00
Roadrunner, 1969	28.00 To 50.00
Robin, 1975	25.00 To 34.00
Rose Parade, 1973	26.00 To 65.00
Safari	10.00
Sahara Golf Invitational, 1976	31.00
Saturday Night Bath	37.00 To 45.00
Secretariat, 1977	40.00 To 43.00
Sheepherder, 1969	48.00 To 140.00
Sheriff, 1969	12.00 To 25.00
Shootout At O.K.Corral, 1971	230.00 To 400.00
Sodbuster, 1969	14.00 To 30.00
Sons Of Freedom, 1975	31.00 To 40.00
Squawman, 1973	26.00 To 35.00
Stage Driver, 1969	13.00 To 60.00
Swallow, Gold Bell	23.00
Swallow, Silver Bell	52.00

Tea Vendor, 1974 .... *Illus* 38.00
Telegrapher, 1969 .... 21.00 To 40.00
Tinker, 1974 .... 25.00 To 32.00
Trader 26.00
Trapper, 1976 .... 31.00
Tribal Chief, 1973 .... 35.00
Turbo Car, STP, Gold, 1972 .... 75.00
Turbo Car, STP, Platinum, 1972 .... 75.00
Turbo Car, STP, Red, 1972 .... 24.00
Valley Forge, 1975 .... 25.00 To 31.00
Vigilante, 1969 .... 13.00 To 30.00
Wells Fargo Man, 1969 .... 13.00 To 35.00
Woodhawk .... 25.00 To 85.00
Woodpecker, 1975 .... 25.00 To 31.00
Woodworker, 1974 .... 20.00

LORD CALVERT, Canada Goose 135.00
Canvasback Duck .... 30.00 To 40.00
Wood Duck .... 30.00 To 75.00

*Luxardo bottles were first used in the 1930s to bottle the Italian
liqueurs. The firm was founded in 1821. Most of the Luxardo bottles found
today date after 1943. The dates given are the first year the bottle
was made.*

LUXARDO, African Head 17.00
Ampulla, 1959 .... 28.00
Apothecary Jar, 1960 .... 11.00
Autumn Wine Pitcher 34.00
Babylon, 1960 .... 14.00
Bacchus 17.00
Bantu, 1962 .... 15.00
Bizantina, 1959 .... 32.00
Burma Pitcher 15.00
Calypso Girl, 1962 .... *Illus* 7.65
Cannon, Brass Wheels 23.00
Cask 14.00
Cellini, 1952 .... 39.00
Cellini, 1968 .... 15.00
Chess Horse, Quartz, 1959 .... 39.00
Clock 13.00
Coffeepot 12.00
Cucciola, 1961 .... 28.00
Deruta Cameo, 1959 .... 28.00
Dolphin, 1959 .... 44.00
Duck, Green, 1960 .... 36.00
Eagle, Onyx, 1970 .... 49.00
Faenza, 1972 .... 8.00
Fakir, 1960 .... 31.00
Fish, Alabaster, 1960 .... 35.00
Fish, Green & Gold, 1960 .... 35.00
Fish, Quartz 37.00
Fish, Ruby, 1961 .... 30.00
Gambia, 1961 .... 11.00
Gondola, 1960 .... *Illus* 7.50
Goose, Alabaster, 1960 .... 30.00
Mayan, 1960 .... 20.00
Mazzo, Amphora, 1954 .... 25.00
Medieval Palace, 1952 .... 34.00
Medieval Palace, 1970 .... 8.00
    LUXARDO, MINIATURE, see Miniature, Luxardo
Miss Luxardo 16.00
Nubian, 1959 .... 12.00
Owl, Onyx 42.00

Lionstone, Tea Vendor, 1974

Luxardo, Calypso Girl, 1962

Luxardo, Gondola, 1960

Luxardo, Torre Tinta, 1962

Paestum, 1959	19.00
Pagliaccio, 1959	18.00
Penguin, 1968	30.00
Pheasant, Black	175.00
Pheasant, Modern	35.00
Pheasant, Quartz	42.00
Pheasant, Red & Gold	35.00
Pierrot, 1959	53.00
Puppy On Base, 1960	34.00
Santa Maria Ship	14.00
Sphinx, 1961	13.00
Squirrel, 1968	35.00
Tamburello, 1959	24.00
Topa Print, 1970	8.00
Torre Bianca, 1962	19.00
Torre Tinta, 1962 ....Illus	8.00
Tower Of Flowers, 1968	16.00
Tower Of Fruit, 1968	17.00
Turkey	34.00
Venetian Gold Rosy, 1952	23.00
Venetian Merletto, 1957	26.00
Venus, 1959	25.00
Venus, 1968	15.00
Wobble Bottle	11.00
Zodiac, 1970	31.00

　　　MBC, see Miniature, MBC

McCORMICK, Abe Lincoln, 1976 .... 29.00 To 40.00
    Air Race Propeller, 1971 .... 16.00
    Air Race Pylon, 1970 .... 9.00
    Alabama Bama 25.00
    Alexander Graham Bell, 1977 .... *Illus* 28.00
    Arizona State Sun Devil 29.00
    Arizona Wildcat 25.00
    Arkansas Hogs, 1972 .... 38.00
    Auburn War Eagle 18.00
    Barrel, With Stand, Gold Hoops, 1968 .... 20.00
    Barrel, With Stand, Plain Hoops, 1968 .... 16.00
    Bat Masterson, 1972 .... 23.00
    Baylor Bears, 1972 .... 29.00
    Benjamin Franklin, 1975 .... 17.00 To 24.00
    Betsy Ross, 1975 .... 29.00
    Billy Mitchell 29.00
    Billy The Kid, 1973 .... 23.00
    Black Bart, 1974 .... 25.00
    Blue Jay, 1971 .... 25.00
    Bluebird, 1971 .... 20.00
    Buffalo Bill, 1979 .... 30.00 To 39.00
    Calamity Jane, 1974 .... 28.00
    California Bears 23.00
    Captain John Smith, 1977 .... 28.00
    Centennial, 1956 .... 138.00
    Charles Lindbergh, 1977 .... 19.95 To 29.00
    Ciao Baby, 1978 .... 22.00 To 38.00
    Daniel Boone, 1975 .... 24.00
    Davy Crockett, 1975 .... 18.00 To 19.00
    Doc Holiday, 1972 .... 17.00 To 22.00
    Drake Bulldogs, 1974 .... 17.00
    Dune Buggy, 1976 .... 19.00 To 29.00
    Eleanor Roosevelt, 1977 .... 14.00 To 30.00
    Elvis, Aloha, Music Box 120.00
    Elvis, Are You Lonesome Tonight, Music Box, 1981 .... 245.90
    Elvis, Bust, Gold 125.00
    Elvis, Bust, White, 1978 .... 20.00 To 32.00
    Elvis, Forever '68, Music Box, 1980 .... 40.00 To 70.00
    Elvis, Gold, Music Box, 1979 .... 185.00 To 275.00
    Elvis, Silver, Music Box, 1980 .... 169.00 To 239.00
    Elvis, Sincerely '77, Music Box, 1978 .... 55.00 To 90.00
    Elvis, Yours '55, Music Box, 1979 .... *Illus* 70.00
    George Washington Carver, 1977 .... 15.00 To 28.00

McCormick, Elvis, Yours
'55, Music Box, 1979

McCormick, Alexander Graham
Bell, 1977

George Washington, 1975	31.00
Georgia Bulldogs	13.00
Georgia Tech Yellowjackets	12.00
Hank Williams, Jr., Music Box, 1980	64.00
Hank Williams, Sr., Music Box, 1980	59.00
Henry Ford, 1977	24.00 To 28.00
Houston Cougars, 1972	30.00
Huck Finn, 1980	20.00 To 33.00
Hutchinson Kansas Centennial, 1972	15.00
Indiana Hoosiers, 1974	15.00
Iowa Cyclones, 1974	34.00
Iowa Hawkeyes, 1974	51.00
Iowa Northern University Purple Panther	32.00
J.R.Ewing, Music Box, 1980	55.00 To 65.00
Jeb Stuart, 1976	25.00 To 26.00
Jefferson Davis, 1976	25.00
Jesse James, 1973	23.00 To 25.00
Jester, Mirth King, 1972	42.00
Jim Bowie, 1975	17.00 To 20.00
John Hancock, 1975	17.00 To 26.00
John Paul Jones, 1975	22.00
Johnny Rogers, No.2, 1973	72.00
Joplin Miner, 1972	24.00
Julia Bulette, 1974	180.00
Kansas City Chiefs, 1969	35.00
Kansas City Royals, 1971	12.00
King Arthur, 1979	22.50 To 35.00
Kit Carson, 1975	19.00
Lobsterman, 1979	22.00 To 38.00
Louisiana State Tigers, 1974	15.00
Mark Twain, 1977	27.00 To 28.00
Meriwether Lewis, 1978	28.00
Merlin, 1979	22.50 To 29.00
Mexican Fighting Bull, 1974	20.00
Michigan State Spartans	13.00
Michigan Wolverines, 1974	17.00
Mikado, 1980	210.00
MCCORMICK, MINIATURE, see Miniature, McCormick	
Minnesota Gophers, 1974	13.00
Mississippi Rebels, 1974	13.00
Mississippi State Bulldogs, 1974	13.00
Missouri Sesquicentennial, China, 1970	7.00 To 10.00
Missouri Sesquicentennial, Glass, 1971	5.00 To 8.00
Missouri University Tigers, 1974	29.00
Muhammad Ali, 1980	46.00 To 51.00
Nebraska Cornhuskers, 1974	15.00
Nebraska Football Player, 1972	25.00
New Mexico Lobo	35.00
Oklahoma Sooner Wagon, 1974	25.00
Oklahoma Southern Cowboys, 1974	19.00
Oregon Beavers, 1974	15.00
Oregon Ducks, 1974	14.00
Ozark Ike, 1979	20.00 To 39.00
Packard, 1937, 1980	64.00
Patrick Henry, 1975	12.00 To 22.00
Paul Bunyan, 1979	22.00 To 38.00
Paul Revere, 1975	25.00 To 36.00
Pioneer Theater Auditorium, Reno, 1972	10.00
Platte Valley, Jug, Fifth	8.00
Platte Valley, Jug, 1/2 Gallon	14.00
Platte Valley, Jug, 1/2 Pint	5.00
Platte Valley, 1953, Jug, 2 Handles, Fifth	10.00

Pocahontas, 1977	36.00
Pony Express, 1978	15.00 To 45.00
Purdue Boilermakers, 1974	15.00
Queen Guinevere, 1979	22.50 To 29.00
Rice Owls, 1972	29.00
Robert E.Lee, 1976	26.00 To 27.00
Robert E.Peary, 1977	28.00
S.M.U.Mustangs, 1972	29.00
Sam Houston, 1977	21.00 To 25.00
Shriner, The Noble, 1976	29.00
Sir Lancelot, 1979	22.50 To 29.00
Skibob, 1971	13.00
Spirit Of '76, 1976	79.00 To 91.00
Stephen F.Austin, 1977	17.00 To 24.00
Stonewall Jackson, 1976	23.00 To 25.00
T.C.U.Horned Frogs, 1972	30.00
Tennessee Volunteers, 1974	13.00
Texas A.& M.Aggies, 1972	28.00
Texas Horns, 1972	29.00
Texas Longhorn Bulls, 1974	35.00
Texas Tech Raiders, 1972	28.00
Thomas Edison, 1977	*Illus* 24.00
Thomas Jefferson, 1975	17.00 To 22.00
Tom Sawyer, 1980	33.00
Tom T.Hall, 1980	65.00
Train Engine, 1969	28.00 To 38.00
Train, Mail Car, 1970	60.00 To 75.00
Train, Passenger Car, 1970	66.00 To 75.00
Train, Wood Tender, 1969	25.00 To 35.00
U.S.Marshal, 1979	20.00 To 35.00
Ulysses S.Grant, 1976	20.00
Washington Cougars, 1974	15.00
Washington Huskies, 1974	14.00
Wild Bill Hickok, 1973	24.00
Will Rogers, 1977	10.00 To 27.00
William Clark, 1978	29.00
Wisconsin Badgers, 1974	16.00
Woman Feeding Chickens, 1980	38.00
Woman Washing Clothes, 1980	*Illus* 34.00
Wood Duck, 1980	25.00 To 47.00
Wyatt Earp, 1972	29.00
Yacht America, 1970	25.00

McCormick, Thomas Edison, 1977

McCormick, Woman Washing Clothes, 1980

Medicine bottles held all of the many types of medications used in past centuries. Most of those collected today date from the 1850-1930 period. Bitters, sarsaparilla, and a few other types of medicine are listed under their own headings.

MEDICINE, A.C.Grant, German Magnetic Liniment, Albany, N.Y., Aqua, 5 In.	75.00
A.E.Smith's Electric Oil, Philadelphia, 3 1/2 In.	24.00
A.Kendall & Co., Electrical Febrifuge, New Orleans, 6-Sided, 3 In.	85.00
A.L.Murdock, Liquid Food, Boston, 12-Sided, Amber, 5 3/4 In.	5.00
Alexander's Tricobaphe, Open Pontil, Aqua	20.00
Allan's Anti-Fat, Buffalo, Cobalt Blue	45.00
Allan's Anti-Fat, Buffalo, N.Y., A.& D.H.C.On Base	9.50
Allen's Lung Balsam	8.00
Allen's World Hair Restorer	2.00
Allison's Cherry Balsam	9.50
Alvert's Derby Cure For Influenza & Colds, English, Aqua	18.00
American Coventry Compound, Open Pontil, Aqua	75.00
American Expectorant, 8-Sided, Aqua	245.00
American Medicinal Oil, Burkesville, Ky., Aqua, 6 1/4 In.	250.00
American Oil, Cumberland River, Kentucky, Rectangular, Aqua	300.00
American Pulmonary Balsam, Round, 5 1/4 In.	40.00
Anderson's Cough Drops, Flared	28.00
Anderson's Cough Drops, Open Pontil, Aqua	85.00
Anderson's Cough Drops, Prepared By I.Mellen, OP, Aqua	85.00
Anderson's Dermador, Round, Open Pontil, Aqua, 5 1/4 In.	28.00
Andrew's G.W.Worm Syrup, Aqua, 4 3/4 In.	105.00 To 125.00
Arctic Frost Bite Cure, Label & Box, Square, Aqua, 2 1/2 In.	6.50
Arentent Druggist, Memphis, Rectangular, Aqua, 4 3/4 In.	75.00
Armour Laboratories, Square, Amber	1.00
Arnold's Vital Fluid, Boston, Indented Panels, 7 In.	125.00 To 145.00
Arthur's Renovating Syrup, Iron Pontil, Blue-Green, Pint	135.00
Asiatic Balsam Compound, Pontil	45.00
Atlas Kidney & Liver Cure, Label, Amber, 9 In.	15.00
Atlas Kidney & Liver Cure, Label, Aqua	12.50
Aunt Ruth's Quaker Pills, Cap, Amber	6.50
Ayer's Ague Cure, Lowell, Mass., Aqua, 7 In.	8.00
Ayer's Cherry Pectoral, Lowell, Mass., Open Pontil, Aqua, 7 In.	26.00
B.A.Fahnestock's Vermifuge, Aqua	10.00 To 20.00
B.Fosgate's Anodyne Cordial	20.00
Bach's American Compound, Auburn, N.Y., Aqua, 7 3/4 In.	110.00
Bailey's American Vermifuge, Aqua	35.00
Baker's Pain Panacea, Open Pontil, Aqua, 5 1/4 In.	40.00
Baker's Vegetable Blood & Liver Cure, Greenville, Tenn., Amber	275.00
Baldwin's Celery Pepsin & Dandelion Tonic, Honey Amber	40.00
Balm Of Thousand Flowers, Irregular Octagon, OP, Aqua, 5 In.	47.00
Balsam Of Wild Cherry & Tar, N.Y., Pontil, Rectangular, 7 1/2 In.	90.00
Banes & Park, Balsam Of Wild Cherry & Tar, Aqua, 7 1/2 In.	125.00
Barry's Pearl Cream, Milk Glass	16.00
Barry's Tricopherous For Skin & Hair, Open Pontil, Aqua	15.00
Bear Oil, Open Pontil	12.00 To 16.00
Beetham's Glycerine & Cucumber	4.00 To 5.00
Bell & Co., Inc., Mfg.Chemists, New York, Rectangular, Green	4.00
Bell & Co., Inc., Orangeburg, N.Y., Papayans, Bell, Amber, 3 1/2 In.	3.00
Belle Of Anderson Sour Mash, 6-Pointed Star, Milk Glass	65.00
Bells Syrup Codeine Company, Clear, Square	1.00
Blodgett's Persian Balm, Great Home Luxury, Rectangular, 5 In.	125.00
Blood & Rheumatism Remedy No.6088, St.Paul, Minn.	12.00
Blood Life The King Of Tonics, Clear, Rectangle, ABM	1.00
Bloodline Liver Pills, Round Wooden Box, Label, Contents	15.00
Bonpland's Fever & Ague Remedy, Full Label, Aqua	45.00
Bonpland's Fever & Ague, Labeled, Open Pontil, 5 In.	40.00
Bonsail's Worm Syrup, Rectangular, 4 3/4 In.	95.00
Braddock's Cough Mixture, Embossed, Open Pontil, Aqua	95.00

Brant's Indian Pulmonary Balsam, Octagon, Aqua, 6 3/4 In. 30.00
Brant's Indian Pulmonary Balsam, Open Pontil, 7 In. .... 80.00 To 90.00
Brant's Indian Purifying Extract, Open Pontil, Aqua, 10 In. 50.00
Brant's Indian Purifying Extract, 8-Sided, Embossed, Aqua 65.00
Brant's Purifying Extracts, Brooklyn, N.Y., Rectangular, 10 In. 125.00
Brewster's Pectoral Mixture For Coughs, Aqua .... 35.00 To 50.00
Brinckerhoff's Health Restorative, High Embossing, Heavy Pontil 350.00
Brinckerhoff's Health Restorative, N.Y., Olive Green, 7 In. 280.00
Bromo-Seltzer, Teal Green 4.00
Bromo, Caffeine, Round, Light Cobalt, 3 In. 2.00
Brown's Essence Of Jamaica Ginger, Open Pontil, 5 1/2 In. 27.00
Brown's Essence Of Jamaica, Philada., OP, Aqua, 5 1/4 In. 21.00
Buchan's Hungarian Balsam, Open Pontil, Aqua, 5 3/4 In. 70.00
Buchu Remedy, Log Cabin Hops, Amber 120.00
Bulter's Balsam Of Liverwort, Aqua 75.00
Burnett Apothecary, Flat, Oval, Open Pontil, Pint, 8 1/2 In. 59.50
Burnett, Cylinder, Green, 3 1/2 In. 10.00
Burnett's Cocaine 10.00
Burrington's Vegetable Cough Syrup, Open Pontil, 5 1/5 In. 37.00
C.Brinckerhoff's Health Restorative, Price 1 Dollar, Green 225.00
C.Ellis & Co., Philadelphia, Cylinder, Aqua, Open Pontil, 8 In. 20.00
C.Heimstreet & Co., Troy, N.Y., 8-Sided, Open Pontil, Cobalt Blue 60.00
C.Pendleton's Tonic, Amber 25.00
C.Sine's Tar Wild Cherry & Hoarhound, Open Pontil, Aqua, 5 In. 50.00
Calvert's Derby Cure 25.00
Cantrell's Ague Mixture, Aqua, Rectangular, Philadelphia 225.00
Carbona Products Co., 12-Sided, Aqua, 6 In. 9.00
Carter's Extract Of Smartweed, Erie, Penn., Open Pontil, Aqua 100.00
Carter's Spanish Mixture, Iron Pontil, Olive Green, 8 1/4 In. 165.00
Carter's Spanish Mixture, Label, Richmond, Va. 250.00
Caswell Hazard Co., Chemists, Deep Cobalt, New York 35.00
Celre-Fo-Md, American Chemical Co., Wis., Round, Amber, 2 1/2 In. 3.00
Chamberlain's Colic, Cholera & Diarrhoea Remedy, Green, 4 1/2 In. 6.00
Chamberlain's Immediate Relief 12.00
Champlin's Liquid Pear, Milk Glass 10.00
Chapman's Cholera Syrup, 4 Salem St., OP, Aqua .... 110.00 To 175.00
Chateau Neuf Skin Lotion, Milk Glass, 4 1/4 In. 15.00
Chaul-Moo-Gra The East India Cure, Aqua, 6 1/4 In. 12.00
Christie's Magnetic Fluid, OP, Aqua, 4 3/4 In. .... 17.00 To 45.00
Citrate Of Magnesia, Light Teal 20.00
Citrate Of Magnesia, Sapphire Blue 125.00
Clark's Anti-Bilious Compound, Label, Contents, Aqua, 9 In. 25.00
Clark's World Famed Blood Mixture, Lincoln, Blue 17.50
Clemen's Indian Tonic, Embossed Indian, Label, 5 1/2 In. 285.00
Clements Tonic, Amber, 8 In. 17.50
Clewley's Miraculous Cure For Rheumatism, Embossed Nun's Head 85.00
Clickener's Sugar Coated Vegetable Purgative Pills, Pontil 50.00
Climax Syrup, Owegy, N.Y., 12-Sided, Aqua, 4 3/4 In. 155.00
Cocoa Beef Tonic 5.00
Coe's Dyspepsia Cure, Aqua 12.00
Coffeen's Chinese Liniment, S's Backward, Aqua, 4 1/2 In. 30.00
Comstock's Vermifuge 25.00
Constitution Life Syrup, Full Label 18.00
Cook's Infallible Eye Water, Aqua .... 50.00 To 60.00
Cooper's New Discovery, Aqua, Pint 7.50
Corbin's German Drops, Liverpool, N.Y., Rectangular, Pontil, 6 In. 225.00
Corbin's Summer Complaint Tincture, C.1860, Aqua, 4 1/4 In. 30.00
Craft's Distemper & Cough Remedy, Amber 10.00
Craig Kidney Cure Company, Amber .... 100.00 To 165.00
Cramer's Kidney & Liver Cure, 7 In. 7.00
Criswell's Bromo-Pepsin Cures Headache 5.00
Croff's Liniment 55.00
Crumpton's Strawberry Balsam, Attica, Ind., Pontil, Square, 5 In. 140.00

Cunningham & Co., Pittsburgh, Applied Lip, Cork Closure, No.722 .... 100.00
Curtis & Perkins' Cramp & Pain Killer, Open Pontil, 4 1/2 In. 30.00
Curtis' Cherry Syrup, Open Pontil, Clear, 7 1/4 In. 100.00
Cuticura For Affections Of The Skin, Label, Square, 9 1/2 In. 9.00
Cutter Laboratory, Berkley, Cal., Embossed, Dark Puce, 1 3/4 In. 25.00
D.Mitchell, Rochester, N.Y., Rectangular, Clear 2.00
Daily's Pain Extractor, Louisville, Open Pontil 30.00
Dalby's Carminative, Etched, Aqua 12.00
Davis Inflammatory Extirpator, Open Pontil, 3 3/4 In. 25.00
Davis Vegetable Pain Killer, Labeled, Open Pontil, 6 3/4 In. 30.00
Davis Vegetable Pain Killer, Open Pontil, Aqua, 8 1/4 In. 85.00
Davis Vegetable Pain Killer, Open Pontil, 4 1/4 In. 20.00
Davis Vegetable Pain Killer, Rectangular, Aqua, ABM 2.00
Delight's Spanish Lustral, Open Pontil, 6 In. 50.00
Dellug & Co., Pharmaceutists, New York, Rectangular, 4 3/4 In. 20.00
Dentist, Ether Bottle, Large Mouth, Open Pontil, 7 In. 10.00
Denton's Healing Balsam, Flared Lip, Aqua, 3 3/4 In. 55.00
DeWitt's Cough Cure, Aqua 3.50
  MEDICINE, DR. W.B. CALDWELL'S, see Medicine, Caldwell's
Dr.A.L.Adam's Liver Balsam, Rectangular, Aqua 275.00
Dr.A.Roger's Liverwort, Tar, & Canchalaqua, IP, 7 1/4 In. 75.00
Dr.Ashbaugh's Wonder Of The World, Pittsburgh, Aqua 30.00
Dr.Atherton's Wild Cherry Syrup, Oval, 5 1/8 In. 75.00
Dr.B.W.Hair's Asthma Cure, Square, Clear 30.00
Dr.Baker's Pain Panacea, Open Pontil, Aqua .... 16.00 To 28.00
Dr.Baker's Pain Panacea, Rectangular, Deep Aqua, 5 3/4 In. 85.00
Dr.Birmingham's Anti-Bilious Blood Purifer, Paneled, Green 20.00
Dr.Blackman's Genuine Healing Balsam, Fruit, 8-Sided, 4 1/2 In. 30.00
Dr.Blackman's Genuine Healing Balsam, Open Pontil, 5 1/4 In. 35.00
Dr.Browder's Compound Syrup Indian Turnip, OP, Aqua, 7 In. 95.00
Dr.C.W.Roback's Scandinavian Blood Purifier, Aqua, 7 1/2 In. 110.00
Dr.Caldwell's, Green & Aqua, ABM 1.00
Dr.Carey's Marsh Root, Elmira, N.Y., Label 10.00
Dr.Chapman's Croup Syrup 28.00
Dr.Chaussier's Empress, Hair, Sapphire Blue, 7 1/2 In. 150.00
Dr.Cheever's Life Root Mucilate, Charlestown, Mass., OP, Aqua 175.00
Dr.Church's Liniment, Cole, Virginia, Nevada, Label, Aqua, 7 In. 30.00
Dr.Craig's Cough & Consumption Cure, Amber, 8 In. .... 300.00 To 350.00
Dr.Curtis Cherry Syrup, N.Y., Pontil, Flint Glass, 7 In. 175.00
Dr.Curtis Inhaling Hygean Vapor, New York, Clear, 7 1/4 In. 225.00
Dr.D.Kennedy's Favorite Remedy, Rectangular, 8 3/4 In. 2.50
Dr.D.Unger's Cinchona Rubra Cure For Drunkenness, Clear, 1/2 Pint 250.00
Dr.Daniel's Liniment, Clear 5.00
Dr.Daniel's Wonder Worker, Clear 5.00
Dr.Davis's Compound Syrup Of Wild Cherry, 5-Paneled, Aqua, 7 In. 22.00
Dr.Davis's Compound Syrup, 8-Sided, 5 Indented, Aqua 75.00
Dr.Dean's King Cactus Oil, Amber 55.00
Dr.E.J.Cox, New Orleans, Aqua, 7 In. .... Illus 60.00

Medicine, Dr.E.J.Cox, New Orleans, Aqua, 7 In.

Dr.Elmore's Rheumatine Goutaline, New York, Dyspepsia & Kidney 55.00
Dr.Evan's Camomile Pills, Square, Aqua, 3 In. 20.00
Dr.Fahrney's Panacea, Deep Blue Aqua 20.00
Dr.Fenner's Kidney & Backache Cure, Amber 15.00
Dr.Fenner's Kidney & Backache Cure, Oval, Amber 50.00
Dr.Fenner's Kidney & Backache Remedy, Oval, Amber 20.00
Dr.Fitch's Female Specific, Open Pontil, Oval, 6 1/4 In. 25.00
Dr.Foord's Pectoral Syrup, N.Y., Rectangular, Aqua, 5 1/2 In. 85.00
Dr.Foord's Pectoral Syrup, New York, Lopsided Lip, 5 In. 95.00
Dr.Forsha's Alterative Balm 65.00
Dr.Fowler's Anti-Epicolic, Canton, New York, Aqua, 6 In. 125.00
Dr.Freeman, Indian Specific For Coughs, Penn., Aqua, 4 1/2 In. 200.00
Dr.Friend's Cough Balsam, Morristown, N.J., Aqua, 6 1/4 In. 200.00
Dr.Gordak's Colombo Drops, Aqua 35.00
Dr.Gordak's Jelly Of Pomegranate, Embossed, Open Pontil, Aqua 100.00
Dr.Gordak's Jelly Of Pomegranate, Pale Yellow Green, Pint 110.00
Dr.Gorve's Anodyne For Infants 5.00
Dr.Hair's Asthma Cure, Hamilton, Ohio 10.00
Dr.Hale's Cough Cure 5.00
Dr.Ham's Aromatic, N.Y., Open Pontil, Aqua, Round, 8 1/2 In. 95.00
Dr.Harter's Dixie Tonic, Dayton, Brown, 7 1/2 In. ....*Color* 200.00
Dr.Harter's Dixie Tonic, Dayton, Ohio, Amber 200.00
Dr.Harter's Fever & Ague Specific 25.00
Dr.Harter's Iron Tonic, Sides Embossed, BIMAL, Amber, 9 X 3 In. 6.00
Dr.Hayner Alterative, Philadelphia, OP 15.00
Dr.Hoofland's Balsamic Cordial, Phila., 7 In. .... 135.00 To 225.00
Dr.Hooker's Cough & Croup Syrup, Indented Panel, Round, 5 1/2 In. 85.00
Dr.Ingham's Vernive Pain Extr., Open Pontil, Aqua .... 15.00 To 18.00
Dr.J.G.B.Siegert & Sons, Miniature, 6 In. 20.00
Dr.J.G.B.Siegert, Embossed On Shoulder, Olive Green 3.00
Dr.J.H.McLeaus Strengthening Cordial, Full Label, 1/2 Pint 14.75
Dr.J.H.McLeaus Strengthening Cordial, Full Label, Pint 14.75
Dr.J.S.Clark's Balsam For The Throat & Lungs, Aqua 8.00
Dr.J.W.Grady & Co., Vegetable Remedies, Boston, New York 12.00
Dr.James, Remedy No.1, Jersey City & London, Green Aqua, 7 In. 95.00
Dr.Jayne's Ague Pills, Aqua 8.00
Dr.Jayne's Alterative, Philadelphia, OP, 7 In. .... 20.00 To 26.00
Dr.Jayne's Carminative Balsam, Open Pontil, Aqua, 5 1/4 In. 25.00
Dr.Jayne's Expectorant, Philadelphia, Pa., Aqua, 6 1/2 In. 16.00
Dr.Jayne's Indian Expectorant, Open Pontil, Aqua .... 75.00 To 80.00
Dr.Jayne's Oleacinous Hair Tonic, Philadelphia, Aqua, 5 In. 25.00
Dr.Jayne's Tonic Vermifuge, Open Pontil, Aqua .... 20.00 To 45.00
Dr.Jewett's Celebrated Pulmonary Elixir, Rindge, N.H. 150.00
Dr.Jewett's Celebrated Pulmonary, Open Pontil, Full Label, Aqua 160.00
Dr.John Bull's Compound, Louisville & New York, IP, 7 1/2 In. 85.00
Dr.John Bull's King Of Pain, Louisville, Ky., Oval, Aqua, 5 In. 180.00
Dr.John Bull's King Of Pain, New York, Pontil, Blue Aqua, 5 In. 85.00
Dr.Johnston's Indian Compound Herbaline, Oval, Aqua, 10 In. 325.00
Dr.Jones' Cough Remedy, Rectangular, Aqua 5.00
Dr.Kaiser Cough Cure, Rectangular, Clear 40.00
Dr.Kelling's Pure Herb Wedicines, Misspelled, Aqua, 5 In. 110.00
Dr.Kelling's Pure Herb, Open Pontil, Aqua, 6 1/2 X 2 1/2 In. 135.00
Dr.Kelsey, Lowell, Mass., Open Pontil 25.00
Dr.Kennedy's Medical Discovery, Aqua 5.00
Dr.Kennedy's Medical Discovery, OP, 8 3/4 In. .... 30.00 To 45.00
Dr.Kennedy's Medical Discovery, Roxbury, Mass., Aqua, 8 1/2 In. 35.00
Dr.Kennedy's Prairie Weed, Aqua, 8 In. 12.00
Dr.Kennedy's Salt Rheum Ointment, Open Pontil, 3 1/2 In., Aqua 40.00
Dr.Kennedy's Salt Rheum Ointment, Widemouth, OP, Aqua, 2 In. 35.00
Dr.Kennedy's Salt Rheumatism Ointment, Jar, Name In Semicircle 85.00
Dr.Kilmer's Complete Female Remedy, Deep Aqua 75.00
Dr.Kilmer's Female Remedy, Binghamton, N.Y., Aqua 18.00
Dr.Kilmer's Indian Cough Cure 12.50

Medicine, Dr.Miles New
Heart Cure, Aqua, 8 In.

Medicine, Dr.Pitcher's Castoria, Boston,
1868, Aqua, 5 3/4 In.

Dr.Kilmer's Kidney, Liver & Bladder, Label	9.50
Dr.Kilmer's Kidney, Liver Cure, London	12.00
Dr.Kilmer's Lung Cure, Label, Deep Aqua	250.00
Dr.Kilmer's Ocean Weed Heart Remedy, 7 1/4 In.	18.00
Dr.Kilmer's Swamp Root, Kidney, Liver & Bladder Cure	6.00 To 8.00
Dr.Koch's, Clear, Square, 9 1/2 In.	2.00
Dr.L.E.Keeley's Gold Cure For Tobacco Habit	35.00
Dr.Langley's Root & Herb, 9 In.	25.00
Dr.Leroy's Compound Mixture, Soda Shape, Aqua	120.00 To 125.00
Dr.Leroy's Specific, Iron Pontil, Aqua	150.00
Dr.Loring's Specific For Dyspepsia, Stopper, 4 1/2 In.	10.00
Dr.M.Bowman's Genuine Healing Balsam, 8-Sided, Clear, 5 1/4 In.	55.00
Dr.M.G.Kerr, Balsam, Rectangular, 4 1/2 In.	30.00
Dr.M.M.Fenner's Peoples Remedies, Light Amber, Large	27.00
Dr.M.M.Fenner's, Kidney & Backache Cure, 1872-1898, Oval, Amber	30.00
Dr.Manley Hardy, Boston, Aqua	80.00
Dr.McLane's American Worm Specific, OP, Aqua, 3 3/4 In.	12.00
Dr.McLane's American Worm Specific, Round, 4 In.	21.00 To 23.00
Dr.McMunn's Elixer Of Opium, OP, Aqua, 4 In.	10.00 To 22.00
Dr.Miles New Heart Cure, Aqua, 8 In.	Illus 6.00
Dr.Miles Restorative Blood Purifier, Aqua	10.00
Dr.Moore's Essence Life, Thin Flared Lip, Open Pontil, Aqua	30.00
Dr.Mowe's Vegetable Bitters, Rectangular, Aqua, 10 In.	125.00
Dr.Munn's Bronchitic Pulmonary Syrup, Veterinary, Aqua, 7 1/4 In.	175.00
Dr.Nywall's Family, Amber, 7 1/2 In.	7.00
Dr.Owen's Horse Linament, London, Aqua	70.00
Dr.Pareira's Italian Remedy, Aqua	85.00
Dr.Peter Fahrney's Teething Syrup For Babes	5.00
Dr.Pierce's Favorite Prescription, Buffalo, N.Y., Aqua, 8 1/4 In.	7.00
Dr.Pierce's Golden Medical Discovery, Partial Label, Aqua	25.00
Dr.Pinkham's Emmenagogue, Deep Aqua, Pontil, Square, 5 3/4 In.	55.00
Dr.Pinkham's Emmenagogue, Open Pontil, Aqua, 6 In.	55.00 To 85.00
Dr.Pitcher's Castoria, Boston, 1868, Aqua, 5 3/4 In.	Illus 3.00
Dr.Porter, New York, Open Pontil	10.00
Dr.Ranney's Botanic Blood & Liver Cure, Tooled Lip, Full	10.00
Dr.Rooke's Pale Newfoundland Cod Liver Oil, Cobalt, 7 In.	25.00
Dr.Rooke's Solar Elixir	7.50
Dr.S.Feller's Electric Liniment, 6-Sided, Deep Aqua, 4 1/4 In.	95.00
Dr.S.M.Gidding's Preparations, N.Y., Oval, Pontil, 7 1/4 In.	24.00
Dr.S.S.Fitch & Co., Broadway, N.Y., Aqua, 3 In.Square	15.00
Dr.S.S.Fitch & Co., 707 Broadway, N.Y., Rolled Flared Lip, 6 In.	25.00
Dr.S.Weaver's Canker & Salt Rheum Syrup, Open Pontil, Quart	35.00

Dr.Sage's Catarrh Remedy, Rectangular, Aqua, 2 1/4 In. 2.00
Dr.Sanford's Invigorator, N.Y., Embossed, Aqua, 7 3/4 In. 40.00
Dr.Sanford's Invigorator, N.Y., Rectangular, Pontil, 6 1/4 In. 80.00
Dr.Sanford's Invigorator, New York, Indented Panels, 7 In. 85.00
Dr.Stewart's Tonic, Amber 50.00
Dr.T.McGown's Essence Of Tar, Memphis, Blue Aqua, 5 7/8 In. 275.00
Dr.Taft's Asthmalene, New York, Tooled Lip, Full 5.00
Dr.Taylor's Chround Thermal Balsam Of Liverwort, 8 1/2 In. 300.00
Dr.Thacher's Liver & Blood, Chattanooga, Tenn., Amber 9.00
Dr.Thompson's Eye Water, Bridgeport, Conn't., OP, Aqua 12.00
Dr.Trafts Ashmalene, Aqua, Rectangle 1.50
Dr.Warren's Ginger Brandy, Red Amber 38.00
Dr.Warren's Pulmonic Cherry Cordial, Pontil, 7 In. 285.00
Dr.Wishart's Pine Tree, Embossed Trademark, Amber, 9 1/2 In. 59.00
Dr.Wishart's Pine Tree, Embossed Trademark, Deep Moss Green 55.00
Dr.Wistar's Balsam Of Wild Cherry, I.B., Open Pontil, 6 1/4 In. 45.00
Dr.Wistar's Balsam Of Wild Cherry, 8-Sided, OP, 6 1/2 In. 30.00
Dr.Wood's Aromatic Spirit, Bellows Falls, Vermont, Oval, 7 1/2 In. 80.00
Duff Gordon Sherry, Medical Dept.U.S.A., BIMAL, Dark Green 250.00
Durang's Rheumatic Remedy Co., Washington, D.C. 4.50
Durflinger 41, Clear, 4 In. 20.00
Durflinger 41, Cobalt, 5 1/2 In. 20.00
E.H.Flagg's Instantaneous Relief, Phila., Rectangular, 4 In. 85.00
E.S.Reed's Sons Apothecary, Atlantic City, Embossed Devil, 6 In. 45.00
Elepizone, A Certain Cure For Fits & Epilepsy 30.00
Ely's Cream Balm, Rectangular, Amber, 2 In. 4.00
Emmert Drug Co., Freeport, Illinois, Citrate Of Magnesia, Green 14.00
Epilepticide, Rectangular, Green, 5 In. 6.50
Evan's Teething Syrup, Aqua .... 8.00 To 10.00
Fahnestock's Vermifuge, Open Pontil, Aqua .... 10.00 To 25.00
     MEDICINE, FAHRNEY'S, see Medicine, Dr. Peter Fahrney's
Fellow's Syrup Of Hypophosphates, Oval, Aqua 1.00
     MEDICINE, FENNER'S, see Dr.M.M.Fenner's
Ferro China Bislari, Round, Dark Green 2.00
Fetridge & Co.Balm Of Thousand Flowers, 8-Sided, Aqua, 5 In. 65.00
Fletcher's Castoria, Aqua & Green, ABM 1.00
Floraplexion, Cures Dyspepsia, Liver Complaint & Consumption 15.00
Foley's Kidney & Bladder Cure, Amber 10.00
Foley's Kidney & Bladder Cure, BIMAL, Amber, 9 In. 8.00
Foley's Kidney & Bladder Remedy 15.00
Foley's Kidney Cure, Full Contents & Label, Amber, 9 1/2 In. 15.00
Folger's Olosaonian, N.Y., Embossed, Long Neck, Aqua, 7 1/4 In. 65.00
Folger's Olosaonian, New York, Aqua, 6 In. .... 25.00 To 30.00
Folger's Olosaonian, Open Pontil, Aqua, 90% Paper Label 140.00
     MEDICINE, FRIEDENWALD'S, see Medicine, Buchu Remedy
From The Laboratory Of G.W.Merchant, Lockport, Green 95.00
Fruitcura, Woman's Tonic, Madame M.Yale, Aqua, 8 3/4 In. 25.00
Fry's Great Rheumatic Cure, Allegheny, Penn. .... 125.00 To 150.00
G.D.E.Konngtilly, Cylinder, Aqua, 2 1/2 In. 10.00
G.K.Wheat, Wheeling, W.Va., Open Pontil 90.00
G.W.David Inflammatory Extirpator Cleanser, Open Pontil, Label 45.00
G.W.Merchant, Lockport, N.Y., Dark Green, OP, 5 In. .... 110.00 To 115.00
G.W.Merchant, Lockport, N.Y., Emerald Green, 5 In. .... 60.00 To 80.00
G.W.Merchant, Lockport, N.Y., Iron Pontil, Green 60.00
Gargling Oil, Lockport, N.Y., Cobalt Blue, Rectangle, 7 1/2 In. 35.00
Gargling Oil, Lockport, N.Y., Emerald Green 15.00
Gargling Oil, Lockport, N.Y., Teal Green 15.00
Genuine Essence, Open Pontil, Aqua, 4 1/2 In. 12.00
Genuine Essence, Open Pontil, 5 In. 15.00
Genuine Russell Spaulding, Boston, Open Pontil, Aqua 12.00
Gibb's Bone Liniment, Embossed, Olive Green, 6 1/2 In. 350.00
Gilbert Bros.& Co., Baltimore, Md., Double Ring Neck, Aqua 7.00
     MEDICINE, GIN, see Gin

Medicine, H.Bonnabel, New
Orleans, Aqua, 4 3/4 In.

Ginseng Panacea, Pontil, Rectangular, 4 1/4 In. 100.00
Glover Medicine Co., Augusta, Maine, Pint 9.50
Glover's Imperial Distemper Remedy, Honey Amber 4.00
Glover's Imperial Distemper Remedy, Teal Blue 25.00
Glover's Imperial Mange Cure, Amber, Rectangular 3.00
Golden's Beef Tonic, Wine Shape, Teal Green 8.50
Graefenberg Children's Panacea, Open Pontil, 4 In. 45.00
Graefenberg Dysentery Syrup, Open Pontil, 4 1/2 In. 20.00
Grant's German Magnetic Liniment, Albany, N.Y., Pontil, 5 In. 85.00
Gray's Balsam Best Cough Cure, Embossed & Labeled 12.00
Gray's Balsam Best Cough Cure, Embossed, 5 1/4 In. .... 6.00 To 12.00
Gray's Balsam For Throat & Lungs, Leroy, New York, Clear 7.00
Great Blood, Rheumatism Cure, West Superior, Wis. 30.00
Great Shoshonee's Remedy Of Dr.Josephus, Aqua, 9 1/4 In. 55.00
Guy's Tonic, Emerald 38.50
H.Bonnabel, New Orleans, Aqua, 4 3/4 In. .... *Illus* 60.00
H.E.Holmes, Walla Walla, W.T., 5 In. 25.00
H.G.Farrell's Arabian Liniment, Peoria, Aqua, 5 In. 85.00
H.G.Farrell's Arabian Liniment, Peoria, OP, Light Green, Large 65.00
H.G.Farrell's Liniment, Peoria, Embossed, Light Green 85.00
    MEDICINE, H.H.WARNER'S, see Medicine, Warner's
H.K.Mulford Chemists, Amber, Rectangular 1.50
H.K.Mulford Co., Soluble Tablets, Screw Top, Amber, 2 1/2 In. 2.00
H.Lake's Indian Specific, Rectangular, Aqua, 8 In. .... 250.00 To 325.00
H.T.Helmbold's Genuine Fluid Extracts, OP, Aqua, 6 1/4 In. 45.00
H.T.Helmbold's Genuine Preparations, 6 1/2 In. 18.00
H.W. & Co.Warranted Pure Cod Liver Oil, N.Y., Pontil, 10 1/4 In. 75.00
Hagan's Magnolia Balm, Rectangular, Milk Glass 10.00
Hair's Asthma Cure, Hamilton, Ohio, Aqua, 8 In. 15.00
Hall's Balsam For Lungs, Medium Cobalt Blue 80.00
Hall's Balsam For The Lungs, Aqua, 7 1/2 In. 10.00
Hall's Catarrh Cure, Aqua, Cylinder 4.00
Hamlin's Wizard Oil, Aqua, ABM 3.00
Hampton's Vegetable Tincture, Baltimore, OP, Olive Amber 235.00
Hand's Pleasant Physic, Label, Wrapper, & Pamphlet 15.00
Handyside's Blood Food, Emerald Green .... 65.00 To 70.00
Handyside's Comsumption Cure, Black Glass, 10 1/2 In. 265.00
Harper's Cough Remedy 65.00
Harper's Cuforhedake Brain Food 7.00
Hart's Swedish Asthma Cure, Amber 15.00
Hartshorn's Family Medicine, Light Green 8.00
Haskell's Capilli Restitutor, Open Pontil, Aqua, Pint 25.00
Hass's Catarrh Cure, Round, Aqua, 4 1/2 In. 2.00
Hawes Healing Extract, Essex, Conn., Thin Flared Lip, OP, Aqua 45.00
Hawks' Universal Stimulant, New Hampshire, Round, 4 In. 26.00
Healy & Bigelow Kickapoo Cough Cure, Aqua 6.50

Healy & Bigelow Kickapoo Indian Tape Worm Secret, Green 5.00
Healy & Bigelow, Indian Sagwa, Embossed Indian 9.50
Healy & Bigelow's Kickapoo Indian Cough Cure 12.00
Heimstreet, Cobalt 24.00
Helmbold's Genuine Fluid Extract, Open Pontil 35.00
Henry Wampole, Philadelphia, Light Blue, 6 In. 10.00
Henry's Calcined Magnesia, Manchester, Clear, 4 In. .... 10.00 To 50.00
Henry's Red Gum Cough Remedy, Guaranteed To Cure, Clear 20.00
Hewling's Genuine Essences, Rectangular, 5 In. 75.00
Hiawatha Blackberry Medicinal Cordial, Norfolk, Va., BIM, Clear 19.00
Hick's Capudine Cure, Label Under Glass, Stopper, Amber, 8 In. 45.00
Himalaya Cure For Asthma, Amber 8.50
Hobensack's Worm Syrup, Open Pontil, Aqua, 4 1/2 In. .... 32.00 To 50.00
Holloway's Ointment Cure, Pottery 15.00
Holman's Natures Grand Restorative, Boston, Mass., Aqua, 6 3/4 In. 125.00
Holme's Dulcified Vegetable Compound, Winthrop, Maine 35.00
Honduras Tonic, W.E.Twiss, Amber, 8 3/4 In. 20.00
Honneywell Universal Cough Remedy, Open Pontil 40.00
Hood's Excelsior Liniment, Whittled 7.50
Hood's Pills Cure Liver Ills 6.00
Hood's Sarsatabs, Round, 4 In. 6.00
Hop-Cel Nerve, Blood & Brain Tonic, Amber, 8 3/4 X 1 3/4 In. 30.00
Hopkin's Chalybeate, Baltimore, IP, Green, 7 5/8 In. 145.00
Hopkin's Chalybeate, Iron Pontil, Medium Olive 200.00
Houseman's German Cough Drops, By J.Davis, Aqua, 6 In.Diam. 155.00
Hull's Lung Tonic 5.00
Hulland Cough & Consumption Cure 12.00
Humphrey Chemical Co., New York, Cobalt Blue, Square, 7 1/4 In. 15.00
Humphrey's Chemical, Bromated Pepsin, Rectangle, Cobalt, 4 1/4 In 8.00
Hunnywell's TU24 Anodyne, Boston, Mass., Flared Lip, 4 In. 33.00
Hunnywell's Universal Cough Remedy, OP, 4 1/4 In. .... 26.00 To 35.00
Hunnywell's Universal Cough Remedy, Open Pontil, 6 1/4 In. 35.00
Hunt's Liniment, Sing Sing, N.Y., OP, Aqua, 4 3/4 In. 32.00
Hunt's Liniment, Sing Sing, N.Y., Pale Green, 5 In. 27.50
Hunt's Remedy, Providence, R.I., BIMAL, Aqua, 7 X 2 1/2 In. 11.00
Hunter's Balsam Or Cough Syrup, J.Curtis, Aqua, 6 In. 140.00
Hurd's Cough Balsam, Open Pontil, Aqua .... 25.00 To 40.00
Hurd's Hair Restorer, Bubbles, Oval, Aqua, 7 1/2 In. 150.00
Hutton-Dixon Wormy Treatment 2.50
Hyatt's AB Double Strength Life Balsam, N.Y. 65.00
Hyatt's Infallible Balsam, Light Green 265.00
Hyatt's Infallible Life Balsam, N.Y., Aqua Green, 10 In. 15.00
Hyatt's Infallible Life Balsam, N.Y., Deep Aqua 60.00
Hyatt's Infallible Life Balsam, N.Y., Iron Pontil, Green 325.00
I.A., Embossed, Aqua, 2 1/2 In. 5.00
        MEDICINE, INDIAN SAGWA, see Medicine, Healy & Bigelow
Indian Root Beer Extract, Aqua 2.00
Ingram's White Pine Cough Balsam, Aqua, 8 In. ....*Color* 3.50
Iroquois Indian Catarrh Remedy, Labeled 8.00
J.B.Wheatley's Compound Syrup, Dallasburg, Ky., OP, Aqua 40.00
J.E.Combault's Caustic Balsam, Aqua 4.00
J.L.Curtis Syrup Of Sassafras, Rectangular, 5 In. 65.00
J.M.Henry & Sons Vermont Liniment, Waterbury, Aqua, 5 1/8 In. 150.00
J.R.Burdsall's Arnica Liniment, New York, Aqua .... 6.00 To 20.00
J.R.Rowand, Hexagonal, Open Pontil, 3 3/4 In. 35.00
J.R.Stafford's Olive Tar, Backwards S, 6 In. 18.00
J.R.Stafford's Olive Tar, Cabin Shoulders, OP, Aqua, 6 In. 22.00
J.S.Jenkin's Resurateur, Philadelphia, Pontil, Aqua 18.00
J.Tilden Co., Paneled Rectangular, Pint 40.00
J.White Chemist & Druggist, Boston, Rectangular, 6 1/2 In. 45.00
Jacob's Cholera & Dysentery Cordial, Indented Panels, Aqua, 7 In. 75.00
Jacob's Cholera, Box & Testament, Open Pontil, 7 In. 100.00
John Graf, 8-Sided, Dark Amber 25.00

John J.Smith, Louisville, Ky., Open Pontil, Green Aqua	35.00
John Wyeth & Bros., Dosage Cap, Cobalt, 6 1/2 In.	10.00
Johnson's American Anodyne Liniment, OP, Aqua, 4 1/2 In.	20.00
Jones' Drops For Humors Or Anti Impetigenes, Flared Lip, 5 In.	44.00
Keasbey & Mattison Co., Ambler, Pa., ABM, Cobalt, 6 1/2 In.	4.00
Kendall's Spavin Cure, 12-Sided, Amber, 5 1/2 In. .... 3.00 To	10.00
Kerr & Bertolet Balsam, Box & Testament, Open Pontil, 4 3/4 In.	40.00
Kerr & Bertolet Compound, Pontil, 4 5/8 In.	42.00
Kerr Balsam, Full Wrapper	40.00
MEDICINE, KICKAPOO, see Medicine, Healy & Bigelow	
Kidder's Dysentery Cordial	80.00
Kier's Petroleum, Open Pontil, 6 1/2 In.	40.00
King's Discovery For Consumption	5.00
King's Royal Patent, 2 1/2 In. ....*Color*	25.00
Kodol Dyspepsia Cure, Pale Green	12.00
Kolmstock's Vermifuge, Aqua, 4 In.	15.00
Landley's Panacea, Rectangular, Squat, Aqua, 7 In.	89.00
Langenbach's Dysentery Cure, Full Label, Embossing, Golden Amber	50.00
Langenbach's Dysentery Cure, Golden Amber, 5 3/4 X 2 1/2 In.	50.00
Lauden & Co.'s Vermifuge, Phila., Open Pontil, Aqua	42.50
Lavol, A.J.White, New York, Cobalt, 7 1/4 In.	10.00
Ledlard's Morning Call, Olive Green, Quart	85.00
Lightning Kidney & Liver Cure, Weston W.Va., Large	29.50
Lindsey's Blood Searcher, Aqua, Large	46.00
Lindsey's Blood Searcher, Pittsburgh, Aqua	35.00
Liquazane, Amber, Round	1.00
Liqufruta Cough Cure, Rectangular, Green, 5 1/4 In.	16.00
Liquid Opodeldoc, Open Pontil, Round, 4 1/2 In.	9.00
Liquozone, Chicago, Round, Amber, 6 In.	2.50
Liquozone, Chicago, Round, Amber, 8 1/2 In.	2.00
Little's White Oil, Scottsville, Va., Nielsen 7-Star, Pontil, 6 In.	290.00
Longley's Panacea, Rectangular, Aqua, 6 1/2 In.	100.00
Longley's Panacea, Rectangular, Aqua, 6 3/4 In.	140.00
Lord's Opodeldoc, Aqua, 5 In.	10.00
Louden & Co.'s Alterative, Philadelphia, Oval, Aqua, 6 1/2 In.	85.00
Louden & Co., Female Elixir, Philadelphia, Aqua, 5 In.	125.00
Louden & Co., Vermifuge, Oval, 5 In.	39.00
Louden's Alterative, Aqua	50.00
Louden's Cherokee Liniment, 4 In.	6.00
Lowerre & Lyon Astringent Mixture, Rectangular, 5 3/8 In.	145.00
Lydia Pinkham's Blood Purifier, Aqua	6.00
Lydia Pinkham's Vegetable Compound, Aqua, ABM, 8 1/4 In.	2.00
Lyon's Powder, B. & P.New York, Open Pontil, Dark Puce	65.00
Lyon's Powder, Open Pontil, Apricot	180.00
Lyon's Powder, Open Pontil, Emerald Green	200.00
Lyon's Powder, Open Pontil, Puce	60.00
M.B.Robert's Vegetable Embrocation, OP	45.00
M.B.Robert's Vegetable Embrocation, Round, Green, 4 7/8 In.	90.00
M.D.Flint's Wild Cherry Compound, Embossed, 8-Sided, Fifth	350.00
Macassar Oil, Open Pontil	15.00
Macassar Oil, Rectangular, Flared Lip, 3 1/2 In.	11.00
Mackenzie's Ague & Fever Mixture, Cleveland, Ohio, Label, Aqua	300.00
Maguire Druggist, St.Louis, Mo., Open Pontil, Aqua, 5 1/2 In.	26.00
Maltine Mfg.Co., Label 3 Sides, Contents, Cork, Amber, 6 1/4 In.	4.00
Marsh's Pain Reliever, Open Pontil, Aqua .... 30.00 To	48.00
Masta's Indian Pulmonic Balsam, Lowell, Mass., Aqua .... 80.00 To	85.00
Masta's Pulmonary Indian Balsam, Lowell, Mass	125.00
Mat.Davis's Liniment Prepared By G.Schaub, Round, Aqua, 5 1/4 In.	225.00
Mayr's Wonderful Stomach Remedy, ABM	2.00
McClintock's Family Medicine, Aqua	50.00
McClintock's Family Medicine, Open Pontil, Clear, 8 1/4 In.	80.00
McClintock's Family Medicines, Clear, 10 In.	110.00
McCombies Compound Restorative, Open Pontil, Aqua .... 65.00 To	68.00

McLean's American Worm Specific, Aqua 25.00
Merrick's Vermifuge, Aqua 65.00
Merrick's Vermifuge, Milton, Pa., Aqua, 3 1/2 In. 55.00
Merrick's Vermiguge, Milton, Penn., 12-Sided 85.00
Mexican Mustang Liniment, Aqua 10.00
Mexican Mustang Liniment, Iridescent, OP, Aqua, 4 In. 10.00
Milk Of Magnesia, Chas.H.Phillips Chemical Co., Cobalt, 7 In. 3.00
Mimmon's Liver Regulator, Brass Horseshoe, C.1880 .... 75.00
Moore's Revealed Remedy, Amber, 9 In. 15.00
Moore's Revealed Remedy, Monogram & Shield, Amber 35.00
Morley's Liver & Kidney Cordial, ABM, Rectangle, Amber 10.00
Morse's Celebrated Syrup, Iron Pontil, Green 275.00
Morse's Celebrated Syrup, Iron Pontil, Light Green 360.00
Morse's Celebrated Syrup, Providence, R.I., Oval, Aqua, 9 1/2 In. 50.00
Morse's Invigorating Cordial, Open Pontil, 7 1/2 In. 57.00
Morse's Perfected Emulsion, Monogram, Blue-Green, 5 In. 15.00
Moxham Pharmacy, Johnstown, Pa., Aqua, 4 1/2 In. 9.00
Moxie Nerve Food, Ice Blue, Quart 30.00
Moxie Nerve Food, Trademark, Clear, 7 1/2 In. 6.00
Moxie Nerve Food, 10 1/2 In. 4.00
Moyer & Hazard, Phila., Open Pontil, Aqua, 4 1/4 In. 18.00
Mrs.Bush Specific Cure For Burns & Scalds, Winder, Georgia, Clear 9.00
Mrs.Dinsmores' Cough & Croup Balsam 4.00
Mrs.E.Kidder Dysentery Cordial, Boston, OP, Aqua .... 55.00 To 65.00
Mrs.Gervaise Graham, Beauty Doctor, Chicago & San Francisco 15.00
Mrs.N.M.Gardner's Indian Balsam Of Liverwort, 5 1/4 In. 70.00
Mrs.Winslow's Soothing Syrup, Aqua .... 4.50 To 10.00
Mrs.Winslow's Soothing Syrup, Open Pontil, Aqua .... 9.00 To 18.00
Mulford's Digestive Malt, Philadelphia, BIM, Amber, 8 1/2 In. 5.00
Munyon's Paw-Paw, Barrel, Original Paper Label, Amber, 10 1/4 In. 20.00
Murine Eye Remedy, Clear 3.00
Murine Eye Remedy, Partial Label, Milk Glass 25.00
Mystic Cure For Rheumatism & Neuralgia, Rectangular, Clear 25.00
N.Jarvis Oris Tooth Wash, Apothecaries Hall, Boston, Aqua, 5 In. 125.00
N.P.Co., Norwich, N.Y., Oval, Cobalt 3.00
N.Y.Pharmacal Association, Cobalt Blue, Pint 19.50
Nathan Tucker's 5 Grains Cocaine, Clear, 4 In. .... *Illus* 10.00
Nerve & Bone Liniment, Open Pontil, Aqua, 4 In. 12.00
Nerve & Bone Liniment, Round, 4 1/2 In. 9.00
New England Cough Syrup, Open Pontil 50.00
New England Cough Syrup, 6 Sides, Olive Amber, Label, Quart 165.00
Nowill's Pectoral Honey Of Liverwort, Aqua 65.00
O'Rourke & Hurley, Cobalt Blue 12.00
Oakley's G.W.Depurative Syrup, Reading, Pa., Aqua 135.00
Odol, Toothpowder, Milk Glass 4.00
Oldrige's Balm Of Columbia, Partial Label, Aqua, 5 1/2 In. 135.00

Medicine, Nathan Tucker's 5 Grains
Cocaine, Clear, 4 In.

Orrick's Worm Destroyer, Aqua 65.00
Osgood's India Cholagogue, N.Y., OP, Aqua, 5 In. .... 15.00 To 40.00
Osgood's India Cholagogue, Open Pontil, 5 In. 25.00
Otis Clap & Son, Square Round-Shouldered, 8 1/4 In. 5.00
Owl Drug Co., Square, Whiskey Type, Label, Fifth 175.00
Owl Pharmacy, Seven Troughs, Nevada, Clear, 6 In. 120.00
Ozomulsion, Coffin Shape, Amber 1.00
P.T.Wright's Carminative Balsam, Phil., Rectangular, 4 1/2 In. 75.00
Page's Vegetable Syrup For Females, Label, Aqua, Quart 75.00
Paine's Celery Compound, Amber 4.00
Paine's Celery Compound, Aqua .... 14.00 To 15.00
Paine's Celery Compound, Reddish Amber 10.00
Parker's Ginger Tonic, Aqua, Rectangle 2.00
Peptenzyme, Fred & Carnrick, Rectangular, Cobalt, 4 1/2 In. 8.00
Peptonoids, Arlington Chemical Co., Rectangular, Amber, 7 1/2 In. 2.00
Perry's Dead Shot Vermifuge 10.00
Perry's Dead Shot Vermifuge, Aqua 10.00
Persian Powder, Red Amber 25.00
Phalen's Chemical Hair Invigorator, OP, Aqua .... 12.00 To 25.00
Phaselin, Rectangular, Light Green 8.00
Phillip's Emulsion Cod Liver Oil, N.Y., Honey Amber 9.50
Phillip's Emulsion Cod Liver Oil, Rectangle, Amber 2.00
    MEDICINE, PINE TREE CORDIAL, see Medicine, Wishart's
Pinex, Aqua, ABM 1.00
Pinkstone's Curechilene, Cures Cattle Diseases 25.00
Piso's Cure For Consumption, Hazeltine & Co., Light Aqua 3.00
Piso's, Trademark, Hazeltine & Co., Green, 5 In. 5.00
Planter's Nubian Tea, Embossed Head, Contents, Box, Amber, 8 In. 25.00
Pond's Extract, Open Pontil, Rectangular, 4 1/2 In. 27.00
Porter's Cure Of Pain, Bundyburg, Ohio, OP, 6 3/4 In. 200.00
Preston Of New Hampshire Smelling Salts, Stopper, Palmer Green 10.00
Preston's Hed-Ake-Cure 10.00
Preston's Veg.Purifying Catholicon, Portsmouth, N.H., Oval, Quart 125.00
Price's, Patent Candle Company, Green-Aqua 95.00
Prickly Ash Poke Root Potassium, Blood Purifier, Amber, 9 3/4 In. 15.00
Primley's Speedy Cure For Coughs & Colds, Elkhart, In., Clear 25.00
Professor Dean's Barbed Wire Remedy 50.00
Professor Degrath's Electric Oil, Philadelphia, Aqua 20.00
Professor H.K.Flagg's Balm Of Excellence, Aqua, 4 7/8 In. 65.00
Professor Mott's Magic Hair Invigorator, 25 Cents, Aqua 250.00
Professor Wood's Hair Restorative, Open Pontil, Aqua 25.00
Professor Wood's Hair Restorative, St.Louis 95.00
Pure Norwegian Cod Liver Oil, Clear 5.00
Queru's Cod Liver Oil Jelly, Round, OP, Aqua, 5 1/2 In. 110.00
Quirye, Dr.Koch Berlin, Dog's Head, Milk Glass 65.00
R.Bernard's Cholera Medicine, N.Y., Outrolled Lip, 6 In.Square 112.00
R.E.Sellers, Druggist, Pittsburgh, Open Pontil, Aqua 35.00
R.E.Woodward's Vegetable Tincture, S.Reading, Mass., Aqua, 6 In. 175.00
R.R.R.Radway's Ready Relief, 50 Cents, N.Y., Rectangular, 6 In. 75.00
R.R.R.Rudway's Renovating Resolvent, Open Pontil, 7 1/4 In. 50.00
R.V.Pierce, M.D., Green, ABM, 9 1/8 In. 3.00
R.V.Pierce, M.D., Prescribed By, Buffalo, N.Y., Citron .... 20.00 To 30.00
Reed's Gilt Edge Tonic 1878, Amber, Square, Quart 9.50
Reed's Gilt Edge Tonic 1878, Olive Green 12.00
Retham Pain Killer, Emerald 19.50
Rev.Hill's Vegetable Remedy, Aqua .... 95.00 To 100.00
Rhode's Fever & Ague Cure, Label, Aqua, 8 1/2 In. .... 90.00 To 145.00
Ricksecker's Skin Soap Cure 10.00
Ridgeway's Acme Liniment, Hyde Town, Pa., Strap Sided, Amber 15.00
Ridgeway's Acme Liniment, Pleasantville, Pa. 17.00
Rival Herb Tablets, Tin, 3 1/4 X 2 1/4 X 1 1/4 In. 20.00
Robert B.Seller's Vermifuge, Pittsburgh, Blue Aqua, 4 In. 65.00

Roche's Embrocation For Hooping Cough 4.00
Rock's Cough & Cold Cure, Aqua .... 8.00 To 10.00
Roger's Vegetable Worm Syrup, Cincinnati, Oh., Pontil, Aqua 25.00
Rohrer's Expectoral, Iron Pontil, Yellow Amber, 3/4 Quart 160.00
Rohrer's Expectoral, Lancaster, Pa., Honey Amber 150.00
Rohrer's Expectoral, Lancaster, Pa., Iron Pontil .... 115.00 To 190.00
Rohrer's Wild Cherry Tonic, Lancaster, Ground Pontil, Amber 130.00
Roswell Vanbuskirk Druggist, Rectangular, 6 1/8 In. 75.00
Royal Schiedam Schnapps, Embossed, IP, Yellowish Olive Amber 250.00
Royces Universal Relief, Wales, Mass. 65.00
Rupturine Cures, Rupture Hernia Cure Co., Dug, 3 1/2 In. 28.00
Rupturine Cures, Westbrook, Maine, 8 Panels, Embossed, 6 1/4 In. 35.00
Rush's Buchu & Iron, Aqua, 8 7/8 In. 5.00
Rushton, Clark & Co., New York, Pontil, Long Neck, 10 In. 70.00
Rushton, Clark & Co.Chemists, N.Y., OP, Green Aqua, 9 1/2 In. 45.00
Rushton, Clark & Co.Chemists, New York, Pontil, 10 In. 16.00
Russ Aromatic Schnapps, N.Y., Deep Olive Green, 8 1/4 In. 125.00
S.B.Catarrah Cure, Smith Bros., Fresno, California 10.00
S.M.Kier Petroleum, Pittsburgh, Pa, Rectangular, Aqua, 6 1/2 In. 65.00
S.O.Bunbar, Taunton, Mass., Fluid Magnesia, Label, Aqua, 6 In. 95.00
S.W.Marsh Pain Reliever, Seed Bubbles, Rectangular, 4 In. 54.00
Sanderson's Blood Renovator, Indented Panels, Oval, 8 In. 130.00
Sanford's Radical Cure, Cobalt Blue, 7 1/4 In. .... 22.00 To 30.00
Sargent & Co., American Canchalacogue, New York, Aqua, 7 1/2 In. 225.00
Save The Horse Treatment For Lameness, Rectangular, 6 1/4 In. 12.00
Sawen's Cough Balsam, Aqua 32.00
Sawyer's Family Cure, Label & Contents 28.00
Scalpine, Log Cabin 90.00
Schaffer's Vermifuge, Aqua 50.00
Schenck's Pulmonic Syrup, Medium Green, 8-Sided, 6 3/4 In. 95.00
Schenck's Pulmonic Syrup, 8-Sided, Open Pontil, Aqua .... 40.00 To 55.00
Schenck's Seaweed Tonic, Aqua, Quart 20.00
Schenck's Seaweed Tonic, Aqua, 8 3/4 In. .... 120.00 To 150.00
Schenk's Pulmonic Syrup, Open Pontil, 7 In. 60.00
Schlotterbeck & Foss Co., Portland, Maine, 7 1/4 In. 8.00
Scott's Emulsion, With Lime & Soda, Embossed Fish & Man, 7 In. 3.00
Scott's Emulsion, With Lime & Soda, 9 1/2 In. 5.00
Scott's Red Oil Liniment, Philadelphia, Aqua, 5 In. .... 48.00 To 65.00
Scovill's Blood & Liver Syrup, Aqua 12.00
Seabury's Cough Balsam, Open Pontil, Aqua 35.00
Seabury's Refined Castor Oil, Jamaica, L.I., Embossed, 5 In. 125.00
Seabury's, Jamaica, N.Y., Open Pontil, 5 1/4 In. .... 22.00 To 35.00
Shaker Anodyne, Enfield, N.H., Aqua 65.00
Shaker Anodyne, Enfield, N.H., Open Pontil 55.00
Shaker Cherry Pectoral Syrup, Open Pontil, Aqua .... 75.00 To 115.00
Shaker Cherry Pectoral, Canterbury, N.H., Protruding Pontil 75.00
Shaker Fluid Extract Valerian, OP, Flange, Aqua, 3 1/2 In. 24.00
Shaker Syrup, Canterbury, N.H., 6-Sided, Open Pontil, 7 In. 100.00
Shaker Syrup, No.1, Canterbury, N.H., Rectangle, Open Pontil, Aqua 85.00
Shecut's Southern Balm For Consumption, Coughs, Colds, Aqua 225.00
Shepherd's Vermifuge, Pittsburgh, Cylinder, Aqua, 4 In. 50.00
Sherman's Lozenges, Oval, 3 In. 65.00
Shiloh's Consumption Cure, Green 5.00
Shirley's Universal Renovator, Front Embossing, Pontil, 6 3/4 In. 90.00
Sim's Tonic, Elixir Pyrophosphate Of Iron, Antwerp, N.Y., Amber 12.00
Simmon's Iron Cordial, Phila., Rectangle, Indented Front Panels 5.00
Sir James Murray Solution Of Magnesia .... 60.00 To 65.00
Skeleton's Pectoral Balsam Of Life, For Lung Diseases, Hampshire 175.00
Smith's Anodyne Cough Drops, Montpelier, Vermont, Aqua 75.00
Smith's Green Mountain Renovator, E.Georgia, Vermont, Aqua 55.00
Smith's Green Mountain Renovator, Iron Pontil, Amber 650.00
Smith's Veterinary Remedy, Contents & Label 5.00
Smolander's Preparations, Embossed Horse, Aqua 7.00

Millville Art Glass, Israel's 25th Anniversary, Honey Amber ; J. F. Kennedy, 10 Yr. Memorial, Cobalt Blue; Watergate, Amethyst; Jersey Devil, Jersey Green

Famous Firsts, Baby Panda, 1981

Ski Country, Goat, Mountain, 1975

Ski Country, Duck, Mallard Family, 1977

Ski Country, Falcon, White, 1977

Old Commonwealth, Hunter, Waterfowler, No. 2, 1980

Ezra Brooks, Snow Leopard, 1980

Ezra Brooks, Macaw, 1980

Ezra Brooks, Old EZ, No. 3,
Snow Owl, 1979

Old Commonwealth, Leprechaun, 1980

Old Commonwealth, Coal Miner, Lunch Time, No. 4, 1980

Hoffman, Sow Grizzly & Cub Fishing, 1981

Beam, Jaguar, 1981

**Beam, Ducks Unlimited,
No. 7, 1981**

Hoffman, Wood Ducks, 1981

Famous Firsts, China Clipper, 1979

Famous Firsts, Fireman, 1981

Ezra Brooks, Train, Casey Jones, No. 1, 1980

Candy Container, Tot Telephone, 2½ In.

Beam, Fire Chief's Car, 1981

Hoffman, Mississippi Bulldogs, 1977 ; Golden Eagles, U.S.M., 1981 ; Mississippi Rebels, 1977

Beam, Telephone, Coin, 1981

Barber, Enamel Flower Decoration, Orange, 7 In.

Medicine, St.Joseph's Assures
Purity, Clear, 5 1/2 In.

Medicine, The Mother's Friend,
Atlanta, Ga., Aqua, 7 In.

Snow & Mason Croup & Cough Syrup, Round, 5 In. 65.00
Spalding's Rosemary & Castor Oil, Aqua .... 23.00 To 35.00
Spark's Kidney & Liver Cure, Camden, N.J., Aqua 5.00
Spark's Perfect Health For Kidney & Liver Diseases, Dose Glass 175.00
Spiller's Golden Cure, Westbrook, Me., Box Label 10.00
St.Andrew's Wine Of Liferoot, BIMAL, Amber 15.00
St.Catherine's Chloride Calcium, Canada, Aqua 85.00
St.Joseph's Assures Purity, Clear, 5 1/2 In. .... Illus 3.00
Stabler & Co.Druggists, Baltimore, Pontil, 6 1/2 In. .... 26.00 To 50.00
Stephen Sweets Liniment, Aqua 10.00
Stieau Pills, Round, Clear 2.00
Stoddard, Open Pontil, Amber, Round, 5 In. 28.00
Swaim's Panacea, Phila., Genuine, Aqua, 8 In. 550.00
Swaim's Panacea, Phila., IP, Light Green, 8 1/2 In. .... 225.00 To 240.00
Swaim's Panacea, Phila., Open Pontil, Apple Green 125.00
Swaim's Panacea, Phila., Open Pontil, Olive Green .... 140.00 To 200.00
Swaim's Vermifuge, Dysentery, Cholera, Morbus, Dyspepsia, Aqua 60.00
Sweet's Blood Renewer, Chicago, Double Ring Lip, Aqua, 8 In. 20.00
Sweet's Infallible Liniment 9.50
Swifts Pharmacy Seattle, Washington, 12 Ounce 5.00
T. & W.Henry, Aromatic Spirit Of Vinegar, Oval, Flint, 3 In. 90.00
T.W.Harper's Cough Remedy, Aqua 65.00
Taylor's Opocura, Square, Aqua, 3 In. 220.00
The Mother's Friend, Atlanta, Ga., Aqua, 7 In. .... Illus 3.00
Thomas Ecletic Oil, Foster Milburn Co., Rectangular, 4 1/2 In. 2.00
Thompson's Compound Syrup Of Tar, Consumption, Aqua .... 75.00 To 90.00
Thompson's Compound Syrup Of Tar, Consumption, Green 120.00
Thompson's Eye Water .... 15.00 To 25.00
Thomson's Compound Syrup Of Tar, Philadelphia, Indented Panels 95.00
Tincture Of Iodine, Embossed, Amber 3.00
Tincture Of Vermifuge, Glass Stopper, Original Contents 15.00
Tobias Venetian Liniment, OP, Aqua, 3 7/8 In. .... 15.00 To 20.00
Tom's Russian Liniment, Indented Panels, Square, OP, 4 1/2 In. 95.00
Tonsiline, Giraffe Embossed On Back, Label, Contents 3.50
Trask's Magnetic Ointment, Dark Aqua, 2 3/4 In. 30.00
Trial Mark Pain Killing, Rectangular, Light Green, 7 1/4 In. 5.00
Tricopherous For The Skin & Hair, Aqua 10.00
Tulu Compound, Wm.Stotswood, Petersburg, Va., Label, Green, 4 In. 65.00
Turner Brothers, New York, Barrel, Golden Amber With Olive Color 125.00
Turner's Balsam, 8-Sided, Aqua, 4 1/2 In. 60.00
Tuttle's Worm Syrup 70.00
U.S.A.Hospital Dept., Blob Top, Collar, Aqua, Pint 125.00
U.S.A.Hospital Dept., Olive Green, Quart 89.50
U.S.A.Hospital Dept., X On Base, Deep Aqua, Quart 43.00
Udolpho Wolfe's Schnapps, IP, Olive Green, 8 In. .... 45.00 To 65.00
Uncle Sam's Nerve & Bone Liniment, Aqua 22.50
United States Medicine Company, N.Y., Aqua, 5 3/4 In. 8.00

University Of Free Medicine, OP, Aqua, 6 In. .... 85.00 To 110.00
University Of Free Medicine, Philadelphia, Partial Label, Aqua 150.00
Vaughn's Vegetable Lithontriptic Mixture 35.00
Vaughn's Vegetable Lithontriptic Mixture, Small 40.00
Vegetable Pulmonary Balsam, Open Pontil, 4 1/2 In. 20.00
Venos Lightning Cough Cure, Cornflower Blue, 5 1/4 In. 15.00
Victor Liver Syrup, Victor Remedies Co., Aqua, 5 1/4 In. 2.00
Viell Cure De Gen, Seal On Neck, Squat, Green, 5 1/4 In. 175.00
Vigor Of Life, Aqua 5.00
Voldner's Aromatic Schnapps, Olive Amber, IP, 9 1/2 In. 75.00
Voldner's Aromatic Schnapps, Olive Green, 8 In. 75.00
W.Bailey's Apothecaries Hall, Rectangular, 5 3/4 In. 100.00
W.F.Lawrence's Genuine Preprations, Rectangular, 8 3/4 In. 110.00
W.F.Lawrence's Preparations, Epping, N.H., Long Neck, 9 In. 65.00
W.R.Warner & Co., Phila., Pa., Teaspoon On Reverse, Cobalt Blue 10.00
Wadleigh's Rheumatic Cure, Alton, N.H., 8 1/2 In. 23.00
Wadworth's Vegetable Croup Syrup, Aqua 20.00
Wait's Wild Cherry Tonic, Amber .... 15.00 To 17.00
Wampole's Liquid Wheat 5.00
Warner's & Boswell's Colorified, Deep Cobalt 18.00
Warner's Animal Cure, Amber, 10 1/2 In. .... 275.00 To 375.00
Warner's Kidney & Liver Cure 10.00
Warner's Log Cabin Extract, Full Label, Contents 85.00
Warner's Log Cabin Extract, Golden Amber, 8 1/4 In. 40.00
Warner's Safe Cure, Amber, 7 1/4 In. .... 5.00 To 22.00
Warner's Safe Cure, Free Sample, Cylinder .... 10.00 To 12.00
Warner's Safe Cure, Left-Handed Safe, Amber 52.00
Warner's Safe Cure, London, Amber, 4 1/2 In. 325.00
Warner's Safe Cure, London, Deep Teal Green, 1/2 Pint 110.00
Warner's Safe Cure, London, Green, Pint 95.00
Warner's Safe Cure, London, Olive Amber, Pint 95.00
Warner's Safe Cure, London, Olive Green, 1/2 Pint 110.00
Warner's Safe Cure, London, Olive Green, Pint 110.00
Warner's Safe Cure, London, Paint, Red Puce 110.00
Warner's Safe Cure, London, Straw Yellow, 1/2 Pint 110.00
Warner's Safe Cure, London, Thick Glass, Dark Green, 1/2 Pint 110.00
Warner's Safe Cure, Melbourne, Amber, Pint 30.00
Warner's Safe Cure, Melbourne, Reddish Amber, Pint 60.00
Warner's Safe Cure, Melbourne, Straw Yellow, Pint 110.00
Warner's Safe Cure, Rochester, Amber, 1/2 Pint 25.00
Warner's Safe Cure, Rochester, Amber, Pint 17.50
Warner's Safe Diabetes Cure, Amber, Pint 25.00
Warner's Safe Diabetes Cure, Amber, 9 1/2 In. 32.50
Warner's Safe Diabetes Remedy 60.00
Warner's Safe Kidney & Liver Cure, Amber, 9 3/4 In. 12.00
Warner's Safe Kidney & Liver Cure, Left-Handed Safe, Blob Top 65.00
Warner's Safe Kidney & Liver Cure, Rochester, N.Y. 12.00
Warner's Safe Kidney & Liver Remedy, Blob Top, Amber, 9 1/2 In. 26.00
Warner's Safe Nervine, Amber, 9 1/2 In. 20.00
Warner's Safe Nervine, Dark Amber, 7 3/8 In. 10.00
Warner's Safe Nervine, Double Collar, Pint 65.00
Warner's Safe Nervine, Honey Amber, Pint 18.00
Warner's Safe Nervine, London, Olive Amber, Pint 110.00
Warner's Safe Nervine, London, Straw Yellow, 1/2 Pint 55.00
Warner's Safe Nervine, Rochester, Light Amber, 1/2 Pint 30.00
Warner's Safe Rheumatic Cure, Amber, 9 3/8 In. .... 10.00 To 45.00
Warner's Safe Tonic, Pint 65.00
Warner's Tippecanoe, Amber .... 68.00 To 70.00
Watermelon Seed Cure, Akron, Ohio, Wooden Vials, Box, Advertising 50.00
Watson's Magic Balsam, Bainbridge, Georgia, Amber 15.00
Webb's A No.1 Cathartic Tonic, Amber .... 30.00 To 45.00
Weedon & Donts, Eufaula, Ala., Emerald Green, 4 1/2 In. 25.00
West's Rheumatic Remedy 5.00

Wheatley's Compound Syrup, Dallasburg, Ky., Aqua, 6 In.	95.00
Wheatley's Compound Syrup, Open Pontil, 5 3/4 In.	55.00
Wheelers Tissue Phosphates, Aqua, Square	1.50
Whitlock Prescription Specialists, SCA, 7 In.	9.00
Whittemore's Eye Water, Label Reads Hawe's Healing Extract	40.00
Whitwell's Original Opodeldoc, Aqua	25.00 To 30.00
Whitwell's Original Opodeldoc, Aqua Clambroth, 4 3/8 In.	65.00
Wilson Botanic Druggist, Boston, B O & G C, OP, Aqua, 7 In.	80.00
Winter's Canadian Vermifuge, Contents, OP, Aqua, 4 In.	48.00
Wishart's Pine Tree Cordial, Amber, Fifth	35.00
Wishart's Pine Tree Cordial, Amber, Label	65.00
Wishart's Pine Tree Cordial, Green	48.00 To 55.00
Wishart's Pine Tree Cordial, Green, Small	50.00
Wishart's Pine Tree Cordial, Label & Contents, Amber	90.00
Wishart's Pine Tree Cordial, Teal Blue	55.00 To 60.00
Wishart's Pine Tree Cordial, Yellow Green	55.00
Wishart's Pine Tree, Bright Green, Small	55.00
Wm.Brown, Chemist & Druggist, Boston, 6-Sided, Open Pontil	65.00
Wm.H.Read's Syrup Of Liverwort, Baltimore, Aqua, 7 In.	150.00
Wm.R.Warner & Co., Philadelphia, Cobalt Blue	5.00
Wm.Radam's Bacteria & Lungus Destroyer, Should Be Fungus	65.00
Wm.Radam's Microbe Killer Cure, Embossed, Amber	25.00
Wm.Radam's Microbe Killer, Honey Amber	70.00
Wm.Radam's Microbe Killer, 100% Label	50.00
Wooten Wells, Blood Purifer, Tonic, Wooten Wells, Texas, Aqua	35.00
Wright's Indian Cough Balsam	10.00
Wynkoop's Iceland, N.Y., Cabin Shoulders, OP, Aqua, 5 1/4 In.	47.00
X-Zalia, Boston, Mass., Clear, 7 1/4 In. ....*Illus*	12.00
Yeth's Granular Effervescent, Contents, Cobalt Blue, 6 1/2 In.	15.00
METAXA, Crescent Decanter	7.00
Floral Decanter	12.00
Greek Girl	44.00
Greek Man	44.00
White Vase	28.00
MICHTER'S, American Legion Doughboy, 1979 ....*Illus*	45.00
Automobile, York Pullman, 1977	129.00
Casinos	34.00
Casinos, Atlantic City, 1980	34.00
Casinos, Bahamas, 1980	34.00
Casinos, International, 1980	34.00
Casinos, Las Vegas, 1980	34.00
Casinos, Puerto Rico, 1980	34.00
Casinos, Reno, 1980	34.00

Medicine, X-Zalia, Boston,
Mass., Clear, 7 1/4 In.

Michter's, American Legion
Doughboy, 1979

Michter's, Goddess Selket,   Michter's, Halloween Witch, 1979   Michter's, New York
Gold, 1980   Policeman, 1980

Christmas Tree, 1978 .... 19.00 To 56.00
Conestoga Wagon, 1976 .... 201.00
Daniel Boone Homestead Barn, 1977 .... 55.00
Death Mask Of King Tut, 1978 .... 35.00
Death Mask Of King Tut, 1978, 1 3/4 Liter 32.00
Easton Peace Candle, 1979 .... 44.00
Fleetwood Packard, 1979 .... 52.00
Football, Delaware, 1979 .... 40.00
Football, Pennsylvania, 1979 .... 40.00
Football, Texas, 1979 .... 40.00
Goddess Selket, Gold, 1980 ....Illus 48.00
Halloween Witch, 1979 ....Illus 65.00
Hershey Trolley, 1980 .... 38.00
Ice Wagon, 1979 .... 30.00
Liberty Bell, Bisque, 1975 .... 80.00
Liberty Bell, Brown, 1969 .... 42.00
New York Policeman, 1980 ....Illus 35.00
Penn State Nittany Lion, 1978 .... 61.00
Pennsylvania Dutch Hex, 1977 .... 15.00
Pennsylvania, Keystone State 33.00
Pittsburgh University Gold Panther, 1977 .... 73.00
Pot Still, Gold, 1980 .... 500.00
Pot Still, 1980 .... 12.00
Queen Nefertiti, 1979, 1 3/4 Liter 98.00
Reading Pagoda, 1980 .... 60.00
Resorts International, 1978 .... 380.00
Stagecoach, Wells Fargo, 1978 .... 64.00
Union Canal Boat, 1977 .... 54.00
V.F.W., George Washington, 1980 .... 44.00
Volunteer Fireman, 1979 .... 72.00

MIDLAND, Eagle, 1971 .... 15.00
Moonwalk, 1970 .... 12.00

MIDWESTERN, Bar, Swirled To Left, Aqua, 10 3/4 In. 40.00
Club Shape, 24 Vertical & 16 Swirled Ribs, Aqua, 8 3/8 In. 120.00
Club, Deep Aqua, 9 In. 230.00
Club, Ribbed & Swirled To Right, Aqua, 8 1/2 In. 20.00
Club, Swirled To Left, Aqua, Quart 5.00
Globular, Aqua, 9 In. 40.00
Globular, Ribbed, Pale Green, 5 3/4 In. 45.00
Globular, Swirled To Left, Calabash Form, Aqua, 10 1/2 In. 30.00
Globular, Swirled To Left, Citron, 8 In. 325.00

Globular, Swirled To Left, Deep Aqua, 7 1/2 In. 170.00
Globular, Swirled To Left, Deep Golden Amber, 7 3/4 In. 250.00
Globular, Swirled To Left, Dense Puce Amber, 7 3/4 In. 275.00
Globular, Swirled To Left, Golden Amber, 7 1/2 In. 360.00
Globular, Swirled To Left, Golden Amber, 8 In. 425.00
Globular, Swirled To Left, Golden Amber, 8 1/4 In. 400.00
Globular, Swirled To Right, Deep Golden Amber, 7 3/4 In. 380.00
Globular, Swirled To Right, Golden Amber, 7 In. 325.00
Globular, Swirled To Right, Light Golden Amber, 7 1/2 In. 300.00
Globular, Swirled To Right, 8 1/2 In. 275.00
Globular, Vertically Ribbed, Olive Yellow, 7 3/4 In. 325.00
Globular, Vertically Ribbed, Smoky Clear, 8 1/4 In. 400.00
Grandfather, Ribbed & Swirled To Right, Golden Amber, Quart 1100.00
Pitkin Type, Swirled To Left, Deep Golden Amber, 1/2 Pint 250.00
Swirled To Left, Golden Amber, 1/2 Pint 275.00
Vertically Ribbed, Yellow Amber, 1/2 Pint 350.00

MIKE WAYNE, April Fool, 1978 .... 25.00
Christmas Tree, 1979 .... 53.00
Christmas Tree, 1980 .... 67.00
Elijah Wayne Keg 52.00
Mercedes Benz 450SL, 1980 .... 61.00
Plumbers, 1978 .... 25.00
Pope John Paul II, 1980 .... 62.00
Tattooist, 1978 .... 25.00
Triple Self-Portrait 25.00

MILK GLASS, see also Cologne; Cosmetic; Drug; Ink; Medicine
MILK GLASS, Mustard, Square, Oriental Man, Woman, Label, 3 3/8 In., Pair 70.00
Rectangular Log Cabin, Original Paint, Mustard Label, 4 In.Tall 53.00
Windmill, Dutch Children, 6-Sided, Original Paint, 4 In. 45.00
World's Fair, 1939 .... 8.00

Milk bottles were first used in the 1880s. The characteristic shape and printed or embossed wording identify these bottles for collectors. Pyro is the shortened form of pyroglaze, an enameled lettering used on milk bottles.

MILK, A Bottle Of Milk Is A Bottle Of Health, Large Letters, 1/3 Quart 8.50
A Bottle Of Milk Is A Bottle Of Health, Large Letters, Quart 12.50
A.B.Chapin, Allegheny, N.Y., Embossed, Round, 1/4 Pint 4.25
A.G.S., Handled, Quart 45.00
A.W.Seeman, Bayonne, N.J., Embossed, Round, 1/2 Pint 2.95
Aber Bros., Sharpsville, Pa., Embossed, Round, Pint 2.50
Adohr Farms, Embossed, Square, Quart 1.25
Adohr Milk, Various Pictures, Yellow & Red Pyro, Round, 1/2 Gallon 20.00
Adohr, Golden Guernsey, Embossed, Maroon Pyro, Round, 1/2 Pint 15.00
Aiea Dairy, Embossed, Round, 1/2 Pint 7.50
Akron Pure Milk Co., Embossed, 12 Ounce 5.00
Akron Pure Milk Co., 24 Body Ribs, Embossed, Round, Pint 4.00
Akron Pure Milk Co., 24 Ribs Full Length, Embossed, Round, Quart 4.00
Akron Pure Milk Co., 3 Stars On Neck, Embossed, Round, Pint 2.50
Alaska Dairy Products, Cream Top, Red & Green Pyro, Square, Quart 75.00
Alber's Milling Company, Red Pyro, Round, 1/2 Gallon 20.00
Alderney Dairy Company, 2 Neck Rings, Embossed, Round, 1/2 Pint 3.25
Alderney Green Meadow Dairy, Cow's Head, Neck Ring, Embossed, Quart 6.50
Alfalfa Farm Dairy, Embossed, Gill 4.00
Algoma Guernsey Farm, Baby & Blocks Spell Algoma, Orange Pyro, Quart 5.00
Alpenrose, Portland, Oregon, Red Pyro, Square, Quart 2.00
Alpenrose, Portland, Oregon, Red Pyro, Square, 1/2 Pint 7.50
Altamont Milk Co.Inc., Carthage, N.Y., Embossed, Round, 1/4 Pint 5.50
Ambort Dairy, Calexico, Calif., Embossed, Round, Quart 7.00
Anchorage Dairy, Matanuska Maid, Orange Pyro, Round, Quart 40.00
Anglo Swiss, New York, Embossed Lady, Quart 12.00
Annapolis Dairy, Embossed, Round, 1/2 Pint 3.00

Antigo Dairy Co., Red Pyro, Round, 1/2 Pint	2.50
Arden Certified Milk, Cow & Calf, 6 Neck Rings, Embossed, Round, Quart	20.00
Arden Farms Dairy Co., Cultured Sour Cream, Arden, N.Y., Embossed, Pint	5.00
Arden, Picture Of Boy, Books, Apple & Glass, Red Pyro, Round, 1/2 Pint	5.00
Armour Creameries, Armour Louisville, Ky., Embossed, Pint	6.00
Associated Milk Dealers Incorporated, Heavy, Embossed, 1/2 Pint	4.00
Astoria Milk Dealers, Embossed, Round, Quart	7.50
Atzingen & Gannon, Picture Of Baby, Brown Pyro, Round, Cream Top	9.00
Augusta Dairies Inc., Staunton, Va., Neck Ring, Black Pyro, Round, Quart	8.50
Avondale Farms Dairy, Cream Top, Embossed, Round, Quart	9.00
Baby Face, Painted, Quart	12.00
Bacon Creamery, Loudon, Tennessee, Red Pyro, Round, Quart	7.50
Badger Farms Creameries, Portsmouth, N.H., Embossed, Round, 1/2 Pint	3.75
Bartholomay Co., Rochester, N.Y., Cream Top	12.00
Bartholomay, 1/2 Pint, 5 1/2 In.	3.00
Beck's Dairy, Picture Of Cloud, Stars, Red Pyro, Round, Quart	7.50
Beebe's Dairy, Norwichtown, Conn., Maroon Pyro, Round, Squat, Quart	6.50
Bell Dairy, Fishbowl-Shaped, Green Pyro, 12 Ounce	5.00
Belle Vernon, In Large Arc, Embossed, 12 Ounce	5.25
Bellevue Dairy, Syracuse, N.Y., Embossed, Round, 1/3 Quart	3.00
Bendora Dairy Farm Inc., Sour Cream, Morristown, N.J., Embossed, Pint	4.25
Bentley & Sons Farm Dairy, Fairbanks, Red Pyro, Round, 1/4 Pint	40.00
Bentley & Sons Farm, Picture Of Cow, Red & Green Pyro, Round, Pint	40.00
Biltmore Dairy Farms, Animal & Swans, 2 Body Rings, Embossed, Quart	6.50
Biltmore Dairy Farms, The South's Finest, Painted, Motto On Rear	2.00
Birmingham Dairy, Manassas, Va., Embossed, Round, Pint	5.00
Birtcherd Dairy, In Script, Embossed, 1/2 Pint	4.50
Blue Bird Creamery Inc., Embossed, Square, Quart	12.50
Blue Island Sanitary Dairy, Embossed, Round, 1/2 Pint	3.25
Blue Ribbon Creamery, Embossed, Round, Quart	6.00
Borden's Condensed Milk Co., Aqua, Quart	35.00
Borden's, Lafayette, Indiana, Embossed On Shoulder	8.00
Borden's, Picture Of Eagle, 1/2 Pint	10.00
Borden's, Stamped On Closure, Clear, Quart	25.00
Borden's, Tin Top, Borden's Stamped On Closure, Quart	25.00
Bowman Dairy Co., Embossed Bow & Arrow, Orange Pyro Picture, Gallon	12.00
Braley's Creamery, Inc., Neck Ribs, Embossed, Round, Pint	4.50
Brighton Place Dairy, Rochester, N.Y., Green	215.00
Brighton Place Dairy, Rochester, N.Y., Green, Quart	170.00
Brookside Certified Dairy, 10 Stars On Neck, Embossed, Round, Pint	6.00
Buena Vista Dairy, Boy, Girl, Mother, Father, Brown Pyro, Round, Quart	8.50
Buffalo Milk Co., Embossed Bison, 1/2 Pint	15.00
Buffalo Milk Co., Embossed Bison, Pint	15.00
Buffalo Milk Co., Embossed Bison, Quart	15.00
Burger's Milk, Plastic Handle, Red Pyro, Square, Gallon	9.00
C.Medson, Roebling, N.J., Embossed, Round, Pint	3.25
C.R.Dean Cloverdale Dairy, So.Portland, Me., Clear, Quart	4.00
Campbell's Creamery Inc., Blake-Hart Square, Embossed, Pint	7.50
Canham's Dairies Inc., 2 Body Belts, Embossed, Round, Quart	5.00
Capitol Dairy Co., Chicago, Embossed, Round, 1/2 Pint	2.50
Capitol Dairy, Cac'to, Cal., Embossed, Round, Quart	5.00
Carnation Co., Oak., Embossed, Amber, Square, Quart	9.00
Carnation Fresh Dairy, Picture Of Bottle, Red Pyro, Round, Cream Top	15.00
Catawha, Hickory, N.C., Amber, 1/2 Gallon	5.00
Central, Red Pyro, Square, 1/2 Pint	1.75
Challenge Harmony Valley Creamery, Elk & Mountains, Red Pyro, Quart	7.50
Chapman's Milk, Warren, O., Neck Ring, Black Pyro, Round, Quart	5.00
Chas.A.Hoak's Dairy, C.H.A.Monogram, Cream Top, Embossed, Round, Quart	10.50
Chester City Dairy, Chester, Ill., Embossed, Round, Quart	4.00
Chestnut Farms Chevy Chase Dairy, Cream Top, Embossed, Round, Quart	8.50
Chestnut Farms Chevy Chase Dairy, 24 Neck Ribs, Embossed, Round, Pint	4.00
Chevy Chase Dairy, Washington, Picture Of Nurse & Baby, Pint	23.00
Cloister Dairies, Amber, Square, Quart	5.50

Cloister Dairies, Yellow Pyro, Amber, Square, Quart 7.50
Clover Blossom, Stylized Clover, 6 Hobnails, Embossed, 12 Ounce 4.50
Clover Brand Dairy Products, 3-Leaf Clover, Embossed, Round, Pint 5.00
Clover Farms Inc., Bridgeport, Conn., Embossed, Round, Squat, Quart 7.50
Clover Leaf Creamery Co., Toledo, O., Embossed, Round, 1/2 Pint 7.50
Clover Leaf Dairy, Baby Pulling Cart, Orange Pyro, Square, Quart 1.00
Clover Leaf Dairy, Painted Green Clovers, Quart 4.50
Cloverlake, 4-Leaf Clover, Wire Handle, Orange Pyro, Square, Gallon 11.00
Cloverland Dairy, 4-Leaf Clover, Ribbed, Clamp Band, Embossed, Quart 9.50
Cloverleaf Dairy, Salt Lake City, Utah, Red Pyro, Square, 1/2 Pint 7.50
Clovis Quality Dairy, Statue Of Liberty, Green Pyro, Round, Quart 16.00
Clovis Quality Dairy, Statue Of Liberty, Red Pyro, Round, Quart 14.00
Collar City Creamery, 2 Body Belts, Cream Top, Embossed, Round, Quart 10.50
Colvert's Pasteurized, Amber, White Pyro, Square, Quart 4.50
Colvert's, Red Pyro, Square, 1/3 Quart 2.75
Comalac, 10 Neck Ribs, Picture Of Girl, Red Pyro, Round, Pint 5.50
Concord Dairy Co.Inc., Embossed, Round, 1/2 Pint 4.00
Concord Dairy Inc., Thatcher, Maroon Pyro, Round, Quart 5.00
Consumers Dairy, Picture Of Baby, Orange Pyro, Round, Quart 5.00
Corbin Milk Company, Corbin, Ky., Quart, 8 7/8 In. 3.00
Country's Delight, Embossed Picture, Maroon Pyro, Wire Handle, Gallon 11.00
Cranford Dairy, Cow's Head & Farm In Shield, Red Pyro, Round, Quart 5.50
Cream Top Dairy, Cream Top, Square, Orange & Green Pyro, Quart 10.50
Creamer's Dairy, Embossed, Round, 1/4 Pint 22.50
Creamer's Dairy, Mountains & Sunrise, Red & Black Pyro, Round, Quart 40.00
Creamer's Dairy, Mountains, Sun, Barn, Black & Red Pyro, Round, Pint 40.00
Creamery Co., Phone Richmond 703, Embossed Eagle, 12 Rib, Pint 20.00
Creamland, Albuquerque, Embossed, Round, 1/2 Pint 5.50
Crisp County Dairies, Man, Woman & Child, Red Pyro, Round, Quart 8.50
Crowley's, Embossed, Round, Pint 4.00
Crowley's, Embossed, 1/2 Pint 3.75
Curles Neck Farm, Picture Of Barns & Silo, Green Pyro, Round, Quart 4.50
Dairyland Creamery Co., 20 Heavy Neck Ribs, Embossed, Round, Quart 5.00
Dairyland Farms, Red & Blue Pyro, Square, Quart 4.00
Dairymen's Association, Red & Orange Pyro, Square, Tall, Quart 10.00
Dairymen's Meadow Gold, Cow's Head, Orange, Red Pyro, Square, 1/2 Pint 7.50
Danville Dairy Products Co., Cream Top, Embossed, Round, Pint 6.50
Dart Farms Dairy, St.Clair County, Orange Pyro, Round, Pint 4.50
Davis Dairy Farm, Anderson, Ind., Embossed, Round, 1/2 Pint 5.00
Deary Bros., Dudley, Mass., Neck Ribs, Embossed, Round, 1/2 Pint 3.25
Deer Creek Dairy, Skyscrapers, Ship, Red Pyro, Round, Squat, Quart 10.00
Deerfoot Farms Southborough, Mass., 1/2 Pint 8.00
Deerfoot Farms, Crown Top, Embossed, Round, 1/2 Pint 10.00
Deger's, Phoenixville, Pa., Cream Top, Embossed, Square, Quart 7.50
Deposit Bottle, Poinsettia Dairy, Embossed Bottom, Orange Pyro, Quart 15.00
Deseret Brand, Picture Of Beehive, Red Pyro, Square, Quart 3.00
Diamond Dairy, Montague, N.J., Embossed, Round, 1/2 Pint 2.95
Dierolf's Dairy, Rock Island, Ill., Straight-Sided, Embossed, 12 Ounce 5.25
Dingley Dell Goat Dairy, Quart 10.00
Douglaston Manor Farm, Picture Of Goose, Black Pyro, Round, Quart 5.50
Driessen Dairy, Appleton, Wis., Embossed, Round, 1/2 Pint 3.50
Driftwood Dairy, 4-Sided, Cow's Head, Yellow Pyro, Amber, Square, Quart 3.00
Dubois Dairy Co., Picture Of Hand, Cream Top, Square, Red Pyro, Quart 8.00
Dunsmuir, 8 Neck Ribs, Embossed, Round, 1/2 Pint 8.50
Durand Dairy, Orange Pyro, Round, 1/2 Pint 2.00
Dutch Maid, Picture Of Dutch Girl, Amber, White Pyro, 1/2 Gallon 7.00
E.D.Comes & Sons Dairy, Orange Pyro, Round, Pint 2.50
E.E.Freimuth, Terryville, Conn., Red Pyro, Round, Quart 4.50
E.L.Tilton & Son, Allenhurst, N.J., Ribbed, Embossed, Round, 1/2 Pint 2.95
E.W.Woolman's, 4709 Lancaster Ave., Cap Seat, Tin Top Closure, Pint 15.00
Eden Valley Dairy, Boy Climbing Stairs, Brown Pyro, Round, Quart 8.00
Ellerslie Dairy Inc., Petersburg, Va., Embossed, Round, Quart 3.00
Ellwood Dairies, Goleta, Calif., Embossed, Round, 1/4 Pint 5.50

Elm Dairy, Amber, Wash & Return 75.00
Embossed, Nebraska, Quart 5.00
Essex Junction, Vermont, White Pyro, Amber, Quart 6.00
Ethan Allen Creamery, Essex Junction, Vt., Orange Pyro, Round, Quart 6.00
Ethan Allen Creamery, White Pyro, Amber, Square, Quart 6.50
F.A.Greene, Guernsey, Adams Centre, Embossed, Round, 1/4 Pint 6.00
F.G.Kimball, Manchester, N.H., 20 Thick Ribs, Embossed, Round, Quart 8.00
Fair Oaks Milk Co., Smiling Face, Orange Pyro, Square, Gallon 6.25
Fairfield Western Maryland Dairy, 14 Ribs, Embossed, Round, 1/2 Pint 4.00
Fairmont Creamery, Red & Yellow Pyro, Round, 1/2 Pint .... 5.50 To 6.50
Fairmont, Woman Doing Exercises, Plastic Handle, Red Pyro, Gallon 10.00
Fairmount Dairy, Mountain, Embossed, Round, Pint 10.00
Fairmount Dairy, Picture Of Mountain, Embossed, Round, Quart 11.00
Fairview Dairy, Cream Top, Embossed, Square, Quart 7.50
Fairview Dairy, Phillipsburg, N.J., Cream Top, Embossed, Round, Quart 10.50
Fairview Farms Inc., J.J.Corkery, Embossed, Round, 1/2 Pint 3.00
Fargo Dairy, Cream Top, Square, Red Pyro, Quart 8.00
Farm Dairies Assn., Picture Of Milk Bottle, Orange Pyro, Round, Quart 9.50
Farmer's Dairy Products, 12 Neck Ribs, Embossed, Round, 1/2 Pint 3.75
Farmer's Dairy, Frenchtown, N.J., Embossed, Round, 1/2 Pint 3.00
Farmer's Dairy, Greensburg, Pa., Picture Of Wreath, Embossed, 1/2 Pint 3.00
Fayette B. Weiss Dairy, Embossed, Round, Pint 3.50
Fenn's Guernsey Dairy, Amber, White Pyro, Square, Quart 5.75
Fetter's Dairies, Girardville, Pa., Embossed, 1/2 Pint 3.75
Flanders' Dairy, Milkman & Horse-Drawn Wagon, Red & Black Pyro, Quart ... 10.00
Flora Pure Milk Co., Flora, Ill., 20 Neck Ribs, Embossed, Round, Quart 3.50
Florida Dairies, Inc., Picture Of Cow's Head, Embossed, Round, Pint 12.00
Florida Store Bottle, Fully Embossed, 1/2 Pint 10.00
Florida Store Bottle, 14 Neck Ribs, 5 Inside Circle, Embossed, Pint 4.50
Flynn Gold Ribbon, Within Ribbon, Cream Top, Square, Orange Pyro, Quart ... 8.00
Fort Smith Pure Milk Co., Ark., Pint 6.00
Frank H.Cantwell, Clayton, N.Y., Embossed, Round, 1/4 Pint 4.75
Frank Pilley & Sons, Inc., Shield, Panther, Embossed, Round, Pint 7.50
Franklin Lake Dairy, In Script, Franklin Lakes, N.J., Embossed, Pint 4.00
Franklin Lake Dairy, N.J., Embossed, Round, 1/2 Pint 3.00
Freeman Buttermilk Dairy Co., Amber, Quart 70.00
French Broad Dairy, Knoxville, Tenn., Embossed, Round, Quart 7.50
Fresh Jersey Milk, Picture, Lavender Pyro, Quart 16.00
G.H.Brown & Son, Nashua, N.H., Embossed, Round, 1/2 Pint 3.25
G.H.Richardson, Dracut, Mass., Round, 10 Ounce 5.00
Gala Borden, Amber, Square, 1/2 Gallon 6.00
Garden Dairy, Santa Maria, Cal., Orange Pyro, Plastic Handle, Gallon 10.00
Gem City Dairy, Baraboo, Wis., Embossed In Slug Plate 8.00
Gibbs' Farm Dairy, Rochester, Mass., Ribbed, Embossed, Round, Pint 3.50
Gillette & Sons Dairy, Eagle, Stars, Orange Pyro, Pint 15.00
Glendale Farm Inc., Lakewood, N.J., Embossed, Round, 1/2 Pint 4.00
Gold Medal Creamery, Long Beach, Embossed, Round, Pint 4.00
Gold Spot Dairy, Woman Drinking Milk, Orange Pyro, Square, Quart 6.00
Gold Star Pasteurized Dairy Products, Orange Pyro, Round, Quart 8.50
Golden State Company Ltd., Embossed, Round, Quart 7.50
Golden State, In Arc, Embossed, Round, 1/2 Pint 4.50
Good Will Dairies, Morganton, N.C., Embossed, Round, 1/2 Pint 3.75
Greeley, Gray's, Colo., Embossed, Red Pyro, Round, Quart 8.00
Greenwell Dairy, Hawaii, Cow's Head, Green Pyro, Square, 1/2 Gallon 15.00
Gridley Dairy Co., Amber, Quart 25.00
H.P.Hood & Sons Dairy, Red Pyro, Round, Squat, Quart 3.50
H.W.Gray, Jacksonville, Fla., Embossed, Round, 1/2 Pint 4.00
Hackett Dairy, 1 Gill, 4 1/2 In. 8.00
Haleakala Dairy, Makawao, 1 Neck Ring, Embossed, Round, 1/2 Pint 7.50
Hamburgh Dairy Registered, Watertown, N.Y., Embossed, Round, 1/4 Pint ... 5.50
Hamilton Hegeman, 4 H's In Diamonds On Neck, Embossed, Squat, 1/2 Pint ... 3.00
Hampden Creamery Co., Cow's Head, Embossed, Tin Top, Round, 1/2 Pint ... 15.00
Hampden Creamery Co., Picture Of Cow's Head, Embossed, Round, 1/2 Pint ... 7.50

Hampton Creamery, Embossed Cow's Head, 1/2 Pint 9.50
Hampton Heights Dairy, 3 Cent Bottle, Embossed, Round, Quart 3.00
Hassenteufel Dairy, P.H.Raritan Township, Embossed, Pint 5.00
Hawthorne-Melody, Chicago, Ill., Castle, Embossed, Round, Squat, Quart 7.50
Hawthorne-Melody, Large Castle, Embossed, Wire Handle, Square, Gallon 6.50
Hazelwood's Farm Dairy, Picture Of Cow's Head, Orange Pyro, Gallon 10.00
Heifer Brand, Embossed Cow 5.00
Hendrick's Dairy, Picture Of Dentist, Red Pyro, Pint 12.50
Henry Becker & Son, Inc., Roseland, N.J., Embossed, Round, Squat, Quart 7.50
Herpy's Dairy, Littleton, Mass., Embossed, Round, 1/2 Pint 3.00
Highland Farm Dairy, Picture Of Barn, Green Pyro, Round, 1/2 Gallon 15.00
Hill Bros., Canton, N.Y., Embossed, Round, 1/4 Pint 5.50
Hill's Dairy, Jersey Milk, Barstow, Neck Ring, Quart .... 5.00 To 7.50
Hilton Hart's Dairy, Ft.Myers, Fla., Round, 6 Ounce 10.00
Hind-Clarke Dairy, 2 Body Belts, Embossed, Round, Quart 7.50
Home Dairy, Monrovia, Cal., Embossed, Round, 1/2 Pint 4.00
Honolulu Dairymen's Assoc., 2 Body Belts, Embossed, Round, 1/2 Pint 7.50
Hopewell Dairy, Taste The Difference, Bellefontaine, Ohio, Amber 5.00
Humboldt Dairy Chicago Products Co., Embossed, Pint 4.50
Humboldt Dairy Chicago Products Co., Embossed, 8 Ounce 4.00
Hurstbourne Farms, St. Matthews, Ky., Embossed, Round, Pint 6.50
Hydrox Dairy, Olean, N.Y., Cream Top, Embossed, Round, Quart 10.50
Hygienic Dairy, Embossed, Round, 1/4 Pint 5.00
Independent Creamery, Chicago, Ill., Embossed, Round, Pint 5.00
Independent Dairies Inc., Kansas City, Mo., Embossed, Round, Quart 4.00
International Dairy, Chicago, Flying Eagle, Pint 8.00
Iowa, Embossed, Quart 5.00
J.A.MacVarish Real Jersey Milk, Embossed, Round, Pint 5.00
J.F.McAdams & Bros., In Script, Cream Top, Embossed, Round, Quart 10.50
J.Paulus, New Brunswick, N.J., 12 Neck Ribs, Embossed, Round, 1/2 Pint 3.00
Jarosz Milk Co., Chicago, Ill., Embossed, Round, Pint 3.50
Jersey Farm Dairy, Fresno, Cal., Round, 10 Ounce 3.00
Jersey Heights Dairy Cottage Cheese, Embossed, 12 Ounce 4.50
Jersey Maid Dairies, Cow's Head, Boy With Carrier, Brown Pyro, Quart 5.50
Jersey Pasteurized, Brown Pyro, Round, Squat, Quart 8.00
Johanna Farms, Flemington, N.J., Embossed, Round, 1/2 Pint 3.00
Jolly Dairy & Ice Cream Co., Tifton, Ga., Squat, Quart 18.00
Kaimia, Hendersonville, N.C., Square, Gallon 3.00
Kensington Farm, Savannah, Ga., Embossed, Round, Quart 7.50
Kingston Dairy & Ice Cream Co., Embossed, Round, Quart 6.00
Klamath Falls, 10 Neck Ribs, Embossed, Round, 1/2 Pint 8.50
Kligerman Dairies, Cream Top, Outline Of New Jersey, Embossed, Quart 9.00
Klondike Farm, Elgin, N.C., Milk For Health, Green Pyro, Round, Quart 8.50
Klondike Farms, 5 Cent Deposit, Embossed, Round, 1/2 Pint 3.75
L.A.Creamery Co., Embossed, Round, Pint 4.00
L.A.Creamery Co., W.C.G.Co., Embossed, Round, 1/2 Pint 3.50
Lackawanna Dairy, F.J.Francisco & Sons, Embossed, Round, 1/2 Pint 3.00
Lake To Lake, Hand, Spoon, Pitcher, Cream Top, Square, Red Pyro, Quart 8.00
Lakeside Dairy, Picture Of Cow's Head, Green Pyro, Round, Quart 5.50
Lakeview Dairy, Palmdale, Calif., 14 Neck Ribs, Embossed, Round, Pint 8.50
Lancaster Creamery, Young Naked Boy, Amber, White Pyro, Square, Quart 5.00
Landgren's 114 Third Street Dairy, Straight-Sided, Embossed, 12 Ounce 5.00
Lang's Creamery, Buffalo, N.Y., Amber, Round 45.00
Lansing Dairy Co., Embossed, Round, 1/2 Pint 3.75
Liberty Milk Co., Cumberland, Md., Embossed, Round, 1/2 Pint 3.75
Liberty Milk Co., 24 Ribs, Statue Of Liberty, Embossed, Round, Quart 10.00
Lincoln Bros.Dairy, Taunton, Mass., Embossed, Round, 1/2 Pint 3.00
Live Oak Riviera Farms, Eagle, Plane & Ship, Red Pyro, 1/2 Pint 6.00
Lone Oak Farm, Embossed, 2 Ounce 8.00
Lost River Dairy, 2 Bands Around Body, Embossed, Round, Quart 8.50
M.H.Renkin Dairy Co., Established 1888, Embossed, Round, Squat, Quart 7.50
Mackinaw City Dairy, Pierce & Sons, Embossed, Round, Quart 4.00
Manchester Dairy, Berney-Bond, Embossed, Round, Squat, Quart 7.50

Milk, Meadow Gold, Amber, Quart

Marble's Dairy, Ribbed, 5 Cent Bottle, Thatcher, Embossed, Round, Pint	4.50
Marshall Dairy Co., Ithaca, N.Y., Cream Top, Embossed, Round, Quart	10.00
Massabesic Lake Farm, Picture Of Baby, Orange Pyro, Round, Quart	5.50
Matthews Selected Dairies Co., Straight-Sided, Embossed, 12 Ounce	4.00
Mayfair Creamery, Boy & Girl Drinking Milk, Orange Pyro, Square, Quart	1.00
McArthur Jersey Farm, Dutch Maid, Churn, Black Pyro, Round, Quart	9.00
McAteer's Dairy, Ocala, Fla., Embossed, Round, 1/2 Pint	8.50
McFarlane Dairy, Mt.Pleasant, Mich., Embossed, Round, 1/2 Pint	4.50
Meadow Brook Farm Dairy, Cow, Farm, Orange Pyro, Round, Quart	4.50
Meadow Dairies, Slanted Neck Ribs, Embossed, Squat, Round, Quart	6.00
Meadow Gold, Amber, Quart ....*Illus*	4.50
Meadow Gold, Embossed & Painted, Wire Bail, Amber, Gallon	8.00
Meadow Gold, Embossed, Amber, Square, Quart	6.00
Meadow Gold, Embossed, No Handle, Square, Gallon	6.50
Meadow Gold, Red Pyro, Square, Quart	2.25
Meadowbrook Dairy, Red-Orange Pyro, Square, 1/2 Pint	1.50
Mercer's Jersey Farm, Red & Yellow Pyro, Square, Quart	5.00
Midwest Purity, Outline Of Illinois, Embossed, Round, Quart	8.50
Milam Dairy, Milk & Cream, Embossed Bottom, Squat, Red Pyro, Quart	18.00
Milk Shed, Moultrie, Ga., 1/2 Pint	10.00
Miller Grade A, Orange Brown Pyro, Square, Heavy, 1/2 Pint	3.00
Millside Farms, Cream Top, Embossed, Square, Quart	7.50
Mission Dairy Inc., Phoenix, Non-Redeemable, Maroon Pyro, Round, Quart	12.50
Mitchell's, Screw Top Finish, Red Pyro, Round, Quart	20.00
Model Dairy Co., Chicago, Ill., Ribbed, Embossed, Round, 1/2 Pint	3.25
Model Dairy, T.B. Tested Cows, Clear, Quart	7.50
Modern Dairy Co., La Crosse, Wis., Orange Pyro, Round, 1/2 Pint	2.50
Modern Dairy, Berlin, Pa., Maroon Pyro, Round, 1/2 Pint	3.00
Momence Dairy, Momence, Ill., Cow In Pasture, Sun, Blue Pyro, Quart	7.00
Monterey Bay Milk Distributors, Hobnailed Neck, Round, 1/4 Pint	5.00
Monticello Dairy, In Script, 2 Body Belts, Embossed, Round, Quart	2.00
Mt.Fern Dairy, Dover, N.J., Embossed, Pint	5.00
Mt.Pleasant Farm, Livingston, N.J., Embossed, Round, 1/2 Pint	5.00
Mueth Dairy, Mascoutah, Ill., Liberty, 1934, Embossed, Pint	4.00
Nebo View Dairy, Nephi, Utah, Orange Pyro, Round, Pint	7.50
New Eden Milk, Thomas McManus, Embossed, Round, Quart	3.25
New Era Dairy, Various Pictures, Black Pyro, Round, 1/2 Gallon	15.00
Newberg Dairy, Newberg, Ore., Maroon Pyro, Square, 1/2 Pint	7.50
Noel Farms Dairy, East Aurora, N.Y., 1/2 Pint, 5 1/2 In.	1.50
North Shore Dairy Co., Cow, Orange Pyro, Round, Squat, 1/2 Gallon	9.00
Northland's, 2 Pine Trees, Cream Top, Square, Red Pyro, Quart	8.00
Oak Hill Dairy, Ashville, N.C., Slug Plated	3.50
Oak Hill Dairy, Grade A Raw Sealed II, Embossed, Quart	18.00
Oakland Creamery Co., Embossed, Round, Quart	4.00
Ohio Valley Dairy, Cream Top, Embossed, Round, Quart	10.50
Old Crown Top, Thatcher Seal, Embossed, Round, Quart	4.50
Olson's Dairy, Butler, Penna., Cream Top, Embossed, Round, Quart	10.50

Otto Milk Company, Cream Top, 2 Raised Belts, Embossed, Round, Quart	8.50
Otto's, 2 Body Ribs, Red Pyro, Round, Cream Top	12.50
Owen Dairy, Le Grand, Calif., 3 Neck Rings, Embossed, Round, Quart	7.50
Ozark Dairy, Picture Of Dairy Building, Red Pyro, Round, 1/2 Gallon	14.00
Palmerton Sanitary Dairy, Cream Top, Embossed, Round, 1/2 Pint	9.00
Palmerton Sanitary Dairy, Cream Top, Embossed, Round, Quart	8.50
Panco Dairy Co., West Paterson, N.J., Embossed, Round, Pint	3.25
Park Farm Dairy, N.Y., Embossed, Round, Pint	3.50
Paskal Dairy, Embossed Cow, 1/2 Pint	12.00
Patapsco Dairy Co., Baltimore, Clear, Quart	7.00
Pearson's Sanitary Dairy, P Inside, Ribbed Neck, 1/2 Pint, 6 1/2 In.	5.00
Peoples Dairy Co., Akron, O., Embossed, Round, Pint	3.00
Peoples Milk Co., Embossed, Round, Amber, Quart	25.00
Peoples Milk, 70 E.Ferry, Amber, Round	20.00
Pet Dairy Products Co., Cream Top, Embossed, Round, 1/2 Pint	9.00
Pet, It Whips, Cream Top, 1/2 Pint	4.50
Petaluma Co-Operative Creamery, Red Pyro, Round, Quart	4.25
Peters Dairy, Man, Woman, & Child, Green Pyro, Round, Quart	4.00
Pevely Dairy Co., Neck Chain, Embossed, Round, Squat, Quart	6.00
Pevely Dairy Co., St.Louis, Mo., Embossed, 10 Ounce	4.75
Phelp's Dairy, Waycross, Ga., Cows, Farm, Orange Pyro, Quart	20.00
Pierce Dairy Products, Inc., Buffalo, N.Y., 1/2 Pint, 5 1/2 In.	3.00
Pine Farm Dairy, Golden Guernsey, Tifton, Ga., Orange Pyro, Quart	18.00
Pine State Dairy, Picture Of Pine Trees, Green, Orange Pyro, 1/2 Pint	5.00
Pioneer Farms, Picture Of Pioneers, Barn, Red Pyro, Round, Quart	8.00
Plainview Farms Dairy, Banner, Cow's Head, Green Pyro, Round, Pint	5.50
Pleasant Home Dairy, Salem, Oregon, Embossed, Round, Quart	7.50
Polk's Best, Amber, Quart	45.00
Polk's Best, Indianapolis Trademark, Cream Top, Embossed, Round, Quart	10.50
Portland Milk Co., Damascus, Embossed, Round, Pint	7.50
Price's Sunset Creamery, Roswell, Orange Pyro, Round, Quart	10.00
Producer's Dairy Co., Double Neck, Ribbed Body, Embossed, Round, Quart	5.00
Producer's Dairy Delivery, Fresno, Calif., Embossed, Round, 1/2 Pint	4.00
Property Of Rhoads Dairy, Ashville, N.C., Slug Plated, Quart	3.50
Purity Dairy, Picture Of Baby, Imperial, Orange Pyro, Square, Quart	7.50
Purity Grade A Milk, Cream Top, Square, Red Pyro, Quart	7.50
Purity Maid, New Albany, Cream Top, Embossed, Round, Quart	10.50
Purity Milk Co., Columbus, Ind., Cream Top, Square, Orange Pyro, Quart	8.00
Queen City Dairy Inc., Embossed, Round, Pint	12.50
Queen's Farm, Deposit Bottle, Pint	8.50
Queen's Farms Inc., 16 Diamonds On Neck, Embossed, 1/2 Pint	4.00
R & S Dairy, Murray, Utah, Embossed, Round, Pint	7.50
R Dairy, Taylorsville, Utah, Picture Of Child, Black Pyro, Round, Pint	7.50
R.H.Taylor, Watertown, N.Y., Embossed, Round, 1/4 Pint	5.50
R.S.Pearson, Sanitary Dairy, Ithaca, N.Y., 1/2 Pint, 6 1/2 In.	5.00
R.W. Jones Inc., Straight-Sided, Embossed, 1/2 Pint	3.00
Reehl's Dairy, Comic Cow, White Pyro, Amber, Square, 1/2 Gallon	8.00
Rieck's Pure Milk & Cream, Fluted Finish, Embossed, Round, Pint	25.00
Rieck's, Embossed, 1/2 Pint	4.50
Ringgold Dairy Farm, Ribbed, Embossed, Round, Quart	7.50
Roberts, Rising Sun, Cows In Pasture, Red Pyro, Round, Quart	8.00
Roelof Dairy, Galesburg, Mich., Embossed, Pint	4.50
Roger Jessup Farms, Picture Of Cow, Maroon Pyro, Square, 1/2 Pint	4.00
Rosedale Dairy Co., Maywood, Ill., Embossed, Round, Pint	3.00
Roth Brothers, Amber	75.00
Roundout Valley Dairy Co., Embossed, Round, Quart	4.00
Royal Dairy, Keyser, W.Va., Orange Pyro, Round, Quart	8.50
Royal Farms, The Better Milk, Orange Pyro, Round, Squat, Quart	7.50
Rutland Hills Co-Operative Inc., Embossed, Round, 1/4 Pint	6.00
S.B.Milk Dealers Assn., Santa Clara County, Embossed, Round, Quart	6.50
S.Seegert's Dairy, Silver Creek, N.Y., Embossed, Round, 1/2 Pint	2.50
S.W.Weiss Farm, Stoneham, Mass., 14 Neck Ribs, Red Pyro, Round, Quart	7.50

Salt Lake Milk Producers Assn., Embossed, Round, Quart 5.00
Sangamon Dairy Products Co., Springfield, Ill., Embossed, 12 Ounce 4.50
Sanida Sanitary Farms, Air, Land, Sea, Wire Handle, Red Pyro, Gallon 25.00
Sanitary Dairy Company, 24 Ribs, Cream Top, Embossed, Round, Quart 12.50
Scott Key Dairy, Frederick, Md., Green Pyro, Round, Quart 5.00
Seiberg's Cream, Cream Top, Square, Red Pyro, Quart 7.50
Seneca Dairy, Canandaigua, N.Y., Embossed, Round, 1/4 Pint 4.25
Shaw's Dairy, Thatcher, Embossed, Round, 1/4 Pint 3.50
Shawsheen Dairy, Indian Head, 2 Body Rings, Embossed, Round, Quart 9.00
Shawsheen Dairy, Picture Of Indian's Head, Orange Pyro, Round, Quart 6.50
Sheffield Farms, Slawson Decker Co., N.Y., Embossed, Round, Quart 4.00
Shrum's Dairy, Jeannette, Penn., Wax Cone, Quart 3.00
Silver Seal Meadow Gold, Cream Top, Embossed, Round, Quart 10.00
Silverside Dairy, Picture Of Policeman, Orange Pyro, Round, Quart 9.00
Skipton Dairy Co., Heavy Neck Ring, Black Pyro, Round, Squat, Quart 8.00
Smalley, A.G.S.& Co., Embossed, Round, Quart 15.00
Smalley, A.G.S., Tin Top, Pint 37.00
Smalley, Handle, Lid, Embossed, Round, Quart 50.00
Smyth Farm Dairy, White Handle, Red Pyro, Square, Gallon 10.00
Sonoma Mission Creamery, Embossed, Round, Pint 5.00
South Side Dairy, Butte, Mont., Orange Pyro, Round, Quart 8.00
Southern California, Hobnailed Neck, Red Pyro, Round, Quart 2.00
Southern Dairies, Sealtest Emblem, Embossed, 1/2 Pint 10.00
Southern Dairies, Sealtest Emblem, Try Cottage Cheese, Red Pyro, Quart 22.50
Southern Maid, Inc., Embossed, Round, 1/2 Pint 6.50
St.Lawrence Milk, Cream Top, Embossed, Round, 1/2 Pint 9.00
St.Louis Dairy Co., Embossed, 10 Ounce 5.00
St.Louis Dairy Co., In Script, Embossed, Pint 5.50
St.Louis Dairy, Lamb, Embossed, Round, 1/2 Gallon 8.50
State Of Conn., Prison Bottle, Orange Pyro, Tall, Square, Quart 12.00
Stebbins Farm, Houghton, N.Y., Embossed, Round, Pint 4.00
Steere's Milk, Picture Of Cone & Sundae, 4-Sided, Red Pyro, 1/2 Pint 2.50
Steffen's, Cream Top, Square, Orange Pyro, Quart 8.00
Streit Milk Co., Sheffield, Ala., Fully Embossed, Quart 22.00
Stroudsburg Sanitary Dairy, Cream Top, Embossed, Round, Quart 10.00
Sun Valley Dairy, Green, Yellow Pyro, 1/2 Gallon .... *Color* 70.00
Sunflower Dairy, Astoria, Oregon, Embossed, Round, Quart 7.50
Sunland Dairy, Sunburst & Sun Picture, Baby, Red Pyro, Round, Quart 4.00
Sunny Farm Dairy, W.Rochester, N.Y., Embossed, Pint 5.50
Sunnymede Farm, Bismarck, Missouri, Red Pyro, Squat, 1/2 Pint 5.50
Sunset Dairy, Picture Of Sun Setting, Embossed, Round, Quart 5.00
Sunset Dairy, Red Pyro, Round, Quart 7.50
Sunshine Dairy, Cream Top, Baby Top, Orange Pyro, Square 15.00
Sunshine Dairy, Half-Risen Sun, Orange Pyro, Round, 1/2 Pint 6.50
T.P.D., Tonopah, Nevada, Embossed, Round, 1/2 Pint 7.50
T.P.D., Tonopah, Nevada, Embossed, Round, Quart 8.50
Tapper's Dairy, Orange Pyro, Square, Quart 2.50
Thompson Jersey Farm, Picture Of Cow's Head, Red Pyro, Square, Gallon 10.00
Tilton's City Dairy, Neck Hobnails, Embossed, Round, 1/2 Pint 3.25
Tober's Dairy, Buffalo, Embossed, Pint 4.50
Tomion's Dairy, Fowlerville, Mich., Diamond Neck, Embossed, Round, Pint 5.00
Tooke's Dairy, Ft.Myers, Fla., Embossed, Round, 1/2 Pint 8.50
Tri-State Milk Bottle Supply.Ashland, Ky., Clear, Quart 5.00
Tucker Dairy Co., Red & Maroon Pyro, Square, Quart 1.50
Tucker's Dairy, Red Pyro, Square, 1/2 Pint 2.00
Tumbling Run, J.H.Brokhaff Park Dairy, Straight-Sided, 1/2 Pint 4.25
Tumbling Run, J.H.Brokhoff Park Dairy, Embossed, Pint 5.00
Twin Palms Dairy, Cow, Barn, Trees, Orange Pyro, Round, 1/2 Gallon 10.00
Twin's Farm, Schenectady, Embossed Cow's Head, 1/2 Pint 10.00
United Dairies, Cedar Rapids, Iowa, Wavy Neck Ring, Embossed, Pint 8.00
Universal Dairy Pak Inc., Jackson, Michigan, Straight-Sided, 12 Ounce 4.00
Universal Store, 5 Cent Bottle, 1/2 Pint, 5 1/2 In. 4.00
Universal Store, 5 Cents, Embossed, Ribbed, Round, Pint 3.50

Upton's Farm, Baby Face, Clear, Pint ....*Illus* 20.00
Uservo Inc., In Oval, Embossed, 12 Ounce 3.25
Vallejo Milk Co., Vallejo, Calif., Embossed, Round, Pint 5.00
Vallotton's Dairy, Picture Of Dentist, Orange Pyro, Quart 12.00
Vallotton's Dairy, Valdosta, Ga., Picture Of Dentist, White Pyro, Quart 12.00
Vallotton's Milk, Picture Of Dentist, Maroon Pyro, Round, Quart 8.50
Vallotton's, Cat, Dog, Cow Jumping Over Moon, Maroon Pyro, Quart 8.50
Velva Brand, H.G.Hill Stores, Embossed, Round, Quart 6.00
Venable Dairy, Salem, O., Embossed, Round, Pint 3.00
Victor Farm Dairy, 1 Neck Ring, Embossed, Round, 1/2 Pint 3.75
Victoria Guernsey, Picture Of Large Poppy, Orange Pyro, Square, Pint 3.00
Victoria Guernsey, Picture Of Poppy, Orange Pyro, Round, Squat, Quart 7.50
Victoria Guernsey, Picture Of Trophy, Poppy, Orange Pyro, Square, Quart 1.00
Victory, Florida Store Bottle, Embossed State, Stars, 3 Cents, Quart 15.00
Voegel's Pasteurized, Cream Top, Baby Top, Black Pyro, Square 15.00
W.A.Ross Dairy, Belmont, Mass., Embossed, Round, Squat, Quart 7.50
Walker-Gordon, Picture Of Bottle Carrier, Embossed, Round, Quart 4.00
Walnut Tree Hill, Picture Of Farm, Amber, White Pyro, Square, Quart 5.00
Waple Dairies Inc., Cream Top, Lightning Bolt, Embossed, Round, Quart 10.00
Wayne Creamery, Outline Of 2 Kids, Blue Pyro, Round, Quart 4.00
Wayne Dairy, Richmond, Ind., World, Stars, Banner, Red Pyro, Round, Quart 3.50
Wayne's, Picture Of Milkshake With Straws, Orange Pyro, Round, Quart 5.75
Weber Milk Co's.Buttermilk, Indianapolis, Ind., Amber, 1/2 Pint 65.00
Welsh Farms, Boy With Cow, Cream Top, Orange Pyro, Quart .... 6.50 To 8.50
Welsh Farms, N.J., Wavy Neck Ring, Embossed, Round, 1/2 Pint 3.00
Western Maryland Dairy 7.00
Western United, Embossed In Script, Chicago, Pint 3.50
Wharton's Dairies Inc., Escondido, Calif., Orange Pyro, Round, Quart 7.00
White's Dairy, Embossed Cow, Pint 9.50
Whiteoak Dairy Farm, Picture Of Tree, Embossed, Round, 1/2 Pint 5.00
Whiting's Milk, Red Pyro, Round, 1/2 Pint 3.00
Wild Oak Dairy, Camp Meeker, Calif., Green Tint, Embossed, Round, Quart 12.00
Willamette Dairy Co., Old Crown Top, Embossed, Round, Pint 4.00
Willis Dairy Farms, Eagle, Girl With Glass, Orange Pyro, Round, Quart 4.50
Willow Farm Dairy Products, Cream Top, Square, Red Pyro, Quart 7.50
Willow Farm, Picture Of Farm Boy, Brown Pyro, Square, Gallon 10.00
Willow Farm's Dairy, Old Dacro Top, Embossed, Round, 1/2 Pint 4.00
Winnisimet, Indian's Head, Amber, White Pyro, Square, Quart 5.75
Wm.Biddle & Sons, Pittsfield, Illinois, Embossed, Round, 1/2 Pint 3.25
Wm.Fitzer Cream, New Lenox, Ill., Embossed, Round, 1/2 Pint 3.25
Wm.Weckerie & Sons, 806 Jefferson, Amber, Round 35.00
Wood's Petersburg Dairy, Black Pyro, Round, Pint 3.00
Woodlawn Dairy, Englewood, N.J., Embossed, Round, 1/2 Pint 3.00
Woodlawn Farm Dairy Co., Embossed, Pint 4.50
Woodlawn Farm Dairy Co., Straight-Sided, Embossed, 1/2 Pint 4.00
Woodside Dairy, C.E.Erickson, Spring Valley, N.Y., Embossed, Pint 5.00
Yerington Dairy, Embossed, Round, Pint 4.00
Youman's Farms, New Scotland, N.Y., Embossed, 12 Ounce 3.50
Zuxerin, Ribbed, Thatcher, Embossed, Round, Quart 4.00

MILLVILLE ART GLASS, Albert Einstein, Numbered, Honey Amber 10.00
  Amelia Earhart, Numbered, Medium Amber 12.50
  American Circus, Honey Amber 15.00
  American Freedom Train Bicentennial, Numbered, Amber 30.00
  Apollo Soyus, Numbered, Dark Amber 85.00
  Apollo XI 10th Anniversary, Amber ....*Illus* 15.00
  Betsy Ross, Flag Day, Bicentennial, Amethyst 15.00
  Betsy Ross, Flag Day, Bicentennial, Light Amethyst 45.00
  Burgoyne, Saratoga Bicentennial, Amethyst 15.00
  Connecticut Bicentennial, Blue 20.00
  Delaware Bicentennial, Chicken Roost, Light Amethyst 650.00
  Delaware Bicentennial, Light Amethyst 15.00
  Eleanor Roosevelt, Numbered, Cathedral Red 10.00

Millville Art Glass, Graf Zeppelin
75th, Numbered, Amber

Milk, Upton's Farm,
Baby Face, Clear, Pint

(See Page 181)

Millville Art Glass, Apollo XI
10th Anniversary, Amber

(See Page 181)

Frank H.Wheaton, Sr., Numbered, Century Amber	12.50
Franklin D.Roosevelt, Numbered, Cathedral Red	10.00
Georgia Bicentennial, Light Yellow	15.00
Gerald R.Ford 38th President, Inside Number, Amethyst	40.00
Good Buddy, CBer, Numbered, Amber	10.00
Good Buddy, CBer, Numbered, Amethyst	10.00
Good Buddy, CBer, Numbered, Aqua	75.00
Good Buddy, CBer, Numbered, Blue	10.00
Good Buddy, CBer, Numbered, Dark Green	10.00
Good Buddy, CBer, Numbered, Light Green	30.00
Good Buddy, CBer, Numbered, Yellow	125.00
Graf Zeppelin 75th, Numbered, Amber *Illus*	30.00
Great American Rip-Off, Numbered, Medium Green	10.00
Hawaii, Captain Cook Bicentennial, Numbered, Amber	15.00
Israel's 25th Anniversary, Honey Amber *Color*	225.00
J.F.Kennedy 10 Yr.Memorial, Cobalt Blue *Color*	40.00
J.F.Kennedy 10 Yr.Memorial, Light Blue	50.00
J.F.Kennedy 15 Yr.Memorial, Numbered, Light Green	25.00
J.F.Kennedy 15 Yr.Memorial, Numbered, Yellow Brown	25.00
Jersey Devil, Jersey Green *Color*	10.00
Jimmy Carter 39th President, Numbered, Amber	10.00
Jimmy Carter 39th President, Numbered, Green	10.00
Jimmy Carter 39th President, Numbered, Light Blue	10.00
Jimmy Carter 39th President, Numbered, Navy Blue	30.00
John Paul Jones, Numbered, Amethyst	12.50
John Wayne, Numbered, Deep Green	12.50
July 4th Bicentennial, Numbered, Blue	45.00
July 4th Bicentennial, Numbered, Honey Amber	35.00
Lake Placid 1980, Numbered, Honey Amber	10.00
Lindbergh 50th Anniversary, Numbered, Light Blue	25.00
Maryland Bicentennial, Amethyst	15.00
Massachusetts Bicentennial, Green	15.00
Mauricetown, N.J., Anniversary, Numbered, Cobalt Blue	12.50
Moscow 1980, Numbered, Honey Amber	10.00
Mt.St.Helens, Numbered, Volcano Gray	10.00
New Hampshire Bicentennial, Medium Amber	15.00
New Jersey Bicentennial, Medium Blue	20.00
New York Bicentennial, Medium Amber	15.00
North Carolina Bicentennial, Green	15.00
Panama Canal Treaty, Numbered, Medium Amber	10.00

Pennsylvania Bicentennial, Green	20.00
Pope John Paul I, Numbered, Medium Blue	12.50
Pope John Paul II, Numbered, Amethyst	50.00
Pope John Paul II, Numbered, Amethyst, 1st Revision	75.00
Pope John Paul II, Numbered, Amethyst, 2nd Revision	10.00
Pope John Paul II, Polish Eagle, Numbered, Red	10.00
Pope John Paul II, U.S.A.Visit, Numbered, Green	12.50
Pope John XXIII, Numbered, Medium Amber	12.50
Pope Paul VI, Numbered, Light Green	200.00
Pope Paul VI, Numbered, Light Yellow Green	12.50
Queen Elizabeth 25th, Numbered, Amethyst *Illus*	550.00
Rhode Island Bicentennial, Amethyst	15.00
Richard Nixon 37th President, Inside Number, Amethyst	40.00
Ronald Reagan 40th President, Numbered, Gold	12.50
Rotary 75th Anniversary, Numbered, Cobalt Blue	11.50
Royal Wedding, Prince Charles, Numbered, Royal Gold	12.50
Salt II, Vienna Summit, Numbered, Honey Amber	10.00
Senator Hubert H.Humphrey Memorial	25.00 To 90.00
Senator Sam Ervin, Senator Howard Baker, Topaz	15.00
Skylab Dies In Australia, Pomono Green	15.00
Skylab 3, Medium Cobalt Blue	20.00
South Carolina Bicentennial, Blue	15.00
Special Apollo XI, Burnt Amber	45.00
Special Apollo XI, Green & Reddish Amber	145.00
Spirit Of '76 Bicentennial, Honey Amber	35.00
Spirit Of '76 Bicentennial, Numbered, Blue	45.00
St.John Neumann, Amethyst	30.00
St.John Neumann, Purple	150.00
Susan B.Anthony, Numbered, Medium Blue	12.50
Tall Ships Bicentennial, Blue *Illus*	15.00
Tall Ships Bicentennial, Olive Green	15.00
U.S.Marine Corps Bicentennial, Numbered, Dark Amber	15.00
U.S.Navy Bicentennial, Numbered, Medium Blue	15.00
U.S.S.Arizona, Numbered, Blue	10.00
U.S.S.Missouri, Numbered, Blue	10.00
U.S.S.New Jersey, Numbered, Green	10.00
U.S.S.North Carolina, Numbered, Green	10.00
U.S.Space Shuttle Columbia, Numbered, Honey Amber	12.50
U.S.Space Shuttle Enterprise, Numbered, Light Amber	20.00
Viking I, Aqua	125.00
Viking I, Light Green	40.00

Millville Art Glass, Tall Ships
Bicentennial, Blue

Millville Art Glass, Queen Elizabeth
25th, Numbered, Amethyst

Virginia Bicentennial, Medium Blue	15.00
Watergate, Amethyst ....*Color*	550.00
Watergate, Medium Blue	50.00
Watergate, Topaz	15.00
Welcome Home Hostages, Numbered, Yellow Ribbon Amber	12.50
Will Rogers, Numbered, Medium Amber	12.50
Wright Brothers 75th Anniversary, Numbered, Blue	20.00
1794 Silver Dollar, Numbered, Orange Amber	10.00
1795 Silver Dollar, Numbered, Light Blue	10.00
1804 Silver Dollar, Numbered, Cathedral Red	10.00
1840 Silver Dollar, Numbered, Cobalt Blue	10.00
1873 Trade Dollar, Numbered, Silver Gray	10.00
1876 Centennial Train, Numbered, Cathedral Red	10.00
1876 Centennial Train, Numbered, Sample, Flint	110.00
1876 Centennial Train, Numbered, Sample, Reddish Flint	125.00
1878 Silver Dollar, Numbered, Amber	10.00
1878 Silver Dollar, Numbered, Amethyst	10.00
1878 Silver Dollar, Numbered, Blue	10.00
1878 Silver Dollar, Numbered, Deep Green	30.00
1878 Silver Dollar, Numbered, Honey Amber	85.00
1878 Silver Dollar, Numbered, Light Green	10.00
1909 Model T Ford, Numbered, Blue	10.00
1909 Model T Ford, Numbered, Light Amber	30.00
1909 Packard, Numbered, Amethyst	10.00
1921 Silver Dollar, Numbered, Amethyst	30.00
1921 Silver Dollar, Numbered, Blue	10.00
1932 Chevy, Numbered, Cobalt Blue	30.00
1932 Chevy, Numbered, Light Blue	10.00
1933 Duesenberg, Numbered, Yellow Green	30.00
1971 Ike Dollar, Numbered, Green	45.00
1973 St.Nick, Topaz	125.00
1974 St.Nick, Green	65.00
1975 St.Nick, Medium Blue	35.00
1976 Campaign Cabin, Carter & Ford, Numbered, Green	85.00
1976 Democrat Campaign Cabin, Numbered, Aqua	80.00
1976 Democrat Campaign Cabin, Numbered, Emerald Green	25.00
1976 Republican Campaign Cabin, Numbered, Green	25.00
1976 St.Nick, Dark Amber	45.00
1976 St.Nick, Olive	90.00
1977 St.Nick, Honey Amber	25.00
1978 St.Nick, Amethyst	75.00
1978 St.Nick, Medium Blue	15.00
1979 St.Nick, Amethyst	15.00
1979 Susan B.Anthony Dollar, Numbered, Honey Amber	10.00
1980 Campaign Cabin, Carter & Reagan, Numbered, Amber	55.00
1980 Democrat Campaign Cabin, Numbered, Honey Amber	20.00
1980 Republican Campaign Cabin, Numbered, Honey Amber	20.00
1980 St.Nick, Ice Gray	12.50
1981 St.Nick, Cathedral Red	10.00

Mineral water bottles held the fresh, natural spring waters favored for health and taste. Most of the bottles collected today date from the 1850-1900 period. Many of these bottles have blob tops.

MINERAL WATER, see also Seltzer; Soda

MINERAL WATER, A.R.Cox, Norristown, Pa., Dark Green, Squat	30.00
Adirondack Spring	30.00
Apollinaris, Rhenish, Prussia, Germany, London	8.00
Artesian, Iron Pontil	140.00
Augusta Lithia, Dr.T.T.Fauntleroy, Staunton, Va.	22.00
Ballston Spa, Emerald Green, Pint	34.00
Blue Lick, Olive, 8 In. ....*Color*	6.00
Boyd & Beard, Green	45.00
C.Allen Browne, Boston, Iron Pontil, Squart, Dark Green	100.00

C.W.Weston, Olive	35.00
Champion Spouting Spring, Saratoga, N.Y., Aqua, Pint	35.00
Chase & Co., San Francisco, Green, Pontil	22.00
Cincinnati, Star, Tall	16.00
Clarke & Co., New York, Dark Olive Green, Pint	20.00
Clarke & Co., New York, Embossed Shoulders, Amber	25.00
Clarke & Co., New York, Green, Quart	34.00
Clarke & Co., New York, Iron Pontil, Medium Green, Quart	70.00
Clarke & Co., New York, Olive Amber, Pint	30.00
Clarke & White, Large C, New York, Dark Olive Green, Pint	32.50
Clarke & White, New York, Green, Pint	34.00
Clarke & White, New York, Green, Quart	49.00
Clarke & White, New York, Olive Green, Pint	17.50 To 20.00
Clarke & White, New York, Pint	15.00
Clarke & White, Saratoga, N.Y., Olive Green, Pint	20.00
Congress & Empire Spring Co., Emerald Green, Pint	20.00
Congress & Empire Spring Co., Green, 7 7/8 In.	20.00 To 28.00
Congress & Empire Spring Co., Saratoga, N.Y., Green	25.00
Congress & Empire, Hotchkiss Sons, Golden Amber	75.00
Congress Spring Co., Saratoga, Embossed, Blue-Green, Quart	15.00
Congress Spring Co., Saratoga, N.Y., Grass Green, Pint	25.00
Congress Spring Water, Kelly Green	20.00
D.A.Knowlton, Saratoga, N.Y., Olive Green, Stubby Neck, Quart	35.00
Dr.Struve's, Light Green, 1/2 Pint	40.00
Dyottville Glass Works, Philadelphia, Deep Aqua	8.50
Empire Spring Co., Saratoga, N.Y., Green, 8 In.	22.00
Empire Water, Amber, Quart	23.00
Excelsior Spring, Saratoga, N.Y., Deep Forest Green, Pint	17.00
Excelsior Spring, Saratoga, N.Y., Yellow Green, Quart	28.00
F.A.Conant, Iron Pontil, Light Teal Green	18.00
F.Brown, Boston, Back, French Water, Front, Shaped Top	250.00
F.Brown, Boston, French, IP, Emerald Green, Whittled	250.00
F.R. & J.F., Slatington, Pa., Pony, Medium Green	35.00
Franklin Mineral Spring, Saratoga, Green, Pint	150.00
Frederick Meincke, 1882, Savannah, Cobalt	120.00
Frost's Magnetic Spring, Eaton Rapids, Michigan, Quart	90.00
G.Klauder, Superior, Cobalt Blue	350.00
G.W.Weston & Co., Saratoga, N.Y., Olive Green, Pint	32.50
G.W.Weston, Olive Green, Pint	35.00
G.W.Weston, Saratoga, New York, Green, Quart	47.00
George A.Kiehl, Lancaster, Pa., Medium Green, Squat	30.00
Gettysburg Katalysine Water, Green, Quart	30.00
Gettysburg Katalysine Water, Yellow Green, 10 In.	15.00
Geyser Spring, Saratoga, N.Y., Aqua, Quart	38.00
Glenrock Cold Spring, Maine, Aqua, Quart	15.00
Granite Rock Spring Bottling, Higganum, Conn., Green Aqua	10.00
Granite State Spring Water, In Script, Crown, Aqua	3.50
Guilford Mineral Spring, Emerald Green, Quart	25.00
Guilford Mineral Spring, Olive Green, Quart	25.00 To 40.00
H. & J.Alwes, Cincinnati, Ohio, Blob Top, Iron Pontil, Aqua	32.00
H.L. & J.W.Brown, Hartford, Ct., Squat, Olive Amber	95.00
H.L.& J.W.Brown, Hartford, Ct., Iron Pontil, Olive Green	120.00
H.Rummel, Charleston, W.Va.	14.00
Hanbury Smith, Vichy Water, New York	20.00
Hanbury Smith's Mineral Water, Light Green, Pint	33.00
Hassinger & O'Brien, O'Fallon Street, St.Louis	14.00
Hathorn Spring, Saratoga, N.Y., Amber, Quart	20.00
Hathorn Spring, Saratoga, N.Y., Black Amber, Pint	15.00
Hathorn Spring, Saratoga, N.Y., Dark Amber, Quart	24.00
Hathorn Spring, Saratoga, N.Y., Emerald Green, Pint	22.00
Hathorn Spring, Saratoga, N.Y., Whittled, Amber, Quart	25.00
Hathorn Spring, Saratoga, N.Y., Yellow Green, Pint	10.00
Headman's Excelsior, Green, Iron Pontil	38.00

Highrock Congress Springs, Citron Green, Pint	50.00
Highrock Congress Springs, Olive Green	50.00 To 60.00
Hiram Ricker, Facsimile, 1st Poland, Amber	*Color*
Honesdale Glassworks, Penn., Aqua, 7 In.	25.00
Hotchkiss, Emerald Green, Pint	29.00
Hunyadi Janos, Contents, Full Label, 1 Pint 6 Ounce	5.00
Hygeia Bottling Works, Pensacola, Fla., Plunger, Aqua	22.00
J. & A.Dearborn, N.Y., 8-Sided, Cobalt, Pontil	75.00 To 120.00
J.Boardman & Co., New York, 8-Sided, Blue-Green	30.00
J.Born, Cincinnati, Aqua, 7 1/2 In.	*Illus* 38.00
J.Born, Cincinnati, Long-Neck Variant, Deep Aqua	15.00
J.Harvey & Co., Providence, R.I., Iron Pontil, Olive Green	150.00
J.Kennedy, Pittsburgh, Aqua	40.00
J.N.Gerdes, San Francisco, Blob Top, 9 Vertical Panels	15.00
J.R.Owens, Parkesburg, Pa., Pony, Iron Pontil, Dark Green	65.00
J.W.Thornley, Holmesburg, Pa., Iron Pontil, Green, Squat	50.00
J.Wise, Allentown, Pa., Cobalt, Squat	45.00
Jackson Bottling Works, Jackson, Miss., Hutch, Aqua	32.00
John Boardman, New York, 8-Sided, Cobalt, Pontil	50.00
John Clarke, New York, Pontil, Olive Green, Quart	65.00
John Clarke, New York, 3-Piece Mold, Pontiled, Yellow Green	55.00
John Ogden's, Pittsburgh, Blob Top, Iron Pontil	30.00
John Ryan, Excelsior, Savannah, Graphite Pontil, Dark Cobalt	100.00
John Ryan, Excelsior, Savannah, Iron Pontil, Cobalt	30.00
John Ryan, 1859, Union Glassworks, Cobalt	20.00
Lancaster X Glass Works, N.Y., Iron Pontil, Aqua	18.00
Lynch & Clarke, New York, Pontil, Olive Green, Pint	100.00
Lynch & Clarke, Pontil, Olive Amber, Pint	85.00
Macon, Georgia, Improved, Iron Pontil, Cobalt Blue	50.00
Magnetic, Spring Lake, Michigan, Wm.F. & Sons, Quart	300.00
Middletown Healing Springs, High-Arched, Quart	195.00
Middletown Healing Springs, Quart	35.00
Middletown Healing Springs, Stoddard, Amber	45.00
Middletown Mineral Springs, Middletown, Vt., Green	125.00
Minevaluater, Troy, N.Y.	5.00
Missisquoi A Spring, Embossed Indian	175.00
Missisquoi A Spring, Olive Green, Quart	38.00
Missisquoi A Spring, Stoddard, Golden Amber, Quart	55.00
Missisquoi Spring, Forest Green, 9 5/8 In.	45.00
Newport Mineral Water Co., Newport, Ky., Cobalt Blue, Round	14.00
O.G.Knowlton, Saratoga, Pint	38.00
O.Tullmann's Water Works, California, Hutchinson, Label	55.00
Oak Orchard Springs, Blue Green	35.00
Overdick, Cincinnati, Iron Pontil, Aqua	25.00
P.Conway Bottler, Philada., Iron Pontil, Cobalt, Squat	65.00
Pavillion & U.S.Spring Co., Saratoga, N.Y., Green, Pint	90.00
Poland Spring 1890, Moses, Clear	65.00
Poland Spring, Figural Of Moses, Aqua	50.00 To 75.00
Red Springs, Green, Pint	32.00
Rice & McKinney, Phila., Green	25.00
Risedorph Bottling Co., Blue, 9 In.	*Illus* 26.00
Roussel's, Philadelphia, Open Pontil, Chartreuse, Large	149.00
S.Moore, Phila., Iron Pontil, Green	30.00
S.Smith Knickerbocker, New York, Emerald Green	200.00
Samuel Soda Springs, Aqua	5.00
Saratoga Star Spring, Olive Green, Pint	60.00
Saratoga Vichy Spouting Spring, Aqua	18.00
Saratoga Vichy Water, Saratoga, N.Y., Amber, Quart	120.00
Seitz & Brothers, Premium, Easton, Pa., Sapphire Blue, 8-Side	60.00
Setters Vichy, L.Cohen & Son, Pitts., 6 1/2 In.	*Color*
Sharon Sulpher, John H.Gardner & Sons, Green	60.00 To 75.00
Star Springs, Amber, Pint	18.00
State Of New York, Whittled, Aqua	20.00

Mineral Water, Risedorph
Bottling Co., Blue, 9 In.

Mineral Water, J.Born, Cincinnati,
Aqua, 7 1/2 In.

Sterling Spring, Crystal Falls, Mich., Baltimore Loop, Amber	15.00
Stoddard Type, Olive Amber, Blob Top	18.00
Sunset Spring, Catskill Mountains, Bail, Stopper, 2 1/2 Quart	20.00
Superior Union Glass Works, Paneled Base, Teal	20.00
Superior, Teal Green, 8 Panels, Iron Pontil	35.00
Superior, 10-Sided, Graphite Pontil, Light Blue	25.00
Syracuse Springs Excelsior, Amber, Pint	95.00
Syracuse Springs Excelsior, Whittled, Amber, Quart	25.00
T.A.W.Napa Soda, Green, 7 1/2 In.	25.00
The Emancipator, Clear, 9 In. ....*Color*	8.00
Tullmann's, Hutchinson, Aqua, Lemon Soda, Paper Label	55.00
Tweedles, Graphite Pontil, Light Green	70.00
Ungersofner, Bitterwasser, Embossed On Bottom, Yellow, Pint	3.00
Union Glass Works, Paneled Base, Blue	30.00
Upsilanti Mineral Water Salts, T.C.Owen, Michigan, Aqua	6.00
Utica Bottling Establishment, Iron Pontil, Green	65.00
Verhage, Cincinnati, Iron Pontil, Aqua	35.00
Vermont Springs, Saxe & Co., Light Green, Quart	65.00
Vermont Springs, Saxe & Co., Olive Green, Quart	45.00
Vermont Springs, Saxe & Co., Sheldon, Vt., Bubbly, Whittled	52.00
Veronica Spring Water, Wraparound Label, Amber, Quart	15.00
Vichy Water, Hanbury Smith, Yellow Green, 1/2 Pint	37.00
Vincent Hathaway & Co., Boston, Green, Round	25.00
W.Eagle, Superior, Iron Pontil, Medium Green, Squat	75.00
W.Eagle, Vestry, Varnick & Canal Sts., Pontil, Dark Green	80.00
W.H.Burt, San Francisco, Iron Pontil, Deep Green	30.00
Washington Spring Co., Bust Of Washington, Emerald Green	325.00
Washington Spring, Saratoga, N.Y., Emerald Green, Pint	65.00
Whitney Glassworks, Glassboro, N.J., Blue Green, Quart	55.00
Windsor Mineral Spring Co., Lewiston, Maine, Hutchinson	34.00
Wm.H.Weaver, Hackettstown, Iron Pontil, Green	100.00
Wm.W.Lappeus, Albany, 5 Flat & 5 Round Panels, Cobalt Blue	75.00
Wooten Wells, Blood Purifier, Tonic, Texas, Aqua	35.00
MINIATURE, Alpha States, California	15.00
Alpha States, Idaho	15.00
Alpha States, Iowa	15.00
Alpha States, Maryland	15.00
Alpha States, North Dakota	15.00
Alpha States, Oregon	15.00
Alpha States, South Carolina	15.00
Alpha States, South Dakota	15.00
Alpha States, Utah	15.00
Alpha States, Wyoming	15.00

Miniature, Beer, Acme, Brown, 4 In.; Pabst
Blue Ribbon, Green, 4 1/2 In.; Burger
Bohemian, Brown, 4 In.

Miniature, Beer, Prager, Brown, 4 In.;
Tech Beer, Wooden, 3 1/2 In.;
Prager, Brown, 3 In.

Armagnac, Lantern	8.00
Armagnac, Windmill	35.00
Bather On Rock	95.00
Beer, Acme, Brown, 4 In. ....*Illus*	5.00
Beer, Arrow, 4 In.	12.00
Beer, Burger Bohemian, Brown, 4 In. ....*Illus*	5.00
Beer, Esslingers, 4 In.	9.00
Beer, Felsenbrau	12.00
Beer, Goebel	15.00
Beer, Hamms	10.00
Beer, Old Export, 4 In.	12.00
Beer, Pabst Blue Ribbon, Green, 4 1/2 In. ....*Illus*	5.00
Beer, Prager, Brown, 3 In. ....*Illus*	5.00
Beer, Prager, Brown, 4 In. ....*Illus*	5.00
Beer, Primo, Stubby	50.00
Beer, Schmidts, 4 In.	9.00
Beer, Senate, 4 In.	40.00
Beer, Tech Beer, Wooden, 3 1/2 In. ....*Illus*	12.00
Beer, WV	22.00
Bitters, Brand Bros., Triangular, Amber	35.00
Bitters, Dr.Loew's, Aqua	55.00
Blown, Chestnut, Wide Mouth, Olive Amber, 3 3/4 In.	90.00
Bull Rider	19.00
Candy Container, War Tank	20.00
Caveman	11.00
Collectors Art, Afghan Hound	26.00
Collectors Art, Angus Bull	24.00
Collectors Art, Basset Hound	26.00
Collectors Art, Blue Bird	25.00
Collectors Art, Blue Jay	27.00
Collectors Art, Brahma Bull	26.00
Collectors Art, Bunting	18.00
Collectors Art, Canary	25.00
Collectors Art, Cardinal	31.00
Collectors Art, Charolais Bull	25.00
Collectors Art, Chipmunk	25.00
Collectors Art, Collie	24.00
Collectors Art, Dachshund	24.00
Collectors Art, Dalmatian	24.00
Collectors Art, German Shepherd	25.00
Collectors Art, Goldfinch	18.00
Collectors Art, Hereford	26.00
Collectors Art, Hereford, Polled	25.00

Collectors Art, Hummingbird	19.00
Collectors Art, Irish Setter	23.00
Collectors Art, Koala	29.00
Collectors Art, Longhorn Bull	28.00
Collectors Art, Meadowlark	32.00
Collectors Art, Mexican Fighting Bull	26.00
Collectors Art, Oriole	17.00
Collectors Art, Parakeet	14.00
Collectors Art, Parakeet, Cologne	9.00
Collectors Art, Pinscher	23.00
Collectors Art, Pointer	25.00
Collectors Art, Poodle	19.00
Collectors Art, Rabbits	31.00
Collectors Art, Raccoons	32.00
Collectors Art, Robin	23.00
Collectors Art, Schnauzer	23.00
Collectors Art, Skunks	31.00
Collectors Art, St.Bernard	24.00
Columbia Catsup	5.00
Crown Distilleries, Crown & Shield, Amber, Slug Plate, 5 1/4 In.	25.00
Cyrus Noble, Assayer	17.00
Cyrus Noble, Bartender	15.00
Cyrus Noble, Bear & Cubs, 1980	11.00
Cyrus Noble, Blacksmith	14.00
Cyrus Noble, Buffalo	13.95
Cyrus Noble, Buffalo, Reissue	15.00
Cyrus Noble, Burro	11.00 To 13.00
Cyrus Noble, Delta Saloon Bar Scene, 4-Piece Set	275.00
Cyrus Noble, Gambler, 1975	11.00 To 13.00
Cyrus Noble, Gambler's Lady, 1977	14.00
Cyrus Noble, Gold Miner, 1974	15.00
Cyrus Noble, Landlady, 1978	18.00
Cyrus Noble, Middle Of Piano, Trumpeter, 1979	14.00
Cyrus Noble, Mine, 1979	15.00
Cyrus Noble, Miner's Daughter, 1976	18.00
Cyrus Noble, Moose & Calf, 1980	11.00
Cyrus Noble, Mountain Lion & Cubs, 1979	13.95
Cyrus Noble, Music Man, 1978	16.00
Cyrus Noble, Penguin Family, 1980	19.00
Cyrus Noble, Violinist, 1978	14.00
Cyrus Noble, Walrus Family, 1980	11.00
Cyrus Noble, Whiskey Drummer, 1977	19.00
Demijohn, Basketweave, Aqua, 3 In.	12.50
Drioli, African Dancer	6.00
Drioli, Bull	12.00
Drioli, Cat	9.00
Drioli, Dog	9.00
Drioli, Donkey	5.00
Drioli, Duck	9.00
Drioli, Eel	7.00
Drioli, Elephant	5.00
Drioli, Englishmen	4.00
Drioli, Fish	7.00
Drioli, Horse	7.00
Drioli, Jazz Band, Set Of 6	138.00
Drioli, Jug, 1968	4.00
Drioli, Minstrels, Set Of 6	45.00
Drioli, Mouse	8.00
Drioli, Orientals	7.00
Drioli, Owl	7.00
Drioli, Pelican	7.00
Drioli, Rock Group, Set Of 6	35.00
Drioli, Teardrops, Set Of 3	26.00
Drioli, Turkey	6.00

Drioli, Venus	4.00
Famous Firsts, Butterfly, 1972	11.00
Famous Firsts, Coffee Mill, 1979	16.00
Famous Firsts, Corvette, 1953	16.00
Famous Firsts, Corvette, 1963	16.00
Famous Firsts, French Telephone, 1973	11.00 To 13.00
Famous Firsts, Geisha Girls, Set Of 3, 1978	33.00
Famous Firsts, Honda Motorcycle, 1979	16.00
Famous Firsts, Hurdy Gurdy, 1979	15.00 To 17.00
Famous Firsts, Liberty Bell, 1976	10.00
Famous Firsts, Medieval Warrior, 1979	17.00 To 20.00
Famous Firsts, Phonograph, 1973	14.00
Famous Firsts, Roulette Wheel, 1980	20.00
Famous Firsts, Spirit Of St.Louis, 1972	20.00
Famous Firsts, Winnie Mae, 1972	22.00
Famous Firsts, Yacht America, 1978	18.00
Fenkhausen & Co., San Francisco, Clear	40.00
Flask, Clam, Original Closure, Amber	135.00
Food, Soy Sauce, 2 3/4 In.	20.00
Galliano, Guard	5.00
George Washington, Figural, Light Blue	7.00
Gin, Case, Light Green, 4 In.	45.00
Grenadier, Dragoon 17th Regiment, 1970	25.00
Grenadier, Frey Junipero Serra	12.00
Grenadier, Frosty The Snowman, 1980	20.00
Grenadier, General George Custer, 1971	25.00
Grenadier, General Jeb Stuart, 1970	25.00
Grenadier, General Lafayette, 1979	20.00
Grenadier, General Robert E.Lee, 1977	11.00 To 15.00
Grenadier, Officer, Scots Fusilier, 1971	30.00
Grenadier, Officer, 3rd Guard, 1971	25.00
Grenadier, Santa Claus, 1980	20.00
Grenadier, Sgt.Maj., Coldstream, 1971	25.00
Grenadier, Teddy Roosevelt, 1977	11.00 To 15.00
Grenadier, Washington Blue Rifles, 1974	20.00
Grenadier, 11th Indiana Zouave, 1975	15.00
Grenadier, 14th Virginia Cavalry, 1975	15.00
Grenadier, 2nd Regiment Sharpshooters, 1975	15.00
Grenadier, 4th Virginia Cavalry, 1975	15.00
Grenadier, 6th Alabama Raccoon Roughs, 1975	15.00
Grenadier, 6th Wisconsin	15.00
Grenadier, 79th New York Highlanders, 1975	15.00
Hoffman, Alfy Afghan, Musical Decanter, 1979	*Illus* 15.00
Hoffman, Bear & Cub, 1978	12.00
Hoffman, Billy Boxer, Musical Decanter, 1979	*Illus* 15.00
Hoffman, Fanny Fox, Musical Decanter, 1979	*Illus* 15.00
Hoffman, Horses, Set Of 6	100.00
Hoffman, Mr.Lucky, Set No.1	66.00
Hoffman, Percy Poodle, Musical Decanter, 1979	*Illus* 15.00
Hoffman, Scotty Terrier, Musical Decanter, 1979	*Illus* 15.00
Hoffman, Terry Terrier, Musical Decanter, 1979	*Illus* 15.00
Hoffman, Wildlife, Set Of 6	72.00
Jesse Moore & Co., Louisville In Circle, Antlers, Trademark	45.00
Johnnie Walker Scotch, Whiskey, T.W.A., Red Label	1.50
Jug, J.W.Palmer, Compliments Of J.W.Sesy, Cream	28.00
Kontinental Classics, Editor, 1976	16.00
Kontinental Classics, Gunsmith, 1977	16.00
Kontinental Classics, Prospector, 1977	16.00
Kontinental Classics, Saddlemaker, 1977	16.00
Lionstone, Barber, 1976	16.00
Lionstone, Bartender, 1969	13.00
Lionstone, Bath, 1976	15.00
Lionstone, Cardinal, 1972	14.00
Lionstone, Cavalry Scout, 1970	16.00

Miniature, Hoffman, Top Row, Alfy Afghan, Billy Boxer, Percy Poodle;
Bottom Row, Fanny Fox, Scotty Terrier, Terry Terrier, Musical Decanters, 1979

Lionstone, Circus, Set Of 9, 1973	110.00
Lionstone, Clown, No.1, Monkey Business, 1978	17.00
Lionstone, Clown, No.2, Sad Sam, 1978	16.00
Lionstone, Clown, No.3, Say It With Music, 1978	17.00
Lionstone, Cowboy, 1970	16.00
Lionstone, Dancehall Girl, 1973	15.00
Lionstone, Dog Series, No.1, Set Of 6, 1975	85.00
Lionstone, Dog Series, No.2, Set Of 6, 1977	85.00
Lionstone, Dog Series, No.3, Set Of 6, 1977	77.00
Lionstone, Doves Of Peace, 1977	15.00
Lionstone, Fire Equipment, Set Of 3, 1976	41.00
Lionstone, Gambler, 1970	16.00
Lionstone, Gold Panner, 1975	14.00
Lionstone, Indian, Casual, 1970	16.00
Lionstone, Indian, Proud, 1970	16.00
Lionstone, Lion & Cub, 1977	8.00
Lionstone, Lonely Luke, 1975	13.00
Lionstone, Lucky Buck, 1975	14.00
Lionstone, OK Corral, Set Of 3, 1971	60.00 To 93.00
Lionstone, Photographer, 1976	15.00
Lionstone, Professor, 1975	14.00
Lionstone, Rain Maker, 1976	15.00
Lionstone, Roadrunner, 1969	15.00
Lionstone, Robin, 1975	17.00
Lionstone, Sheepherder, 1975	13.00
Lionstone, Sheriff, 1970	16.00
Luxardo, Amphora	18.00
Luxardo, Apothecary Jar	14.00
Luxardo, Bear	7.00
Luxardo, Buffalo	7.00
Luxardo, Burma Ash Tray	9.00
Luxardo, Cat, Black	13.00
Luxardo, Dinosaur	12.00
Luxardo, English Bull	6.00
Luxardo, Frog	6.00
Luxardo, Fruit	28.00
Luxardo, Gambia	5.00
Luxardo, Gondola	6.00
Luxardo, Hippo	7.00
Luxardo, Lion	7.00
Luxardo, Mud Bucket	15.00
Luxardo, Rhino	7.00
Luxardo, Turkey	31.00
Luxardo, Twist	3.00
Luxardo, Venus, 1969	6.00

Lynde & Putnam, Mineral Water, San Francisco, Dark Green	40.00
MBC, Aladdin	6.00
MBC, Circus Circus	6.00
MBC, Dunes Hotel	6.00
MBC, Fox, Pennsylvania Dutch, Pair	12.00
MBC, Geisha, Set Of 6	31.00
MBC, Globe	9.00
MBC, Hacienda Hotel	7.00
MBC, Horseshoe	6.00
MBC, Karate Fighter	6.00
MBC, King Tut	6.00
MBC, Kung Fu Fighter	6.00
MBC, Landmark Hotel	7.00
MBC, Laurel & Hardy, Pair	27.00
MBC, MGM Grand	7.00
MBC, Peddler	10.00
MBC, Poodle	7.00
MBC, Rooster	6.00
MBC, Savemost Man	6.00
MBC, Ship	8.00
MBC, Slot Machine, Reno, Las Vegas, Paul's	6.00
MBC, Stardust Hotel	7.00
MBC, Stein, Blue	7.00
MBC, Tropicana Hotel	8.00
MBC, Vase	7.00
McCormick, Ben Franklin, 1976	17.00
McCormick, Betsy Ross, 1976	35.00 To 50.00
McCormick, Charles Lindbergh, 1978	12.00 To 14.00
McCormick, Confederates, Set Of 4, 1978	38.00
McCormick, Dog, Set Of 6	90.00
McCormick, Elvis No.1, 1979	25.00 To 30.00
McCormick, Elvis No.2, 1980	27.50 To 33.00
McCormick, Elvis No.3, 1980	29.00
McCormick, George Washington, 1976	35.00 To 39.00
McCormick, Gunfighter, Set Of 8, 1977	122.00 To 125.00
McCormick, Henry Ford, 1978	12.00 To 15.00
McCormick, John Hancock, 1976	17.00
McCormick, John Paul Jones, 1976	16.00 To 17.00
McCormick, Jupiter Train Set, 1980	49.00 To 67.00
McCormick, Mark Twain, 1978	14.00
McCormick, Patrick Henry, 1976	17.00
McCormick, Paul Revere, 1976	35.00 To 50.00
McCormick, Pony Express, 1980	23.00 To 25.00
McCormick, Rose Collection, 1980	27.00
McCormick, Spirit Of 76, 1977	19.00
McCormick, Thomas Jefferson, 1976	17.00
McCormick, Will Rogers, 1978	12.00 To 13.00
McLech, Arch	5.00
McLech, Big Ben Tower	5.00
McLech, Burn's Cottage	6.00
McLech, Football	4.00
McLech, Joan Of Arc	10.00
McLech, Mermaid	6.00
McLech, Pistols, Pair	18.00
McLech, Tower Of London	7.00
McLech, World Cup	5.00
Michter's, King Tut	6.00 To 14.00
Midwestern Pattern Mold, 16 Vertical Ribs, Dark Amethyst, OP	750.00
Morse's Indian Root Pills, Amber	4.50
Nehi Bottle On World Globe, Columbus, Georgia, Glass	25.00
Old Commonwealth Coal Miner, No.1	50.00
Old Pepper Whiskey, Jas. E.Pepper & Co. In Shield, Amber	65.00
Pabst Brewing Co., Amber, 4 1/4 In.	6.00

Paul Jones, Blob Seal	6.00
Perfume, Edrehis Pocket, Pumpkinseed, Label, Flint, Clear, 3 In.	20.00
Perfume, Peacock, Clear	35.00
Potter's, Dog Sled	40.00
Potter's, Goose Family	18.00
Pottery, Chas.Grover Liquor Merchants	25.00
Pottery, Jug, Sweet Mash Corn, Jacksonville, Florida	45.00
Pottery, Parker Rye, Louisville, Handle	25.00
Raintree, Clown No.1 ....*Illus*	25.00
Raintree, Clown No.2 ....*Illus*	25.00
Rockingham, Mermaid	300.00
Ski Country, Badger Family	18.00 To 27.00
Ski Country, Blackbird	18.00 To 27.00
Ski Country, Bluejay	35.00 To 47.00
Ski Country, Bob Cratchet	18.00 To 33.00
Ski Country, Bobcat	28.00
Ski Country, Bonnie	15.00 To 21.00
Ski Country, Bull Rider	18.00 To 33.00
Ski Country, Burro	22.00 To 25.00
Ski Country, Cardinal	36.00 To 50.00
Ski Country, Caveman	11.00 To 20.00
Ski Country, Chukar Partridge	15.00 To 24.00
Ski Country, Clown	28.00 To 30.00
Ski Country, Clyde	15.00 To 27.00
Ski Country, Condor	26.00 To 35.00
Ski Country, Coyote Family	22.00 To 27.00
Ski Country, Dove	35.00
Ski Country, Duck, American Widgeon	13.00 To 27.00
Ski Country, Duck, Blue Teal	45.00
Ski Country, Duck, King Eider	28.00
Ski Country, Duck, Mallard	36.00 To 50.00
Ski Country, Duck, Mallard Family	36.00 To 40.00
Ski Country, Duck, Merganzer	30.00
Ski Country, Duck, Pintail	19.00 To 30.00
Ski Country, Duck, Redhead	45.00
Ski Country, Duck, Wood	125.00
Ski Country, Eagle, Easter Seal	20.00 To 33.00
Ski Country, Eagle, Harpy	85.00 To 100.00
Ski Country, Eagle, Majestic	135.00 To 165.00
Ski Country, Eagle, Mountain	100.00 To 125.00
Ski Country, Eagle, On Drum	42.00 To 55.00
Ski Country, Eagle, On Water	33.00

Miniature, Raintree, Clown No.1,
Clown No.2

Ski Country, Elephant, Circus	40.00 To 45.00
Ski Country, Elk	22.00
Ski Country, End Of Trail N	30.00 To 70.00
Ski Country, Falcon, Peregrine	17.00 To 25.00
Ski Country, Falcon, Prairie	30.00 To 35.00
Ski Country, Falcon, White	22.00 To 35.00
Ski Country, Ferret	29.00 To 33.00
Ski Country, Flycatcher	15.00 To 28.00
Ski Country, Fox, Family	15.00 To 24.00
Ski Country, Fox, On Log	150.00 To 200.00
Ski Country, Goat, Mountain	40.00 To 45.00
Ski Country, Goose, Canada	20.00 To 70.00
Ski Country, Goose, Canada Family	24.00
Ski Country, Great Spirit	11.00 To 20.00
Ski Country, Grouse, Ruffed	28.00
Ski Country, Hawk, Eagle	45.00 To 55.00
Ski Country, Hawk, Red Shoulder	45.00 To 50.00
Ski Country, Hawk, Redtail	45.00
Ski Country, Horse, Lippizaner	30.00 To 40.00
Ski Country, Horse, Palomino	29.00 To 40.00
Ski Country, Indian, Buffalo Dancer	16.00 To 24.00
Ski Country, Indian, Chief, No.I	13.00 To 19.00
Ski Country, Indian, Chief, No.2	13.00 To 19.00
Ski Country, Indian, Cigar Store	15.00 To 26.00
Ski Country, Indian, Dancers, Set Of 6	150.00 To 185.00
Ski Country, Indian, Eagle Dancer	15.00 To 30.00
Ski Country, Indian, Lookout	14.00 To 20.00
Ski Country, Indian, North American, Set Of 6	100.00 To 125.00
Ski Country, Jenny Lind, Blue	40.00
Ski Country, Jenny Lind, Yellow	100.00 To 170.00
Ski Country, Kangaroo	27.00 To 30.00
Ski Country, King Eider Duck	33.00
Ski Country, Labrador, With Duck	20.00 To 24.00
Ski Country, Labrador, With Pheasant	15.00 To 26.00
Ski Country, Lady, Blue	18.00
Ski Country, Lady, Brown	18.00
Ski Country, Lion, Circus	20.00 To 27.00
Ski Country, Meadowlark	25.00
Ski Country, Mountain Goat	45.00
Ski Country, Mrs.Cratchet	27.00 To 30.00
Ski Country, Muskie	20.00 To 22.00
Ski Country, Oriole	20.00 To 30.00
Ski Country, Osprey	100.00 To 125.00
Ski Country, Otter	14.00 To 25.00
Ski Country, Owl, Barn	20.00 To 27.00
Ski Country, Owl, Horned	100.00 To 150.00
Ski Country, Owl, Saw-Whet	32.00 To 34.00
Ski Country, Owl, Screech Family	39.00 To 85.00
Ski Country, Owl, Snow	95.00 To 100.00
Ski Country, Owl, Snow Baby	32.00 To 35.00
Ski Country, Owl, Spectacled	43.00 To 75.00
Ski Country, P.T.Barnum	16.00 To 30.00
Ski Country, Peacock	40.00 To 75.00
Ski Country, Pelican	28.00
Ski Country, Penguin	17.00 To 27.00
Ski Country, Pheasant, Fighting	22.00 To 40.00
Ski Country, Pheasant, Standing	60.00 To 70.00
Ski Country, Political Donkey	25.00
Ski Country, Political Elephant	25.00
Ski Country, Prairie Chicken	28.00 To 37.00
Ski Country, Ram, Bighorn	29.00 To 33.00
Ski Country, Ringmaster	15.00 To 23.00
Ski Country, Robin	55.00

Ski Country, Ruffed Grouse	20.00 To 28.00
Ski Country, Sage Grouse	34.00 To 40.00
Ski Country, Salmon	20.00
Ski Country, Sheep, Dall	20.00 To 28.00
Ski Country, Sheep, Desert	20.00 To 30.00
Ski Country, Skier, Blue	35.00 To 40.00
Ski Country, Skier, Red	35.00 To 40.00
Ski Country, Skunk Family	16.00 To 27.00
Ski Country, Snow Leopard	16.50 To 20.00
Ski Country, Submarine	19.00 To 24.00
Ski Country, Swallow, Barn	29.00
Ski Country, Swan, Black	27.00 To 30.00
Ski Country, Tiger, Circus	37.00 To 39.00
Ski Country, Tom Thumb	19.00 To 20.00
Ski Country, Trout, Brown	22.00 To 27.00
Ski Country, Trout, Rainbow	18.00 To 20.00
Ski Country, U.S. Ski Team	15.00 To 20.00
Ski Country, Widgeon Peregrine Falcon	15.00 To 16.00
Ski Country, Wild Turkey	100.00 To 125.00
Ski Country, Woodpecker, Gila	30.00 To 32.00
Ski Country, Woodpecker, Ivory Bill	23.00 To 28.00
W.A.Lacey, Log Rabbit, 1980	11.00
W.A.Lacey, Log Raccoon, 1980	11.00
Whiskey, Apricot Brandy, Embossed, BIMAL	8.00
Whiskey, Crown Distilleries Co., Crown & Shield, Amber, 5 1/4 In.	25.00
Whiskey, Crown Distilleries, Squat Shape, Amber	20.00
Whiskey, Crown Distilleries, 5 3/4 In.	20.00
Whiskey, Dallemand's Cream Pure Rye, Amber	8.00
Whiskey, Detrick, Pilgrim Motto, 4 1/2 In. *Illus*	27.50
Whiskey, Detrick, Prosperity Motto, 4 1/2 In. *Illus*	27.50
Whiskey, Duffy Malt, Embossed, Dug, BIMAL	13.00
Whiskey, Duffy Malt, Golden Amber, 3 3/4 In.	15.00
Whiskey, F.Stearns, Embossed, Dug, BIMAL	6.00
Whiskey, G.O.Taylor, Amber	5.00
Whiskey, Gilka, Berlin, Rectangle, Light Amber, 3 1/2 In.	16.00
Whiskey, Gordon's Dry Gin Special, Green	8.00
Whiskey, J.Rieger & Co., Kansas City, ABM, Clear	8.00
Whiskey, J.Rieger, Embossed, BIMAL	8.00
Whiskey, Jesse Moore & Co., Louisville, Ky., Light Amber, 6 1/8 In.	45.00
Whiskey, Keller Strasse Distilling, Embossed, Dug, BIMAL	10.00
Whiskey, Light Olive Yellow, 4 1/2 In.	3.00
Whiskey, M.Shaughnessy & Co., St.Louis, Amber, BIMAL	10.00
Whiskey, Manshach & Co., Philadelphia, Emerald Green, 4 1/2 In.	50.00

Miniature, Whiskey, Detrick, Pilgrim Motto, Prosperity Motto, 4 1/2 In.

Whiskey, Mt.Vernon Rye, Embossed, BIMAL 9.00
Whiskey, Old Fiddler, Fiddle Shape, Label, Amber, 1/18 Pint 10.00
Whiskey, Old Pepper, Jas.E.Pepper & Co., Light Amber, 4 5/8 In. 65.00
Whiskey, Paul Jones, Embossed, BIMAL 6.00
Whiskey, Sterling Scotch, 2-Tone, Pottery 22.00
Whiskey, Taylor & Williams, Embossed, Dug, BIMAL 4.00
Whiskey, Tonita, Embossed, Dug, BIMAL 7.00
Whiskey, Western Whiskey, Crown Distilleries, Stopper, 4 1/2 In. 25.00
Whiskey, Western Whiskey, Crown Distilleries, 5 3/4 In. 20.00
White Horse Scotch, T.W.A. 1.50
Zara Type Seal, Sea Green, 6 In. 25.00

NAILSEA, Clear With White Swags, Pint 20.00
Gemel, Clear With White Stripes, 7 1/2 In. 30.00

Nursing bottles were first used in the second half of the 19th century.
They are easily identified by the unique shape and the measuring units that
are often marked on the sides.

NURSING, American Feeding Bottle, Turtle, Light Aqua 15.00
American Oval Feeder, Turtle Shape 19.00
Babe's Companion 35.00
Baby's Delight 35.00
Best, Patent September 1, 1891 .... 35.00
Blown, Aqua, 9 In. 40.00
Blown, Light Yellow Green, 7 1/2 In. 35.00
Blown, White, Blue And Cranberry Looping, 6 1/4 In. 65.00
Burr's, Pat.Nov.26, 1872, 5 1/2 In. 25.00
Eagle, Acme, & Diamond Sparkler, Set Of 3 .... 40.00 To 60.00
Embossed Cat 8.00
Embossed Dog 8.00
Embossed Frog & Rabbits, 1 To 8 Ounce, Embossed Vertically 7.50
Embossed Rabbits 8.00
Franklin Nurser, Clear 8.00
Good Luck, Embossed Horseshoe, Turtle Shape, Clear 18.00
Graduated Nursing Bottle, SCA, 6 1/2 In. 9.00
Green, 14 Ribs 125.00
Hagerty Bros. & Co., New York, Aqua, 5 1/2 In. 15.00
Harvest Feeder, Compliments I.W.Harper, Kentucky, Jug 35.00
Little Papoose Nurser 150.00
Oval American Feeder, The, Clear, 8 Ounce 14.00
Owl Drug 25.00
Rabbit 5.00
Ribbed Teardrop Shape, Open Pontil, Lies Flat, Aqua 35.00
Submarine, Blown, C.1850 .... 105.00
Sunshine Dairy, Red Pyro, Picture Of Baby, Cap, Nipple, 8 Ounce 3.00
Teddy's Pet Nurser, Testimony Ceremony 25.00
Tube Feeder, Embossed Crystal, 18-Star Shield, Aqua 75.00

OBR, Balloon, 1969 .... 6.00 To 9.00
Caboose, 1973 .... 17.00
Eastern Kentucky University, 1974 .... 18.00
Fifth Avenue Bus, 1971 .... 15.00
Football Player, Nebraska 15.00
Georgia Tech 15.00
Georgia University 15.00
Green Bay Packers 13.00
Hockey Player, 1971 .... 11.00
Locomotive, General Sherman, 1974 .... 13.00 To 17.50
Missouri University 20.00
Music City Guitar 17.00
NFL Football 15.00
Ohio State 11.00
Pierce Arrow, 1969 .... 21.00 To 25.00

Prairie Wagon, 1969 .... 8.00 To 14.00
River Queen, Gold, 1969 .... 15.00 To 20.00
River Queen, 1967 .... 7.00 To 12.00
Santa Maria, 1971 .... 14.00
Titanic, 1976 .... 32.00 To 40.00
Trolley Car 32.00
W.C.Fields, Bank Dick, 1976 .... 10.00 To 14.00
W.C.Fields, Top Hat, 1976 .... 15.00

OIL, Huffman Mfg.Co., The, Spout, Clear, Quart 7.00
Macassar, Aqua 15.00

OLD BARDSTOWN, Affirm & Alydar, 1980 .... 150.00
Bulldog, 1 3/4 Liter, 1980 .... 125.00
Bulldog, 750 Ml, 1980 .... 50.00
Christmas Card .... 12.00 To 14.00
Delta Queen, 1980 .... 47.00
Fighting Gamecock, Pair, 1980 .... 150.00
Football Player 36.00
Foster Brooks, 1978 .... 32.00 To 40.00
Georgia Bulldog 64.00
Georgia Bulldog, 1 3/4 Liter 154.00
Horse, Citation, 1979 .... 65.00 To 74.00
Iron Worker, 1978 .... 33.00 To 37.00
Keg, With Stand, 1/2 Gallon, 1977 .... 27.00
Keg, With Stand, Gallon, 1977 .... 37.00
Kentucky Colonel, No.1, 1978 .... 29.00 To 39.00
Kentucky Colonel, No.2, 1979 .... 54.00
Kentucky Derby, 1977 .... 14.00 To 15.00
Razorback Hog, 1980 .... 48.00
Surface Miner, 1978 .... 34.00 To 36.00
Tiger, 1980 .... 38.00
Trucker, 1978 .... 35.00 To 38.00
Wildcat No.1, 1978 .... 47.00
Wildcat No.2, 1979 .... 37.00
Wildcat No.3, 1980 .... 135.00

OLD CHARTER, Decanter, Gold 5.00

OLD COMMONWEALTH, Alabama National Champ 60.00
Chief Illini, 1979 .... 55.00
Coal Miner With Lump Of Coal, No.3, 1977 .... 37.00
Coal Miner With Pick, No.2, 1976 .... 36.00
Coal Miner, Lunch Time, No.4, 1980 ....Color 43.00
Coal Miner, 1975 .... 133.00 To 150.00
Coins Of Ireland .... 15.00 To 18.00
Dogs Of Ireland, 1980 .... 21.00
Fireman, Cumberland Valley, 1976 .... 48.00
Fireman, Heroic 41.00
Fireman, Valiant Volunteer, 1980 .... 48.00
Fisherman 46.00
Golden Retriever, 1979 .... 42.00
Houston University, 1977 .... 28.00
Hunter, Waterfowler, No.1 .... 41.00
Hunter, Waterfowler, No.2, 1980 ....Color 44.00
Kentucky Peach Bowl, 1977 .... 30.00
Leprechaun, 1980 ....Color 50.00
Louisville National Champs 22.00
Lumberjack, 1979 ....Illus 45.00
Maryland Terps, 1977 .... 28.00
North Carolina, 1975 .... 28.00
Princeton University, 1976 .... 26.00
Sons Of Erin II, 1978 .... 19.00
Thoroughbreds, 1977 .... 36.00

Old Commonwealth, Lumberjack, 1979
(See Page 197)

U.S.C.Trojan Centennial, 1980	50.00
Walking Horse, 1977	36.00
Western Logger	52.00
OLD CROW, Car, Bugatti Royale, 1974	220.00
Chess Rug	75.00
Chess Set, Rug	75.00
Chess Set, 32 Piece	300.00
Chessman, Bishop, Dark	9.00
Chessman, Bishop, Light	9.00
Chessman, King, Dark	9.00
Chessman, King, Light	9.00
Chessman, Knight, Dark	9.00
Chessman, Pawn, Dark	12.00 To 15.00
Chessman, Pawn, Light	15.00 To 22.00
Chessman, Queen, Dark	9.00
Chessman, Queen, Light	9.00 To 12.00
Chessman, Rook, Dark	9.00
Chessman, Rook, Light	9.00 To 12.00
Crow, Royal Doulton	47.00
Crow, 1974, Red Vest	11.00
OLD FITZGERALD, America's Cup, 1970	21.00
American Sons, 1976	13.00
Birmingham, 1972	45.00
Birmingham, 2nd Edition	40.00
Blarney, 1970	11.00
Cabin Still, Anniversary, 1959	11.00
Cabin Still, Anniversary, 1960	10.00
Cabin Still, Bourbon, 1963	6.00
Cabin Still, Copper Still, 1957	6.00
Cabin Still, Deer Browsing, 1967	7.00
Cabin Still, Deer, Double Image	14.00
Cabin Still, Demijohn	10.00
Cabin Still, Diamond, 1961	10.00
Cabin Still, Diamond, 1970	6.00
Cabin Still, Dog, 1958, Left	14.00
Cabin Still, Dog, 1965, Right	8.00 To 10.00
Cabin Still, Ducks Unlimited, 1972	47.00
Cabin Still, Ducks Unlimited, 1973	42.00
Cabin Still, Early American, 1970	4.00
Cabin Still, Fish, Double Image	14.00
Cabin Still, Fish, 1969	5.00
Cabin Still, Gold Coaster, 1955	13.00

Cabin Still, Hillbilly, Dull Finish, Fifth	10.00
Cabin Still, Hillbilly, Fishing, Quart	95.00
Cabin Still, Hillbilly, Gallon	752.00
Cabin Still, Hillbilly, Pint	35.00
Cabin Still, Hillbilly, Quart	35.00
Cabin Still, Hillbilly, Shiny Finish, Fifth	14.00
Cabin Still, Hospitality	5.00
Cabin Still, Mallards	12.00
Cabin Still, Pheasant, 1956	6.00
Cabin Still, Pheasants Rising, 1964	12.00
Cabin Still, Quail, 1972	6.00
Candlelite, 1955	18.00
Candlelite, 1961	11.00
Classic, 1972	6.00
Colonial, 1969	5.00
Crown, 1957	9.00
Davidson, North Carolina, 1972	37.00
Diamond, 1959	10.00
Double Candlelite, 1956	8.00
Eagle, 1973	4.00
Executive, 1960	7.00
Flagship, 1967	5.00
Fleur-De-Lis, 1962	5.00 To 10.00
Florentine, 1961	9.00
Four Seasons, 1964	5.00
Geese, 1970	6.00
Gold Coaster	12.00 To 13.00
Gold Web, 1953	16.00
Golden Bough, 1970	6.00
Hospitality, 1958	5.00
Hostess, 1977	5.00
Huntington, West Virginia, 1971	25.00 To 28.00
Illinois, 1972	17.00
Irish Charm, 1977	13.00
Irish Counties, 1973	14.00
Irish Luck, 1972	16.00
Irish Patriots, 1971	10.00 To 13.00
Irish Wish, 1975	12.00 To 15.00
Jewel, 1951	8.00
L.S.U., 1970	27.00
Leprechaun, Plase God, 1968	23.00
Leprechaun, Prase Be, 1968	23.00
Lexington, 1968	6.00
Man Of War, 1969	6.00
Memphis, 1969	11.00 To 14.00
Monticello, 1968	4.00 To 5.00
Nebraska, 1971	34.00
Nebraska, 1972	25.00
Ohio State, 1970	15.00 To 17.00
Old Cabin Still, 1958	12.00
Old Cabin Still, 1972	50.00
Old Cabin Still, 1973	45.00
Old Ironsides	5.00
Old Monterey, 1970	*Illus* 14.00
Pheasant, 1972	5.00
Pilgrim Landing, 1970	15.00
Ram, Bighorn, 1971	5.00
Richwood, West Virginia, 1971	30.00 To 35.00
Rip Van Winkle, 1971	*Illus* 45.00
Songs Of Ireland, 1969	15.00
Sons Of Erin, 1969	13.00 To 15.00
South Carolina, 1970	13.00
Texas University, 1971	16.00

(See Page 199)

Old Fitzgerald, Old Monterey, 1970   Old Fitzgerald, Rip Van Winkle, 1971

Tournament, 1963	8.00
Tree Of Life, 1964	5.00
Venetian, 1966	4.00
Vermont, 1970	17.00
Virginia, 1972	17.00
West Virginia Forest Festival, 1973	20.00
OLD HICKORY, Old Hickory	18.00
OLD MR.BOSTON, Amvet, Convention, Iowa, 1975	11.00
Anthony Wayne, 1970	12.00
Assyrian Convention, 1975	18.00
Bart Starr No.15	15.00
Bell, Freedom	14.00
Berkeley, West Virginia	24.00
Bingo In Illinois, 1974	14.00
Black Hills Motor Classic, 1976	22.00
Clown Head, Signature, 1974	29.00
Clown Head, 1973	18.00
Cog Railway, 1978	16.00
Concord Coach, 1976	18.00
Dan Patch, 1970	15.00
Dan Patch, 1973	12.00
Daniel Webster Cabin, 1977	18.00
Deadwood, South Dakota, 1975	14.00
Eagle Convention, Atlanta, 1972	15.00
Eagle Convention, Boston, 1971	9.00 To 12.00
Eagle Convention, 1975	12.00
Eagle Convention, 1976	12.00
Elkins, West Virginia, Stump, 1975	21.00
Fire Engine	19.00
Green Bay No.87	11.00
Greensboro Open, 1976, Golf Bag	40.00
Greensboro Open, 1978, Golf Shoe	40.00
Guitar, Music City, 1968	15.00 To 17.00
Illinois State Capitol	13.00
Lamplighter	12.00
Lincoln Rider, 1972	10.00
Lion, Sitting	16.00
Lion, Sitting, With Signature	20.00
Miss Madison, Boat, 1973	19.00
Miss Nebraska	18.00
Mississippi Bicentennial, 1976	14.00
Molly Pitcher, 1975	9.00

Monticello, 1974 .... 13.00
Mooseheart, 1972 .... 11.00 To 13.00
Nathan Hale, 1975 .... 10.00 To 12.00
Nebraska Czechs 15.00
Nebraska No.1, Gold, 1970 .... 13.00
New Hampshire Frigate, 1975 .... 13.00
New Hampshire Independence, 1976 .... 16.00
New Hampshire Liquor Commission, 1974 .... 15.00
Paul Bunyan, 1971 .... 7.00
Paul Revere, 1973 .... 11.00
Polish American Legion, 1975 .... 19.00
President Inaugural, 1953 .... 15.00
Prestige Bookend, 1970 .... 7.00
Race Car No.9 .... 21.00
Red Dog Dan 11.00
Sherry Pitcher 4.00
Ship Lantern 18.00
Shriner AAONMS Camel, 1975 .... 14.00 To 17.00
Shriner With Star 20.00
Shriner With Triangle 20.00
Shriner, Betash Temple 25.00
Steelhead Trout, 1976 .... 16.00
Tennessee Centennial 12.00
Town Crier, 1976 .... 12.00
Venus 15.00
West Virginia National Guard 35.00
York, Nebraska 14.00

OLD RIP VAN WINKLE, Bay Colony, 1975 .... 13.00
Cardinal, 1974 .... 14.00
Colonial Virginia, 1974 .... 12.00
Kentucky Sportsman, 1973 .... 25.00
Kentucky University Wildcat, 1974 .... 30.00
New Jersey Bicentennial, 1975 .... 16.00
New York Bicentennial, 1975 .... 16.00
Rip Van Winkle, No.1, 1975 .... 47.00
Rip Van Winkle, No.2, 1975 .... 35.00
Rip Van Winkle, No.3, 1977 .... 33.00
Sanford, North Carolina, 1974 .... 14.00

PEPPER SAUCE, Aqua, 8 3/4 In. 25.00
Beehive, Aqua 8.00
Cathedral 39.50
Cathedral, Aqua 20.00
Cathedral, C. & Dl., New York 35.00
Cathedral, Green Aqua 25.00
Cathedral, Iron Pontil, Hexagonal, Blue Aqua, 8 1/2 In. 49.00
Cathedral, Lime Green, 7 In. 55.00
Cathedral, Rolled Lip, Open Pontil, Aqua, 6 1/2 In. 10.00
Cathedral, 20 Rings, Aqua 6.00
Cathedral, 4-Sided, Open Pontil, Aqua 25.00
Cathedral, 6-Sided, Aqua 25.00
Diamond Packing Co., Bridgeton, N.J., Aqua 8.00
Durkee's, Beehive Shape, Blue Green 40.00
Durkee's, Light Blue 22.00
Emerald Green .... 18.00 To 25.00
G.Co., Pat.Sept.28, 1875, Aqua 28.00
Partial Neck Label, Light Green 24.00
Ridgy, Blue Green 24.00
Ridgy, Patent Applied For, S. & P., Emerald Green 25.00
Roped Corners, Stars On 3 Sides, Rolled Lip, OP, 5 3/4 In. 42.00
S. & P., Spiral, Kelly Green 17.00
Teal 17.00

W.K.Lewis, 8-Sided, Open Pontil, Aqua 50.00
Wells Miller Provost, Open Pontil, 8 Rounded Panels, Aqua 45.00
8 Lobed Sides, 3 Rings On Neck, Aqua, 8 In. 15.00
8-Sided, 3 Neck Rings, Aqua 30.00

PEPSI COLA, Anderson Junior College 3.00
Bicentennial 5.00
Birmingham, Alabama, Amber 70.00
Cincinnati Reds 6.00
Clemson Tigers 3.00
Dallas Cowboys 6.00
East Tennessee Street 6.00
Emerald Green, 12 Ounce 12.00
Escambia Bottling Co., Pensacola, Fla., Hutchinson .... 450.00 To 600.00
Fiesta Bowl, 1972 .... 9.00
Florida Rowdies 8.00
Furman 3.00
Iowa Vs. Iowa State 3.00
Kentucky, 1974-76 .... 3.00
Macon 4.00
Nebraska University 5.00
New Bern, N.C., Amber 35.00
North Carolina, Straight-Sided 6.00
Pepsi Escambia, Pensacola, Florida 35.00
Richmond, Va., Embossed On Each Of 8 Panels, Green 35.00
St.Louis Blues 5.00
Virginia Presidents 4.00
Washington, D.C., Amber 35.00
75th Anniversary 3.00

PERFUME, see also Cologne; Scent
PERFUME, Art Deco, Tapering Square, Frosted Figural Nudes & Geometrics 30.00
Bell Shape, Clear 15.00
Blue Opaque Ribbons, Alternate White Latticinio, 3 1/4 In. 50.00
Colgate & Co.Perfumers, Amber, 7 1/4 In. 6.00
Corset Shape, Pewter Cap, C.1860, Purple, Sandwich, 2 3/4 In. 50.00
Court Jester, Clear 50.00
Crown Perfumery, London, Ground Crown Stopper, Palmer Green 10.00
Daphene Powder Sachet, California, Cap, Label, Contents 65.00
Dunmore, Basket Weave, Handled, Open Pontil 22.00
Ed.Pinaud, Paris, Embossed Flowerbasket, SCA, 6 3/4 In. 6.00
Freeman The Perfumer, Cincinnati, Clear Stopper 8.50
G.W.Laird, N.Y., Embossed, Milk Glass, 5 In. .... 5.00 To 8.00
Genuine Essence, Open Pontil, Aqua 15.00
Globular, Blown, Blue Swirls, White Cased Interior, 3 3/8 In. 45.00
Harmony Of Boston, SCA, 6 In. 3.00
Heart Shape, Black Opaque, 3 1/2 In. 15.00
Heather Bloom Toilet Water, Koken's Barber Supply, Crown Stopper 15.00
Japanese Perfumes, Ground Stopper, Lady & Fan, Peacock Blue .... Illus 35.00
Lalique, Guerlain, Gray Enamel, Signed, 4 1/4 In. .... Illus 1100.00
Lalique, Intaglio, Blue Enamel, Signed, 9 1/2 In. .... Illus 900.00
Larsen Cognac, Genuine Limoges China, Stopper 12.50
Memorial Hall, Embossed Building In Oval, 1876, 6 In. 135.00
PERFUME, MINIATURE, see Miniature, Perfume
Mirror Front, Clear, 4 1/2 In. .... Illus 12.50
Palmer's, Deep Green, 7 In. 12.00
Palmer's, Green, 5 1/4 In. 4.00
Richard Hudnut, 2 7/8 In. 4.00
Seahorse Scent Bottle, White Stripes, Rigaree, Clear 65.00
Seahorse, McKearin Plate 101 No.2 .... 60.00
Seely Mfg. Co., Detroit, Clear Stopper 10.00
Strawberry Point Hearts, Rimmed In Gilt, Stopper, 4 5/8 In. 7.50

PICKLE, Barrel, 10 Hoops, Widemouth, Olive Green, 8 In. 18.00

Perfume, Lalique, Guerlain, Gray
Enamel, Signed, 4 1/4 In.

Perfume, Lalique, Intaglio, Blue
Enamel, Signed, 9 1/2 In.

Perfume, Mirror Front, Clear, 4 1/2 In.

Bunker Hill, Embossed Monument, Yellow Amber, Round, Pint	10.00
Cabbage Rose, Milk Glass	16.00
Cathedral Arches, Crosses, Green, Quart	80.00
Cathedral Arches, Florals Above Arches, 8-Sided, Green, 1/2 Pint	55.00
Cathedral Arches, Green, 11 1/2 In.	395.00
Cathedral Arches, Laid-On Ring, Clamshell, Green, 1/2 Pint	150.00
Cathedral Arches, R.& F. Atmore, Philadelphia, Embossed, Blue	175.00
Cathedral Arches, Rolled Lip, Amethyst, 13 3/4 In.	29.50
Cathedral Arches, Swirls, Branches, & Leaves, Green, 1/2 Gallon	140.00
Cathedral Arches, 4 Different Designs, C.1821, Aqua, Pint	175.00
Cathedral Arches, 4-Sided, Embossed Fleur-De-Lis, Aqua, Quart	85.00
Cathedral Arches, 8-Sided, Chain Link Design, Aqua, Quart	135.00
Cathedral, Aqua, 7 In.	45.00
Cathedral, Aqua, 9 In.	55.00
Cathedral, Aqua, 9 1/2 In. ....Color	100.00
Cathedral, Aqua, 12 In.	90.00
Cathedral, Aqua, 13 In.	47.00
Cathedral, Bulb Neck, Rolled Lip, 4-Sided, OP, 8 3/4 In.	45.00
Cathedral, Clock Type, Medium Green, 13 3/4 In.	400.00
Cathedral, Deep Aqua, 11 1/2 In.	85.00
Cathedral, Floral Over Plain Arch, Iron Pontil, Green, 12 In.	195.00
Cathedral, Fluted Panel 3 Sides, Pontil, Greenish Aqua, 3/4 Pint	69.50
Cathedral, Gherkins, Wm.Davis, Boston, 6-Sided, Metal Label	350.00
Cathedral, Green Aqua, Quart	60.00
Cathedral, Green, 12 In.	200.00
Cathedral, Green, 13 In.	67.00
Cathedral, Hatmore, Open Pontil	350.00
Cathedral, Iron Pontil, Aqua, 3 1/4 X 3 1/4 X 10 In.	200.00
Cathedral, Iron Pontil, Dark Aqua, 8 In.	80.00
Cathedral, Iron Pontil, Deep Aqua, 11 1/2 In.	175.00
Cathedral, Iron Pontil, Medium Green, 12 In.	125.00
Cathedral, Kemp Day, New York, 6-Sided, Embossed, Aqua, 13 In.	105.00
Cathedral, Lattice Design On 4 Sides, Aqua	59.50
Cathedral, Light Green, 11 1/2 In.	145.00
Cathedral, Medium Green, 9 1/4 In.	150.00
Cathedral, Yarnall Bros. On 1 Panel, Gallon	275.00
Cathedral, Yellow Green, 13 3/4 In.	40.00
Cathedral, 4-Sided, 16 Vertical Petals, Iron Pontil, 1/2 Gallon	59.50

Cathedral, 6-Sided, Aqua, 3/4 Gallon 64.50
Chace & Duncan, N.Y., Base Embossed, Barrel Shape 25.00
Cross-Hatched Panels, Bulb Neck, 6 1/2 In. 30.00
Crosse & Blackwell, London, Label, Square, Clear 3.00
Dove With Olive Branch On Shoulder, Aqua, 9 In. 25.00
Embossed, R. & F.Atmore, Aqua, 11 In. 165.00
Fortnum & Mason, Est.1801, Piccadilly, London, Cylinder, Quart 14.50
Globe, St.Louis, Label, Aqua, 1/2 Gallon 10.00
Goofus Glass, 7 In. 8.00
Grapes, Light Aqua, 9 1/2 In. 30.00
Heinz & Noble, Pittsburgh, Indented Panel, Aqua, 2 1/8 X 7 1/2 In. 100.00
Heinz, Clear, 7 1/2 In. ....Color 8.00
Indented Ovals, Vines Around, Iron Pontil, Aqua, 11 In. 175.00
J.J.W.Peter's Hamburg, Oval, Dog Trademark On Bottom, Red Amber 25.00
New England, Free-Blown, Open Pontil, Large Mouth, Green, 9 3/4 In. 600.00
Paneled With Floral Desing, 6-Sided, Aqua, 18 In. 250.00
S.Wardell, San Francisco, Graphite Pontil, Aqua, 1/4 Pint 200.00
Ship, Waves, & Seagulls, Goofus Glass 65.00
Skilton Foote & Co., Bunker Hill, Embossed Monument, Amber 12.50
Skilton Foote & Co., Bunker Hill, Light Amber, 8 In. 30.00
Spatter Milk Glass, 15 In. 110.00
Squire Pickles, Sun-Colored Amethyst, 7 1/2 In. ....Illus 8.00
Statue Of Liberty, Goofus Glass 60.00
Tulip, Open Pontil, Aqua, Small 125.00
Vasiform, Floral Design, Aqua, Gallon 39.50
W.M.& P., N.Y., Embossed, Open Pontil, 7 1/2 In. 100.00
W.Numsen & Son, Baltimore, Embossed, Fluted Shoulder, Aqua, 9 In. 285.00
Whitney Glass Works, 6-Sided, Aqua, 12 In. 40.00
Wm.Underwood & Co., Boston, Aqua, 32 Ounce 75.00
Wreath Paneled, 2 Quart 110.00
1 Panel Embossed Vertically, Square, Gallon 275.00
4-Sided, Aqua, Pint 59.50
8 Flattened Petals At Throat, Double Lattice Design, Aqua, Pint 165.00
8 Rounded Panels, Iron Pontil, Aqua, 7 1/2 In. 65.00

*Poison bottles were usually made with raised designs so the user could feel
the danger in the dark. The most interesting poison bottles were made from
the 1870s to the 1930s.*

POISON, A.B.M., Tinct.Iodine, Embossed Skull & Crossbones, Stopper, Amber 6.00
Aqua, 4 1/2 In. ....Illus 45.00
Carbolic Acid, Cobalt Blue 25.00
Chestnut Flask, Raised Design, 1/2 Post, 5 1/4 In. 45.00
Coffin, Amber 2.00

Pickle, Squire Pickles,
Sun-Colored Amethyst, 7 1/2 In.

Poison, Aqua, 4 1/2 In.

Coffin, Cobalt, 3 1/2 In. 25.00
Coffin, Labeled, Cobalt Blue 50.00
Coffin, Partial Label, ABM, Cobalt Blue 25.00
Dicks Ant Destroyer, Finlay Dicks & Co., New Orleans 30.00
Fishscale Design, Folded Lip, Sapphire Blue, 5 1/2 In. 160.00
Front & Back Labels, Embossed Twice, Cork, Cardboard 10.00
Gift Flask, 6-Sided, Emerald, 2 Skulls, 6 In. 25.00
Golden Amber, 2 Panels, Ridges On 3 Corners, Pint 10.00
John M.Frost, Buffalo, N.Y., Round, Clear, 2 1/2 In. 3.00
Laudanum, McCormick & Co., Baltimore, 3-Sided, Label, 4 In. 25.00
Leaven's English Vermin Destroyer, Oval, Aqua, 5 1/4 In. 75.00
Leavin's English Vermin Destroyer, Open Pontil, Oval, Aqua, 9 In. ... 175.00
Melvin Badger Apothecaries, Boston, 8-Sided, Cobalt Blue, 5 1/2 In. 18.00
Mulford, On Base, Skull & Crossbones, Cobalt Blue 15.00
Norwood's Insect Liquid, Full Label, Open Pontil 20.00
Not To Be Taken, Embossed, Cobalt, 6-Sided, 3 1/2 In. .... 7.00 To 18.00
Not To Be Taken, Oval, Amber 12.00
Not To Be Taken, Star Figures, 6-Sided, Cobalt Blue, 3 In. 12.50
Owl Drug Co., Carbolic Acid Label, Cobalt Blue 65.00
Owl Drug Co., Cobalt Blue, 3 1/4 In. 15.00
Owl Drug Co., Embossed Owl, Deep Cobalt Blue, Triangular, 4 3/4 In. 65.00
Owl Drug Co., Owl With Mortar & Pestle, 3-Sided, Cobalt Blue, Quart 375.00
Paneled, Chinese Lettering Front & Back, Cobalt Blue, 7 In. 125.00
Quick Death Insecticide 2.00
Quilted, Cobalt Blue, 4 In. 8.00
Rectangular, Labeled, Embossed, Cobalt Blue 20.00
Skull & Crossbones, Amber 3.00
Skull, Cobalt 325.00
Triangle, Cobalt Blue, Quart 45.00
Triloids, Cobalt, 3 1/2 In. ....*Illus* 8.00
Triloids, Label & Contents, Cobalt Blue 8.00
Triloids, Triangular, Cobalt Blue 5.00
Triloids, 3 Labels, Cobalt Blue 13.00
Wyeth, Cobalt 10.00
Wyeth, Cylinder, Amber 20.00
Wyeth, Partial Label, Wooden Top, ABM, Cobalt Blue, Cylinder 15.00
3-Sided, Amber 3.50
3-Sided, Cobalt Blue 6.00

POTTER'S, Canoe 38.00
 Clydesdale 40.00
 Clydesdale Family 42.00
 Dog Sled 130.00
 Gold Panner 40.00

Poison, Triloids, Cobalt, 3 1/2 In.

Pottery, Greybeard, Whiskey, 7 1/2 In.

Pottery, Kintore Scotch, 7 1/2 In.

Goose Family	45.00
Indian Plaque	40.00
Polar Bear	26.00
Polar Bear Cubs	35.00
POTTERY, As You Like It Horseradish, 2-Tone	5.00
Ballantine Scotch	15.00
Brookfield Rye 1867, Canteen Shape, Left-Handled, Brown Glaze	75.00
Glen Forest Sour Mash, St.Louis, Gold Trim, Quart	22.00
Greybeard, Whiskey, 7 1/2 In. *Illus*	25.00
Hallenbeck & Messier, Albany, N.Y., Embossed Stag's Head On Reverse	15.00
Happy Days Famous Rye, Professors Drinking, Quart	60.00
Hoffman House Pure Rye	25.00
Holloway's Ointment For Cure Of Scrofula	20.00
Horse Head Malt Syrup, Stenciled, Mug	35.00
Ink, Lovatt & Lovatt Ltd., Debossed, Dark Brown, 4 3/4 In.	12.00
Ink, Rolled Lip, Round	5.00
Jug, Owensboro Club Bourbon, Owensboro, Kentucky	60.00
Kintore Scotch, 7 1/2 In. *Illus*	30.00
Klein Bros., Cincinnati, Keystone Rye, Painted Flowers, Quart	60.00
POTTERY, MINIATURE, see Miniature, Pottery	
Moutard's Maille, Paris, Sarreguemines	10.00
Mug, Bovox Makes Real Strength, Dragon Handle, Embossed Dragon	20.00
Mug, Knudsen's Buttermilk, Blue Bands, Black Lettering	40.00
Mug, Old Colony Brewing Co.	10.00
O'Keefe's Pure Malt Whiskey, Blue Transfer, Oswego, N.Y., Quart	60.00
Radium Ore Revigorator, Brass Faucet & Lid, Blue & Cream Glaze	75.00
The Fleischman Co., Cobalt Blue Glaze, Quart	65.00
PURPLE POWER, Wildcat On Basketball	9.00
Wildcat On Football	9.00
Wildcat Walking	19.00
ROYAL DOULTON, Crow, Old Crow	57.00
Jug, Special Best Procurable, Hudson Bay Co., Quart	150.00
RYNBENDE CHERRY, Blown, Fox	7.50
Blown, Goose	7.50
Blown, Hare	7.50
Blown, Owl	7.50
Blown, Swan	7.50
RYNBENDE DELFT URN, Apricot	6.00
SANDWICH GLASS, see Cologne; Perfume; Scent	

SARSAPARILLA, A.H.Bull, Extract Of Sarsaparilla, Hartford, OP, 7 In. 35.00
A.H.Bull, Extract Of, Hartford, Conn., OP, Aqua, 6 In. 15.00
Allen Co., Woodfords, Maine, Aqua 13.00
Ayer's, Open Pontil 45.00
Bristol's Extract, Buffalo, Open Pontil, Aqua, 5 1/2 In. 50.00
Burr & Waters, Buffalo, N.Y., Pottery, Gray Salt Glaze 100.00
Corwitz, Aqua 22.00
Dalton's, & Nerve Tonic 8.00
Dana's, Aqua, 9 In. .... 2.00 To 5.00
Dr. Copper's 20.00
Dr. Greene's, Full Label 28.00
Dr.Belding's Wild Cherry, Aqua, 9 1/4 In. 45.00
Dr.F.A.Wood's 15.00
Dr.Guysott's Yellow Dock 3.00
Dr.Ira Baker's Honduras, Aqua, 11 In. 40.00
Dr.Miles' Wine, Aqua 28.00
Dr.Townsend's, Albany, N.Y., Blue-Green, 3/4 Quart .... 110.00 To 220.00
Dr.Townsend's, Albany, N.Y., Green 65.00
Dr.Townsend's, Albany, N.Y., No.1, Light Yellow 115.00
Dr.Townsend's, Albany, N.Y., Square, Olive Green, 9 1/2 In. 100.00
Dr.Townsend's, Albany, New York, Olive Green 55.00
Dr.Townsend's, Iron Pontil, Bright Green 60.00
Dr.Townsend's, Iron Pontil, Emerald Green 130.00
Dr.Townsend's, Iron Pontil, Green .... 150.00 To 160.00
Dr.Townsend's, Iron Pontil, Teal Blue 185.00
Dr.Townsend's, N.Y., Square, Iron Pontil, Green, 9 1/2 In. 90.00
Dr.Townsend's, Olive Amber, 3/4 Quart 50.00
Edward Wilder & Co., Log Cabin 175.00
Emerson's 35.00
F.Brown Sarsaparilla & Tomato Bitters, Open Pontil, Aqua 110.00
Foley's, Chicago, BIMAL, Labeled, Contents, Red Amber 35.00
Gooch's, Blue 150.00
Graefenberg Compound, New York, Aqua 40.00
Guysott's, Iron Pontil, Whittled, Deep Aqua 140.00
H.T.Helmbold's Genuine Preparation, Label, Aqua, 6 1/4 In. 95.00
Hood's, London, 5 1/2 In. 15.00
Hurd's, Aqua 50.00
J.L.Kelley & Co., Open Pontil, Aqua 265.00
J.L.Kelley & Co.Chemists, Portland, Me., Pontil, 7 3/4 In. 215.00
John Bull, Extract Of, Aqua 20.00
John Bull, Extract Of, Louisville, Ky., Green 35.00
John Bull, Extract, Louisville, Ky., Iron Pontil, Light Blue 225.00
Joy's, The Edwin W.Joy Co., San Francisco 9.00
Mack's 290.00
Merchants, Iron Pontil, Green 140.00
Merchants, Open Pontil, Green 150.00
Primley's, Milwaukee 25.00
Recamier, Amber 28.00
Riker's Compound, Rectangle, Aqua 20.00
Sand's Genuine, Rectangular, New York, Quart, 10 In. 85.00
Sand's, N.Y., Open Pontil, Aqua, 6 In. .... 28.00 To 42.00
Sawyers Eclipse, Aqua 32.00
Skoda's .... 25.00 To 28.00
Skoda's, Light Amber 26.00
Spanish, Embossed T.H.Taylor, Brattleboro, Vt., OP, Aqua 65.00
Taylor's, Root Beer, 4 3/4 In. 20.00
Wetherell's, Exeter, Aqua 38.00
Yagers, Clear 30.00

SCENT, see also Cologne; Perfume
SCENT, Blown, Applied Rigaree, 2 5/8 In. 40.00
Blown, Swirled Ribs, Flattened Blob, 1 3/4 In. 55.00
Blown, Swirled Ribs, 3 1/4 In. 25.00
Blown, White Looping, Coiled, Applied Rigaree, 2 7/8 In. 95.00

Blown, White Looping, 2 3/8 In.	35.00
Shield Shape, Sunburst, Sapphire Blue, 2 3/4 In.	90.00
Swirled Ribs, Violet Cobalt, 2 3/8 In.	40.00

SEAL, A.S.C.R., 3-Piece Mold, Open Pontil	80.00
Jos.Ridson 1818, Black, McK Plate 221, No.II, 10 In.	450.00
M.Daniel, Open Pontil, 3-Piece Mold, Black Glass, 10 1/2 In.	125.00

SELTZER, see also Mineral Water

SELTZER, Atoka Ice & Power Co., Atoka, New Mexico	75.00
Brooklyn, N.Y., Fluted, Green	35.00
Brooklyn, N.Y., Round, Green	30.00
Coca-Cola, Winona, Minnesota, Emerald Green	27.50
Connecticut, Blue	19.50
Hathorn Spring, Saratoga, N.Y., Amber, Quart	12.00
J.L.McCarthy & Perry, No Siphon	100.00
J.L.McCarthy, Mercantile Co., O.K.City	100.00
J.L.McCarthy, Perry	100.00
Kinney Bottling Works, McCurtain, Oklahoma	90.00
Larvex, Cobalt Blue, 7 1/2 In. *Color*	8.00
New Jersey, Blue	19.50
New York, Blue	19.50
Norwalk, Connecticut, Fluted, Green	35.00
Pittsburgh, Pa., Embossed, Round	35.00
Poteau Bottling Works, Poteau	80.00
Red Dragon, Washington, D.C., 6-Sided, Amber, 3 In.	4.00
Water, Saratoga, Blue-Green, Embossed Shoulder, Pint	40.00

SHOE POLISH, Bixby, Aqua	3.00
Bixby, Colorful Label, Box, Contents, Applicator	7.00
Cylindrical Body, Sheared Top, Open Pontil, Olive Amber	80.00
Dark Amber, Pontil, 1 7/8 X 4 7/8 In.	65.00
Olive Amber, Pontil, 5 In.	55.00
Osborn Polish, Black Glass, Open Pontil	125.00
Race & Sheldon's Magic Waterproof Boot Polish, OP, Teal	350.00
Shulife For Shoes, Amber, Round	8.00
Square, Aqua, 4 In.	25.00
Square, Blacking, Aqua, 4 1/2 In.	25.00
Trade Klenzo Mark, Raven Gloss Mfg.Co., Aqua, 3 1/3 In.	5.00

SICILIAN GOLD, David	18.00
Guard, Gallon	80.00
Moses	19.00
Pieta	24.00

SKI COUNTRY, American Elk	90.00
Antelope, Wyoming, 1979	40.00 To 65.00
Arizona Ceremonial Eagle Dancer, 1978 *Illus*	110.00
Badger	55.00 To 64.00
Baltimore Oriole, 1975	33.00 To 60.00
Banded Mallard	75.00
Basset Hound, 1978	36.00 To 60.00
Bear, Brown, 1974	25.00 To 35.00
Birth Of Freedom, Gallon	2500.00
Birth Of Freedom, 1976	65.00 To 100.00
Blackbird, Red-Winged, 1977	37.00 To 50.00
Blue Jay, 1978	44.00 To 65.00
Bob Cratchit	34.00 To 60.00
Bobcat	55.00 To 64.00
Bonnie, 1974	20.00 To 33.00
Buffalo Dancer, 1979	85.00 To 125.00
Bull Rider, 1980	50.00 To 65.00
Burro, 1973	39.00 To 42.00
Cardinal, 1979	65.00 To 85.00

Ski Country, Arizona Ceremonial
Eagle Dancer, 1978

Caveman, 1974	14.00 To 30.00
Charolais Bull	55.00
Chukar Partridge, 1979	33.00 To 55.00
Cigar Store Indian, 1974	27.00 To 40.00
Circus Lion, 1975	35.00
Circus Tiger, 1975	40.00 To 47.00
Circus Wagon, 1977	25.00 To 35.00
Clown Bust, 1974	36.00 To 45.00
Clyde, 1974	30.00 To 37.00
Condor, 1973	41.00 To 55.00
Coyote Family, 1977	44.00 To 65.00
Dall Sheep, 1980	65.00 To 85.00
Dancers Of The Southwest, Set Of 6	375.00
Desert Sheep, 1980	75.00
Duck, Blue-Winged Teal, 1974	73.00 To 135.00
Duck, King Eider, 1977	49.00 To 65.00
Duck, Mallard Family, 1977	Color 70.00
Duck, Mallard, 1973	50.00 To 75.00
Duck, Pintail	57.00 To 75.00
Duck, Pintail, 1979, 1/2 Gallon	225.00 To 250.00
Duck, Redheaded, 1974	63.00
Duck, Widgeon, Gallon	175.00
Duck, Widgeon, 1979	25.00 To 57.00
Duck, Wood, 1974	150.00 To 230.00
Eagle & Egret, Easter Seal, 1980	40.00 To 80.00
Eagle On Drum, 1976	125.00 To 135.00
Eagle On Water	120.00 To 135.00
Eagle, Bald	135.00
Eagle, Harpy, 1973	95.00 To 145.00
Eagle, Hawk, Ornate, 1974	131.00 To 150.00
Eagle, Hawk, 1974	45.00 To 135.00
Eagle, Majestic	325.00 To 395.00
Eagle, Majestic, Gallon	1770.00 To 2000.00
Eagle, Mountain, 1973	124.00 To 175.00
Elephant On Drum	38.00 To 45.00
Elk, 1979	53.00 To 65.00
End Of The Trail, 1976	100.00 To 150.00
Falcon, Peregrine, 1980, Fifth	48.00 To 75.00
Falcon, Peregrine, 1980, Gallon	350.00 To 500.00
Falcon, Prairie	75.00 To 80.00
Falcon, White, 1977	Color 75.00
Fire Engine	110.00
Flycatcher, Scissortail, 1979	48.00 To 75.00
Fox Family, 1979	39.00 To 65.00
Fox On Log, 1 3/4 Liter	235.00 To 291.00
Fox On Log, 1973	85.00 To 250.00

Gamecocks, Fighting, 1980 .... 100.00 To 136.00
Goat, Mountain, 1975 .... *Color* 60.00
Goat, Mountain, 1975, Gallon .... 555.00 To 700.00
Goose & Chicks, Canadian, 1980 .... 53.00 To 65.00
Goose, Canadian, 1973 .... 67.00 To 125.00
Grand Slam No.1, Desert Sheep, 1980 .... 57.00
Grand Slam No.2, Dall Sheep, 1980 .... 61.00
Grand Slam No.3, Mountain Sheep, 1980 .... 68.00
Great Spirit, 1975 .... 90.00 To 150.00
Hawk, Osprey, 1976 .... 150.00 To 175.00
Hawk, Red-Shoulder, 1972 .... 70.00 To 100.00
Hawk, Redtail, 1977 .... 70.00 To 100.00
Holstein Cow, 1973 .... 33.00 To 50.00
Hooded Merganser .... 70.00 To 75.00
Horse, Lippizaner, 1975 .... 45.00
Horse, Palomino, 1975 .... 40.00 To 50.00
Idaho Snake River Stampede, 1980 .... 64.00 To 70.00
Indian Dancers, Set Of 6, 1975 .... 293.00 To 300.00
Indian Warrior On Horse, No.1, With Hatchet .... 165.00 To 175.00
Indian Warrior, No.2, With Lance, 1979 .... 135.00 To 170.00
Indian, Deer Dancer .... 50.00 To 80.00
Indian, Eagle Dancer .... 109.00 To 250.00
Indian, Lookout, 1977 .... 80.00 To 90.00
Indian, North American, 1977, Set Of 6 .... 227.00 To 250.00
Indian, Shield Dancer, 1975 .... 50.00
Jenny Lind, Blue .... 56.00 To 60.00
Jenny Lind, Yellow .... 103.00 To 165.00
Kangaroo, 1974 .... 19.00 To 40.00
Koala, 1973 .... 17.00 To 37.00
Labrador With Mallard, 1977 .... 114.00 To 135.00
Labrador With Pheasant, 1976 .... 74.00 To 90.00
Leadville Lady, Blue Dress, 1973 .... *Illus* 23.00
Leadville Lady, Brown Dress, 1973 .... *Illus* 23.00
Lion, Mountain .... 45.00 To 50.00
Meadowlark, 1980 .... 42.00 To 56.00
Mill River C.C., 1977 .... 37.00
     SKI COUNTRY, MINIATURE, see Miniature, Ski Country
Mrs. Cratchit, 1978 .... 53.00 To 57.00
Muskie, 1977 .... 29.00 To 40.00
Otter, River, 1979 .... 39.00 To 60.00
Owl, Barn .... 50.00 To 70.00
Owl, Horned, 1974 .... 85.00 To 125.00
Owl, Horned, 1974, Gallon .... 800.00 To 1300.00
Owl, Near Miss, 1979 .... 42.00 To 50.00
Owl, Northern Snow, 1972 .... 95.00 To 125.00
Owl, Saw-Whet, 1977 .... 40.00 To 49.00
Owl, Screech Family, 1977 .... 57.00 To 95.00
Owl, Screech Family, 1977, Gallon .... 410.00 To 475.00
Owl, Spectacled, 1975 .... 85.00 To 110.00
Owls, Barred 64.00
P.T.Barnum, 1976 .... 29.00 To 35.00
Peace Dove, 1973 .... 36.00 To 60.00
Peacock, 1972 .... 75.00 To 100.00
Pelican, 1976 .... 40.00 To 45.00
Penguin Family, 1978 .... 33.00 To 52.00
Pheasants, Fighting, 1977 .... 75.00 To 77.00
Pheasants, Fighting, 1977, 1/2 Gallon .... 175.00 To 199.00
Political, Donkey, 1976 .... 20.00 To 33.00
Political, Elephant, 1976 .... 20.00 To 33.00
Prairie Chicken, 1976 .... 42.00 To 70.00
Raccoon, 1974 .... 39.00 To 55.00
Ram, Bighorn, 1973 .... 55.00 To 90.00
Ringmaster, 1975 .... 25.00 To 30.00

Robin, 1975	43.00
Ruffed Grouse	48.00 To 65.00
Sage Grouse, 1974	49.00 To 65.00
Salmon, Landlocked, 1977	35.00 To 42.00
Scrooge, 1979	39.00 To 55.00
Skier, Blue, 1975	33.00
Skier, Gold, 1975	122.00 To 125.00
Skier, Red, 1975	26.00 To 35.00
Skunk Family, 1978	23.00 To 55.00
Snow Leopard, 1980	*Illus* 55.00
Submarine, 1976	22.00
Swallow, Barn	31.00 To 55.00
Swan, Black	24.00 To 38.00
Tom Thumb, 1974	20.00 To 30.00
Trout, Rainbow, 1976	36.00 To 47.00
U.S. Ski Team, 1980	22.00 To 45.00
Wild Turkey, 1976	120.00 To 195.00
Woodland Trio	55.00 To 65.00
Woodland Trio, Music Box	60.00
Woodpecker, Gila	30.00 To 90.00
Woodpecker, Ivory Bill, 1974	33.00 To 55.00
Wyoming Bronco, 1979	30.00 To 65.00
Wyoming, Cowboy Joe	70.00 To 110.00

Snuff bottles have been made since the 18th century. Glass, metal, ceramic, ivory, and precious stones were all used to make plain or elaborate snuff holders.

SNUFF, Chinese, Porcelain, Hand-Painted	20.00
Chinese, 18th Century, Cinnabar	165.00
Doct. Marshall's, Aromatic Catarrh, Head-Ache, OP, Aqua	24.50
E.Roome, Troy, N.Y., Open Pontil, Olive Green	90.00 To 155.00
E.Roome, Troy, New York, Pontil, Golden Amber, 4 1/4 In.	140.00
Free-Blown To Flattened Ovoid Form, Pontil, Olive Amber, 4 7/8 In.	135.00
G.W.Merchant, Open Pontil, Green	95.00
Gephalic	55.00
Jar, Lorillard's, Brown, 6 1/2 In.	*Color* 75.00
Keene, Open Pontil, Olive Green, 3 1/4 In.	80.00
Light Green, Heavy Rolled-Out Lip, OP, Cylinder, 6 1/2 X 3 1/4 In.	49.50
Lip Style, Light Olive-Yellowish Green, OP, 18th C., 5 3/8 In.	79.50
O.Lorroaid, Amber, Quart	8.00
Offset Neck, Open Pontil, Yellow Green, 4 3/4 In.	55.00
Olive Green, Lip Style, OP, 18th C., Cylinder, 7 1/8 In.	129.50
Open Pontil, Green, 4 1/4 In.	25.00

Ski Country, Leadville Lady, Blue
Dress, Brown Dress, 1973

Ski Country, Snow Leopard, 1980

Snuff, Tobacco, Scotch &
Rappee, Brown, 4 In.

Open Pontil, Light Amber, 3 3/4 In. 25.00
Open Pontil, Olive Green, 4 1/4 In. 25.00
Open Pontil, Rectangular, Olive Amber 34.00
P.Lorillard, Handmade, Amber, Pint 13.00
Rectangular, Chamfered Corners, Olive Amber, 5 3/4 In. 50.00
Rectangular, Chamfered Corners, Pontil, Medium Amber, 4 3/4 In. 55.00
Rectangular, Chamfered Corners, Pontil, Olive Amber, 6 In. 115.00
Rectangular, Concave Chamfered Corners, Pontil, Yellow Green, 6 In. 70.00
Rectangular, Pontil, Olive Amber, 4 In. 40.00
Seed Bubbles, Snap Case, M Debossed On Bottom, 4 1/4 In. 25.00
Square, Chamfered Corners, Pontil, Green, 2 3/4 X 5 In. 80.00
Stoneware, 2 Cobalt Blue Bands, Pewter Cap, Cork Insert, Gray, 7 In. 120.00
Tobacco, Scotch & Rappee, Brown, 4 In. .... *Illus* 3.00
True Cephalick, King's Pat., Open Pontil, Aqua 60.00
Z On Bottom, 1860, Green Amber 20.00

Soda bottles held soda pop or Coca-Cola or other carbonated drinks.
Many soda bottles had a characteristic blob top. Hutchinson stoppers and
Coddball stoppers were also used.

SODA, see also Mineral Water; Pottery

SODA, A.C.Gilligan, Cincinnati, Embossed Eagle On Back, Aqua 30.00
A.D.Simmons, Denver, Colo., With Eagle, Amethyst, Hutchinson 50.00
A.Hain & Son Lebanon Co., Iron Pontil, Cobalt 150.00
A.Ludwig, Napa, Cal., Hutchinson 25.00
A.M.Farland, Phila., Iron Pontil, Blue Green 49.50
A.R.Andrews, Detroit, Michigan, Hutchinson 20.00
A.R.Cox, Norristown, Graphite Pontil, Green, Squat 25.00
A.R.Cox, Norristown, Pa., Light Emerald Green 25.00
A.R.Cox, Norristown, Pa., Light Teal 13.00
A.Ratner, Albany, N.Y., Hutchinson 7.00
ABL Myers, A.M.Rock Rose, New Haven, Pontil, Deep Green 850.00
Alabama Bottling Co., Birmingham, Ala., Eagle On Reverse, Hutchinson 20.00
Alabama Bottling Works, Birmingham, BIMAL 7.00
Alaska Distilled Soda Water, Hutchinson 495.00
Albert Von Harten, Savannah, Ga., Blob Top, Green .... 15.00 To 65.00
Amanule College, Seal, Pontil 50.00
American Bottling Works, Louisville, Kentucky, Hutchinson 14.00
American Soda Fountain Co., Amber 15.00
American Soda Works, S.F., Hutchinson, Embossed Flag, Aqua 25.00
Amsterdam, N.Y.Bottling Works, BIM, Aqua, 9 1/2 In. 3.00
Andrew Lore Bottling Co., Cairo, Ill., Pictured Wreath & Bottle, Aqua 25.00
Andrew's, Philadelphia, Green 60.00
Arizona Bottling Works, Phoenix, Aqua, Crown Top 7.50
Arizona Bottling Works, Phoenix, Arizona, Bubbles, Hutchinson 150.00
Arthur Christean, Chicago, Ill., 8 Panel, Aqua 17.50
Ashland Bottling Works, Wis., Amber 22.50

Atoka Ice & Ower Co., Atoka, Crown Top	75.00
Aurora Springs Bottling Works, Meriden, Conn., Clear	6.00
B.Gross, Louisville, Kentucky, Hutchinson	18.00
Babb & Co., San Francisco, Pontil, Green	28.00
Baer & Stegmayer, Wilkes-Barre, Emerald Green, Squat	125.00
Baldy & Bowles Acme, Shelton, Conn., Clear	6.00
Bartley & Clancy, Danbury, Conn., Hutchinson	4.00
Beach & Litchfield, Newark, N.J.	20.00
Bennington Bottling Co., North Bennington, Vt., Hutchinson, Aqua	52.00
Bick & Riebel, Cincinnati, Ohio, Squat	10.00
Bogardus Bottling Works, Eldorado, Kansas, Hutchinson	30.00
Bower & Spencer, Kewanee, Illinois, Ice Blue	30.00
Breig & Schafer, S.F., Embossed Fish, Blob Top, Aqua	22.50 To 25.00
Bridgeton Glassworks, N.J., Embossed	10.00
Bridgeton Glassworks, New Jersey, Teal, 7 In.	40.00
Brock's Bottling Works, Comanche, Texas, Amethyst, Hutchinson	20.00
Bryant Root Beer, Detroit, Amber	1.50
Buffum & Co., Pittsburgh, Blob Top, Iron Pontil	15.00
Burgin & Sons, Phila.Glass Works, Iron Pontil, Blue-Green	18.00
C.B.Huggan's, Fullerton, California, Hutchinson, Aqua	95.00
C.B.Owen & Co.Bottlers, Cincinnati, Iron Pontil, Cobalt Blue	60.00
C.C.Habenight, Columbia, S.C., Aqua, Hutchinson	30.00
C.Cleminshaw, Troy, N.Y., 8-Sided, Ribbed & Paneled, Aqua, 7 In.	50.00
C.Geise & Son, Council Bluffs, Iowa, Hutchinson	13.00
C.M.S.Co., Alliance, Ohio, Embossed Crown On Front, Aqua	15.00
C.Volkman, Eau Claire, Wis., Quart, Aqua	20.00
Cairns Timmerman Block, St.Louis Soda Co.	14.00
California Bottling Works, T.Blauth	10.00
California Bottling Works, T.Blauth, Hutchinson	16.00 To 20.00
California Soda Works, Eagle, Lime Green With Gold Swirls, Hutchinson	150.00
California Soda Works, Embossed Eagles, Hutchinson, Aqua	35.00 To 45.00
Calnon & Cronk, Detroit, Light Green, Pontil	300.00
Camer & Jacky, Phillipsburg, Mon., Hutchinson, Aqua, 6 1/2 In.	40.00
Canada Dry, Carnival Glass	10.00
Canon City, Colorado, Hutchinson	125.00
Cape Argo Soda Works, Marshfield, Ore., Hutchinson	50.00 To 55.00
Cape City Bottling Works, Cape Girardeau, Mo., Aqua	9.00
Capital City Bottling Works, Baton Rouge, La., Hutchinson	28.00
Capital S.W.Co., Columbus, Ohio, Aqua, Hutchinson	6.00
Carson Brewing Co., Carson City, Nevada, Clear	25.00
Carson Carbonating, Jonesboro, Arkansas, Aqua, 6 3/4 In., Hutchinson	20.00
Champion Bottling Works, Williamsport, Pa., 10-Sided, Clear	15.00
Chas.Bernard, San Francisco, Hunnewell Type, Bubbly, Ice Blue	20.00
Chas.Grove, Cola, Pa., Iron Pontil	65.00
Chas.H.Mayer, Hammond, Ind., Hutchinson	8.00
Chas.Joly, No.9, So.7th, Phila., Green	15.00
Chas.Pape Bottling Works, Marietta, O., Aqua, Hutchinson	10.00
Cherokee Bottling Works, Cherokee, Iowa, Hutchinson	8.00
Cincinnati Soda Water & Ginger Ale Co., 6-Pointed Star, Aqua, 7 In.	7.50
City Bottling Works, Denver, Hutchinson, Clear	10.00
City Ice & Bottling Works, Georgetown, Texas, Aqua, Hutchinson	14.00
Clapp, Stubby, Red Amber	95.00
Clark & Roberts, Boston, Blob Top	10.00
Clarksburg Bottling Works, Clarksburg, West Virginia, Hutchinson	15.00
Classen & Co., San Francisco, Re.Pacific Soda Works, Aqua	10.00
Clicquot Club Soda, Millis, Mass., Crown Top, BIMAL, Teal Blue	12.00
Cloversville Bottling Works, Hutchinson	20.00
Coca Mariani, Dark Green	7.50
Colorado Springs, Colorado, Hutchinson	125.00
Columbia Soda Works, San Francisco	60.00
Concord Bottling Co., Concord, New Hampshire, Star, Hutchinson	25.00
Consolidated Bottling Co., Huron, South Dakota, Hutchinson	35.00
Consolidated Bottling Co., Leavenworth, Kans., Baltimore Loop, Aqua	18.00

Constitutional Beverage, Cabin Shape, Scroll, Amber 65.00
Constitutional Beverage, Golden Amber 80.00
Corcoran Bros., Pittston, Pa., Aqua 12.00
Crafton Bottling Works, Grafton, W.Va., Light Green 15.00
Cream Ale, Diehl & Lord, Nashville, T., 10 Panel, Amber 65.00
Cripple Creek, Colorado, Hutchinson 35.00
Crown Bottling Mfg.Co., Ardmore, Okla., Embossed Crown, Hutchinson 50.00
Crown Bottling Works, Cincinnati, Embossed Crown On Front, Aqua 15.00
Crystal Bottling Co., Lexington, Ky., Hutchinson 5.00
Crystal Bottling Works, 10-Sided, Hutchinson, Aqua 27.50
Crystal Bottling, Pine Bluff, Arkansas 24.00
Crystal Ice & Bottling Works, New Iberia, La., Aqua, Hutchinson 12.00
Crystal SJD, Uniontown, Pa., Clear, Hutchinson 10.00
Crystal Soda Water Co., Windber, Pa., Tombstone Panel 10.00
Crystal Springs Bottling Co., Barnet, Vt., Baltimore Loop Seal 65.00
Crystal, Blob Top, Amber 310.00
Cypress City Bottling Wks., Plaquemine, La., Must Not Be Sold 12.00
D.F.Shields, Rochester, New York, Hutchinson, Aqua 15.00
D.Palliser, Mobile, Alabama, Hutchinson .... 2.00 To 12.00
D.S. & Co., San Francisco, Aqua 50.00
D.S. & Co., San Francisco, Green 25.00
Dan Gallagher, Texarkana U.S.A., Hutchinson 20.00
Dan McPalin, Park City, Utah, Hutchinson 30.00
David Boyle, Patterson, N.J., Embossed, Quart, Hutchinson 10.00
Dearborn, 83 30 Ave., N.Y., Dark Teal Blue 60.00
Delta Bottling Works, Yazoo City, Miss., Hutchinson 18.00
Denhalter Bottling Co., Salt Lake City, Utah, Hutchinson, Amethyst 22.00
Dennis & Co., Mt.Morris, N.Y., BIM, Amber, 9 3/4 In. 3.00
Dennis & Co., Mt.Morris, N.Y., BIM, Blob Top, Honey Amber, 9 1/2 In. 4.00
Detroit, Central, Cobalt Blue 90.00
Diamond Bottling Works, Miami, Oklahoma, Hutchinson .... 60.00 To 115.00
Distilled Soda Water Co.Of Alaska, Aqua, Hutchinson .... 450.00 To 850.00
Dixon & Carson, 41 Walker, N.Y., Blue Green 35.00
Dixon, Carson, 41 Walker St., N.Y., Blob 30.00
Dr.Pepper, King Of Beverages 35.00
Droger Bros, Butte, Montana 50.00
Dyottville Glassworks, Phila., Aqua 5.00
E.Lester, St.Louis, Flare Top 14.00
E.Ottenville, Nashville, Tenn., Cobalt Blue, Hutchinson 90.00
E.Postens & Co., Providence, R.I., Gravitating Stopper, Hutchinson 110.00
E.S. & H.Hart, Superior Soda Water, Union Glass Works, Green 55.00
E.S.Hart, Canton, Ct., Superior Soda Water, U.G.W., Pontil, Aqua 85.00
E.Wagner, Manchester, Amber, Blob Top 8.00
E.Wagner, Manchester, New Hampshire, Amber, Blob Top 8.00
Eagle Bottling Works, Lawton, Crown Top 70.00
Eagle Bottling Works, Tacoma, Washington, Embossed Eagle, Hutchinson 16.00
Eagle Bottling, Buffalo, Embossed Eagle, Hutchinson 15.00
Eagle Soda Water & Bottling Co., Santa Cruz, Cal., Eagle, Hutchinson 150.00
Eagle Soda Water & Bottling Co., Santa Cruz, Eagle 65.00
Eastern Cider, Blob Top, Amber 30.00
Ebberwein Ginger Ale, Brown 20.00
Edward Taylor, Genuine Aerated Waters, Tangier, Torpedo, Aqua 8.00
Elting, Hudson, New York, Hutchinson, Aqua 8.00
Empire Soda Works, San Francisco, Aqua 50.00
Empire Soda Works, Vallejo, Hutchinson, Aqua .... 8.00 To 10.00
EWA Bottling Works, Hutchinson 40.00
Excelsior Soda Works, Los Angeles, California 35.00
Excelsior Water, The, 8-Sided, Green .... 35.00 To 45.00
Excelsior, Los Angeles, California, Aqua, Hutchinson 13.00
F.A.Conants Soda Water, New Orleans, Green 35.00
F.Bauman Soda Works, Santa Maria, Cal., Hutchinson 30.00
F.F.Fischer Bottling Works, Alvin, Texas 30.00
F.Schmidt, Leadville, Colo., Hutchinson 25.00

F.Sherwood, Bridgeport & New Haven, Pontil, Teal Green	85.00
Fabrica De Son Joes, Oaxaca, Mexico, Hutchinson	19.00
Field's Superior, Charleston, S.C., 8-Sided, Cobalt Blue	35.00
Finkenstadt Bros., New York, Blob Top, BIM, Aqua, 9 1/4 In.	4.00
Fred Schorr, Cincinnati, Embossed Lion On Back, Aqua	25.00
Fred W.Witte Ginger Ale, Bail, Aqua	10.00
Fredrich Rau, Philadelphia, Pontil, Green	45.00
G.A.Bode Bottlers Extracts, Chicago, Hutchinson	5.00
G.A.Bode Bottlers Extracts, Clear	3.00
G.Ebberwein, Savannah, Georgia, Gingerale, Amber, Blob	25.00
G.Geise & Son, Council Bluffs, Iowa, Hutchinson	10.00
G.Lauter, Reading, Pa., Green, Squat	35.00
G.Norris & Co., Detroit, Michigan, Cobalt Blue	50.00
G.Norris & Co.City Bottling Works, Detroit, Mich., Light Cobalt Blue	75.00
G.Recker, Vincennes, Indiana, Hutchinson, Aqua	10.00
G.Simons, Hartford, Ct., Pontil, Green	80.00
G.Sudhoff Soda Water Co., St.Louis, Mo.	5.00
G.Thomas, Truckee, California, Hutchinson	200.00
G.Van Benschoten Premium Soda Water, Pontil, Light Teal	75.00
G.Voelker, St.Louis, Missouri, Aqua	30.00
G.W. & W.W.Boynton, Providence, R.I., Light Green	12.00
G.W.Brandt, Carlisle, Pa., Iron Pontil, Emerald Green	50.00
G.W.Wells, Santa Ana, California, Fluted Bottom, Aqua	18.00
Gannet & Morse, Diamond, Augusta, Maine, Marble Top, Embossed, Aqua	20.00
Genuine Belfast Ginger Ale, G.D.Dows & Co., Boston, Round	20.00
Geo.Meyer, Farmington, Mo., Aqua, Hutchinson	22.50
Geo.Schmucks Ginger Ale, Cleveland, O., 12-Sided, Hutchinson, Amber	85.00
Geo.Van Benschoten, Blue-Green, Iron Pontil	110.00
Geo.Van Benschoten, Bridgeport, Conn., Bluish Green	100.00
Geo.Van Benschoten, Bridgeport, Conn., Iron Pontil, Blue-Green	110.00
Geo.Van Benschoten, Bridgeport, Conn., Iron Pontil, Dark Green	65.00
Geyser Bottling Works, Duluth, Minnesota, Hutchinson, Italian Green	45.00
Gimlich & White, Pittsfield, Mass.	13.00
Ginger Beer, Ledicott's, Southend, Stopper, Pint	8.00
Golden Gate, Green, Blob Top	35.00
Golden West, San Francisco, Hutchinson	30.00
Gravel Springs Bowling Pin Type, BIMAL, Amber	10.00
Gridley Soda Works, California	60.00
Guyette, Detroit, Cobalt Blue, Hutchinson	90.00
H L & J W Brown, Hartford, Ct., Pontil, Green	80.00
H.Aman, Cheyenne, Wyo.	45.00
H.Delmeyr, Brooklyn, N.Y., Squat	20.00
H.Denhalter & Son, Salt Lake City, Utah, Hutchinson, Aqua	90.00
H.Denhalter & Son, Salt Lake City, Utah, Lime Green	55.00
H.E.Scaife, Union, S.C., Hutchinson	15.00
H.Epping, Louisville, Kentucky, Hutchinson	10.00
H.Grone & Co., St.Louis, Mo., Iron Pontil, Aqua	10.00
H.Lyford & Co., Worcester, Mass., Iron Pontil, Dark Green	65.00
H.Maillard, Lead City, S.D., Light Aqua, Hutchinson	35.00 To 45.00
H.O.Krueger, Grand Forks, Dakota, Hutchinson, Aqua	170.00
H.O.Krueger, Grand Forks, Dakota, Whittled	190.00
H.P.Disboro, Frienhead, New Jersey, Hutchinson	6.00
H.Verhague, Seltzer Water, Cin., Squat	10.00
Hamilton's Beverages Of Waldorf, Maryland, Clear, 6 1/2 Ounce	5.00
Hanford Soda Works, J.S., Hutchinson	10.00
Hanigan Bros., Denver, Spelled Vertically	12.00
Hannigan Bros., Denver, Co., SCA, Hutchinson	15.00
Hartlet & Cheltra, Bath, Maine, Hutchinson	17.00 To 38.00
Hassinger & Petterson, St.Louis, Paneled, 5-Sided, 2 Teardrop Panels	20.00
Hawaiian Soda Works, Honolulu	75.00
Heiss, Philada., U.G.W. On Reverse, Iron Pontil, Medium Blue	65.00
Henry Grader, Columbus, Ga., Hutchinson	10.00
Henry Kuck, Savannah, Georgia, 1878, Dark Green	12.00 To 25.00

Soda, Henry Schramm,
Fullersburg, Ill., Aqua, 6 In.

Soda, Hofmann Bros.,
Chicago, Eagle, Aqua, 7 In.

Henry Schramm, Fullersburg, Ill., Aqua, 6 In. .... *Illus* 8.00
Henry Verhage, Cincinnati, Aqua 25.00
Herman Winter, Savannah, Ga., Blob Top, Aqua 10.00
Hickory Bottling Works, Hickory, N.C., Stopper, Embossed Star, Aqua 35.00
Hires, Crown Top, BIMAL, Fluted Base, Amber 10.00
Hobart Bottling Works, A.E.Fritsche, Hobart, Okla. 45.00
Hoffman & Joseph, Albany, Oregon, 1880-81, Embossed Lion, Aqua 50.00
Hofman Bros., Cheyenne, Wyoming, Etched 190.00
Hofmann Bros., Chicago, Eagle, Aqua, 7 In. .... *Illus* 12.50
Hofmann Bros., Chicago, Embossed Eagle, Hutchinson 15.00
Holden's G.A.Capital Soda Works, Sacramento, Cobalt Blue 98.00
Hollister & Co., Honolulu, Aqua, Hutchinson 30.00
Horan, N.Y., Teal Blob 30.00
Houppert & Smyly, Birmingham, Ala., Aqua, Hutchinson 10.00
Hubbbell, Phila., Saratoga Type, Green 45.00
Hygeia Soda Works, Kahului, Hutchinson .... 60.00 To 75.00
I.Ottenville, Nashville, Tenn., Cobalt Blue, Hutchinson 110.00
I.T.Fosler, Richmond, Ind. 10.00
Idaho Springs, Colorado, Hutchinson 50.00
Imperial Bottling Works, Portland, Oregon, Hutchinson 55.00
Ira Harvey, Pontil, Black Glass 75.00
Isaac Crams, Middleton, New York, Aqua 10.00
J & K Langdon, Youngstown, Ohio, 5-Point Star On Neck, Aqua, Hutchinson 15.00
J. & B.Winnemucca, Nevada, Aqua 50.00
J.A.Lomax, 14 & 16 Charles Place, Chicago, Cobalt Blue, Hutchinson 16.00
J.A.Seitz, Easton, Pa., Squat, Teal Green 25.00
J.A.Wallis, Bangor, Maine, Hutchinson .... 25.00 To 45.00
J.C.Buffum, Pittsburgh, Aqua 25.00
J.C.Port, Costa Soda Works, Hutchinson 80.00
J.Cairn, Block & Co., St.Louis, Missouri 16.00
J.Cairns, St.Louis, Mo., Refired Pontil, Teal Blue 35.00
J.D.Crowl, Westminster, Md., Aqua, Hutchinson 20.00
J.F.Batterman, Brooklyn, New York, Teal, 6 1/2 In. 35.00
J.F.Herrmann & Son, Washington, D.C., Aqua, Hutchinson 26.00
J.G.Schoch, Philadelphia, Pontil, Blob Top, Cobalt Blue 500.00
J.H.Yale, Middletown, Ct., Pontil, Light Green 70.00
J.L.McCarthy, Norman, Applied Crown Top, Aqua 50.00
J.Manke, Savannah, Dark Green 15.00
J.McLaughlin, Phila., Iron Pontil, Deep Green, Squat 40.00
J.Moran, Burlington, Vt., 13-Star American Flag, Aqua 35.00
J.Pablo & Co., Man & Dog In Boat, Aqua 5.00
J.Steel, Easton, Pa., Graphite Pontil, Green, Squat 65.00
J.T.Nusbaum & Brothers, Weissport, Tiny Air Bubbles, IP, Green, Squat 75.00
Jackson's Napa Soda Springs, Aqua 12.00
Jacob Ries, Shakopee, Minnesota, Hutchinson .... 6.00 To 8.00

James H.Holmes, Auburn, N.Y., Metal Stopper, BIM, Amber, 9 1/2 In.	5.00
James Ray Ginger Ale, Cobalt	15.00
John Clancey, New Haven, Conn., Aqua, Hutchinson	8.00
John Fehr, Reading, Iron Pontil, Medium Blue	60.00
John Fehr, Reading, Single Tapered Top, Blue, Pony	120.00
John Forthoffer, Mt.Vernon, Ind., Aqua, Hutchinson	12.00 To 14.00
John Graf, Milwaukee, Wis., 8-Sided, Embossed, Amber	20.00 To 35.00
John Graf, Milwaukee, Wisconsin, Hutchinson	18.50
John O'Brien, St.Louis, Round Bottom, Aqua	20.00
John Ryan Ginger Ale, 1852, Olive Amber	95.00
John Ryan 1866, Excelsior Soda Works, Savannah, Georgia, Pale Blue	35.00
John Ryan, Savannah, Georgia, 1866, Cobalt Blue	85.00
John Ryan, 1866 Porter & Ale, XX, Saratoga Lip, Green	45.00
John S.Baker, Boardman, New York, 8 Panels, Iron Pontil, Aqua	55.00
John Volpert, Minersville, Pa., Squat, Green	90.00
Johnston & Co., Phila., Iron Pontil, Green, Pony	40.00
Johnston & Co., Philadelphia, Collar, Aqua	25.00
Joliet Slovenic Bottling Co., Joliet, Ill.	6.00
Jos.James Bottling Works, Red Jacket, Michigan	10.00
Kanawha Carbonating Co., Aqua	25.00
Keach, Torpedo, Baltimore, Light Green	225.00
Kearney, Shamokin, Pa., Hutchinson, Amber, Quart	185.00
Keenan Mfg.Co., Butte, Mont., Aqua, Hutchinson	25.00
Kelley & McWilliams, Rome, Ga., Hutchinson	15.00
Kelso, Wash., Crown Top	3.00
Kessler & Son, Carlstadt, N.J., Embossed Deer Head, Aqua, Hutchinson	15.00
King Of Beverages, Dr.Pepper	35.00
Kingston Bottling Works, Kingston, N.C., Aqua, Hutchinson	40.00
Kinney Bottling Works, McCurtain, Hutchinson	135.00
Kinston Bottling Works, Kinston, North Carolina, Hutchinson	35.00
Kohl & Beans, Easton, Pa., Iron Pontil, Green, Squat	45.00 To 60.00
L.C.Arny, New Orleans, Louisiana, Paneled Base, Hutchinson	12.00
L.Cohen & Son, Pittsburgh, Pa., Embossed Lion, Hutchinson	30.00
La Siberia Fabrica De Casseosas, Mexico	5.00
Lahaina Ice Ltd., Lahaina, Maui, 4-Piece Mold	20.00
Lancaster Glassworks, Phila., Blue	15.00
Lancaster Glassworks, Phila., Green	25.00
Lancaster X Glass Works, Aqua	35.00
Lattonia Ice Co.Ltd., Lahaina, Maui, Hutchinson	20.00
Leonard Voos, Natchez, Miss., Aqua, Hutchinson	25.00
Lewis & Scott, Phila., Green, Squat	25.00
Liberty Soda Works, Picture Of Eagle, San Francisco, Aqua	35.00
Lihue Ice Co., Hawaii, Hutchinson, Aqua	25.00
Lomax, Chicago, Blob, Iron Pontil, Cobalt Blue	65.00
Lone Star Bottling Works, Galveston, Texas	10.00
Longmont Bottling Works, Longmont, Colorado, Hutchinson	10.00
Lord, Diehl & Danbury, Memphis, Tenn., Aqua, 6 3/4 In., Hutchinson	10.00
Louis Fritz & Co., Covington, Ky., Hutchinson	25.00
Louis Masuthe, Pacific, Mo.	22.00
Luke Beard, Howard Street, Boston, Emerald Green, Squat	32.50
Lyford, Worcester, Ma., Iron Pontil, Emerald Green	65.00
M.Cronin, 230 K St., Sacramento, Aqua, Hutchinson	10.00
M.M.Batelle, Brooklyn, N.Y., Union Glass Works, Graphite, Teal Blue	75.00
Magic Soda Works, Weiser, Idaho, Crown Top	5.00 To 6.00
Mansfield Bottling Works, Mansfield, Ark., Aqua, Hutchinson	16.00
Marble Ball Inside, Embossed, 6 Ounce, Set Of 10	100.00
Marion Bottling Works, Marion, N.C.	22.00
Maui, Hawaii, Hutchinson	15.00 To 17.00
McCarthy & Moore, Waterbury, Connecticut, Hutchinson	18.00
McGrath Bros.1890, Hoosick Falls, N.Y., Aqua, Hutchinson	8.00
McNally & Co., Camden, N.J., Green Pony	45.00
Meincke Ebberwein Ginger Ale, Savannah, Amber	20.00
Merritt & Co., Helena, Montana	10.00 To 45.00

Meyer & Radcliffe, Wheeling, W.Va., Hutchinson	8.00
Miami Bottling Works, Miami, Oklahoma, Hutchinson	75.00
Michael Radigan, Shawnee, Ohio, Hutchinson, Green	55.00
Miguel Pons, Mobile Alabama, Pontil	15.00
Milk Glass, 10 In.	10.00
Millirons Bottling Works, Macon, Georgia, Hutchinson	20.00
Minnesota, Standard, Amber	90.00
Monroe Cider & Vinegar Co., Ferndale, Cal., Aqua, Hutchinson	17.50
Monroe's Distilled Soda Water, Eureka, Cal., Hutchinson	15.00 To 18.00
Monroe's Distilled Soda Water, Eureka, Cal., Lime Green, Hutchinson	50.00
Montana Territory, Hutchinson	75.00
Morris, Detroit, Mich., Cobalt, Hutchinson	26.00
Moscow Bottling Works, Moscow, Ida., Early Crown, Aqua, 8 Ounce	5.00
Mrs.B.Zimmerman, New Brunswick, New Jersey, Hutchinson	3.00
N.Hilo, Aqua, Tall, Hutchinson	25.00
N.Richardson & Son, Trenton, N.J., Green Aqua	10.00
Napa Soda, Phil Caduc, Cobalt Blue	70.00
National Bottling Works, Ruon Mattson, Hancock, Michigan, Hutchinson	10.00
Negaunee Bottling Works, Negaunee, Mich., Hutchinson, Quart	18.00
Nevada City Soda Works, L.Siebert, Blob Top, Apple Green	35.00
New Liberty Soda Works, Embossed Liberty Head, Hutchinson	85.00
Nitz & Co., Milwaukee, Wis., Best By Test Motto, Hutchinson	17.00
Norris, Detroit, Violet Cobalt, Hutchinson	100.00
North Western Bottling Co., Butte, Mo.	18.00
Northrop & Sturgis Company, Portland, Oregon, Aqua, Hutchinson	15.00
Northwestern Bottling Co., Butte, Mont., Hutchinson	22.00
Northwestern Bottling Co., Kremmling, Colo., Hutchinson	25.00
Northwestern Bottling, Butte, Mont.	15.00
O.P.Rushton, Clarke & Co., New York, Aqua, 7 In.	25.00
Omaha Bottling Co., Omaha, Neb., Aqua, Hutchinson	24.00
Owen Casey, Eagle Soda Works, Cobalt	30.00
P.Connell, Bordenton, New Jersey, Light Green	8.00
P.Conway, Bottler, Phila., Iron Pontil, Medium Blue	49.50
P.Ebner Bottler, Wilmington, Delaware, Paneled Base	20.00
P.Seasholtz, Pottstown, Pa., Squat, Blue Green	55.00
Pacific & Puget Sound Soda Works, Seattle, Hutchinson	125.00
Pacific Bottling Works, Tacoma, Washington, Hutchinson	17.00
Pacific San Francisco, Green	20.00
Pacific Soda Works, Portland, Oregon, Hutchinson	30.00
Pacific Soda Works, San Francisco, Aqua	35.00
Parker & Sons, New York, Blue	15.00 To 18.00
Parker, Iron Pontil, Cornflower Blue	45.00
Parker, Sapphire Blue	145.00
Pearson's Soda Works, California, Hutchinson	17.50
SODA, PEPSI COLA, see Pepsi Cola	
Perkins, Tannersville, N.Y., Star, Hutchinson	6.00
Perth Amboy Bottling Co., N.J., Monogram, P.A.B.Co., Deep Aqua	7.00
Peter J.Kelly, Stanhope, N.J., Aqua, Hutchinson	5.00
Phil Caduc, Napa Soda, Deep Aqua	35.00
Philip Young, Savannah, Eagle, Shield, Flags, Green	125.00
Phoenix Bottling Works, Mobile, Alabama, Hutchinson	19.50
Pioneer Bottling Works, Victor, Colorado, Aqua	20.00
Pioneer Soda Water Co., Embossed Walking Grizzly Bear	65.00
Pioneer Soda Works, Anchor With Initials G.B.	15.00
Pioneer Soda Works, P.O., Aqua, 6 In. *Illus*	15.00
Pioneer Soda Works, San Francisco, Embossed Shield, Hutchinson	10.00
Pioneer Soda Works, San Francisco, Shield, Hutchinson	9.00
Pioneer, Bisbee, Arizona, 4-Piece Mold, Crown Top	10.00
Pittsburgh, Pa., Lion Holding Seltzer Bottle, Hutchinson, Amber	400.00
Pormy & Segekly, Omaha, Nebraska, Hutchinson	19.00
Port Huron, Michigan, Andrae, Cobalt Blue	125.00
Port Huron, Zuber, Cobalt Blue	110.00
Portland Bottling Works, Portland, Indian, Hutchinson	10.00

Soda, Pioneer Soda Works, P.O., Aqua, 6 In.

Portland Soda Works, Eagle, Dark Green	35.00
Portland Soda Works, Large Eagle, Spread Wings, Whittled, Hutchinson	20.00
Poteau Bottling Works, Poteau	80.00
Preuss F.Hoeffer, N.Y., Stopper, Blob Top, BIM, 9 1/4 In.	4.00
Pride Bottling, Chicago, Embossed Elk, Hutchinson	10.00
Priest Napa Natural Mineral Water, Aqua	5.00
Puget Sound, Seattle, Hutchinson	125.00
Pure Drink Mfg.Co., Aqua	26.00
Queen City Bottling, Cincinnati, Julias Weber On Reverse	7.50
Queen City Bottling, Cincinnati, Wm.Heckerman On Reverse	7.50
Queen City Pure Water, 2 Quart	13.00
R & W Las Vegas, Light Blue, Hutchinson	375.00
R.E.Gatewood, Phoebus, Va.	10.00
R.Forster, Poughkeepsie, Gin Top, Blue Green, Squat	30.00
R.Kearney, Philada., Dark Green	40.00
R.Robinson's XXX Ginger Ale, Brooklyn, N.Y., Act Of Congress, Aqua	13.00
Rapide's Bottling Works, Alexandria, Louisiana, Hutchinson	17.00
Raub & Eckert, Easton, Pennsylvania, Pontil, Green, Pony	50.00
Raub & Eckert, Green, Squat	125.00
Red Seal Soda Water Co., Salt Lake City, Sun Pattern, Amethyst	14.00
Richardson Bottling Co., Mansfield, Ohio, Ice Blue, Hutchinson	3.00
Richardson W.Morton, Trenton, New Jersey, Green	18.00
Robert Schultz, Sheboygan, Wis., Hutchinson	6.00
Robinson Wilson, Lagalee, Boston, Iron Pontil, Teal Green, 6 1/2 In.	65.00
Rocky Mountain Bottling, Butte, Mont.	15.00
Ryberg, Peckham, New York	8.00
S.A.Smith, Doylestown, Pa., Squat, Green	110.00
S.C.Palmer, Washington, D.C., Hutchinson	25.00
S.Maas, Philada., Amber	5.00
S.Martinalli, Watsonville, California, Hutchinson	15.00
S.Smith, Knickerbock Mineral & Soda Waters, N.Y., Embossed	200.00
Sacramento Type, Embossed Eagle, Iron Pontil, Green	90.00
Salinas P.S.Soda Works, California, Hutchinson	20.00
San Francisco Soda Works, Hutchinson, Aqua	20.00
San Jose Soda Works, John Balzhauser, Hutchinson	14.00
Sandusky, Bubble Burst, Cobalt Blue, Quart	200.00
Sapulpa Bottling Works, Applied Crown Top, Amethyst	80.00
Saratoga Seltzer Water, Embossed Shoulder, Blue-Green, Pint	40.00
Schick & Fett, Reading, Green, Squat	15.00
Schlitz, Crown Top, BIM, Aqua	5.00
Schramm & Schramm Bottling Co., Farmington, Mo., Amethyst, Hutchinson	35.00
Scripture & Parker, Boston, Squat, Teal Green	30.00
Sea Horse, Embossed, Bullet Stopper	16.00
Seattle Soda Works, Blue Aqua, Hutchinson	10.00
Seitz & Bro., Easton, Pa., Sapphire Blue	50.00

Seitz Bros., Easton, Pa., Graphite Pontil, Dark Blue, Squat, Blob Top 30.00
Seitz Bros., Easton, Pa., Green, Squat 15.00
Seitz Bros., Easton, Pa., Squat, Dark Aqua 6.00
Sels & Sons Redding, California, Lime Green 25.00
Silver State, Reno, Embossed Miner & Mule, Clear, Machine-Made 10.00
Simon & Co., Murphysboro, Ill., Aqua, Hutchinson 9.00
Sloup, Sherry Bottling Co., Omaha, Hutchinson 15.00
Smith & Co. Premium, Charleston, 8-Sided, Blue-Green 30.00
Smith, New York, Cobalt Blue 200.00
Soult & Zerbe, Lewistown, Pa., Emerald Green, Squat 135.00
South Bend Soda & Bottling Works, South Bend, Wash., Hutchinson 15.00
Southwick & G.O.Tupper, N.Y., 10 Panels, IP, Electric Blue, 7 1/4 In. 132.00
Speidel Bros., Wheeling, W.Va., Aqua, Hutchinson 12.00
St.Helena Soda Works, California 80.00
St.Louis Soda Co., Cairns Timmermann Block, Large 15.00
Standard Bottling Co., Denver, Colo., Hutchinson, Aqua 12.00
Standard Bottling Co., Denver, Colo., Hutchinson, Clear 14.00
Standard Bottling Co., Fort Bragg, Hutchinson 10.00
Standard Bottling Works, Minneapolis, Amber, Hutchinson .... 85.00 To 110.00
Standard Bottling Works, Minneapolis, Dark Amber 95.00
Star Bottling Co., Seattle, Wash., Hutchinson, Clear 12.50
Star Bottling Works, Houston, Texas, Embossed Star, Hutchinson 15.00
Star Bottling Works, St.Paul, Minn., Hutchinson, Aqua 6.00
Steinmetz & Herrmann, Newark, N.J., Star On Back, Light Aqua 10.00
Success Bottling, Chicago, Embossed Pig, Hutchinson 12.00
Swidler & Bernstein, Chicago, Embossed Walking Bear, Hutchinson 12.00
T & R Morton, Newark, Graphite Pontil, Light Green 18.00
T & W, 141 Franklin St., N.Y., Bluish-Aqua, Blob Top, 7 1/4 In. 7.00
T. & S.Port, Townsend, Washington, Hutchinson 100.00
T.Burns, Tucson, Ariz., Aqua, Hutchinson .... 55.00 To 110.00
T.C.Fox, Knoxville, Tenn., Aqua, Hutchinson 12.00
T.J.Tanner, Port Townsend, Wisconsin, Bubbles, Hutchinson 190.00
T.W.Gillett, New Haven, Iron Pontil, Blue-Green 35.00
Tacoma, Wash., Hutchinson 15.00
Taka-Kola, Farmille, Va., 8-Sided, Clear 5.00
Tarr & Smith, Pontil, Green 65.00
Tawasentha Springs Co., Cincinnati, Embossed Indian Maiden, Green 45.00
Taylor Soda Water Mfg.Co., Boise, Idaho, Hutchinson, Clear .... 75.00 To 90.00
Teller's, Detroit, Blob, Cobalt Blue 200.00
Teller's, Pontiled Cobalt Blue Blob, Taper Top 200.00
Ten Pin, Embossed M. & W., St.Louis, Emerald Green, IP 700.00
Ten Pin, M. & W., St.Louis, Iron Pontil, Emerald Green 700.00
Thomas Leonard Sonora Soda Works, California 40.00
Thomas Maher, Graphite Pontil, Dark Green 50.00
Thoth, Philadelphia, Deep Green, Squat 30.00
Tonopah Soda Works, Nev., Hutchinson 275.00
Trinidad, Colorado, Hutchinson 20.00
Tucson, Ariz., Hutchinson 125.00
Tweooles Celebrated Soda Water, Graphite Pontil 55.00
U.& I.D.Clinton, Woodbridge, Conn., Emerald Green, Iron Pontil 45.00
U.& I.D.Clinton, Woodbridge, Conn., Iron Pontil, Dark Green 55.00
U.& I.D.Clinton, Woodbridge, Conn., Iron Pontil, Teal Blue, 7 In. 75.00
Uncle Sam's Beverages, Pictures Uncle Sam, Painted Label, Houston 4.00
Union B.Works, Houston, Tex., Hutchinson 10.00
Union Glass Works, Phila., Aqua 10.00
Union Glass Works, Phila., Green 20.00
Usona Bottling Works, Fort Smith, Ark., BIMAL 24.00
Utopia Grape, Amber, 8 In. .... *Color* 5.00
Vincent Hathaway & Co., Boston, Round Bottom, Emerald Green 45.00
Virginia Brewing Company, Roanoke, Va. 25.00
Vogel Bottling Works, Houston, Texas 15.00
Von Harten & Grogan, Savannah, Ga., Green 15.00
W.A.French & Co., Red Bank, N.J., Aqua Blue 30.00

Soda, Western Bottling Works,
Chicago, Ill., Aqua, 6 In.

Soda, William H.Baxter, Haslingden,
Aqua, Codd, 9 1/2 In.

W.B.Hays Bottling Co., Poplar Bluff, Missouri, Hutchinson	30.00
W.E.Brockway, New York, Graphite Pontil, Teal Green	35.00
W.E.Brockway, New York, Iron Pontil, Light Green, 6 3/4 In.	27.50
W.F.Roesen, Jefferson City, Mo., Embossed Woman & Cannon	70.00 To 95.00
W.H.Burt, San Francisco, Iron Pontil, Olive Green	20.00
W.H.Darling & Son, Newport, Vermont, Hutchinson	30.00
W.H.Darling & Son, Newport, Vermont, Paper Label	42.00
W.H.Donovan, Halifax, Aqua, Hutchinson	15.00
W.H.Hutchinson & Son, Bottlers Supplies, Chicago, BIMAL, Aqua, 13 X 6	22.00
W.H.Sparks, Irondale, Mo., Aqua, Hutchinson	20.00
W.J.Laws, Crown Point, Indiana, Hutchinson	10.00
W.L.Rose & Co., Wheeling, W.Va., Aqua, Hutchinson	12.00
W.M.Blanchfield, Salem, New York, Aqua	8.00
W.M.Rex, 525 Green St., Phila., Pontil, Blue, Squat	60.00
W.Schlieper, , St.Louis, Mo., Blob Top, Aqua	12.00
W.Sievers, Cincinnati, Ohio, Hutchinson	5.00
W.Walker Soda Water, Atlanta, Ga., Hutchinson	70.00
Waldron Bottling Works, Waldron, Arizona, Hutchinson	15.00
Waldron Bottling Works, Waldron, Ark., Amethyst	17.00
Waldron Bottling Works, Waldron, Ark., Hutchinson	15.00 To 16.00
Waneta Cocoa, Boston, Honey Amber	12.00
Weiss Bier, F.Kutscher, New Haven, Ct., Double Ring Lip, Aqua	10.00
Western Bottling Works, Chicago, Ill., Aqua, 6 In. ....*Illus*	9.00
Westey Cunningham, Hampton, Va., Clear	5.00 To 20.00
White Rock Water, Crown Top, Labels, Amber	6.00
William Eagle, New York Premium, 8-Sided, Emerald Green	50.00
William H.Baxter, Haslingden, Aqua, Codd, 9 1/2 In. ....*Illus*	10.00
William's, Kalamazoo, Pontil, Peacock Blue	300.00
Williams & Severance, San Francisco, Cal., Dark Blue	40.00
Williams & Severance, San Francisco, Graphite Pontil, Cobalt Blue	55.00
Wm.Eagle, New York, Premium Soda Water, 8-Sided, Medium Green	32.00
Wm.Eagle, Vestry, Varick & Canal St., Iron Pontil	45.00
Wm.Everhart, Easton, Pa., 2 Embossed Stars, Light Bluish-Green, Squat	25.00
Wm.Griffeths Bottler, Virden, Ill., Clear, Hutchinson	6.00
Wm.McCully & Co., Pittsburgh, Pa., 3-Piece Mold, Black Glass	30.00
Wonsitler & Co., Doylestown, Pa., Squat, Green	45.00
Yuncker Bottling Co., Tacoma, Washington, Green	25.00
Zeis & Sons, Redding, California, Green	30.00

SPIRIT, see also Seal

SPIRIT, Dutch Squat, Olive Green, 7 In.	25.00
Emmanuel, Deep Olive Amber, Quart	40.00
M., Olive Amber, Pint	100.00

STIEGEL TYPE, Flowers, Hearts, & Birds, Polychrome Enamel, Half Post, 6 In. 135.00

STONEWARE, Grumman's Bottling Works, S.Norwalk, Conn., Cream, Quart 25.00

Jug, Incised Label, From Louisville, Ky., Brown Glaze, 3 3/8 In. 22.50
McGuire Bros.Lemon Beer, Debossed, Gray 38.00
Motto Jug, Detrick Distilling Co., Brown & White, 4 1/2 In. 22.50
National Wine Co., Lima, Ohio, Barrel Shape, Stand, 4 In. 50.00
Weiss Beer, Baltimore, Washington Bottling 25.00

TARGET BALL, New Brunswick Glass Works, 2 1/2 In. ....*Color* 60.00

TOBACCO JAR, Globe Tobacco, Amber, 8 In. ....*Color* 25.00

TONIC, Baldwin's Celery Pepsin Dandelion 50.00
Burdock's Blood, Clear 15.00
Dr.H.C. Stewart's, Amber 55.00
Dr.Palmer's, Full Label, Clear 12.00
Halls Wine, Olive Green, Round, 12 In.Diam. 39.00
Honduras Mountain, Rectangular, Aqua, 9 In. 10.00
Hood's Blood & Nerve 10.00
Hoopland's German, Aqua, Square 30.00
Hoptonic Royals Shape 55.00
Howe's Arabian Tonic Blood Purifier 18.00
Imperial Wine, Amber, Oval, 10 In. 30.00
Jones Red Clover, Amber, Square 35.00
Mitte & Kanne, St.Louis, Amber, Oval, 8 In. 25.00
Mrs.Miller's Herbal, Kokomo, Indiana, 9 1/2 In. 25.00
Mull's Grape, Rock Island, Ill., Amber 10.00
Orange Tonica, Risley & Co., N.Y., Lady's Leg, Round, Amber, 10 In. 50.00
Smith's Columbo, Square, Amber 25.00
Waits' Wild Cherry, Amber, Square 20.00
Webb's Cathartic 15.00
Dr.Palmer's, Full Label, Clear 12.00

VIAL, Blown, White Latticinio, 5 3/4 In. 45.00
Concentric Circles, 3 5/8 In. 15.00

VINEGAR, Bluegrass Belle, SCA 15.00
Heinz, Barrel Shape, Pour Spout, Frosted, Gallon 125.00
White House, Ballerina, Green 12.00
White House, Clear, 7 In. 3.50
White House, Embossed House, 1/2 Gallon 8.00
World's Fair 1939, Milk Glass, 9 1/2 In. 8.00
Yacht Club, Brown & White, 3 1/4 In. 22.00
    W.A. LACEY, MINIATURE, see Miniature, W.A. Lacey
    WARNER BROTHERS, see Alpa
    WATER, MINERAL, see Mineral Water
    WATER, MOSES, see Mineral Water, Moses

*Wheaton Commemorative bottles have been made by hand since 1977 at
Wheaton Village, Millville, New Jersey. Earlier commemorative
bottles were machine made and sold under the name Wheaton Nuline.*

WHEATON COMMEMORATIVE, Abraham Lincoln 10.00
Alexander Graham Bell 7.00
Andrew Jackson 6.00
Andrew Johnson ....*Illus* 8.00
Apollo 11, Blue 21.00
Apollo 11, Burnt Amber 45.00
Apollo 11, 10th Anniversary, Emerald 75.00
Apollo 12, Red 43.00
Apollo 13, Burley 8.00
Apollo 14, Aqua ....*Illus* 6.00
Apollo 15, Green 6.00
Apollo 16, Flint 6.00
Apollo 17, Amethyst 13.00
Ben Franklin, Aqua 6.00
Betsy Ross, Red 7.00

Wheaton Commemorative,
Andrew Johnson

Wheaton Commemorative,
Apollo 14, Aqua

Billy Graham	6.00
Charles A.Lindbergh	6.00
Charles Evans Hughes	6.00
Christmas, 1971	12.00
Christmas, 1971, Not Frosted	16.00
Christmas, 1972	16.00
Christmas, 1973 ....*Illus*	8.00
Christmas, 1974	8.00
Christmas, 1975	10.00
Christmas, 1976	10.00
Christmas, 1977	10.00
Christmas, 1978	10.00
Christmas, 1979	10.00
Christmas, 1980	10.00
Clark Gable	7.00
Democrat, 1972, Eagleton, McGovern ....*Color*	15.00
Democrat, 1972, Shriver, McGovern ....*Color*	15.00
Douglas MacArthur	6.00
Dwight Eisenhower	7.00
Frank H.Wheaton	25.00
Franklin Roosevelt	10.00
George S.Patton	6.00
George Washington	6.00
George Washington, Clear	30.00
Gerald R.Ford, Amethyst	40.00
Gerald R.Ford, Red	8.00
Harry S.Truman	10.00
Helen Keller	6.00
Herbert Hoover ....*Illus*	6.00

Wheaton Commemorative,
Christmas, 1973

Wheaton Commemorative,
Herbert Hoover

Humphrey Bogart	7.00
James K.Polk	10.00
James Madison	10.00
James Monroe	50.00
Jean Harlow	7.00
Jimmy Carter, Amethyst	10.00
Jimmy Carter, Blue	10.00
Jimmy Carter, Navy Blue	30.00
John Adams	8.00
John Paul Jones, Green	6.00
John Quincy Adams	10.00
John Tyler, Dark Amber	25.00
Lee W.Minton	10.00
Lyndon B.Johnson	6.00
Mark Twain	6.00
Martin Luther King	6.00
Martin Van Buren	10.00
Millard Fillmore	10.00
Paul Revere, Cabin	10.00
Pope John Paul VI	13.00
Republican, 1972 ....Color	15.00
Richard M.Nixon	9.00
Robert E.Lee	6.00
Ronald Reagan	10.00
Sheriff's Assoc.	13.00
Sky Lab No.1	7.00
Sky Lab No.2	8.00
Sky Lab No.3	12.00
Sky Lab No.3, Sample	175.00
Southern 500	14.00
Spirit Of 76, Amber	15.00
St.John	13.00
St.Luke	13.00
St.Mark	13.00
St.Matthew	13.00
Thomas A.Edison	6.00
Thomas Jefferson	11.00
Ulysses S.Grant	6.00
Vietnam, Dark Blue	15.00
Vietnam, Red	10.00
W.C.Fields	8.00
William Henry Harrison	10.00
William McKinley	8.00
Woodrow Wilson	10.00

Whiskey bottles came in assorted sizes and shapes through the years. Any container for whiskey is included in this category.

WHISKEY, see also modern manufacturers by brand name

WHISKEY, A.Fenkhausen & Co., San Francisco, Monogram, Amethyst, 12 In.	20.00
A.Groe & Co., Old Governor 1879 Sour Mash, St.Louis	30.00
A.H.Powers & Co.Importers, Sacramento, Picnic, Clear, 5 1/4 In.	25.00
A.Mattei, Fresno, Cal., In Circle, Mold Error, Round, Quart	5.00
Absolutely Pure, Albany, Denver	130.00
Adams, Taylor & Co., Royal Sour Mash, Handmade, Clear, Squat	15.00
Adolph Harris & Co., San Francisco, Deer Head, Light Amber, 12 In.	135.00
Aidee's Scotch, Mac The Knife, 1969	4.00
Albert Pick & Co., Chicago	100.00
Alf's Brune, Wholesale Liquor Dealers	500.00
Alfred Greenbaum & Co., Monogram Through Keystone, Blob Top	15.00
Americus Club, Light Amber, 11 1/4 In.	20.00
Argonaut, E.Martin & Co., San Francisco, Amber, 11 1/8 In.	20.00
Avon Hoboken Gin, Label	35.00
Ballantine's Scotch, Brown Glass	2.00

Barnett & Lumley, Mist Of The Morning, Barrel, Yellow Amber	225.00
Barry & Patton, San Francisco, Seed Bubbles, Green	140.00
Belle Of Anderson, Milk Glass	75.00
WHISKEY, BININGER, see Bininger	
Black & White Scotch, Braniff Airlines, Green	1.50
Blumauer & Hoch, Portland, Oregon, Inside Threads, Amber, 11 1/2 In.	20.00
Bluthenthal & Heilbronner, Memphis, Tennessee, Bulge Neck, Amber	10.00
Bonnie Bros., Light Amethyst	7.00
Bourbon, Copper	165.00
Brookfield Rye 1867, Left-Handled, Footed Canteen Shape, 4 In.	65.00
Brooklyn Glass Bottle Works, Golden Amber, 3/4 Quart	130.00
Bushwick Glass Works, Base Embossed, Golden Amber, 3/4 Quart	65.00
Cartan, McCarthy & Co., San Francisco, Blob Top, Amber, 11 3/4 In.	35.00
Cashmon Distributing Co., It's Pure, That's Sure, Denver, Colorado	70.00
Casper's, Cobalt Blue	135.00 To 200.00
Casper's, Made By Honest N.Carolina People, Cobalt Blue, 1/5 Quart	345.00
Chapin & Gore Sour Mash, 1867, Amber, 1/2 Pint	35.00
Chapin & Gore Sour Mash, 1867, Stopper, Fifth	70.00
Chapin & Gore, Amber, 3/4 Quart	15.00
Chapin & Gore, Applied Inside Threads, Amber, Fifth	45.00
Chas.Cove, Boston, Mass., Samples Of Our Fine Whiskey	35.00
Chas.Moul Pure Wings Liquors, York, Pa., 2 Tone	65.00
Chivas Regal Scotch, 12 Yr.Old, Round, Clear	2.00
Choice Old Cabinet, Amber	350.00
Circle Miller's, Thomas No.20, Olive Green	600.00
Coblentz & Levy, Portland, Oregon, Clear, 11 1/2 In.	20.00
Cognac, Label Under Glass, Embossed, Bright Amber	70.00
Columbian Expo, 1492-1892 Columbus	75.00
Congress Hall, Fleischman & Co., Maryland Rye, Amber, 11 1/4 In.	10.00
Connymede, 76, Square	25.00
Constitutional Beverage, Yellow	180.00
Cordova VO Rye, Acid-Etched, Square, Clear	10.00
Cottage Brand, Cabin, Embossed, Aqua	130.00
Crigler, Merry Christmas, 1/2 Pint	15.00
Cronan & Co., Sacramento, California, Amber, 11 3/4 In.	15.00
Crown Distilleries Company, Crown & Shield, Amber, 11 1/4 In.	8.00
Crown Distilleries, Inside Threads, Amber, Fifth	25.00
Cummin's Old Process Sour Mash, Clear, Pint	17.00
Cumminghams & Ihmsen, Pitts, Base Embossed, Golden Amber, Quart	45.00
Cutter Bird, Amber	135.00
Cutter Bird, Honey Amber	100.00
Cutter, Old Bourbon, A No.2, Tooled Top, Amber, Fifth	10.00
D.Sachs & Sons Distillers, Louisville, Amber, Squat	12.00
Dallemand & Co., Cream Pure Rye, Honey Amber, Pint	8.00 To 12.00
Dave D.Gibbons & Co., San Francisco, Monogram, Amber, 11 In.	40.00
Davy Crockett Pure Old Bourbon, Hey, BIMAL, Amber, Fifth	100.00
Davy Crockett Pure Old Bourbon, Hey, Grauerholz & Co.	35.00
Davy Crockett Pure Old Bourbon, Light Amber, 12 In.	30.00
Davy Crockett Pure Old Bourbon, San Francisco	35.00
Deep Spring Tennessee, Amber	15.00
Dewar's White Label Scotch, Round, Clear	2.00
Don Q, P.R.Rum, 1936	1.50
Drinkometer, Germany, Pottery, 7 In.	*Illus* 65.00
Duffy Malt, ABM, Quart	7.00
Duffy Malt, Rochester, Amber, Fifth, 10 1/4 In.	5.00
Duffy Malt, 1/2 Pint	14.00
Dutch Porter, Long Neck, Open Pontil	49.50
E.A.Fargo Co., San Francisco, Dark Amber, 11 3/4 In.	15.00
E.G.Booz's Old Cabin, Golden Amber, Quart	*Illus* 425.00
E.G.Booz's Old Cabin, 1840, Philadelphia, Amber, 3/4 Quart	60.00
E.G.Lyons, S.F., Clear	25.00
Eagle Glen, Picture Of Eagle, San Francisco, Amber, 11 3/4 In.	150.00
Ebner Bros., Sacramento, Coffin, Clear, 5 7/8 In.	15.00

Whiskey, Drinkometer,
Germany, Pottery, 7 In.

Whiskey, E.G.Booz's Old Cabin,
Golden Amber, Quart

(See Page 225)

Edw.E.Hall, Estab.1842, New Haven, Ct., Cylinder, Amber	12.00
Edward Heffernan, Lynn, Mass., Rectangular, Clear, Quart	7.00
F.Chevalier & Co., Hebe Brand, Embossed Shoulder, Green, 11 7/8 In.	15.00
F.Chevalier Co., San Francisco, Picture Of Castle, Amber, 11 In.	20.00
F.Chevalier Co., San Francisco, 25 Ounce, Amber, 11 1/8 In.	25.00
Flattened, Handle, Tooled Mouth, Iron Pontil, Apricot, 3/4 Quart	100.00
Fleckenstein And Mayer, Portland, Or., Amber, 1/2 Pint	110.00
Flora Temple, Embossed Horse, Handled	275.00
Fred Raschen, Sacramento, Monogram, Amber, 11 3/4 In.	12.00
Fritz Theis, Sole Proprietor, Old Nectar, Denver, Colorado	115.00
G.F.Heublein & Bro., Hartford, Conn., 3-Piece Mold, Citron	65.00
G.W.Chesley Importer, Sacramento, Cal., Picnic, Amethyst, 5 1/4 In.	20.00
G.W.Chesley Importer, 51 Front St., Sacramento, Pumpkinseed, Pint	32.00
Geo.Pfeiffer, High Grade, Colorado	130.00
Geo.Wissemann Co., Sacramento, Monogram, Amethyst, 12 In.	15.00
Geo.Wissemann, Sacramento, Monogram, Inside Threads, Amber	25.00
Giffith Hyatt & Co., Olive Amber, Label	475.00
Gilka, Amber, Quart	11.00
Gilka, Shaped, Unembossed, Amber	5.00
Gill Measure, Golden & Co., Order House, San Francisco, 1 Quart	25.00
Glass Label, Clear, 6 In. ....*Color*	125.00
Glen Forest Sour Mash, St.Louis, Missouri	35.00
Golden Dome Rye & Bourbon, Boston, Trademark, Light Amber	30.00
Golden Star, Embossed Star, Squat, Handled	65.00
Golden Wedding, Carnival Glass	8.00
Gordon's, Embossed Manhattan, Frosted	6.00
Gothic, 6 Embossed Arches, Each Contain Monk, Amber, 9 3/4 In.	5.00
Greeley's Bourbon, Copper Puce	145.00
Greeley's Bourbon, Dark Amethyst	290.00
Green Ribbon Liquor Co., Chicago, Denver, Green	85.00
Griffith & Hyatt Co., Baltimore, Front & Back Label, Olive Amber	475.00
Griffith & Hyatt, Amber, Handle On Right Side	265.00
H.Brickwedel & Co., San Francisco, Medium Amber, 7 3/8 In.	85.00
H.Brickwedel, Wholesale Liquor Dealers, S.F., Crude Amber, Pint	125.00
H.F.& B., N.Y., Hexagonal, Dark Red Amber, 3/4 Quart	150.00
H.Guggenheimer, Cincinnati, Swiveled Neck, Clear, Squat	10.00
H.L.Nye Bourbon, Inside Threads, Dark Amber, 11 In.	15.00
Hall, Luhrs & Co., Monogram, Sacramento, Blob Top, Stretch Marks	20.00
Hall, Luhrs & Co., Sacramento, Inside Threads, Amber, 11 3/8 In.	20.00
Hartebilt Goldlikeur, Embossed Leiden, Holland	1.50
Harwig & Son, Portland, Ore., BIMAL, Amber, Fifth	50.00
Hayner's, 12-Panel Base, Original Lock Top	27.00
Hilbert Bros.Bourbon, Louisville, Ky., Clear, 11 In.	20.00
Hildebrandt Posner & Co., San Francisco, Monogram, Fifth	25.00

Hoffman House Pure Rye, Cincinnati	30.00
Hollywood, Amber	30.00
Hotchkiss, Fenner, & Bennett, Dew Drop, 8 1/2 In. ...._Color_	150.00
House Of Koshu, Cherry, Lady's Bust, Frosted, 7 In.	11.00
I.Goldberg, Amber	35.00
I.Trager Co., Cincinnati, Amber, Quart	7.50
J.A.Gilda, Light Amber	15.00
J.Boissiere Vermouth, Sample Not For Sale	1.50
J.F.Cutter, E.Martin, Large Star	10.00
J.F.Cutter, Estra, Star & Shield Trademark, Blob Top, Amber, 12 In.	45.00
J.F.Cutter, San Francisco, Cal., Shield, Amber	9.00
J.F.T.Co., Philadelphia, Applied Handle, OP, Amber .... 275.00 To	310.00
J.H.Cutter Extra, Star, Shield, Old Bourbon, Medium Amber, Blob Top	45.00
J.H.Cutter, A.P.Hotaling & Co. Sole Agents, Amber, 12 In.	50.00
J.H.Cutter, A.P.Hotaling, 4 Mold	45.00
J.H.Cutter, Blob Top, Dark Amber	275.00
J.H.Cutter, Bottled By A.P.Hotaling & Co., Amber, Fifth	10.00
J.H.Cutter, Cutter O.K. Whiskey, Crown, Trademark, Barrel	30.00
J.H.Cutter, E.Martin, Amber	200.00
J.H.Cutter, Honey Amber	175.00
J.H.Cutter, Hotaling, A No.I, 4-Piece Mold .... 50.00 To	60.00
J.H.Cutter, Old Bourbon, Bottled By A.P.Hotaling, Amber, 12 In.	20.00
J.H.Cutter, Old Bourbon, C.K.Whiskey, Blob Top, Dark Amber	65.00
J.H.Cutter, Old Bourbon, Crown, A No.1, Tooled Top, Amber, 12 In.	12.00
J.H.Cutter, Swirls, Crown Shoulder, Amber, 1/5 Quart	350.00
J.Kellenberger, Durango, Colo., Quart	40.00
J.M.Gellert, Portland, Oregon, 4 Mold, Bulge Neck, Amber, 10 3/8 In.	20.00
J.N.O.T.Barbee & Co., Louisville, Ky., Embossed, Round, Quart	6.00
James & Co., Wine Merchants, Boscombe, Green, Inside Threads	10.00
James De Fremery & Co., San Francisco, Monogram, Amber, 10 7/8 In.	15.00
James De Fremery, San Francisco, Monogram, 1/5 Quart	25.00
James Woodburn Co., Sacramento, California, Monogram, Clear	8.00
Jas.Durkin Wines & Liquors, Spokane, Wash., 32 Ounce, Amber	15.00
Jesse Moore & Co., Louisville, Ky., Trademark, Amber, 11 3/4 In.	12.00
Jesse Moore & Co., Louisville, Ky., Trademark, Dark Amber, Blob Top	60.00
Jesse Moore & Co., Whittled	12.00
Jesse Moore Old Bourbon, Moore Hunt, Blob Top	40.00
Jno.F.Horne, Knoxville, Tenn., Anchor Design, Light Amber	50.00
Johann Hoff, Dark Green	10.00
John Gillon, King Wm.IV, 3-Piece Mold, Olive Green	20.00
John Schweyer, Clear	7.00
Johnny Walker Scotch, Red Label, Square, Clear	2.00
Jones Garvin & Co., Square, Golden Amber, 3/4 Quart	40.00
Jones Garvin & Co., Yellow Amber, Square, Pint	30.00
Jos.A.Magnus & Co., Cincinnati, Ohio, Lion & Figures, Dark Amber	15.00
Jos.Agress Wines & Liquors, New York, 8-Sided, Brown	25.00
Joseph Calway, New York, Honey Amber, Square	15.00
Jug, Fine Old J.R.D. Scotch, Doulton, Lambeth, Quart	140.00
Jug, Special Best Procurable, Hudson Bay Co., Royal Doulton, Quart	150.00
Julius Kessler & Co., Light Purple, Fifth	10.00
Kane O'Leary, Amber, Fifth	400.00
Keen Glass, Open Pontil, 3 Mold, Amber	50.00
Kellogg's Extra Bourbon Whiskey, 5 In.	70.00
Kellogg's Extra Kentucky Bourbon, Inside Threads, Amber	20.00
Kellogg's Nelson County Kentucky Bourbon, Red Whittled, Blob Top	250.00
Kellogg's, W.L.Co., Red Amber	50.00
Kennel Club, San Francisco, Monogram, Amber, 11 5/8 In.	30.00
Kiefer & Co., Los Angeles, Hood River Vinegar Label, Fifth	75.00
Kummerow & Menge Wholesale Wines, Wisc., Beehive Shape	45.00
L.Kornhauser, 968 Main St., Peekskill, N.Y.	35.00
Landregan & White, Oakland, Cal., Coffin, Clear, 6 1/8 In.	15.00
Levaggi Co., San Francisco, Monogram, Amber, 11 In.	20.00
Lilienthal & Co., Distillers, 4 Mold, Blob Top, Amber, 11 1/2 In.	40.00
Louis Taussig & Co., Inside Threads, Square Slug, Amber, 12 In.	45.00

Louis Taussig & Co., San Francisco, Clear, 11 1/4 In.	10.00
Louis Taussig & Co., San Francisco, Inside Threads, Medium Amber	45.00
Louis Taussig & Co., San Francisco, Monogram, Union Label, Amber	25.00
M.McPhelemy, Danbury, Conn., Squat, Amber, 9 1/4 In.	40.00
M.Salzman Co., Swirled Neck, Amber	15.00
M.Shaughnessy Co., St.Louis, Amber, Sample	15.00
Macy & Jenkins, New York, Handled, Amber	15.00 To 18.00
McAuliffe's Pure Irish Whiskey, 48 Nassaust, N.Y., Olive Amber	195.00
McDonald & Cohn, San Francisco, Inside Threads, Light Amber	12.00
McKenna Sour Mash Bourbon, White Jug, Blue Letters	2.50
McKenna's, Nelson County, Amber	100.00
McLech Scotch Whiskey, Mermaid On Rock, 3 3/4 In.	10.00
McLech, Arlando Cherry Brandy, Jug, Behold The Angler	4.00
McLech, Thistle, Scotland, 1969	5.00
McLeod-Hatje Co., San Francisco, Amber, 11 7/8 In.	12.00
Melcher's Schnapps, 7 1/4 In.	40.00
Mellow Corn, 1956, Partial Label	5.00
Merideth Diamond Club, Porcelain, Pint	40.00
Miller's Extra Old Bourbon, Monogram, Medium Amber, 7 1/8 In.	65.00
Miller's Game Cock Whiskey, Boston, Aqua, 6 3/4 In.	9.00
Miller's Game Cock Whiskey, Boston, Long Neck, Round, 11 1/2 In.	11.00
WHISKEY, MINIATURE, see Miniature, Whiskey	
Missisquoi A Springs, Embossed Papoose, Yellow Olive, Quart	225.00
Mohawk Creme-De-Menthe, Green Bottom, White Top, Handled	3.50
Moore & Alexander, Fort Smith, Ark., 1/2 Pint	25.00
Morgan's Maryland Rye, Sheared Lip, Clear	15.00
Mount Vernon Pure Rye, Sample, Amber	35.00
Mount Vernon, Amber, Quart	18.00
Myer's & Co., Pure Fulton, Kentucky, Wooden Carrying Case, Aqua	30.00
N.B.Dursley, 1783, McK Plate 221, No.7, Deep Olive Amber, Quart	525.00
Nabor Alfs Brune, Wholesale Liquor Dealers	500.00
Nathans Bros.1863, Phila., Embossed, Amber	125.00
New Geneva, Pontiled Kick-Up, Deep Blue Aqua, 8 1/4 In.	40.00
O'Reilly & Sons, Queenstown, 3-Piece Mold, Deep Gold	15.00
Old Bourbon, Phoenix, Coffin, Honey Amber, Pint	115.00
Old Bushmill Distillery, Embossed Still	7.50
Old Continental, Embossed Soldier & 1776, Golden Amber	1150.00
Old Gaellic Smuggler, Green	10.00
Old Hardie, Clear & White Enamel Lettering, Pinch	15.00
Old Joe Gideon, Amber, 1/2 Pint	10.00
Old Overcoat, Rye Whiskey	1.50
Old Plantation Distilling Co., My Old Kentucky Home, Amber	35.00
Old Plantation Distilling, Goodnight Los Angeles, Amber	35.00
Old Quaker, Embossed At Base, Rectangular, 9 1/2 In.	8.00
Old Tom Parker, Deer Head, Trademark, Amber, 11 3/4 In.	60.00
Otto Schatz, Welton Street, Denver, Colorado	155.00
Owl Florida Waters, Aqua, 7 In	25.00
Owl Florida Waters, Aqua, 8 1/2 In.	25.00
Oxford Rye Whiskey, 1880s, Full Label, 11 1/2 In.	20.00
P.Claudius & Co., San Francisco, Monogram, Threaded Inside, Amber	25.00
Passport Scotch, American Airlines	1.50
Peacock, Honolulu, Monogram, Cylinder, Light Amber	70.00
Pepper Distillery, Carroll & Carroll, Sole Agents, San Francisco	60.00
Pepper Distillery, Lexington, Ky., 4 Mold, Medium Amber	75.00
Pepper, Embossed In Shield, Hand-Made Sour Mash, Amber, 11 3/4 In.	75.00
Perrine's Barley Malt, Amber	5.00
Peter's Schnapps, 7 1/2 In.	40.00
Phoenix Bourbon, Bird, Coffin, Clear, 7 1/4 In.	55.00
Phoenix Bourbon, Bird, Picnic, Clear, 6 1/2 In.	25.00
Phoenix Bourbon, Bird, Small, Dark Amber, 11 3/4 In.	65.00
Phoenix Old Bourbon, Bird, Coffin, Honey Amber, Pint	115.00
Phoenix Old Bourbon, Bird, Coffin, Light Amber, 6 1/4 In.	125.00
Phoenix Old Bourbon, Bird, Large, Blob Top, Honey Amber, 11 3/4 In.	200.00

Whiskey, Platte Valley, 6 In.

Pioneer Bear A Finkhausen, Medium Amber, Fifth	390.00
Platte Valley, 6 In. *Illus*	2.00
Pride Of Kentucky, Yellow Amber	750.00
R.B.Cutter's Pure Bourbon, Open Pontil, Handled Jug, Amber	225.00
R.M.Rose Pure Liquors, Atlanta, Ga., Square, Quart	15.00
Rex Distilling Co., Boston, Emerald Green	75.00
Rhum-Des Plantation Rum, St.James, Embossed	3.00
Richardson, Brunsing Co., San Francisco, Monogram, Amber, 11 In.	25.00
Rosemond, A In Circle On Shoulder, Square, Amber, 11 1/2 In.	35.00
Rosenblatt Co., San Francisco, Light Amber, Square, 11 1/2 In.	35.00
Roth & Co., Double Rolled Collar, Amber, 1/2 Pint	100.00
Roth & Co., Monogram, Dark Reddish Amber, Blob Top, 11 5/8 In.	50.00
Roth & Co., Monogram, Inside Peel Effect, Amber	20.00
Roth & Co., Monogram, 25 Ounce, Aqua	15.00
Rothenberg & Co., San Francisco, Judge, Blob Top, Medium Amber	110.00
Rothenberg Co., Old Judge Kentucky, Pictures Judge, Amber, Fifth	75.00
Rothenberg Co., San Francisco, Light Amber, Square, 11 1/2 In.	35.00
Rum Carioca, P.R.Rum, Lamp & Shade	7.50
S.C.Dispensary, Strap-Sided, 1/2 Pint	35.00
Schmol Of Distinction, The First Under The Bar	1.50
Security Distilling, Clear	10.00
Shea Bocqueraz & Co., San Francisco, Vertical Embossing, Amber	10.00
Shea Bocqueraz & McKee, Tea Kettle Old Bourbon, Amber, 12 In.	175.00
Sheehaus, Duffy Shape, Clear	5.00
Silver Dollar Pure Rye, Screw Top, Embossed Silver Dollars, Pint	8.00
Simmond's Nabob, 4 Mold, Blob Top, Medium Amber, 10 1/2 In.	45.00
Sir Robert Burnett & Co, , Old Tom Gin, Aqua, Embossed, Label	15.00
Slater's Premium Bourbon, San Francisco, Inside Threads, Amber	20.00
Smuggler's Gaelic, Black, Quart	5.00
Sour Mash 1867, Barrel Shape, Hawley Glass Co., Amber, 8 1/4 In.	20.00
Spruance Stanley & Co., 1869, San Francisco, Tooled Top	25.00
Sudden Discomfort	1.50
Taylors Distillers, Brown, Quart	3.00
Theodore Netter, Barrel, Clear, 8 Ounce	25.00
Thos.L.Smith & Sons, Boston, Mass., 3 Mold, Honey Amber	20.00
Turner Brothers, New York, Barrel, Pale Yellow Amber	125.00
U.Wolfe Schnapps, Full, Label	28.00
Van Bell's Rock & Rye, Embossed	10.00
Van Buren, Kummel Whiskey, Chicago, Full Label, Amber, Quart	20.00
Van Dunck's Coachman, Dark Amber	65.00
W.C.Peacock, Honolulu, Territory Of Hawaii	75.00
W.D.B., Monogram, Monument, Cylinder, Deep Golden Amber, 3/4 Quart	30.00
W.J.Van Schuyver & Co., Portland, BIMAL, Amber, Fifth	60.00
W.J.Van Schuyver & Co., Portland, Oregon, Crown, Shield, Amber	15.00
W.M.Watson Co., Oakland, Cal., Monogram, Amber, 11 3/4 In.	20.00
W.M.Watson Co., Oakland, Cal., Monogram, Dark Amber, Square	25.00
Waldorf & Tavern, Reno, Nevada, Flat, Amethyst, 6 1/4 In.	25.00
Watrous, High Grade Liquors, Denver, Colorado	155.00
White Horse, Clear, 1/2 Pint	5.00

White Label Scotch, American Airlines 1.50
Whitlock & Co., Old Mill, Handled 140.00
Whitney Glassworks, Inside Screw Top, Pat.Jan.1861, Cylinder, Quart 29.50
Wichman Lutgen, Sole Agents, Gilt Edge 300.00
Wichman, Lutgen & Co., Old Gilt Edge, Inside Threads, Amber 20.00
Willington Glassworks, On Base, Cylinder 35.00
Willington Glassworks, Stoddard, 3 Mold, Olive Amber 30.00
Wilmerding, Loewe Co., Kellogg's, San Francisco, Inside Threads 15.00
Winedale Co., Oakland, Cal., Monogram, Amber, 11 In. 15.00
Wm.H.Spears & Co., Old Pioneer, Picture Of Bear, Clear, 11 7/8 In. 100.00
Wm.Maher, High Grade Liquors, Absolutely Pure, Denver ....*Color* 80.00
Woiter's Bros. & Co., 115 & 117 Front St., S.E. 110.00
Wolfe's, 8 In. 12.00
Wolfschmidt Vodka 1.00
Wollfale, Black Glass, Quart 5.00
Wood Cock, Paper Label, Pumpkinseed Flask 25.00
Wormser Bros., San Francisco, Double Ring, Bubbles, Amber, 8 3/8 In. 90.00
Wright & Taylors, Distillers, Brown, Quart 3.00

WHYTE & MCKAYS, Cheater 10.00
  Driver 10.00
  Slicer 10.00

WILD TURKEY, Baccarat Crystal, 1979 .... 150.00 To 209.00
  Charleston Centennial, 1974 .... 57.00 To 65.00
  Crystal Anniversary, 1955 .... 1980.00
  Liggett & Meyers 312.00
  Lore Series, No.1 .... 39.00 To 60.00
  Lore Series, No.2 .... 40.00 To 45.00
  Mack Truck 10.00
  No.4, With Poult .... 90.00 To 100.00
  No.5, With Flags .... 30.00 To 42.00
  No.6, Striding .... 20.00 To 32.00
  No.7, Taking Off .... 18.00 To 34.00
  No.8, Strutting .... 35.00 To 44.00
  North Carolina, 1972 .... 300.00
  South Carolina, 1974 .... 70.00
  Tom Turkey In The Straw, No.1 ....*Illus* 250.00
  Turkey On Log, No.2 ....*Illus* 350.00
  Turkey On The Wing, No.3 ....*Illus* 125.00
    WILLETT, see Old Bardstown

WINE, Blown, Applied Foot, Wafer Stem, 4 1/8 In. 5.00
  Boehmke Wine Co., Naked Lady On Keg, Lady's Leg, Amethyst, Quart 25.00
  Crescent Wine Co., Los Angeles, Amber, Net Contents, 25 1/2 Ounce 40.00

Wild Turkey, Tom Turkey In The Straw, No.1

Deacon-Scotland Yard, Embossed, 3 Mold, Black Glass, Squat 50.00
Dr.Solomon's Indian, Aqua 120.00
Eagle, Amber 25.00
Globe, Leather 20.00
Goldberg, Bowen & Co., Merchants, San Francisco, Coffin, Clear 16.00
Goodwin & Edgerly, N.Y., Turkish, Olive Amber, 10 In. 85.00
Nuyens & Cie, Bordeaux, France, Green 30.00
Owl, Fancy Label, Sherry, Amber, 11 3/4 In. 200.00
P.Welty & Co., Jobbers & Importers, Wheeling, Oval, Clear, Quart 12.00
Stockton's Port 90.00
Tall Cat 10.00
Tall Dog 10.00
Tall Fish 10.00
United Cal.& Montebello Vineyards Consd., S.F., Cal., Amber, 11 In. 35.00
Zeller Schwarze Katz, Green, 13 In. ....*Color* 10.00

Wild Turkey, Turkey On The Wing, No.3

Wild Turkey, Turkey On Log, No.2